THE CANVAS FALCONS

THE CANVAS

THE MEN AND THE PLANES

STEPHEN

FALCON: Any of several diurnal birds of prey of the family *Falconidae*

FALCONS

OF WORLD WAR I

LONGSTREET

BARNES
&NOBLE
BOOKS
NEW YORK

This edition published by Barnes & Noble, Inc.,
by arrangement with Stephen Longstreet

1995 Barnes & Noble Books

ISBN 1-56619-669-8

Printed and bound in the United States of America

M 9 8 7 6 5

ACKNOWLEDGMENTS

For particular help in fleshing out my own collection of material, I am indebted to the following:

The Imperial War Museum and the Royal Aeronautical Society, London; the National Archives, the Library of Congress, the Smithsonian Institution, and the National Air Museum; all of Washington, D.C.; the New York Public Library; the West Point Museum; the Musée de la Guerre and the Bibliothèque Nationale, Paris; the Musée Royale de L'Armée, Brussels; the Historische Bildarchiv, Handke; the Nationalbibliotek and the Heeres Museum, Vienna; and the Bayerisches National Museum, Munich.

Thanks are also due to John Ross, whose collection of World War I diaries, newspaper and magazine clippings, letters, photographs, and drawings has been invaluable in focusing on the individual flier; to Lewis H. Glaser for the use of material collected on World War I planes by Revell, Inc.; and to "W. W. Windstaff" (a pseudonym) for the extracts printed in Chapter 17—A Personal Narrative. In the late twenties, I helped this ace to write his memoirs, which he called *A Flier's War*. Years later I adopted a small section of *A Flier's War* to fit into a novel I had written. The original text is the source of the excerpts used here to give a close-up of one fighter pilot's life.

OFFICIAL PUBLICATIONS

Of the official publications mined for background, the following should be mentioned:

France: Ministère de la Guerre; Etat-major de l'Armée, Service Historique, Les Armées Françaises dans la Grande Guerre (Paris, 1922–25).

Germany: Generalstaab, *Kriegsbrauch im Landkriege (Usages of War)* translated as *The German War Book* (London, 1915).

Great Britain: Foreign Office, *British Documents on the Origins of the War* (London, 1927–38). H. O. Jones, *The War in the Air* (the official history of the war in 6 vols., London, 1922).

United States: Department of State, *Papers Relating to the Foreign Relations of the U.S., World War, 1914* (Washington, D.C., 1928). Carnegie Endowment for International Peace, *Diplomatic Documents Relating to the Outbreak of the European War* (Oxford, 1916). The assembled and selective *German White Book*, the *Austro-Hungarian Red, Belgian Grey, French Yellow, German White, British Blue I and II, Italian Green, Russian Orange I and II,* and *Serbian Blue Books.*

OTHER PUBLICATIONS

A. Russell Bond, *Inventions of the Great War* (London).
Cross & Cockade Journal. Vols. I–V, Society of World War I Historians, California, 1964.
John R. Cuneo, *The Air Weapon, 1914–1916* (Harrisburg, Pa.).
O. G. Thetford and E. J. Riding, *Aircraft of the 1914–1918 War.*
W. L. Wade, *The Aeroplane in the Great War.*

CONTENTS

Photos following page 210

INTRODUCTION

Those were days of glory . . . All the thrill of the hunt, coupled
with the speed and danger of flying . . . we had superbly brave
and finely trained enemies, as anxious to kill as we were . . .
— SILVIO SCARONI, ITALIAN FLIER

The first version of this history of events in the air and of the
fliers of World War I was begun when I was a schoolboy, by
collecting all the news items, magazine stories, photographs, drawings, and personal impressions I could find. (I also illustrated the
material with pen and ink sketches.) Whenever French or English
fliers came to our town to help us rally to the cause of victory, or
an American ace was given a parade down the main street, I tried
to interview as many as I could. That early manuscript is long
lost, but I still have many of the yellowing printed news clippings.
They have the value of most nostalgia, but rarely do they contain
the full facts, as later research proved.

I have planned this version of the book for over twenty-five
years, and—to delay writing it—have piled up an impressive collection of texts, journals, official documents, old letters, books by
air flight specialists, histories, and war memoirs of those who were
there and often died flying and fighting. In addition, there are the
French, German, Italian, and Russian sources of material, from
which I had sections translated, not to mention the old photographs of young men facing box cameras, and those images of
frail war planes now prized like their weight in gold.

To me it seemed there was a long-felt need for a book on the
Great War that was not technical or dedicated to the field of the
specialists, not entangled in the endless listing of names, insignia,
and the documentary red tape. I have tried to give the basic facts,

while also retaining the human element so often missing from the accounts of contemporary historians.

The book is not intended to be taken as a history of World War I. Actually, the airmen above the muck and misery of the ground offensives and losses going on "down there" knew little of the all-over strategy or campaigns. There is just enough of the land war here to give a background to the fliers' setting.

Nor is this a study of the power politics, the powder-keg situations, the double crossing around green-felt conference tables. For the most part, those who brought on the war and continued their strange fumbling efforts while it was in progress are missing. They, too, have been written about in detail elsewhere.

It is the flier himself who is on the central stage, the flier and the machines he flew, the weapons he used; the leaves or AWOL he took in Paris and London, the taut, nerve-destroying life in the airdromes; the horseplay, hobbies, and something of the drinking and womanizing he hunted out so desperately before the dirty business of dying.

Two historian friends have helped to check dates and names; and model makers and World War I flying buffs have gone over the text for details of planes, weapons, and insignia. However, as the material is vast, complex, and often translated from another language, whatever errors have crept in are mine. I have tried to identify and give credit wherever names are available.

There are no invented scenes, no interior monologues, no imaginary dialogues. Often agreement among the specialists and historians as to versions of a story differs. Did a British ace, when asked to drink a toast to "Baron von Richthofen, our worthy opponent," answer, "I'll not drink a toast to that devil" (as one British historian reports it)? Or did he say, "I'll not drink a toast to that sonofabitch" (the second version is the one three other historians agree upon)? Or take the death of Garros, the great French ace. Did he die diving into a Zeppelin, blowing it and himself up? Or was he shot down by a Fokker D-VII? Most historians accept the second account. For the reader who would like

to extend his knowledge of such niceties, some books still avail-
on the subject are listed at the end of this volume.

STEPHEN LONGSTREET

PART I:
Prologue:
How It Began

How easily it all began—like a ballet of toy figures in uniform, falling down in a row, domino-style. There was the Dual Monarchy, a mixed-language nation called Austria-Hungary "made up of eight nations, seventeen countries, twenty parliamentary groups, twenty-seven parties." The name of the Bosnian town where the war fever incubated is remembered, even by airmen: Sarajevo.

The leaders of the European nations were eager for warlike gestures, some even earnestly hoping for battle, a short pageant of power. Every schoolboy knows how the Great War began . . . Using the excuse of an assassination, the Austrians saw a chance to punish and grab off more of Serbia, and even when Serbia offered to meet *all* terms, the Austrians wanted war. The Russians came proudly to the aid of their Slavic brothers in Serbia. Russia was still medieval, autocratic (the czarina wrote to Grigori Efimovich Rasputin, that lecherous priest, in words worthy of Dostoyevsky: "How tiresome it is without you . . . I wish only to fall asleep in your arms"). The Germans announced they must aid brother Austrians if the Great Slavic Bear moved, so the French gave notice they held to a treaty of aid to Russia. England stood firmly proud to its assistance alliance with France. Doomsday for the twentieth century had come.

Sir Edward Grey stood gloomily at his London window. "The lamps are going out all over Europe. We shall not see them lit again in our lifetime."

In a crisis the English, masters of a strong and splendid prose, have never failed to come up with the proper sentence for the schoolbooks of the future. The war could not now be stopped.

All the nations had plans, all had long-studied charts, maps for victory. In the main it was to be—as they saw it—a war of foot-slogging infantry, flanked by fine horsemen, with a great deal of artillery. Of the embryo air forces little was expected. Perhaps some scouting of the weather and the roads might do no harm, if they stayed out of the way of the serious business. In February 1912, a Captain Murry Sueter addressed part of the German Committee of Imperial Defense:

> In case of a European war between two countries, both sides would be equipped with large corps of aeroplanes, each trying to obtain information of the other and to hide its own movements. The effort which each would exert in order to hinder or prevent the enemy from obtaining information would lead to the inevitable result of a war in the air, for the supremacy of the air, by armed aeroplanes against each other. This fight for the supremacy of the air . . . will be of the first and greatest importance . . .

But the committee—set in the mood of the God of Kipling's "Recessional"—seems not to have taken him seriously. Not one armed airplane was in the sky over Europe the day war broke out.

The mood of those who were to fly the skies or fight on land was as fuzzy as that of the warmakers. Today, in a meaner, harder time, it is not easy to recapture their reactions and emotions. Of the eager young Americans of those days John P. Marquand said: "The nice thing about a war is that when one comes, you can drop everything and go to it, and everyone will say that you were exactly right."

This gay, dedicated, almost unbelievably innocent mood was not to last much beyond the sight of the first dead man, a burned-out plane—the intimate realization of how permanent death can be.

The Great War produced four major innovations in warfare, almost absentmindedly, from a sort of melange of ideas that were around and available. No one was too sure at the time as to how they would work out. They were the airplane, the machine gun (based on models fifty years old), chemical warfare (poison gas and the flamethrower) and the land tank, moving like a metal turtle on an endless belt, a road it laid in front and picked up behind itself. The plane was the only one that exceeded expectations. "There shall be wings. If the accomplishment is not for me, for some other . . ." said Leonardo da Vinci.

The Great War—condensed, tidied away as time recedes year upon year—has taken on the color of the last of the romantic wars. The grim realities of the trenches, millions living like demented moles in their own filth, have become transmuted into chipped monuments, a lean marble abstraction: The Unknown Soldier.

The words of those old songs, "It's a Long Long Trail Awinding," "Smiles," "Pack Up Your Troubles in Your Old Kitbag," "There Are Smiles That Make You Happy," have almost slipped away. Beyond the parapets of the trenches that stretched and zigzagged from the Channel to the Swiss border come faint echoes, very faint, of the tunes. But there are no songs of the fliers and their planes.

In letters, personal accounts, we come across the fleeting impressions: flying above puffs of Archie (antiaircraft fire), taxiing over a rough field on a cold ice-blue morning, the stink and vapor of the castor-oil lubrication plumes as the props were spun and the petrol caught, the whole motor rotating with its shaft attached directly to the propeller. All experiences become legend.

The war had long been anticipated and the young men had hoped it would not flicker out before they got there. It was the talk of men in spiked helmets or those carrying swagger sticks made in India, the gossip of fat generals in horizon-blue uniforms, belching from the wine at lunch. All the nations of Europe had plans, great plans, of attack, of sweeps around a nation or through nations, around forts, the power of Krupp and Skoda guns. Plans to defend sacred soil. The general talk was not at all of planes but of the beauty of the cavalry Uhlans, Hussars, crack Moroccan regiments of Berber steeds, British polo ponies, and old regiments whose colors recalled Waterloo, Yorktown, the Great Mutiny.

There was a general trooping of the flags at Aldershot, Potsdam, St. Petersburg, even a few airplanes flying past above.

The heroes-to-be were Kipling's bloody bastards, or the Prussian in march step, the French poilu in his long-tailed blue coat and little cap. War on foot would be backed by the cavalry tactics that had proved their worth among "the lesser breeds without the Law." Backed, if you will, by the French 75's, Krupp's heavy ugly shapes. All this would make it a short land war. "Home by Christmas," both sides were told in the August heat as the great armies massed and eyed each other like dusty lions waiting to pounce. It was the last war, too, of the gay uniforms; the white of the Hungarian Hussars, the polished brass helmets of the German General Staff, the Cossacks with chest armor of cartridge cases trotting by the Winter Palace where the czar of all the Russias took their salutes and cries, the tainted pale heir at his side. The czarina and her daughters were robed in white, twirling their sunshades. And overhead was Igor Sikorsky's flying machine, the Ilya Mourometz, carrying sixteen passengers and a dog.

H. G. Wells might predict, in some far-off future, tanks, landships of steel that rolled over battlefields, and clouds of planes, those toys of canvas and bamboo and birch and ash with their piddling little nasty-smelling motors. But war had small use for such toys. War meant infantry, horsemen, maps and plans, men marching off in 8-pound jackboots along the Berlin streets, girls kissing the French reserves' long mustaches in the Paris railroad stations. Soon the posters of Lord Kitchener, that "noble homosexual," would show him pointing his finger imperiously at the farm lads, the Whitechapel toffs, the young manhood of a whole generation destined to destruction: YOUR COUNTRY WANTS YOU!

The opinion of flying was that aeroplanes had indeed crossed the Channel, had been set as part of the military on the fringes. Perhaps useful for scouting, for observing the lay of the land, the puffs of smoke on the horizon. But they were flimsy things, gadgets rather than solid instruments of war. Good enough to kill the young men in training, excite the sports who had seen the Wright brothers fly, or some hairy Frenchman, a Russian or two, those who had been to the flying exhibitions in Germany at the time of the Balkan War of 1912. No detailed plans existed for a striking force in the air. The damn things could barely take off with the man jammed in at the balky controls.

Eager young fanatics wrote reports and elbowed their way into war departments, pleading for someone to listen and understand the value of these canvas gliders with motors added. Someone remembered that Leonardo da Vinci had made some drawings of flying machines—never did build one, though. There might be some war aeroplanes to fly—if one knew who to ask and where to go.

But the Americans, who had started the whole flying racket, were not too keen on the aeroplane as a war weapon. There had been some bad accidents, an army major killed. A U.S. expedition to Mexico against the bandit-patriot Pancho Villa had used a force of eight U.S. planes. They had achieved little of value; always sand in the motors, or bad gasoline, and more on the ground than in the air. The main point was that they hadn't succeeded in finding Pancho Villa for General Pershing (who avoided flying himself).

There was gossip that the German War Office in its stolid way had been impressed and was engaged in some semisecret project for actually using the airplane. The French, gallant and always adventurous, could boast of several noted fliers who had flown long distances in various planes of strange design.

But no one dreamed that the airplane would become one of the important features of the Great War, as it was soon to be called. That the plane would be a probing warrior of the air, the dropper of explosive destruction from a sky with no mercy. Or that airships would even jeopardize the safety of the folks left at home, ostensibly far from battle.

PART II:
The Early Years

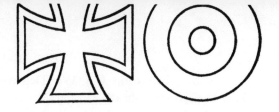

CHAPTER 1

THE WRIGHT BROTHERS

We thought we were introducing into the world an invention
which would make further wars practically impossible . . .
—ORVILLE WRIGHT

There is no irony like God's irony, wrote Heine, and no irony
in modern times is as potent as the remark of Orville Wright. In
December 1903 the Wright brothers flew for a few seconds in
their motor-powered flying machine on the Kitty Hawk dunes on
the Atlantic shore and thus opened up an age of fearful possibilities for stretching the range and the deadly destructive power of
the warmakers.

It was an event little noticed, and the newspapers hardly believed it. The word "practical" is the cue to the Wright brothers'
success in making a practical flying machine of a simple practical
design. They did not, of course, invent the airplane. Men had
been building machines that they hoped would fly almost since
the beginning of the industrial age; machines to be powered by
some kind of steam drive, or compressed air, or alcohol, or some
form of gasoline engine. Most never got off the ground, and those
that did crashed. The practical side of the Wright brothers' perfection of a true flying machine was its control in the air by wing
warping to steer and balance, using wing and rudder flaps created
by their study of original scientific data (they made the first wind
tunnel to test models).

Men who had flown gliders and tried out motors were intrigued
by the Wrights' claims as the brothers calmly went about building
further flying machines. In 1905 the two offered their powered

flight with wings to the U.S. War Department. Three times the War Department told the Wrights it was *not* interested.

The Wright brothers had evidently changed their minds about the use of their invention to prevent wars. Later they wrote to Octave Chanute, the glider expert and a backer of theirs: "We stand ready to furnish a practical machine for use in war at once; that is, a machine capable of carrying two men and fuel for a fifty mile trip . . ." The key word as always with the Wrights is "practical." It now seemed practical to them to send their planes to war, so they planned to take one of their cloth-covered machines to Europe.

They were strange brothers, self-educated, but with a genius for improving inventions in the manner of Yankee tinkerers; they made do with baling wire, bicycle chains, homemade engine blocks, and bicycle-tire repair cement on their early models. But they differed from colonial clockmakers and Kentucky rifle designers in being remarkably scientific, with an original vision of things. They never married, never seemed interested in any sexual adventures. They lived together with their father, a bishop of some local creed, and a spinster sister. They were noted for their silence—at a banquet given in their honor one of the brothers, asked to make a speech, said, "The parrot is the bird that talks the most and flies the worst." Yet there was an almost mystic bond between them, for they were said to communicate at times without speech.

The other side to the Wrights was their practical American desire for wealth, for the full exploitation of their inventions, and for the preservation of their rights to the wing-warping steering devices, which they defended in costly law suits. Their rewards, they felt, were here on earth. A kind of righteous greed, earned reward for their smartness, was part of their accepted creed.

In 1907, having been again rebuffed by the American War Department, they shipped a plane to Europe and went over to sell the idea of an air force to the war offices of European nations. (It may seem less than idealism to sell what could have been a potential weapon to nations that would one day fight the United States—as Germany, Austria-Hungary, and Turkey eventually did—but the American business ethic, symbolized by the Morgans, Rockefellers, the Duponts and others, was suitably expressed by the new radicals in Greenwich Village as "The flag follows the dollar.")

If the brothers were practical in inventions, their business methods were a little odd. They demanded $250,000 for their machine and rights to reproduce it, but refused to demonstrate it until they had a contract. The flying machine remained in its crates, and the Wrights came home, firm but emptyhanded.

Meanwhile French glider men and other dreamers of flying machines with motors began to build their own ideas of the Wrights' version. The engineers Robert Esanult-Peltérie and Léon Levavasseur and their admirer Ernest Archdeacon set out to build a Wright-type plane, working without blueprints. Nothing much came of it.

A showman-sportslover named Louis Blériot began to tow gliders behind motorboats, on floats made by two avid sky-lovers, Gabriel Voisin and his brother Charles. Names like Henri Farman and Léon Delagrange also should concern us for their interest in these floaters, for all the men we have mentioned became the pioneers of the French flying world.

The Brazilian Alberto Santos-Dumont had experimented with gas bags and dirigibles before he turned to a glider with a motor, an Antoinette engine made by Levavasseur. By 1906 near Paris he had flown 8 feet, then 200, then 722. Was there any end in sight to wonders in the air?

In 1907 Blériot decided to specialize in monoplanes. Most flying machines had been like the Wright's plane, biplanes, up to that time. Blériot's third version had all the features of the plane of World War I, though without the better metals, the fairly decent engines, the fancy instruments. Blériot's plane already had a closed body and a tail with rudders and ailerons. It crashed after less than a half dozen flights. Crashing was an occupational hazard; a few fliers nearly always landed the same way: with a crash and a prayer.

In England, too, daring men were building flying machines. J. W. Dunne, A. V. Roe, and an American character, S. F. Cody, who dressed like Bronco Billy Anderson, a cowboy star of the silent screen, were all at work at this time. For the British War Office Cody built, as the records show, "British Army Aeroplane No. 1." The term "flying machine" was becoming old hat and "aeroplane" was coming into use, as well as another form, soon dropped: "avroplane." "Airplane" and "plane" would be in popular use during the Great War. The cowboy-outfitted Cody took off in October 1908 for the first motored flight in the British Empire. His luck held. (It ran out in 1913 when he crashed and was killed, the obituary of so many pioneers.)

A. V. Roe built planes that also kept crashing, so that a public ordinance was proclaimed and he came before a court charged as "a menace to public safety." Scarred and stubborn, Roe went on building planes; Avro fighter planes later did good service in both world wars.

By 1908 the American War Department had finally reconsidered; there might be something to the Wright brothers' "damn-fool contraption," after all. The U.S. army took the brothers' bid to build a machine for military purposes. But the army demands were tough. The plane was to carry two men and enough fuel to stay in the air for 125 miles. It was to fly at one shot 10 full miles at a speed of about 40 miles an hour. Meanwhile the brothers sold the French patent rights of their plane to a French group for $100,000; flying was on the verge of becoming big business. With two orders now on hand to show off their planes, the brothers separated for the first time in their lives for any long period. Wilbur went to France to unpack the crates still holding the plane of their first visit. Orville stayed at home to take on the U.S. army's idea of its first war plane. But first, since they hadn't been flying for over two years, they went back to Kitty Hawk for a refresher course in their 1905 machine. From lying prone in their machine in flight they now took to sitting up. Before, they had used skids, not wheels, on their machine, and a catapult powered by a weight to toss themselves into the air. Wheels and a direct takeoff from earth would come. They could turn and bank their flying machine in the air, do figure eights, and all in all were perfecting their skills as fliers as they improved their plane.

In May 1908, Wilbur received a cold reception from the French. But when he got his plane into the air, the cheers and champagne followed. The French flier-designers had to admit that Wilbur beat them with the grace and ease with which a Wright airship took off and flew. Delagrange tapped his brow and murmured: "We are beaten. We do not even exist."

There began to be talk of "airpower." In England Major B. F. S. Baden-Powell declared that the fact "that Wilbur Wright is in possession of a power which controls the fate of nations [was] beyond dispute."

At home, Orville was proving to the U.S. army in the test flights at Fort Myer, Virginia, that the plane was no mere toy. Early in September 1908, in a series of flights before officials (pompous stuffed shirts and fat cats from Washington), flying alone Orville showed what the machine could do. Banking, going around in a circle, he amazed the onlookers. He even broke several of his own endurance records.

The next day Orville took up Lieutenant Thomas Selfridge, a West Point product who was wild about flying machines. As the plane circled the field the propeller cracked, the engine went into convulsions, and with a swoosh and a shaking the plane crashed down to the ground. Orville Wright was badly injured and the lieutenant killed. (Today Selfridge Field is named for him, the first passenger to die in a plane crash.)

Before a year was up Orville, scarred and limping, was back at Fort Myer in a new plane finishing the series of tests the army had asked for. So the army acquired an air force; anyway, its first plane.

In 1909, it seemed, people were flying someplace, everyplace. Fliers were taking up their version of a plane in England, Canada, Austria, Russia, Roumania, Sweden, Portugal, even Turkey. In Germany Wilbur flew straight up 1,000 feet, and Willie, the Crown Prince, presented him with a diamond and ruby stickpin.

London's *Daily Mail* offered £1,000 for any daredevil who could fly the Channel, a risky 20 miles or more. A man who believed he was dying of tuberculosis was looking for a spectacular method of committing public suicide. He was half French, half

English, and his name was Hubert Latham. On July 19, 1909, he took off from near Calais in a plane Léon Levavasseur had built with a titanic engine—50 horsepower. The engine gasped and died a third of the way across. The plane, however, floated and Hubert, living dangerously, puffed on a cigarette until picked up. (Abandoning death by plane he went hunting on an African safari and was obliged by a wounded buffalo which finally stomped him to death.)

By July 24 a new rival for the Channel prize was ready. Louis Blériot, still limping from a bad burn on his leg, was waiting for the right wind. At 2:30 in the morning, being unable to sleep and finding that the wind had slackened, he went to his monoplane. By 3:30 he was flying a few circles to see how his Anzani three-cylinder motor was performing. Landing to refuel just after 4:30 in the morning, he headed toward England. He was flying without instruments. The Channel chopped below, the propeller's breeze went smashing past his helmeted, goggled head. The chalky cliffs appeared ahead, and as a wind had drifted him east of his planned landing, he came down near Dover Castle. His flying time for the 20 miles was just thirty-seven minutes. He was met by customs officers demanding an inspection.

Military personnel from all over were also present to greet him, as well as future Prime Minister Lloyd George. Blériot was the Lindbergh of his day, but he avoided the "absurd political nonsense" of the latter, though he enjoyed being lionized. In London 120,000 people came to see his plane on exhibition.

After Blériot's great feat, flying became the popular sport of the daring. In August, at Rheims, France, the world's first meet was held; it ran, or rather flew, a week. There were enough flimsy planes and earnest fliers by then. But the field was so soggy for the first few days that some planes could not take off. Blériot flew, as did the suicidal Latham (in plane 13, of course). Eugène Lefebvre, in a stiffish breeze, did a 6¼-mile circle in nine minutes. Henri Farman in his own designed biplane won the endurance test by staying aloft for over three hours. Then he took on two passengers, unnamed heroes. Also present in one of his *June Bug* models was Glenn Curtiss, the Wrights' American rival, who was after the speed prize set up by James Gordon Bennett of the *New York Herald.* Curtiss won it at an average 43 miles an hour.

Very worried and impressed, a British flier said: "The day Blériot flew the Channel marked the end of our insular safety, and the beginning of the time when Britain must seek another form of defence besides ships." Was he hinting at the warplane? someone asked.

Latham, trying for *something,* claimed he had reached a height of 1,200 feet. The judges decided he hadn't gone beyond 500 feet.

There were accidents. Blériot's fuel line broke and caught fire, and he was badly burned as the gasoline tank exploded. Henri Fourneau smashed his ship. Léon Delagrange had his propeller shattered while flying; he was only slightly injured in a quick landing. No one at this air meet was killed.

But the next year, 1910, was an unlucky one. Thirty-two fliers were killed. Among them such early folk heroes as Lefebvre, Ferber, Delagrange. But at Dominguez Field, Los Angeles (where motion pictures were also pioneering), the First International Air Meet was held. Glenn Curtiss reached a record 55 miles an hour. The Frenchman Louis Paulhan got up to 4,165 feet.

Cross-country flying for another *Daily Mail* prize was also popular. USN Ensign Eugene Ely flew a Curtiss off the deck of a cruiser at Hampton Roads in November, and in January 1911 he landed a plane on a platform built onto the afterdeck of the USS *Pennsylvania.* The pattern for carrier warfare had been set.

At this point the Wrights and Curtiss both set up flying schools. Harry Houdini, master of magic, was flying his own Voisin from show appearance to show appearance. ("You need magic," remarked one viewer, "to stay up in *them* things.") Exhibition teams toured country fairs. By 1911 Curtiss was putting floats on some planes and making possible the seaplane. In the same year Galbraith P. Rodgers made the first transcontinental flight across the United States; because of forced stops and crash landings, it took him two months.

And serious businessmen were going into the industry of making planes. Those whose names and products have survived into history were Sopwith, de Havilland, Bristol, Vickers, and Handley Page. In Russia there was Sikorsky, in Holland Fokker, in France Deperdussin. The coming Great War would make considerable use of their skills and machines.

In 1913, with military aviation busy taking its small part in the race toward the war urge now gripping Europe, the military plane was finally off the designers' board and into production. Roland Garros of France crossed the Mediterranean in under eight hours, flying a route of 453 miles. In Russia, Igor Sikorsky was making designs for giant planes to carry as many as sixteen passengers.

With the year 1914 the world resounded to the angry buzz of Europe moving toward the final tragedy—war clearly in the offing. But the diplomats, the journalists, the political philosophers insisted the world was too civilized to go to war on any large scale. The *Daily Mail* had another idea—it offered $50,000 for any flier who could fly nonstop (what else?) in a transatlantic flight. And the Panama-Pacific Exposition offered a prize of $150,000 for a round-the-world flight to be done in ninety days. (Jules Verne's hero had made it in eighty days, but he wasn't using the frail, cranky flying machine of pre-1914.)

However, some of the planes were showing the advantage of good design and builders had improved their skills. The best were the Morane-Saulnier L, the Deperdussin, the Sopwith Tabloid; also the German Rumpler Taube, the Farnsborough, and in America the seaplane Curtiss-America, the Martin TT.

As the motorcar bore a fat archduke and his wife through the Serbian town of Sarajevo, the air armadas of the European nations were not too modest. Germany had 1,200 combat machines, and France and Britain combined counted 1,000 planes. Only a portion of these were ready for action, however. The top speed was 125 miles an hour, and some could fly 1,000 miles and climb to 25,000 feet. But these claims were for special ships so that the figures are in a sense very misleading. In August 1914, on the Western Front, France and Great Britain together had only 220 planes actually ready for flight, the Germans 260.

England had trouble breaking down the cherished tradition that the British square of infantry, bayonets at the ready—the "thin red line"—could be improved upon, or that a gallant charge of horsemen, sabers high, could be replaced by some petrol-reeking gadget. In 1910 the British Secretary of War had made it clear: "We do not consider that aeroplanes will be of any possible use for war purposes." Yet in 1912 the British, a sporting people, had set up the Royal Flying Corps, depending on the de Havilland F-2, which in a tight fit could carry two men, a camera, and some sort of gun at 75 miles an hour with a time range of three hours. They also had the Avro 504, the Bristol Scout, and the Sopwith Tabloid; all 90-mile-an-hour single-seaters.

The French liked the Morane-Saulnier, the Nieuport Scout biplane, and the Farman "pusher," which had its propeller in the rear.

The Germans were the best supplied. They had heavy reconnaissance planes, and for scouts the Albatros and the Taube monoplane with set-back wings that made it look like its name, a dove. Observation and scouting was the duty planned for such machines. No one was too sure just how bombing would work. And no one envisaged aerial duels with deadly weapons in the sky.

America showed little interest in the idea of airpower either as scout or weapon. After three years of war, when the U.S.A. entered in 1917, it ranked fourteenth on the chart of world airpowers. Not one American-designed plane was to fly in combat in Europe; despite the Wright brothers' original impetus, American fliers were to use French and British models exclusively.

CHAPTER 2

THE WORLD OF ANTHONY FOKKER

The history of the Great War, regarded as an intensifying clash between old forms and new forms, still remains to be written . . .

—H. G. WELLS

One of the strangest figures to emerge as a major personality of the Great War was Anthony Herman Gerard Fokker. He was a Dutchman, and Holland remained rich and neutral throughout the struggle. Yet it has been said that without Fokker, "the war against Germany could have been shortened by as much as a year."

For him the *nuova scienza*, the true science, was flying. He seemed never to have smelled the bestial stench of war, or to have been aware of his contribution to the death of a generation or so of Europe's youth. For Fokker, life was an aviary of canvas and wooden hawks let loose. He never deeply considered the terror and unreason of armed conflict. When the challenge was put to him of getting bullets through the spinning speed of a plane's propeller, he never thought much about what flesh and bone those bullets would strike and penetrate. He was a scientist.

Anthony Fokker was born in 1890 in the then Dutch-held island of Java. His father was one of those roving colonial tea planters, fat with the good and easy life. When the boy was six, the family and their loot moved back to Holland, to settle down in Haarlem. Here, Anthony Fokker remembers, "I sat in my father's attic furiously flying a kitchen chair rigged with Wright controls." His was one of those inventive minds whose skills fitted a practical universe. By twelve, he was building his own electric trains out of scrap. He was a poor student at school; the early years of lordly freedom in Java had spoiled Anthony for rigid, scholarly ways. He tried to tap an electric cable passing by the house, but was prevented just in time. He did put electric charges into doorknobs and nearly killed a relative. But above all, he wanted to fly.

He experimented with small gas-combustion engines and almost set the house on fire with his Bunsen burner. He tapped into a nearby gas main when his father objected to the gas bills.

Bored with lessons and studying, he invented a schoolroom cheating machine of circular sheets with the proper answers that came into position as he needed them. (After passing his examinations and leaving school, he showed the invention to the school staff!)

While still a schoolboy, young Fokker discovered that a friend's father owned an early Peugeot (1908), a brand-new model. Riding in this car, the boy decided to invent a puncture-proof tire. The first tires fell apart, but finally he and his father went into the tire business in a serious way. When the friend's car died, Fokker took it apart, made new parts, and got it running for the tire tests at 40 miles an hour. But the project lost money for his father—a pattern that was to be repeated.

Fokker changed directions when he saw a Latham plane in the air over Brussels. He began making paper and wooden models of planes, using the Wright ideas as a start, and soon came to the conclusion that "a sweepback wing with a pronounced dihedral, combined with a high center of gravity, would give me an airplane of perfect stability."

Just as he had embarked on a flying machine, the Dutch army called him in for a year's service as a soldier. Fokker said he was too ill, in poor shape, with dismally deformed feet; quite unfit to serve. He was sent to a hospital ward and put on a diet of rice until he admitted he wanted to be a soldier. By smuggling in food, he held out until one day while going AWOL he fell off a streetcar and sprained his ankle. This was his chance: he bribed a doctor for 100 guilders to give him a certificate stating he was now really unfit for military service. Fokker was discharged with a half dollar's pay.

The family decided first that the boy should study engineering at Bingen on the Rhine, then switched to a school at Zalbach where there was an airplane engine but as yet no airplane. Fokker's father was asked to put up 1,000 marks in case his son broke any of the machines, but having enrolled in the aviation class, the boy turned out to be the only pupil. The teacher was Hugo Buchner who claimed (fraudulently) to have been at the Flying School at Berlin and licensed by the Fédération Aeronautique Internationale. Fokker, a con man himself, shrugged it off, and the two of them set to work to build a plane around the school's precious engine. When it was completed, Buchner wasn't too happy about testing it in a cow pasture near Wiesbaden, but as he was sure the plane couldn't get off the ground he rode it up and down the field. They called it *The Grass Cutter*.

Giving up on Buchner, Fokker and another student got hold of a 50-horsepower water-cooled Argus engine (naturally, the other student paid for it), and they went to work to build a plane around it. They found their machine could hop around and actually leave the ground a bit. Buchner took it up a first time to find out how its controls functioned, but in secret, before flying it again in front of the students. A speed of 50 miles an hour was needed for takeoff. Flying the plane for the students, Buchner forgot to pull back the stick and ran the machine into a ditch and wrecked it. After this debacle, he packed and left the school in disgrace.

Fokker, disgusted with the school, got back 500 marks on his tuition and found an Oberleutnant von Daum who was willing to produce further money. He also begged his father for 1,000 marks, and in partnership with the oberleutnant began to build a plane with a tubular frame in the Zeppelin hangar in Baden-Baden while the airship itself was away on tests. On the first trial, Fokker found out that he had forgotten a steering gear; as he admitted, the machine predictably ran wild "like a headless chicken."

In December 1910 the official test of the new plane was to take place; but the engine would not start. When he got it going, Fokker felt overelated and took the plane off wearing only his light clothes. The flight in the open cockpit soon chilled his overheated body. He developed a cold followed by pneumonia and was close to death.

A telegram came from the oberleutnant saying that he had tried out the plane and run it into a tree. Still sick, Fokker went back to Baden-Baden and rebuilt the wreck. He asked for a flying license. Passing the tests, he was issued license No. 88.

Fokker flew every day, often at 300 feet, and people came to see "the crazy Dutchman" and his flying machine. But von Daum wanted some glory for himself, and after much insisting, he took the plane up and promptly crashed it. As he walked away from the machine, he remarked that he was sick of flying and very sick of Herr Fokker.

Fokker offered him 1,200 marks for his interest in the wreck, so that Fokker now became the sole owner of the remains. Papa Fokker was tapped from time to time for money to keep the company going, and young Anthony, a man with a sense of publicity, saw to it that he was invited to fly for Queen Wilhelmina's birthday party in Amsterdam. The city was not known for its dryness, and Fokker had to take off from a bog. Only a fool or a superego would have tried taking off from the mire. Fokker did. The wheels sank into the muck and he was nearly killed. But he managed to fly over Amsterdam, shaking and wagging his wings at 300 feet while the crowd cheered.

Returning home he flew over Haarlem, his mother and father watching him fearfully. His father rushed up to him as he landed and handed over a family heirloom to his son, a butter-gold watch and chain. Anthony Fokker was now, in his father's eyes, a man.

At this point (1912), Fokker received an invitation to work at the famous Johannesthal Airfield near Berlin. Before the war, Johannesthal was a kind of carnival where young men mad about flying took up crates of their own making supervised by others who had, they hoped, some practical ideas about the theory of flight. Weekends, holiday crowds came to watch and some were even brave or foolish enough to pay for a ride in the rickety machines, while the rest stood by with high hopes of a crash.

Fokker arrived at this scene with his machine, but when the plane was unpacked and the Germans saw the odd sweep-back wing, he was assured the damn thing wouldn't fly. On the first trial, it failed even to leave the hangar. Fokker stripped down the engine and found sugar in the carburetor. (The kingpin pilot of the place, Willi Rosenstein, was suspected of this deed.)

Nonetheless, Fokker finally succeeded in flying his machine, and rapidly became the top pilot of the field. His prewar plane was the superior model, and he made the most money in flying members of the crowd. But his ambition was to sell planes to those nations who wanted to build up an air force.

He hired over two dozen men, most of whom he had to train to his methods, and sent out notices to say that he had formed a plane-building company, Fokker-Aeroplanbau. The Germany army sent officers to look over his plant, and orders for two planes at 10,000 marks followed. But that wasn't enough. Fokker decided to go to Russia, where an air meet was being held, for orders. Over twelve makers of planes were entering their brain-children, and the rules were stiff: climb to 3,000 feet in twelve minutes, bank and turn at very tight angles. Igor Sikorsky was after the government contracts for his own company, and as a Russian he had an obvious advantage. Fokker, never much of a flier, dropped out, but did get a score that placed him third. However, no orders from the czar's air force followed. Although Fokker was short of cash, he turned down jobs with Rumpler and Albatros, who were eager for his knowledge, and went out on flying stunts and exhibitions to keep from going broke.

Meanwhile, German businessmen had been watching the aircraft industry with the impression that a golden goose would be ready for plucking soon, whether war came or not. If it came, so much the better. One day, a puzzled Fokker was invited to one of the big Berlin banks, offered cigars, brandy. He faced a solemn business group, heavy solid citizens of the Reich. They assured him they had great faith in the airplane, that the *Vaterland* would need many planes in war and peace, and that the army and the navy—God bless and protect Kaiser Wilhelm II—would be buying planes by the score; perhaps there would even be a *Luftstreikrafte* —an air combat force. Would Herr Anthony Fokker be in a position to serve as the head of a new airplane plant, starting salary 12,000 marks a year? Herr Fokker said he would.

Alas, it was a trap. The money men were merely surveying the idea, lining up personnel. They did not put up the millions of marks needed, and the 20,000 marks they did find as capital proved insufficient even to pay Fokker's bills. Reluctantly, in order to get a release from this Simon Legree contract, Fokker had to pay *them* 4,000 marks!

But there was always Papa back in Holland, who had now already dumped 100,000 marks of his Java-made coffee fortune into Anthony's business schemes. Once more Fokker asked Papa for money. The answer was firm—a final one. "I have had enough . . . I am not going to believe in any more promises." An uncle, however, proved a willing pigeon, sending 20,000 marks. Finally war talk, and then the rush to actual war itself, saved Fokker. He began to train officers to fly. They were mostly men of the Prussian caste system, whose stiff-necked pride caused many crashes and deaths. They were even known to subdue a plane with their spurs as if riding a balky horse. *Kein Rauch ohne Feuer!*

The German military command decided the time had come to put airplanes into its armed forces, but insisted on stern tests. The winner of the 250-mile course would get 45,000 marks. This time Fokker won. And so he set up in 1913 what was to become an official flying school at Schwerin Airfield, Mecklenburg, close to the Baltic coast. It was a barren windy spot where trees had to be cut down, the ground leveled, hangars and houses built for staff, students, and planes. Bismarck's grandson came, flew, and bought a plane. Others also put in orders for planes. The money was coming in, but Fokker spent it all and still needed more. Again Papa was approached and conned into forming a company, with friends, to put in 300,000 marks; at least that was the announced capital.

Fokker was now turning out planes for the German army and

the German navy; also seaplanes, and planes for private customers. But he remained constantly short of money. Protesting strongly, Papa and his friends forked up 100,000 more marks. Fokker wrote back that he was sure that by the end of 1914 he would be able "to show 40,000 marks profit." By the end of 1914 the Great War was just beginning to devour planes and Fokker was figuring his income in millions. He was then twenty-four.

When Europe erupted into flames, Fokker found himself an Aladdin with a magic lamp. The German government issued orders to confiscate *all* of Herr Fokker's planes for military purposes. No terms were specified, so Fokker sat tight and let the various branches of the army and navy inspect his goods, his factory, staff, and supplies. The army and navy—rivals—began to raise their bids higher and higher. Fokker waited for the cash payments to be made. Then he planned to scoot home to Holland with the money.

However, the government stepped in again, taking over all of Fokker's assets and dividing everything share and share alike between the two services. Fokker was paid more than the combined bids of the army and navy! With so much wealth, Holland seemed the next stop; but with all those young Germans asking to be trained, and so many more demands for his planes, what was a man to do? He stayed on. In his training program he emphasized that planes were magnificent weapons, not to be used merely for looking around at the enemy below. But this was considered the talk of a dreamer. What was needed were practical flying lessons, not advice.

Fokker had orders for two dozen planes for the German Signal Corps. He wrote home that the war would last less than three months, and the German banks would give him enough credit to finish the scout planes on order. They'd be rich. Papa and his friends thanked Anthony and replied that they'd prefer to take their money out *now*—with interest. Fokker talked of their making barrels of marks if they stayed with him; but, as usual, they felt the boy was dreaming again. . . . We shall see.

CHAPTER 3

THE FIRST SOLDIERS
OF THE AIR
AND THEIR WEAPONS

1. | The Men

What sort of young men faced the first Fokkers in the air? ". . . The adventurous spirits, the devil-may-care young bloods of England, the fast livers, the furious drivers—men who were not happy unless they were taking risks. This invested the [Corps] with a certain style (not always admirable). We had the sense of being the last word in warfare, the advance guard of wars to come, and felt, I suppose, that we could afford to be a little extravagant . . ." was how Cecil Day Lewis put it in *Sagittarius Rising*.

What kind of men flew to war on both sides? In the main they were volunteers, these young men who had come forward to fly the first war planes of August 1914. Many had been cow-pasture fliers, part-time inventors, dreamers with blueprints. They flew in various kinds of crates, often with smudged faces grimed with grease, hands roughed raw by the continual tinkering and baling-wire repairs early engines needed. They were intense, mostly callow youths, starry-eyed, with little digested experience of any kind behind them.

We seek them today in faded photographs and sense the ebullience of their youth; its impetuous, romantically steered yearning toward the unknown. Unseeded adolescents mostly, uncontaminated as yet by a corrupted hemisphere at war. They wear the famed insignia of the Jagdstaffel 2, the Escadrille Américaine, the Royal Flying Corps, the Groupes de Chasse.

They were among the first to fly, the first to die. The survivors, broken and scarred, were never again to show those smooth eager faces. Today, more than half a century separates us from these young men. It is difficult in a more cynical, sicker age of the popular nonhero, the degenerate Portnoys, to understand the stance of pride taken up in front of those canvas, wire, and bent-wood contraptions; youth proud in its adjustment, its self-consciousness; unaware of the future—as was its society, even the warmakers themselves, of the coming brutality and horror of the twentieth century.

For the most part they were from the middle or upper middle class, some conventional types, some eccentric mechanics strong in camaraderie, college students dedicated to their fantasies of flying. There was no diffusion or dilution in their dedication to the theory of flight, the game of the air. As for the ordeal by fire ahead—well, that was the one drop of poison in the cup; the chance of death in war.

Soon their names would be listed as heroes (a few) or casualties (many) in their Spads, Sopwith Camels, Fokkers, de Havilland 2's, Morane-Saulniers, Nieuports, Rumpler Taubes, Albatroses. Heroes: War's pseudonym for the impermanence of things.

These first fliers—their names unknown except for long-filed-away records—are all gone. Rare among them was a von Richthofen, Immelmann, Fonck, Guynemer, Nungesser, Garros, Bishop, Mannock, Ball, Luke, Rickenbacker. The heroes-to-be in that stifling August heat were still unknown to fame, unmarked by the myths and mystiques of the popular historian.

The term "ace" would not appear until June 1915, when a French newspaper dubbed Adolphe Pégoud *l'as de notre aviation*, and the ace or top card of the deck became the favor bestowed with journalistic logic on that flier, who had five confirmed kills —later ten—of enemy aircraft to his credit. But the method of counting victories was not always proven, and any flier who had been over the lines was known as an "ace" in most newspaper stories.

Officially the British, not given easily to change, had no ace set-up, but unofficially they stayed at five kills as the qualifying figure. Official scores were supposed to be for confirmed kills.

Few serious historians accept the official or semi-official records of aces on either side. The Germans padded their lists shamelessly. And even British and French "confirmed" kills were often guesses. Planes seen to fall were often not destroyed, and made it back to base. Eyewitness accounts were often weak. So the records of the leading aces, from von Richthofen to Rickenbacker, have been challenged by some historians as being merely somewhere near the range of their actual kills. No one after the war seriously accepted the German lists of air victories. The British official experts stated that twenty-one of von Richthofen's victories are not listed on any documents or records in the Berlin archives.

The Germans questioned William Bishop's record of three enemy planes shot down and three damaged on a raid on a German airfield, stating he left in such a hurry he had no way of knowing what he had destroyed and what merely fired on.

The Service de l'Aviation of the French, later renamed the Armée de l'Air, ever on the romantic side, but it too did not accept all figures. (René Fonck, their top flier, was given 75 kills on the record. But in his book, *Mes Combats* [1920], he insists that the *success* he had in the air amounted up to 127 air victories!)

The American records, some claim, have been brazenly doctored. Just after the war the U.S.A. claimed it had sixty-eight aces, figuring anyone knocking down five or more enemy planes as an ace. The record now reads that there were eighty-two aces; no reason is given for this sudden increase in heroes. The records of Rickenbacker, Frank Luke, and Bill Thaw have grown since the end of the war. This is no reflection on the fliers; it was "official" policy for the air force to polish up the records. In dogfights no one really knew for sure who had shot down what, and how many planes had fired on one enemy. Or how many "kills" just dived out of battle and went home.

The Germans had the easier task in keeping records. Most German fighters stayed in their own back yard, waiting for the enemy to come to them across the lines. Also the prevailing wind was usually from west to east, so that many Allied fighters ended up in German territory, victorious or not.

It was easier to become an ace in 1914 and 1915. Planes and weapons were simple, and many inexperienced men flew in the air. By 1916, 1917, the terms were tougher when you engaged an enemy. The opposition hardened to a science and a skill on both sides. (By 1918 the German air force was outclassed and out-fought.)

Why were there so few survivors from the earliest period of the war? The answer was that if the training planes did not kill them, the accidents of weather, of engine failure, hastily sited air-fields carved from farm fields, the mistakes of mechanics, the balking conditions of so many of the early aircraft—all claimed a heavier toll than the enemy in those days from August 1914 to January 1915. Certainly, the weapons used could hardly be con-sidered dangerous: revolvers, signal pistols, and army rifles which had to be fired standing up in the open cockpits of bucking ma-chines in an attempt to potshot the enemy while studiously avoiding one's own propeller, struts, and exposed controls.

Besides the danger in the air, many were dying because of the bicycle-type wire wheels on their planes. Wild grass and weeds would, on takeoff, often become entangled in the spokes, wreck-ing the plane and killing or injuring the pilot. Then some ground-force genius thought of the solid-disc wheel and takeoffs became just a little less dangerous.

The first virgin planes soon were marked with national insignia and colors, to be followed by the decor of some mascot motif or personal fetish. But initially all was wonder and hope, sky-struck youths or dedicated, stiff-backed fanatics of the motorized kite, that object the Wright brothers had brought into being on the sand dunes of Kitty Hawk in 1903, watched by none but a few indifferent witnesses and gawking sea gulls. From those few sec-onds of uneven airborne flight, with a man prone on his stomach, arose the force to change the face of warfare. But only in those first years could it have the crazy glow of knighthood, of tournament, a personal gallantry between two individuals alone in an immense sky.

Adolphe Pégoud, five times mentioned in an Order of the Day, kept a diary. The text of December 27, 1914, points up the danger of those early flying days:

Weather cloudy. Morning observation at Verdun. No Boche aeroplane about. 12.20 leave with eight shells for Nantillois. At 4,200 feet over Bras I get into clouds. Fog and rain continue over Nantillois. More than beastly. My machine in all positions. Can see nothing. Am continually wiping my glasses; compass jammed. After one and one-half hours of all sorts of worry, dive to get my position. I notice 1,800 feet under the clouds a fine captive balloon and drop my eight bombs. General panic in the company. Several guns are fired at me, and I rise up into the fog. Lost again. Dive down to see, and continue flight at 3,000 feet. Up again among the clouds, and dive down to 2,400 feet. I steady the machine and compass and take the direction S.W. I have an hour's petrol left. Swearing like a pickpocket. It's the limit. I don't know where I am and am fired at. I am 2,400 feet up. Up into the clouds. Down again. Note a rather large station. Am shot at.

Up into the clouds again. Dive twenty-six minutes later and see am again over the station. I'm like a roaring wild beast. Only fifteen liters of petrol left. Don't know where I am; am shot at. I make up my mind, and am going to fly under the clouds at 2,400 feet S.W. till petrol gives out, despite shots. I note a village far off, and as I get nearer recognize Etain. I can use my lungs to breathe now. Saved! Good Heavens, to think how mad I have been with rage. I dive with the motor at full speed. The wind is in my nose. I keep on wiping the glasses and break one case and all. Pass over Etain at 1,450 feet, still diving with motor at full speed. Reach Verdun in fog at 150 feet, and get hail and rain. Can see nothing. One of my eyes is hurting very badly. Land. It's a splendid feeling after all. I can breathe now with my face to the wind and take in lungfuls of air. But to think how I've sworn. Another lesson for me, and I shall keep my eyes open more than ever. Report made at once. Captain astonished, and boasts about it to other officers and makes his report.

Food. At my ease, very pleased to be by the fireside at Verdun. Smoke several pipes, which are excellent. Bed.

In August of 1915, Pégoud was not that lucky—and France said prayers for the death of one of its earliest air heroes.

The French had gathered together a sort of *corps élite* of fliers. They had been trained in 80-horsepower Gnome, rotary-powered Blériot planes that could reach just over 65 miles an hour. The planes were controlled in the air by wing warping, which seemed at this stage to work better than the British system of control surfaces. The French had concentrated their flying school at Pau, just outside Paris. From there fliers went on to become *pilotes aviateurs* at Chartres. Neither side—the Anglo-French idea of rapprochement or the German cry of Encirclement: *Deutschland ganzlich einzukreisen!*—realized how impossible true national isolation would become with the airplane in the sky. The French were more concerned with uniforms than with understanding airpower. When there was talk of eliminating the red pants of the infantry because they were "too easy a target," a former War Minister shouted, Never! *"Le pantalon rouge c'est la France!"* He was one of those who had not been impressed by talk of the plane as a war weapon.

In Russia the czar was not aware of what the Kaiser, the All Highest, the War Lord, had said of him: "The Czar is fit only to live in a farmhouse and grow turnips." Yet the Russians had a talented plane designed in Igor I. Sikorsky, who received a gold watch in 1913 from the czar personally for his work with flying machines. It was Sikorsky who built the first four-engine plane, the Russian Knight, and in February 1914 his Ilya Mourometz, with a wing span of 105 feet, had climbed 6,500 feet, circled Moscow for five hours, and averaged just over 62 miles per hour; all this while carrying the sixteen passengers and dog. Nearly seventy-five of these giants were built, each armed with two Maxim guns and able to carry 1,120 pounds of bombs. They had the first enclosed space for pilot and crew. Sikorsky also designed a fighter plane, the only Russian one to be made.

Aside from Fokker's activities, the German War Office had set up a flying school as early as 1910 in Doberitz, and a year later other schools at Metz and Meresburg. By 1913 Teutonic organization had mounted a good flying service, even including sausage balloons. Five Luftschaffe Bataillonen hot-air bag units (actually using hydrogen) were added, with technicians and flying crews. In charge was a divided command: the Inspektion des Luftschiffe-truppe and the Inspektion der Fliegertruppe. By some bureaucratic logic, overall control was in the hands of the Railroads and Transport Section—so little was the value of airpower understood. On the training and flying level, each section got a Stabsoffizier der Flieger, or staff officer.

The four squadrons that the RAF sent to France at the outset of war turned out to be thirty-seven planes actually ready on English fields, with twenty-six more set to join them in a couple of days. They were painted a dull olive in color and were numbered in squadrons from 2 to 5. The honor of being the first British machine to join the war in France went to a BE-2A, numbered 347, of No. 2 Squadron. The pilot was Lieutenant H. D. Harvey-Kelly (official records seldom give the full first and middle names of fliers). Just before 6:30 in the morning of August 13, 1914, Harvey-Kelly's plane roared into the air outside Dover, to come down at Amiens two hours later, less five minutes. The rest of the squadrons followed, some that day and some two days later. They were flying a motley collection of planes: BE-2's, Morane-Saulnier Parasols, Blériots, BE-8's, Avro 504's, and Farmans; all secondary and third-stage versions of the Wright brothers' ideas of flying. Engines none too reliable, frames of wood with stretched canvas wings, varnished, struts and wires hardly strong enough to take the strain of pressure or diving speed. The fixed wheels did not look tough enough to withstand the jolt of landings in the pastures that passed for airfields. The machines stank of petrol and shook like nervous dogs; yet they flew.

Every British flier had an official list of what he was to carry: extra flying goggles, some sort of tool kit, field glasses, boiled water in a canteen, a form of cooking stove (here the list reminds one of the junk-laden White Knight in *Alice*), biscuits, cans of corned beef, chocolate bars. As for weapons: a revolver and cartridges to load it with. Not officially on the list were the metal mirrors which so many fliers and soldiers carried in a pocket over their hearts to divert bullets.

Four City of London vans had been provided to transport luggage and gear that could not be carried by plane. No time had been taken to paint out their London lettering—BOVRIL BEEF CUBES, LAZENBY'S SAUCE, STEPHEN'S BLUE BLACK INK, PEAK FREAN'S BISCUITS. By late 1914 the British had 63 planes in France; 105 pilots and the extra man then called an observer. There were nearly 800 mechanics, including supervisors, and over 300 lorries and autocars.

The German fliers had the sacred word of their Kaiser: "You will be home before the leaves fall from the trees," which he repeated to his fighting forces. The men shouted "Hoch, Kaiser, Folk and Country!" The French flew dashingly, and on the ground rushed with bayonets into machine guns, crying: "*C'est l'Alsace et la Lorraine!*" The cavalry in shiny cuirasses, black horse plumes, sat waiting as the band played *Sambre et Meuse*, and they looked up at the pitiably few French scout planes. The great cavalry battles would decide this thing in a few weeks, before the snow fell and they could go into winter quarters.

The French General Staff agreed: "*Il faut piquer dedans*—We must hit them where it hurts." But the truth was there was as yet no aerial strategy. Even the Germans in their Allgemeine Elektrizitäts Gesellschaft machines, their Aviatiks, first Fokkers, carried only hand weapons, sometimes silver-mounted shotguns as if for deer or grouse hunting. Their Luftverpehrs Gesellschaft biplane at first came up with nothing but pistols all round. Lethal airpower seemed impossible, out of place, as the enemy fliers waved to each other passing in the air.* The Spandau machine

---

* In November 1914, a German newspaper carried an account of an early "duel with a British machine. . . . When the combatants had exhausted all their rifle and revolver ammunition, they blazed away with their Very flare pistols, which made for very poor shooting. After a while, both pilots realized that the only chance of a hit was to get close up, but when they laid their machines alongside, the humor of the situation struck von Leutzer, so that he roared with laughter at the sight of two observers solemnly taking deliberate aim, a green light answering a red one. . . . The observers were also too amused to shoot straight . . . neither got near his mark."

guns were not yet in mass production. Above the roar of the mortars the German fliers sang *Heil dir im Sigelkrantz*, and once back at their flying field messes with steins of beer and nips of cognac and kummel *Die Wacht am Rhein*, while the gramophones ground out Strauss waltzes or Offenbach.

The Allies spread stories of German *Schrecklichkeit*, news of whole towns destroyed, churches ground to rubble. But the Germans themselves knew that all enemy spies, all hostages shot, were civilian bandits who used arms and sniped. The damn French and Belgian people had no *Rassenstolz* (race pride). In flying messes one heard of all those "armed priests, and the thirty German officers lying in hospitals, their eyes put out by Belgian women and children." Both sides were already busy sharpening their propaganda pens.

The British fliers, less infused with fury, scouted and looked down on the Poor Bloody Infantry, known with affection mixed with disdain as the PBI. They flew from Amiens and Mons over Louvain and Brussels, and always below them were the regular German infantry columns, supply trains, the dust of armies in the August heat. And refugees—the first of generations. The small British Expeditionary Army, commanded by General Sir John French, almost walked blindly into the teeth of the German advance at the start of the war. The French had pulled out on their left flank and only General French's scouting planes' report of the retreat kept him from catastrophe. French was an old-line stiff-upper-lip type, not, according to historians, very bright. Warned by his fliers that the German First Army under von Kluck was aiming for a strangling pincer move to gather in the enemy, General French pulled out and back, getting his men to some sort of safety just in time. The retreat from Mons took place just seven days after the first British plane set down on French soil.

There are those who claim that French's rescue of his forces by means of scout plane reports saved the Allies from losing the war in the first few weeks. If the British *had* been destroyed, the French, left weaker, would have faced the full fury of the enemy at their heels with no possibility of diverting the German forces. We leave that theory to the specialists. The fact is that the airplane had already drastically changed the information-seeking methods of armies in the field.

By September, the German armies were only two dozen miles from Paris. All the French planes available were at the fronts; those mobile, shifting fronts with troops charging into machine-gun fire to die by the thousands with desperately brave last stands and resulting immolation. Not one plane could be spared to patrol the skies over Paris.

The German air force sent out a scout plane, the early Taube, to see Paris. The Taube usually came winging over the city at the *apéritif*—the cocktail hour. It flew just above the rooftops to excite the Parisians. The pilot was Leutnant Karl von Hiddessen. Crowds, cocktail glasses in hand, gathered in the streets to watch the plane perform as the pilot swooped and flew up and down just over the chestnut trees of the grand boulevards, past the kiosks of the Gare de l'Est. Impotent machine guns set up on the Eiffel Tower fired on the little plane with the delta-patterned tail as it dropped its "bomb," which consisted of a sandbag containing a public notice to the people of France. It read: SURRENDER! THE GERMANS ARE AT YOUR GATES! TOMORROW YOU WILL BE OURS!

The crowds cheered the message loudly.

The next Taube flier, Oberleutnant Dressler, did carry small 4-pound bombs; they fell on the edge of the city and did no damage. This, incidentally, represented the first bombing of a capital city from the air.

At Ostend the Germans solemnly set up a bombing command and named it, in the usual jaw-breaking German way, the *Brieftauben Abteilung-Ostende*, which could be translated as the Carrier Pigeon Unit—a cover-up for its real hopes as a bombing command. The secret plan was to take Calais and there set up a base from which its Albatros D-II's could cross the Channel and drop bombs on England until it surrendered. (An idea that had to be postponed until World War II, when the Germans actually took Calais.)

The Pigeons did bomb Dunkirk—the first night raid—and they began to go after the French and British airfields. In December, a few days before Christmas, the Germans sent over a gift to England, an Imperial Navy seaplane, and Dover's High Street got one bomb, no damage. On Christmas Day itself, an Albatros seaplane scouted England and the Thames estuary and dropped two bombs at Cliffe Station. Civilization and society were not yet prepared to accept total war and objected to bombing on sacred holidays. The reading of Dickens's *Christmas Carol* was the only established tradition for Christmas Day.

The Royal Navy Air Service of the British retaliated from the Isle of Grain with several planes that tried to destroy the enemy flier who had dared to attack Christmas, shooting at him and his plane with pistols and rifles. There were no hits.

What is chiefly remembered today of the Ostend Carrier Pigeons are the four young untried fliers who began the war there before passing on to greater fame or notoriety: Manfred von Richthofen, who was to become the folk hero of the comic strip *Peanuts* as the Red Baron; Ernst Udet, flier and tester of deadly planes; Bruno Loerzer, an ace, forty-one kills in the air; and Hermann Goering, who became Hitler's number-two man in the rise and fall of the Third Reich, and commander of the Luftwaffe that was to try to bomb England into submission in the Battle of Britain in World War II.

The French, in spite of warnings, had misjudged the German plans for the opening attacks of the war. Their planes were mostly stacked between Verdun and Nancy in the Côte de Meuse sector. Here they waited fruitlessly while the Germans, with the plans of Alfred von Schlieffen long prepared, pressed their attacks through Belgium. Up north, just before the attacks at Mézières, French scout planes were kept from the air by bad weather, and so failed to observe the Germans massing sixteen army corps and five cavalry divisions for their early version of *blitzkrieg*.

Those French scout planes that did take to the air sent back misinformation and bad guesses. Air scouting as a science was still in its infancy and there were as yet no trained observers. On September 5 the Germans were in sight of Paris and General Joffre stood at the Marne. The short war that would "be over by Christmas" had begun its first year of the grinding destruction that was to haunt the rest of the twentieth century. In the first three months of the war the British and French together suffered a million casualties; mass slaughter would become a commonplace for the next fifty years.

For millions of men, war was to become a way of life. The young as they became adults in uniform soon seemed to have no other world, but for some dim memory of boarding school and Mum's worry over warm clothes. The trench, the airfield were the true world—the first-aid station, the hasty burial of some chum under a sodden sky.

The airmen hurried off on leave and then hurried back as if they were missing some fearful sacred rite; war gave to many a free rein, to some an obsession for brutality. The fliers were almost dispossessed beings away from their squadron, away from that vacuum of horror, a sky that lacked a ceiling.

Their talk, their very language became a cosy private code, as at school, apart from their family life and suspended between the jarring challenge of two realities—home and the front. In time for most it was home that lost the edge of truth.

Many terms of that special world have entered the history of air warfare. Some are confusing. The accepted definition of the word "dogfight," for example, came to mean, from loose usage, any battle in the air in which three to six aircraft were engaged in dodging, diving, and moving around, trying to shoot each other down. But Arch Whitehouse, who fought with the RAF, firmly demanded a tighter formula. ". . . When I speak of a dogfight I mean an aerial engagement in which at least fifty aircraft take an actual part, and the action must be confined to the diameter of a few hundred yards—not miles!"

Specialists, and the fliers themselves, have written a great deal about the art of air warfare, and the science of battle with planes as it existed in that war. By later standards, the speeds were not excessive, the fighter planes small and frail, normally flying at from 75 to 100 miles an hour. (Near the end of the war, the best speed was that of the Spad 12, leveling off at 120 miles an hour, more or less.) Most planes could reach 15,000–20,000 feet at times, but air battles were generally fought, according to reports, from a climb of 10,000 feet on down. "You always look over the ground —in case you have to fly at tree top level to sneak home." The basic air battle, under ideal conditions, was begun by diving at the enemy out of the sun, getting on his tail if possible, and shooting him down. If that failed to inflict a mortal wound as one passed him by, then try to climb again and blast him with bursts of machine-gun fire from below as one rose. If this, too, failed, the battle could result in an ever-tightening circling. Each opponent tried to keep on the other's tail, get the gun sights on target, and fire. One trained oneself to look up and over to keep on the enemy tail. To escape, one went into false stalls and spirals, as if hit and out of the fight. Only the comparatively low speed of those planes could keep them circling and maneuvering in a dogfight.

The journals give us some valuable facts. "Killing range in the air with a machine gun, single or twin, had to be from ninety yards to sixty yards." This was very close, and unless a flier got in his bursts and pulled up and away, there could be a mid-air collision, as indeed there often was.*

The French flier Charles Nungesser, who was an expert at taking proper advantage of the classic air fight, in his early days gave some sound advice to the Belgian Willy Coppens. Nungesser had a very sound argument, said Coppens: "that a two-seater airplane when attacked over enemy territory by a single-seater possessed of greater speed, must accept fight and turn steeply whenever the single-seater dives on it; the single-seater, in effect, can only fire straight ahead, along its axis of flight; it follows that it cannot hold a two-seater for long in its sights, if the two-seater twists and turns, while the observer in the latter keeps the Scout under fire by means of his movable gun." And Coppens added, of a specific battle:

I remembered this piece of advice, and kept continuously turning—first one way and then the other—rarely coming back

---

* The system of measurement as set down in most texts may seem confusing. A meter is about 39 inches, 1,000 meters makes 1 kilometer, and a kilometer is ⅝ of a mile. Time too, in most air forces, was measured on a 24-hour clock; midnight, or 12 o'clock, was 2400 hours.

for more than a second onto an even keel; for we were subjected to repeated attacks from all four of our adversaries. At the first burst, hearing the crack of the bullets, I had the impression that I was being sprayed with molten lead. Being under fire is bad for the nervous system. I could do nothing by way of retaliation myself, having no machine gun, but my observer's fire maintained with the utmost calmness throughout.

There is some confusion as to just when and how the opposing air forces began to put identifying insignia on their wings. At the outset (as we have seen), no planes carried national markings. Anyone within a plane's range, if he had a weapon, fired up at it. It was the English who first painted red, white, and blue streaks on their wings. Some used the Union Jack, which in time was modified to become the red, white, and blue roundel. The French, who had the same national colors, reversed the order, making the outer circle red, the center blue. The Germans could think of nothing better than the symbol of the cross, combining in their practical minds the cross of Calvary used as a religious symbol and a bit of uniform decor called the Iron or Maltese Cross. (When the Americans later set up the Escadrille Lafayette, they added a personal Wild West touch; the head of a feathered shouting Indian, copied from an ammunition box bearing the trademark—an Indian chief —of the Savage Arms Company.)

Baron von Richthofen's all red plane was to become famous, but actually one of the Navarre twins, probably Jean, flew an all-red Nieuport at the Verdun front. Von Richthofen's Jasta all had some red splash of color, either a wing, or tail, or a band on the fuselage. Other groups each later had a dominant color that identified them. Jasta 2 favored yellow; Jasta 3 was Op Art long before its time with black and white checkerboard design; Jasta 6 liked its black put on in stripes.

A French escadrille, the Spa. 48, called itself *Les Coqs*, and had a crowing rooster as its decor in the clouds. The most amazing plane paint was, for a short time, on the British A Flight Camels. The whole body of the ship was done in wide white stripes, and the wheels painted like circus wagons with stars and rays. The

wing commander, a proper Colonel Blimp of his time, took one
look and howled to have all bloody decoration removed!

The French fliers of Les Cigognes, of course, had a flying stork
insignia. As the war progressed, many of the German planes no
longer carried the flaring Iron or Maltese Cross, but adopted the
familiar cross bars of the Red Cross painted in black.

Some fliers named their planes after girls, and a few were obscene in choice of titles. Actually, no flier could long use an
individual plane, for damage and the aging process under hard
conditions could shake a plane to ruin in no time. The aces flew
several favorite planes. Von Richthofen at times had a series of
planes, like a cowboy, ready at roundup time. The first planes
were fragile, and the muslin or canvas had to be constantly
patched. The Germans experimented with plywood bodies, but
there is no record of any all-metal planes. If enemy fire didn't do
damage, the planes also deteriorated from rough fields, poor shop-
work; and those sputtering engines that killed many a pilot and
observer made matchwood and torn canvas of the structure.

Wrote Rupert Brooke, of his sacrificed generation:

> *Honour has come back,*
> *And Nobleness walks in our way again.*
> *And we have come into our heritage . . .*

A heritage of crashing cloth and wood and motor oil spurting
over a broken body on some farmer's meadow scarred by plane
wheels. The British fliers had a more realistic set of verses:

> *The young aviator lay dying*
> *Beneath the wreck he lay.*
> *These last parting words*
> *He did say:*
> *"Take the cylinder out of my kidney,*
> *The connecting rod out of my brain . . .*
> *From my arse remove the crankshaft,*
> *Assemble the fucking*
> *Engine again!"* *

---

* In politer printed versions "back" and "goddam" are used instead of the
soldier's favorite expressions in all wars, long before modern novelists made
the four-letter word chic.

2. | Their Weapons

In drawings Leonardo da Vinci hinted at a primitive machine gun. But it was the practical Americans of the nineteenth century who really brought the chain-shot killer to its ultimate deadly perfection. In 1862 Richard Jordan Gatling of North Carolina was looking for a weapon to mow down more men in the War Between the States. His Gatling gun was the first rapid-fire weapon to use a metal cartridge. Purists on military weapons say that as a hand-cranked bullet sprayer, it was not a true machine gun; that had to wait for the utilizing of the power and kick of expanding the gas at combustion in the gun barrel. Thus the recoil was used to reload and fire automatically as long as the finger remained on the trigger or firing button.

Four Americans perfected this weapon, and their versions, or improved adaptations of them, were to dominate the machine-gun fire of the Great War (and all wars to date). Benjamin Hotchkiss, Hiram Maxim, John Moses Browning, and Isaac Newton Lewis (West Point, Class of '84) cannot be counted as great benefactors of mankind. But their military importance is clear in that they produced a weapon that, until the atomic bomb came on the scene, was capable of, in the Elizabethan phrase, "calling many down to death."

The Hotchkiss machine gun was a small weapon. It fired by means of a springload clip containing twenty-five cartridges. This was the machine gun carried in the early days of air warfare, arming the single-seaters of such men as Garros, Quenault, and Frantz.

The true heavy hitters were the Lewis gun and the Maxim. The United States War Department had not been interested in the Lewis gun of 1911, fired by a flat round drum rotating as it was fired. But it was a good weapon and by 1916 it carried a king-size drum of machine-gun cartridges into air battles and dogfights. Like most guns it also carried a muzzle damper that held back the combustion gas under pressure and so gave it a faster firepower.

Vickers and Sons and Maxim Limited produced the gun known

as the Vickers, based on Maxim patents. In a friendly cartel exchange of the licensing business the Vickers weapon was also produced in an arsenal at Spandau in Germany, and so was called the Spandau. A lighter version was also made, named from the Latin: *Si vis pacem, para bellum—If you wish for peace, prepare for war.* The Parabellum gun was very popular on early German planes. The Maxim for plane use was the only gun that was water-cooled and belt-fed on an enclosed track. Downed fliers, short of water, cooled the weapon with their urine. (The Browning hardly ever got into the air, remaining chiefly a ground weapon.)

But initially the planes still had little method for knocking each other out of the sky. The soldiers on the ground fired at what looked like the enemy's planes. Rifle fire from the ground brought down the first plane on August 12, 1914, when Leutnant Reinhold Jahnow was shot down by French infantry. A little later Sergeant Major D. S. Jilling was wounded by German ground fire. Then a British flying sergeant took a slug up his arse, and for that reason perhaps his name is not recorded.

The British forced down two Taubes by flying above them as if to crash onto them. In September a Bréguet scout plane of the French had dangerous holes made in its wings when a German pilot threw a brick down on it. French fliers carried slingshots, and mean steel darts called *flechettes.* The hand grenade came into use, demanding a skill in baseball pitching the Allies and Germans both lacked. Some grenades were dragged behind on cables, to become, it was hoped, entangled in enemy propellers and so explode. No actual results were reported from these egg drags. Grappling hooks were also tried to gash and tear at enemy wing surfaces. One German put an old-fashioned gramophone horn onto his carbine, but while this secret terror weapon looked frightful, it proved ineffective.

It was not until April 1915 that the French flier, Roland Garros, first proved the deadly effectiveness of the machine gun; the days of scouting planes of opposite forces waving to each other, tossing bricks, or taking potshots with a pistol were by then already over. Garros was piloting an armed MS-2 single-seater. Carrying a load of bombs, he sighted French antiaircraft batteries firing at an Aviatik two-seater. The German Aviatik was 1,500 feet higher than Garros, so he began his climb, and in about six minutes was level with the enemy plane. Moving in he began firing a clip of twenty-five from his Hotchkiss, reloaded, and got off another clip. The German dived steeply to escape, but the Frenchman followed him down to 3,000 feet and gave him a lot of the third clip. Flames exploded the Aviatik, and trailing a black plume of smoke it began its death spin, a fearful fall which lasted nearly a half minute. Garros wrote of his kill:

> I went up by autocar to view the wreck. Those there first were stealing souvenirs—I took strong steps to get these back. The two corpses were exposed in a horrible state—so naked and bloody! The observer shot through the head, the pilot too horribly mutilated to be examined. The plane, what was left of it, was everywhere pierced by bullet holes.

The macabre scene did not prevent Roland Garros from shooting down two more enemies in the next two weeks. His secret (and it was a vital one) was that he had steel plates screwed to sections of his propeller. He could fire straight through the propeller, knowing that if he hit it, the plates would automatically deflect the shot. It all went back to Garros's study of the problem of shooting from the air. The propeller on the machine, he figured, revolved 1,200 times a minute. Why, he wondered, don't I try firing *through* it? The chances of hitting the prop are there, but enough shots will get through to strike the enemy, if I aim my plane and its fixed machine gun properly. He would hit his propeller forty times a second; if he used a Hotchkiss gun, the odds against himself went up even higher.

Early in 1915 Garros had demanded a Hotchkiss *mitrailleuse*. "Firing a clip of twenty-five rounds, I figure enough will pass the propeller blades to destroy an enemy plane. The gun fixed perfectly along my line of flight; to get a hit, all I need to do is to fly straight for just that fraction of a second."

He was told he would surely destroy his own propeller in such a process.

"Ah, so what. I will make a glide landing. If I stay over French-held territory, I've got no problem. The cost of a propeller against the wiping out of a German plane and its crew."

It was suggested he try an old experiment, screwing steel protection plates to part of the propeller to deflect any bullets hitting it. Garros found a new Morane-Saulnier series N monoplane and mounted a Hotchkiss .303 machine gun right behind the propeller with its steel blade protectors. Starting on April 1, 1915, in eighteen days Roland Garros made five kills among the unwary Germans. The enemy could hardly believe reports of a plane firing through its propeller. The higher-ups said the German pilots were either drunk or suffering the "hallucinations of old women." But the Germans in the air began to avoid contact with Allied planes.

Then on April 19, after his sixth air victory, Garros's engine died in the air and he was forced to land behind the German lines. He tried to set fire to his plane, but it and he were captured unharmed.* The plane was shipped to Berlin and Anthony Fokker was sent for to examine the wonder machine and its magic gun.

Fokker shook his head as he looked at the steel wedges attached to the propeller. Garros, he said, had been a lucky fool. Deflected slugs would sooner or later have killed him. If not him, the odds

---

* An official account of the capture was given in the *Kriegszeitung*, the newspaper of the German Fourth Army:

April 18, 1915, at about seven o'clock in the Sainte Catherine Landelede region two aeroplanes appeared at a great height. One disappeared in the direction of Menin, pursued by antiaircraft fire. The other, piloted by Roland Garros, headed toward Landelede. At this moment a train was passing on the Ingelmunster-Courtrai line from the north. Immediately on seeing the train, Garros made a descent at an angle of 60 degrees, coming down from 2,000 meters to 40, executing a series of tight turns over the train. Garros dropped one bomb upon the rails, digging a crater one meter deep and two across. Some guards opened fire on him at 100 meters. The aviator dropped a second bomb and climbed to 700 meters.

Suddenly his motor stopped. The aeroplane wavered and fell into a glide in the direction of Hulste. On touching ground Garros set fire to his machine and took refuge in a peasant's home. The soldiers pursuing him looked for some time, finally discovered him crouching in a ditch behind a hedge. The soldiers asked if he did not have a companion. Garros gave them his word he had been alone in the machine, the engine being only of 80 horsepower and able to carry but a single passenger. Garros said that at 700 meters his motor had been hit and this had forced him to land. . . .

The soldiers of the *Landsturm* who had made the capture were awarded a bonus of 100 marks. So by his fall he had given away his invention of the steel plates screwed into his propeller.

were in favor of bullets bouncing back and smashing the engine or the structure of the plane. Somehow, *somewhere,* Fokker felt, there should be a better system for firing through one's own propeller.

He took a Parabellum machine gun and carefully stripped it down to its basic parts. He didn't know what he was looking for, but he was a great player of hunches. He remembered that as a boy he had flung rocks between the moving vanes of Dutch windmills; it had all been a matter of timing, of figuring out when he was free to toss a rock to miss the great vanes. If he could figure out how to time the passing of the bullets through the propeller flow when the blades were not in front of the machine gun, he'd have it. But how?

Back at the Schwerin plant, Fokker and three assistants tackled the problem. They attached the Parabellum to the engine hood of an E-I plane. Fixing two studs to the propeller shaft opposite each other in alignment with the blades, Fokker figured out that as the shaft revolved, the studs could alternately hit a cam. This cam would work a pushrod connected by wire to the hammer of the machine gun. When the propeller activated the pushrod— which was every time the blade passed the gun—it stopped the hammer from hitting the firing pin. No matter how much pressure there was on the trigger, the gun wouldn't fire. In other words, as he explained to his assistants, the propeller controlled the gun.

In forty-eight hours the new interrupter was tested and found to work. For the mechanically minded, here is Fokker's own description of his invention:

> I attached a small knob to the propeller which struck a cam as it revolved. This cam was hooked up with the hammer of the machine gun, which automatically loaded itself. Thus, as I slowly revolved the propeller, I found that the gun shot between the blades. During the night I found out the basic operation, and began next morning to perfect the device. One blade was enough to strike the cam, because the gun could shoot only 600 times a minute while the blades passed a given point 2,400 times a minute. To the cam was fastened a simple knee lever, which operated a rod, held back by a spring. In order that the pilot

could control the shooting, a piece of the rod which struck the hammer was hinged to hit or miss as the operator required. That was the entire device . . . an immense feeling of pride to invent something which I knew would have a fundamental effect on strategy in the air, . . .*

Fokker got out his battered Peugeot and towed his gun-mounted plane to Berlin. The staff officers were disappointed at the sight. Where were the steel plates? He said later, "I had not figured on the conservative military mind." But he fired three bursts of ten shots each through the spinning prop. When the officers wondered if he was afraid to fire more, he used up the rest of the belt. They then shot off a whole belt.

Yes, fine on the ground, but would it work up there? Fokker promptly took the plane up nearly 1,000 feet, and, aiming at some old wings laid on the ground, he began shooting. It was rocky ground and slugs ricocheted among the staff officers, who discarded dignity and ran for shelter. Fokker landed and showed that the propeller was untouched.

But, "Herr Fokker," the officials now said, "the true test is *you* go up and shoot down an enemy machine from the sky." It was clear; credit and money for his invention would come only if Fokker went to the front in actual combat and made a kill.

It is hard to believe that the Germans would risk their best plane maker, their brightest troubleshooter. Fokker was against the scheme. But like most inventors, he was intrigued by the idea of a true test for his invention. Also, as always with Fokker, there was the vice of greed, of having payment for his work. So he accepted the plan, which required him to commit a criminal action: to kill someone that his nation was not at war with.

A day later he arrived with his machine and gun at Laon, the headquarters of General von Heeringen. By now Fokker thought less and less of the validity of the test plan. After an untouched lunch (cold ham, potato salad) at the château (the castle from

---

* Some time later Fokker learned that this discovery was in fact no invention. Half a dozen inventors in Germany, Austria, and France had done the thing and no one had paid any attention to them. Franz Schneider had patented the Fokker-type cam and pushrod fire control as early as 1912, but it was not called to anyone's attention in military aviation.

which Crown Prince Willie commanded), the prince's own car took Fokker to the waiting plane, motor running. Fokker tried to explain that as a good neutral Dutchman he had no right to go up and kill Frenchmen or Englishmen. He'd be put against a wall as a spy if captured.

"No, Herr Fokker, you are now in the service." He was hastily put into a German oberleutnant's uniform, air force wings on the jacket, and a military identification card in the correct pocket in case of capture.

Luck was with Fokker for a week. Seven times he went up; seven times there was no sign of any enemy plane. On the eighth day, over Douai, at 6,000 feet he spotted a Farman two-seater. Fokker cursed and began his dive for the kill. As he later described the scene:

> . . . the plane grew larger in my sights. My imagination could picture my shots puncturing the gasoline tanks. . . . Even if my bullets failed to kill the pilot and observer, the ship would fall down in flames. I had my finger on the trigger. What I imagined recalled my own narrow escapes; the time the gasoline tanks burst; the breaking of the wing at Johannesthal when my passenger was killed. I had no personal enmity toward the French. I was flying merely to prove that a certain mechanism I had invented would work. By this time I was near enough to open fire, and the French airmen were watching me curiously, wondering, no doubt, why I was flying up behind them. In another instant it would be all over for them. Suddenly, I decided that the whole job could go to hell. It was too much like "cold meat" to suit me. I had no stomach for the whole business. . . . Let them do their own killing.

So Anthony Fokker experienced a split-second of awareness of horror. For the first time he realized fully what his planes and guns actually achieved in use. Abstractly planning and perfecting his work, he had relegated to the background the end results of his drive, his greed. But up there, faced with an easy kill, finger on the trigger, he fled.

Oswald Boelcke, who was to become one of the biggest scorers of the war before his death (forty kills), was sent up instead as an eager pigeon to test the Fokker synchronizer. On his third time up he knocked an enemy plane out of the air with the fixed gun. Now it was official. Orders went out to put as many of the new inventions as possible on German fighter planes. Max Immelmann, another scorer-to-be, got the second fixed weapon set up on a Fokker E-II, with a 100-horsepower Oberursel engine replacing the weaker Argus power plant.

From then on for some time the Germans ruled the skies. Allied planes fell like ducks under the impact of the deadly synchronizer. There was talk in high places that the Fokker invention would "win the war" (this represented the first appearance of the nonsense about "victory through airpower" as the deciding factor in a major war).

The Allied pilots began to call themselves "Fokker Fodder" as more of their comrades died. German pilots were ordered *not* to fly over enemy lines and beyond, so that the French and British would not shoot down and capture one of the newly armed planes and discover its secret. A secret that was kept for just four months. What followed was one of those military blunders that baffle historians when they try to sift out the strange lack of foresight and numbness of war departments and general staffs. A German pilot caught in a thick fog landed at a French airfield. He, his plane, and the secret of the Fokker gun invention were all captured. The firing gear was looked over, tested, drawings made of it, reports drawn up. Then all was solemnly filed away. Not one member of the military personnel did anything about getting the invention to the Allied fliers! Certain civilians nonetheless somehow saw to it that the information and drawings of the gear were leaked to French magazines, which printed them. The French War Ministry was not very impressed by the magazine stories, however, and nothing much was done to arm French fighter planes with the new synchronizer. If the English generals were "brainless donkeys," slaughtering whole generations in their suicidal frontal attacks on the enemy, the French headquarters staff seem equally venal in another way. Furthermore, this black comedy was repeated in England, where the Fokker invention became known to Parliament. The War Office, Parliament was informed, felt that

the Dutchman Anthony Fokker was a neutral, technically anyway, and the patents were his. (The War Office had turned down
him and his planes in 1912.) Yet he *might* do business. Parliament,
respecting business rights, put forward a motion to acquire from
Fokker licenses on his patents for use in the English war effort;
a sad-faced, humiliated member then had to report that all the
test Fokker patents were exclusively licensed to the Germans. It
would not be sporting or even legal to make the offer. As to using
them without such licenses—it was just not cricket. The motion
was rapidly withdrawn and shelved, permanently.

In time—costing many lives by the delay—the British, French,
and American fighter planes were to use a Fokker-type synchronizer. Meanwhile Fokker—the neutral—went on making thousands
of versions of his gear for the Germans in a piano factory. He
gladly spent German money building and taking over factories,
and soon had nearly 2,000 men working in them. (During the
war he was to build about 4,000 Fokker aircraft himself, and by
licensing agreement with other *Vaterland* factories the wartime
total of Fokker planes turned out was 7,600.)

The Fokker in the air became a plane that the enemy was not
too happy to meet. A flying officer, Rothesay Wortley of the
RFC, wrote there were two things about a Fokker that were special:

> First it is difficult to spot. A thin black line with a blob in the
> middle, very like a cormorant on the wing, was all that could be
> seen. Secondly it was fitted with an "interrupter gear" by means
> of which the machine gun could be fired directly ahead . . . the
> trigger automatically stopped when the blades came opposite
> the barrel of the gun. This is a development of the first impor-
> tance. . . .

In 1915, the RFC officer Duncan Grinnell-Milne studied the
appearance of the new Fokker fighters, monoplanes with rotary
motors:

> It was very fast, very maneuverable, with a gun firing through
> the propeller by means of a mechanism captured, it was said,
> from the French. For these good reasons the machine was prov-

ing almost certain death to our BE's, particularly when it was flown by a German pilot named Immelmann. Very vaguely, it was being rumored that this young officer (who had already brought down the incredible number of six machines) had invented a new method of turning . . . he certainly had a remarkably clever way of throwing his machine around so as to appear suddenly, almost sitting on his enemy's tail, with his machine gun banging away through the propeller . . . it opened up a new set of problems in aerial fighting. . . .

To bring down an enemy machine at any time required luck, persistence, a fast airplane, and a well-aimed machine gun; but to bring down a Fokker or even to defend oneself successfully against it required something much more. It required from the scientist a better war machine. . . .

Flying Officer R. S. Wortley in a letter gives further details of how the RFC felt about the new Fokkers.

At first our pilots were not much impressed by this new apparition. They had been far more concerned with "Two-tails," a frightful-looking contraption with a double fuselage, which forged its way through the air.

Artillery observation machines were shot down in full view of our men in the trenches, while long-distance bombers frequently failed to return from patrol. The Fokkers were gaining a complete ascendancy over our machines. They had a superior performance both in climb and speed. . . . The tactics of the pilots seldom varied. They would climb to a height of about 10,000 feet whence they would swoop, hawklike, upon our machines as they passed below them, firing continuously as they dived. They could dive at and pass their opponents, continuing straight onwards and downwards until well out of range; then they would climb again at their leisure to repeat the process later on. The Fokkers hunted in pairs, sometimes even three of them would fly together. . . .

How best to tackle the Fokker with all its advantages in speed and climb? Whether, when dived on from above, to fly straight on, risk being hit, and trust to the observer's expertness in gunnery to bring the enemy down; or to "turn in" under the enemy to avoid his field of fire, but in so doing to deprive one's own observer of his chance of destroying an enemy machine?" . . .

The early Fokkers also posed problems for this anonymous flier:

There were five of us and we ran into five Fokkers at 15,000 feet. We both started climbing, of course. And they outclimbed us. We climbed up to 25,000 feet and we couldn't get any higher. We were practically stalled and these Fokkers went right over our heads and got between us and the lines. They didn't want to dogfight but tried picking off our rear men. Inglis and Cal were getting a pretty good thrill when we turned back and caught one Hun napping. He half-rolled slowly and we got on his tail. Gosh, it's unpleasant fighting in that altitude. The slightest movement exhausts you, your engine has no pep and splutters; it's hard to keep a decent formation, and you lose five hundred feet on a turn.

The other Huns came in from above and it didn't take us long to fight down to 12,000 feet. We put up the best fight of our lives but these Huns were just too good for us. Cal got shot in his radiator and went down and Webster had his tail plane shot to bits and his elevator control shot away. He managed to land with his stabilizer but cracked up.

Fokkers can dive as fast as we can. First you must turn, bank ninety degrees and keep turning. They can't keep their sights on you. Watch the sun for direction. Now there's one on your right—shoot at him. Don't try to hit him—just spray him—for if you try to hold your sight on him you'll have to fly straight and give the others a crack at you. But you put the wind up him anyway and he turns. Quick, turn in the opposite direction. He's out of it for a moment. Now there's another one near you. Try it on him—it works! Turn again, you are between them and the line. Now go for it, engine full on, nose down.

Two of them are still after you—tracer getting near again. Pull up, zoom and sideslip and if necessary turn and spray them again. Now make another dive for home and repeat when necessary. If your wings don't fall off, and you are gaining on them, pull up a little. Ah, there's Archie [antiaircraft fire], that means they are behind you—woof—that one was close—you now have another gray hair—they've been watching you—better zigzag a bit. You can laugh at Archie, he's a joke compared to machine guns. You dodge him carefully and roll in derision as you cross the lines and hasten home for tea. . . .

CHAPTER 4

AIR ACTIONS

Searching in the old files, one can grasp a picture of the first raids on Paris, and of steps taken to raid Germany.

In the first raid of August 30, 1914, two women were wounded and windows broken. "Attila's visiting card," was the comment made by the Parisians. The following day another German appeared over the city, letting off three bombs which did no material damage. On September 4, an aviator reached the center of the city; two bombs exploded behind the store Au Printemps and in the Avenue de l'Opéra. Again, no great damage. A gun mounted on the roof of the Crédit Lyonnais opened fire and two British privates fired from the boulevard without effect. That night it was announced that a squadron of armored planes with machine guns had been organized to pursue intruders. On September 2, the raider came in at about six o'clock in the evening, first over the Invalides on the south side of the river, where he dropped one bomb, then over the Elysée, and finally over the Grand Boulevard. Hundreds of shots were fired, none hit. Thousands of Parisians witnessed the pigeon-shooting match with ironical smiles: the chances seemed to favor the pigeon.

On October 8, four (or five) Allied aeroplanes started for Germany, one section making for Dusseldorf and the other for Cologne. The first city bombs were dropped on an air shed in Dusseldorf by a Lieutenant Marix. A burst of flames and the collapse of the roof resulted. The attacking planes were badly hit, but they succeeded in reaching the British line. The Cologne party circled the city at a height of 600 feet, being fired upon heavily, and succeeded in wrecking part of the military railway station. The attacks were announced as reprisal for German air raids on London and Paris.

Many of the early reports of air action and air raids are not too trustworthy. An eyewitness account of one reaction is given by Stephen Graham, reporting a German raid in October 1914 on the city of Warsaw:

> Aeroplanes were sailing in and out of light clouds like cranes passing over high mountains. Down below people stood and gazed at them all day long, pointing, gesticulating and looking through field-glasses. Suddenly one of these human birds in the sky stopped in its flight, staggered and fell. . . . There was a great rush and many cries of—"This way is quicker, this way is quicker"; and then everybody rushed in the straightest line possible for the point where the flying machine appeared to have fallen. Out of restaurants and cafés dashed officers and with them ladies, who jumped into waiting motor-cars to follow the crowd. Every cab was taken. Droshkis had a dozen or fifteen passengers standing on them. Policemen left their posts, hawkers their stalls, barbers came out in aprons, Jews in square hats and black cloaks, students, schoolboys, 50,000 of them, and the crowd increasing every moment.

A German aeroplane had been shot down, but it hit the earth ten miles outside Warsaw.

In December 1914, French planes gave Metz and its garrison an aerial bombardment in return for a German bombardment of Nancy, an unfortified town. They came from Verdun and flew east for 37 miles until they were over the German stronghold, where they showered powerful bombs on aviation hangars, on the railroad station where troops were in movement, and on barracks at the outskirts of the city.

A raid that much impressed the Germans was made by French airmen on Karlsruhe, on June 15, 1915. Estimates of the number of planes from German and French sides varied from 7 to 23, and of the bombs from 80 to 130. But what aroused chief German press reaction to the "crime of Karlsruhe" was not the material damage (relatively slight) nor the casualty list. It was the attack made on four Ducal palaces.

Of the palaces, only one—that of Prince Max of Baden*—was actually struck. One bomb fell close to the back door of this palace, but did not explode; a second exploded in a small garden; a third, more effective, blew in the roof of the main building. Princess Max was at home. The bomb cut through the tin roof. In exploding it damaged the stone cornice outside, shattered two wooden beams in the garret, drilled two small holes through the floor of the garret, and pierced the ceiling of the room below— that of little Prince Berthold and the Princess Marie-Alexander. By good fortune the bomb stuck fast in the ceiling, only a sharp point showing. The little Princess and Prince had a narrow escape from death, since the ceiling of the room in which they had slept was pierced.

"Even more sensational and dastardly" was the attack on the Grand Ducal Palace where the old grand duchess, mother of the reigning grand duke, lived, and where the Queen of Sweden was a guest at the time. "One bomb fell into the backyard—the *Faisanderie* or Pheasantry—causing casualties among the birds. A second dropped about a hundred yards from the Residenzschloss on the Schlossplatz within fifteen feet of the Karl Friedrich monument, taking the crease out of Karl Friedrich's bronze right trouser leg and pockmarking the foundation. . . ."

Thirty people were killed in an early German raid on Staffordshire, and at least fifty injured. Some families were wiped out altogether. One man was coming out of his house when a bomb fell at his feet and killed him. His little boy, who was following him, had his arm blown off. The first intimation people had of this raid was when the bombs burst among them; many of the victims were women and children. At an inquest on thirteen of the persons who had been killed, the coroner urged the jury to return a verdict to the effect "that death in each case was due to the explosion of a bomb dropped from German aircraft." The jury refused to accept this suggestion and brought in instead a verdict of "Murder against the Kaiser and the Crown Prince, as being accessories to and after the fact."

---

* Prince Max succeeded Count von Hertling as Chancellor in 1918; in October of that year he asked President Wilson to secure an armistice for Germany.

The year 1916 saw the first serious attempts by Allied planes to bomb behind the enemy lines. Reports show that heavy bombs were being used. On March 30, Metz-Sablons and Pagny-sur-Moselle were attacked, and on April 1 and 2 the targets were the station of Étain, the German bivouacs in the neighborhood of Nantillois, and the villages of Azennes and Brieulles-sur-Meuse. Thirty-one Allied machines dropped eighty-three bombs of heavy caliber on the enemy cantonments of Keyem, Essen, Terrest, and Houthulst. On the night of April 23–24, forty-eight heavy-caliber bombs fell on the station of Vifwege, east of the forest of Houthulst, in the environs of Ypres. The German lines of communication in the Verdun region received twenty-one shells and eight incendiary bombs on the station of Longuyon, five shells on Stenay, twelve on the camps to the east of Dun, and thirty-two on German establishments in the Montfauçon region and on the station of Nantillois.

The struggle for mastery of the air was reaching a pitch of considerable intensity. At the Battle of the Somme, which dragged on from July to November 1916, the French and English employed fighter planes to break up German aerial reconnaissance, as troop movements and masses of ammunition supplies were spotted by German fliers on the barren plain of Picardy. Twenty-two French fliers were shot down behind the German front. The French and English also raided German lines of communication. Every night (weather conditions permitting), French squadrons were in action dropping bombs on railways and bridges behind the Germans. The short bright nights favored these excursions; early dawn, too, became a favorite time at which to drop bombs.

A Lieutenant Marchal in June 1916 flew from France over Berlin dropping proclamations, then continued in flight, intending to land behind the Russian lines. He was forced to descend in Poland, however, where he was taken prisoner by Austrians. An official communication in Paris on July 24 described his achievement:

On June 20 at 9.30 in the evening, Sub-Lieutenant Marchal ascended at Nancy on board a Nieuport monoplane of a special type, taking with him a supply of fuel sufficient to last fourteen hours. His mission was to cross Germany at a low altitude in order to drop proclamations on the capital at Berlin and then to descend in Russia. This audacious flight was accomplished point by point, and, after flying all night, Lieutenant Marchal was compelled to descend at 8.30 in the morning of June 21, near Chelm, Russian Poland, at least 100 kilometers [62 miles] from the Russian lines. He was made a prisoner. The proclamation which Lieutenant Marchal dropped on Berlin began with the words: "We could bombard the open town of Berlin and thus kill women and innocent children, but we are content to throw only the proclamations."

Marchal had covered a distance of 1,300 kilometers (807 miles), in continuous flight, mostly at night.

Now the bomber, either escorted by fighter planes or alone, took on a more intense part in the war effort. Again and again the big manufacturing centers of Germany were the targets.

The most daring air raid carried out against the huge Krupp munition works at Essen occurred in the first week of July that year. Sergeant Maxime Gallois defied the German antiaircraft defenses and bombarded the heart of the German armament-producing factories with high explosives. He crossed the German front line twice, flew over Rhenish cities, and returned home; a flight that lasted seven hours. Gallois was guided by the moon and stars and a compass, since the raid was made in the darkest hours of night. He flew at an altitude of 1,200 meters, passing over Metz and Thionville above the course of the Moselle. Batteries fired at him over the Rhine, and above Metz searchlights played about the sky. He could see the reflection of the moon on the Rhine and identified Bonn. From there to Dusseldorf there was a sea of light, which increased as he got further north. Cologne was incandescent; Dusseldorf had blue, red, and white lights. The antiaircraft guns were blazing and Cologne gunners were nearly accurate in their range. The newspaper report read:

> Over Essen he rose to 2,000 meters, circled, searching for where the lights from the shops appeared densest. He dropped the first bomb. Counting ten he dropped the second, the remainder at similar intervals. It was impossible to see their effect

over the flaming furnace chimneys. He flew back, fired at many times.

Gallois drank alcoholized coffee and ate sandwiches and chocolate during his flight. He landed almost blind from the pressure of the wind on his eyes, having lost his goggles early in the flight.

Other French planes made raids into Germany "in reprisal for German attacks on open French towns." Sixty-seven thousand pounds of bombs were dropped in one night on many points of military importance and two machines failed to return. The principal centers hit were Treves, Essen, and Coblentz: eleven planes raided Treves, dropping over 5,000 pounds of bombs. Seven fires broke out, one in the Central Station. Six other planes attacked Ludwigshafen, destroying among other places the Badische Aniline factory.

But no matter how the Germans or French might behave, the British still retained a feeling for pomp and ceremony, as shown in the press description of the burial of the crew of the Zeppelin L-21 in September 1916.

The bodies of men who fell in airship raids received an orderly Christian burial . . . with impressive ritual the sixteen bodies of the men recovered at Cuffley from the wreckage of an airship were interred at Potter's Bar. The traditions of the British army were maintained in doing honor to an enemy. A hundred officers and men of the Royal Flying Corps stood silent and motionless while two buglers sounded "The Last Post." The sun of a perfect afternoon shone on a scene which presented striking contrasts. Within the burial enclosure, to which only a limited number of parishioners were admitted in addition to military, there was perfect quiet. In the public thoroughfare outside there was the hum of a thousand voices and occasional cries from itinerant vendors of souvenirs. An airplane was seen in the distance. As the bodies of the dead were committed to the grave, there could be heard the throbbing strokes of its engine. Splendid order was maintained. Over 1,000 members of the Metropolitan Constabulary, including about 400 special constables, had arrived, and long stretches of the route through which the funeral procession was to pass on its way from Cuffley were lined by officers. The funeral did not attract the general public in such numbers as had been anticipated. By twelve o'clock a crowd of spectators had assembled outside the little iron church of St. Andrew's at Cuffley, wherein were resting the bodies of the crew in coffins of polished Japanese ash—a wood resembling elm. They had been placed in the center aisle, while that of the commander, whose identity had been discovered by small pieces of his tunic found on his breast, rested near the altar. Of the sixteen coffins only that of the commander bore a breastplate. This was of brass with the following inscription: "An unknown German officer, killed while commanding Zeppelin L-21, 3d, September, 1916."

In the roadway immediately in front of the main entrance to the church there was a lorry and to the rear of this a flat trailer about 12 feet long and 6 feet wide. These two vehicles were to convey the bodies of the crew to the cemetery. Twelve were placed on the lorry and three others on the trailer. That with the body of the commander was brought out last and placed on the smaller car, which preceded the other vehicles. For a mile towards Potter's Bar the road was lined by a large number of spectators, chiefly women and children. The majority uncovered as the vehicles passed. Near the entrance to the cemetery were assembled about a hundred officers and men of the squadron of the Royal Flying Corps, to which Lieutenant [Leefe-] Robinson, VC, who brought down the airship, was attached. The general public was not admitted to the cemetery. The coffin of the commander was borne to the grave by six officers of the Royal Flying Corps, and those of the crew by men of the same corps. Nearly half an hour was occupied in this operation. When it had been completed, the remaining officers and men of the Corps marched into the cemetery and took up a position immediately in front of the graves. The majority of the civilians present uncovered, though a few who did not remove their hats immediately did so at the suggestion of the Vicar. . . .

"Forasmuch as it hath pleased Almighty God to take unto Himself the soul of this unknown German officer, here departed, we therefore commit his body to the ground, earth to earth, ashes to ashes, dust to dust, in sure and certain hope of of the resurrection of the dead, and the Day of Judgment. Through our Lord Jesus Christ."

A similar prayer was said by the Vicar over the grave of the members of the crew, after which he read the following:

"Almighty God, Father of all men, we beseech Thee to have mercy upon the souls of these men, whose mortal bodies we have just laid to rest, and grant them, if it be Thy will, forgiveness of their sins. Through Jesus Christ our Lord."

The "Last Post" sounded by two buglers immediately followed, and the service was at an end.

If the first pilots were unprepared to use machine guns, those who were ordered to carry bombs encountered even more confusion. There were simply no true aerial bombs. Cans of gasoline were dropped in the hope that they would burst and catch fire. Tins of explosives were also tried, wrapped in a cover of tarred hemp rope. The French used a melinite shrapnel shell from their artillery, with a nose that was supposed to set it off on landing. Some of these went off before the carrier plane even got off the ground. As for bomb racks, some bombs were tied on with grocer's twine; once over target, the flier cut them loose with his pocketknife. True bombing came in when the RFC attacked German-held Brussels in with a flight of planes, each carrying six 20-pound bombs.

Soon there were also bigger weapons which never were in large supply. The French had a 1-pound pom-pom in the air, called by the fliers the Cow Gun. The Coventry Ordnance was a 1½-pounder automatic quick-fire weapon, able to fire five shells a load. It had a 37-millimeter bore, a nearly 2,000 feet per second muzzle velocity. Its drawback was that the contraption weighed 200 pounds, which in the early planes meant a plane-wrecking load.

The French had a 37-millimeter air cannon, but there doesn't seem to have been much use made of it. Later, it was adopted into an engine's hollow crankshaft as used on the Spad. Its drawback was that after firing, the fumes from the exhaust made the pilot deadly ill!

Firing at an enemy plane with fast bullets from a moving plane at another moving plane made it hard to follow one's aim, or correct it. So tracers were introduced, one tracer to every three bullets being the usual loading pattern (a tracer normally consisted of eight parts barium peroxide to one part magnesium). They glowed when fired and could be followed by sight in flight, although initially they did not glow for long enough and often did not fly true as aimed.

For firing at Zeppelins and balloons incendiary bullets were to be perfected, and since pointed bullets made small holes that did little damage, a flat-nosed bullet was issued.

Early in the war, with time short for expert training, British infantry machine gunners were lured from the trenches—all too eager to leave behind the mud and fleas and be offered flight pay of six shillings a day (about $1.50).

The Germans were systematic in trying to get the best out of their fliers, setting up controls that ranged from a Chef des Feldflugwesens (Chief of Field Aviation) to a Stabsoffizier der Flieger (Staff Officer for Air), now under the eye of the Deutsche Luftstreikrafte—the German air force. Control came down even to the single-seater fighter command, called the Kampfeinsit zu Kommando.

Signalling from scout planes was primitive. The French used a chemical smoke system, perhaps learned from their reading of the Indian warfare of the American frontier.

A magazine reported:

> A device used in these tactics was a battery of twelve small glass bottles set in a wire rack within easy reach of the operator. The bottles contained a liquid which exploded five seconds after the cork was drawn, emitting a little round puff of smoke, or a short trail of smoke. This was the method used for aerial telegraphing. The smoke-puffs were dots; the smoke-trails dashes. Thus the pilot talked back to a far-away land battery, in dots and dashes of smoke, telling watchers that their shots were too high, or too low, or too far to the left, or right, and giving them the exact range.

From letters home, from journals kept by fliers on both sides, a glimpse of the inner emotions of those who were aware of the short life ahead of them emerges. In the air one is poignant under pressure of one's loneliness. "The sky becomes a prison, the plane a cell. . . . There is a sense, as one prepares to meet the enemy so far above the earth, of taut hysterics that one tries to hide on the ground, at the drome . . . those moments of eternity measured off in fragments of seconds by bursts of machine gun fire."

The young fliers were not prepared for the ultimate reality, no matter how many stories they heard of experiences related to air battle. "At first you feel all pudding-like inside—your heart in your shoes . . ." Their letters speak of the monstrous malice they feel at the sight of enemy insignia, symbols on winged surfaces. They learn, in becoming targets, "war's ironic circumstance—to kill quickly, clearly . . . war is the madness of moral inertia, an absolute commitment . . ." When the air battles were transformed into armed attacks, the service life of a flier with his unit lasted on the average four to six weeks. Death came with a clean hit, or dreadfully in the long plunge to earth of shattered man and plane. "I keep dreaming this dream I'm burning, falling . . ." Some escaped with wounds, some became prisoners. It was soon clear to the new men with the squadron that in air warfare one is at the center of an intolerable universe, where "shock in some chaps takes many forms, such as freezing at the controls, or even a loss of speech. Alcohol is only a breather to one's jiggling nerve ends, and those debauches on leave hardly satisfied beyond the moment."

Yet it is amazing how even at the tightest times, when replacements were hard to get and train, there were young men willing to go up again and again into the air, as the odds closed in against them. "The worst is the waiting, the grey life in the barracks of the airdrome, the wall notices of chaps in bad shape in hospital. . . . Bursts of action come to us, then nerve-racking boredom, fearful dreams . . ."

The sky and clouds framed for the sensitive a Blakean vision. For others, "the possession of power over someone that your plane and guns gave was overwhelming—the ability to dominate, to destroy was, I'm ashamed to say, a song of glee . . ."

For the sporting bloods who had ridden after the fox, the plane was truly their modern substitute for riding to hounds, the polo pony, or the cavalry regiment stationed in "Injah." A few English airmen even managed to hunt, tapering off from major killings in the air by blasting the native hare and potting the Gallic fox. There was a diversity of men and classes, cultures and habits, that the pathetically faded letters and journals still show. Other voices, other times, another war, all come into focus as we turn over printed or handwritten yellowing papers:

2.4.17. Breakfasted on coffee and omelettes. The Eternal Omelette. By the way, they are good. Left at 4 p.m. Quite punctual. Arrived at St. Omer at 8.30 p.m. feeling very fed up and tired. Rotten journey at 2 mph. After portering luggage and practicing my execrable French, reported to No. 1 AD. Orders to put up for the night on our own. Proceeded by tender and devious ways to Hotel de France. Horrible place—*déjeuner* worse— and filled with subalterns of all sorts, sizes and descriptions. No room for me—so to Hotel de Commerce. Small, cold room. Candles and damp sheets, ugh!

And they all griped or boasted or went about their business. An American:

. . . they promoted the jackasses on seniority and put men in charge of important technical affairs just because they have spent their lives doing infantry drill . . . and transferred to the aviation section a week ago to get a soft berth and more pay? Why should they worry about their mistakes? They aren't the ones that get killed. . . .

A German: "After 300 shots, the enemy plane caught fire. The plane burned to pieces in the air, and the occupants fell out." An Englishman: "The height was . . . 4,000 feet. As I knew that my fuel must be running low, I reluctantly made for our lines . . ." And Edward Mannock (chief British ace) wrote home:

Dear Mum, I haven't heard from you in reply to my last letter (2nd), so I suppose that it has gone astray. I wrote you from Boulogne, as I hadn't time to send you a line from the other side, before being packed off to France. You will see from the address above that we are prohibited from giving the name of the place at which we are stationed, but I can say that we are in the actual thick of it, and I go across the lines every day (sometimes three times) when the weather is not actually prohibitive. . . .

Now I don't want you to send me anything along, as there is plenty of everything here—tobacco, food, music, sports (when the weather is bad) but no girls, so don't waste what little cash you have in needless expense. I'm all right here. There are lots of interesting things I should like to tell you, but the censor forbids, so I'll leave it to your imagination. In the meantime . . . get ready for my leave, as I promise calling at the first opportunity. Love, Edward.

In the official press releases the early days seem like the images of a sleepwalker's nightmare. The news is bloody, but as yet it does not register; the language is that of a boy's adventure book:

September 5. A French aviator struck a bivouac of a company of the Guards, with the result that eight men and eight horses fell, while thirty-two soldiers were wounded.

September 12. A German non-commissioned officer showed his men a coat almost torn to tatters, which belonged to one of some sixty men wounded by a projectile that had just been hurled by one of our aviators.

End of September. At Autry a bomb killed some thirty soldiers at the edge of the Seriut, another projectile killing or wounding twenty soldiers. A staff major installed there had to change his quarters in all haste.

October 15. To the southeast of Lille a cavalry division which had been pursued and fired on during the whole of the day was at length prevented from carrying out its object by a bomb.

October 23. While reconnoitering the enemy's lines . . . [Raymond] was struck by a Prussian bullet, but made a final effort to regain the French camp. His strength failing, the machine fell at an equal distance between the two opposing armies. The result was a fierce combat for the possession of the fallen airplane and fallen aviator, as the Germans were quick to recognize the value of the information he had obtained. In the struggle the French were finally successful, and . . . Raymond was carried back to the French lines, where he had still the strength to furnish to his superiors a detailed and precise report, which proved of the utmost value. . . .

In contrast, from Albert Ball to the folks at home:

Cheerio dears . . . Really, I am having too much luck for a boy. I will start straight away, and tell you all. On August 22 I went up. Met twelve Huns.

No. 1 fight. I attacked and fired two (ammunition) drums, bringing the machine down just outside a village. All crashed up.

No. 2 fight. I attacked and got under machine, putting in two drums. Hun went down in flames.

No. 3 fight. I attacked and put in one drum. Machine went down and crashed on a housetop.

I only got hit eleven times in the plane, so I returned and got more ammunition. This time luck was not all on the spot. I was met by fourteen Huns, about fifteen miles over their side. My windscreen was hit in four places, mirror broken, the spar of the left broken, also engine ran out of petrol, But I had a good sport and good luck, but only just, for I was brought down about one mile over our side. . . .

Oh, la, la. Topping, isn't it?

Never show how you really feel was the genuine if clichéd British code of conduct. Try to laugh it off. This one cheerful drinking song of British fliers is enough to illustrate the tone:

Beneath a busted Camel, its former pilot lay:
His throat was cut by the bracing wires, the tank had hit his
    head,
And coughing a shower of dental work, these parting words
    he said:
"Oh, I'm going to a better land, they binge there every night,
The cocktails grow on bushes, so everyone stays tight,
They've torn up all the calendars, they've busted all the clocks,
And little drops of whisky come trickling down the rocks."
The pilot breathed these last few gasps before he passed away;
"I'll tell you how it happened, my flippers didn't stay,
The motor wouldn't hit at all, the struts were far too few,
A shot went through the petrol tank and let it all leak through.
Oh, I'm going to a better land, where motors always run,
Where the eggnog grows on the eggplant, and the pilots grow
    a bun.

They've got no Sops, they've got no Spads, they've got no DH-4's,
And the little frosted juleps are served at all the stores."

Finally, a word about the common jargon of the fliers of World War I and their ground crews. This is of interest because it was gutsy, true to the events and lives, and vividly clear without using fancy words. Also, some technical flying terms have changed.

What has survived are such terms as *Boche, Hun, Heinie, Kraut, Squarehead, Fritz* for the Germans, and *Limey* and *Tommy* for the English, even if no longer in common use. Americans were *Yanks, Doughboys, Colonials.* Antiaircraft fire was called *Archie* (a term that did not survive into the next war where it became *flak*, or *ack-ack*). Modern war planes go to hangars only for repair, but then the planes were often housed in canvas *Bessenaus.* A flier who had the *breeze-up* was frightened, *bung off* was to get going; a *brolly*, the English term for an umbrella, later was adopted for a parachute. *Sod, old sweat, matey* were terms of affection among soldiers.

To chandelle was to climb into a corkscrew in the air; *to coupez* was to cut off ignition on landing. We have explained the true meaning of *dogfight.* Gasoline was *petrol* to the British, *essence* to the French, and *fuel* or *juice* to the Americans. *To fish-tail* was to swing the tail of the plane about to come in slower. *Glide angle* was the safest glide, with an engine cut off. *To hoick* was to zoom, the *joystick* was the control column, *kanone* was German for ace, the *kiwi*, a flightless bird, was any nonflying RFC man, also called a *ground squirrel.*

The infantry were *foot-sloggers, gravel-crushers*, but mostly the PBI (Poor Bloody Infantry), *Tommies, roost robbers, smelly feet.* A *quirk* was a dumb flier student. *Tiffin* was lunch, *pips* were the marks of officers' ranks. *Fuckin'* was the most used word in the war, oddly enough with no sexual connotation most of the time.

Women were known as *bints*, as well as by anatomical terms not seen in print in those early times. *Blighty* was a simple wound that got one sent back to England. *Cooties*, of course, were the body lice; *joy-rags* the splendid uniforms saved for leaves. *The donkeys* was the term applied to British generals in the early years of the war. Needless to say, the list of obscene humorous terms could be endless.

CHAPTER 5

THE FIRST BRITISH ACES

> *Had several exciting moments since writing the last notes. Led*
> *the patrol yesterday (five machines) and had a scrap.*
> *Emptied a full drum of rounds into a big coloured two-seater*
> *Hun from about 25 yards. Must have riddled the bus, but*
> *nothing untoward happened. She put her nose down and went*
> *straight. "Melbourne" Bassett got hit in the leg in this scrap.*
> *Made a good show by flying all the way back to the field and*
> *landing, and this with a shattered leg! It was just bad luck*
> *that this shot was the only one on the machine.*
>
> —PILOT'S REPORT

Among the first, if not the very first, of the famous aces, was the Mad Major, as he liked to be called. Actually he was Captain A. A. B. Thomson of the La Gorgue Airdrome near Lestrem, where after the war started he was attached to the RFC's 16th Squadron. He was a wisp of a man, overlean, somewhat in the "Mr. Chips" schoolteacher style. There were rumors he was a scholar. A loner, he didn't talk much, or join in the pubcrawls or dirty stories of whores and cocksmen in the mess hall.

He liked to go up in the sky alone as dawn broke, to skim over the earth just a few feet above the bushes or meadow grass until he met clusters of enemy troops, at which point he would begin strafing with not too deadly an effect. The air base's top brass hauled him over the coals for his personal war games, but he gave the proper excuse. "Well, gentlemen, my machine was out of control. Wouldn't rise at all. Awfully sorry."

The Mad Major lodged by himself in a ruined house near the

air base, living contentedly with some boxes of books which he read with a philosophical calm. The myths and epics of the Greeks, the Romans, the Vikings were his favorite subjects. Perhaps he saw how low had fallen *la guerre à la bourgeoisie*. His most animated moment in quarters came when before retiring for the night he'd have several large gins in the officers' mess bar. And if he felt like talking, it was usually a low-voiced, earnest monologue about Vulcan or Thor, or war beneath the walls of Troy. He was a genuine eccentric, in the true tradition of Samuel Johnson, William Blake, T. E. Lawrence. As dawn broke he would walk toward his waiting BE-2 with his schoolmaster's gait, reading a book and turning a page as he went, then stop to finish a paragraph before handing over the volume to his mechanic, to be placed in the proper box.

"Morning to you, sir," the mechanic would say.

"Morning. Not too bad a morning."

The major would get into the cockpit, placing an extra cushion under his bony rump. Most of the time the plane was a riddled, patched-up affair. His low-flown runs produced many bullet holes in the fabric. If it had been a really close strafing, he would lean out to inspect and ask the mechanic, "Was she properly patched up yesterday?"

"Yes, sir."

Instruments in his planes were shot to bits, fuselage was often in tattered ruins, canvas flapping in the propeller wash. Yet Major Thomson flew well, circling the field once at takeoff to show things were functioning. He hardly ever got above 2,000 feet, liking best his hedge-hopping, his attacks on men at very low level.

One morning the major, on the tail of an enemy flying an Albatros, moved into firing range but just slid past the enemy giving a happy wave. Looking back he saw the damn German outraged and gesturing at him with his fist. It seemed dishonorable to the German that he had been ignored; the warlike thing was to have been shot down. The German pilot now tried to force the Mad Major down by rushing him, and this hound-and-hare chase went on at great speed just over the heads of the soldiers dug in below, who expected the two planes to crash locked together into the churned-up earth. Meanwhile each side picked its target in the air and banged away at the two of them. Moving over and behind the German lines, both pilots now must have felt this would end in a death as they made their moves. First one had the advantage, then the other. Getting 20 feet above the Albatros, the major began to come down in hawklike swoops, making it clear he was going to ram the German ship into the ground with his wheels. He had his loaded pistol but didn't use it—like shooting a mother plover on her eggs. He would use his plane as a weapon to bash the Hun down.

The German pilot, now aware of the madness of the flier in the British plane, was forced to land. He leaped from the Albatros and stood there bewildered. No use running; it was open country and there was no hiding place, and the mad *Englander* was flying back toward him. The major made a swooping run over the grounded craft. His fury was almost gone now as he cheerfully waved again at the puzzled German pilot and headed for home.

When he landed, his mechanic said, "Sir, you'll need a new machine in the morning."

He would. He saw that there were huge holes in the canvas covering of the plane's flying area made by ground fire; had he been a bird and the lost canvas feathers, he could not have flown home. As for petrol, the mechanic measured the tank with a dip stick. "Couldn't have stayed in the air another five minutes, sir. Juice nearly gone."

There isn't much more in the records available about the Mad Major. It is to be hoped he went back to some secluded bedsitter in Bayswater, or a quiet school, to continue reading the myths of the gods.

Not much behind the major in eccentric RFC behavior was another British ace, Captain Gordon Bell, who in public always kept a monocle in place over one eye. Once, walking back from behind enemy lines, Captain Bell, who had wrecked his plane, filed his report thus:

"Sir: While flying my BE-2C I got into the backwash of a sparrow. My machine got out of control, spun, and crashed. The pilot is doing well. G.B."

On another occasion, running into a losing battle with an enemy plane, the captain tried to make it back to base but found the damn ship would respond to control only if flown upside down. He flew it back that way, head down, getting dimmer and dimmer reflexes because of his upside-down position. The monocle was still in place, he claimed later, as he passed out and the plane slowly sank into the treetops. Recovering consciousness and making sure his eyeglass was safe, he began to climb down to the ground, where he found a pink-cheeked British lieutenant taking in the wreck scene.

"I say, have you crashed or something?"

Captain Bell looked down at him. "No, you damn fool, I always land like this."

But for all the P. G. Wodehouse trimmings, Captain Bell was a true ace. In one day he shot down six German planes. His great ambition was to knock Max Immelmann, "inventor" of the Immelmann turn, out of the air. But search as he might, Bell never did find Immelmann within range of his gun, or himself come under the German's firepower. Captain Bell survived battle to die in the wreck of a test plane.

Not all of the early British fliers were pink-cheeked boys or eccentrics, however. Major Lanoe George Hawker, born in 1890, came of a family that served a navy not too far removed from Gilbert and Sullivan's *H.M.S. Pinafore.* As a boy Lanoe was always around machines, electrical hookups, and mechanical devices with which he played, fantasizing about their uses or possibilities. He first saw an airplane on a cinema screen, followed by an actual plane in flight at Bournemouth in 1910. He began to build and fly kites and put together model planes, and he enjoyed the drawings of Bernard Partridge in *Punch.* Hawker entered the Royal Military Academy at Woolwich and became a member of the Royal Aero Club. By 1913 he held a ticket as a pilot. The day war broke out he had just been ordered to Upavon's Central Flying School.

A hasty scramble took place to bring together whatever planes and fliers were available, and Lieutenant L. G. Hawker left with a squadron of the RAF when it flew across the Channel to France on October 5, 1914. It was ordered to stand ready to fly into action from the racetrack at Bruges. In the end it moved to St. Omer.

Hawker was one of the early fliers to take along a pistol when scouting in the air. His score was zero. When the RAF set up headquarters at Bailleul, there were new planes, BE-2C's. Hawker received a bad leg wound from soldiers' ground fire (either side; the Allied and German infantry fired at anything in the sky in those early days, friend or foe). Despite his wound, Hawker insisted on flying, so he was carried to his plane and lifted in, and after flight lifted out again.

At last he was issued a Bristol Baby Biplane, or Scout—a fast single-seater, good and speedy for its day. At Abeele Airdrome he figured out a machine-gun mount for his Baby. He fixed a light Lewis gun to the left of his engine in front of the cockpit, pointed slightly downward so as to miss the propeller, he hoped. He controlled the plane with his right hand on the joystick while firing with his left. It was awkward, but he had a machine gun in the air.

Near the end of July 1915, Hawker was prowling on patrol between tragic Passchendaele and bloody Ypres. At dusk he sighted an enemy two-seater over the German lines. He dived and began firing. The German twisted away in a roll and dive. Hawker went back to his patrol. Twenty minutes later he sighted and fired on another enemy machine over Houthulst Forest. British ground gunners reported the German plane had fallen to earth. Flying at 11,000 feet, the lucky Hawker at seven o'clock in bad light found his third German. With the dying sun behind him, Hawker came down firing from 100 yards: the German burst into flames and fell like a flaming torch to the cheers of regiments of British troops.

Hawker wrote home of one of his kills: "I felt very sorry for him when he fell in flames, but war is war and they have been very troublesome of late . . ."

In August 1915 he was gazetted with the Victoria Cross.

Hawker was a great tinkerer, an inventor of gunsights, of canvas-protected propeller tips. He helped to develop the double

drum of ammunition for the Lewis gun, new gun brackets, and a
new type of link machine-gun belt that did away with most guns'
jammings. He designed plane hangars, laid out airfields. To allevi-
ate the suffering of freezing DH-2 pilots, he designed fleece-lined
flying boots that were soon in full use as standard gear. The DH-2
was a monster, known by its fliers as the "Spinning Incinerator."
Powered by second-hand, cast-off engines from the French 100-
horsepower Gnomes, it often balked and came apart in the air.
Frequently, one or two cylinders could fall away in flight, damag-
ing the rudder controls. One had to be precociously eager to want
to take it up.

Later Hawker was relegated to administration head, but he still
flew whenever he could sneak in a flight. He organized patrols to
try to chase the German machines on the enemy side of the front.
The fighting in the air was growing desperate as the Germans
brought up newer planes, the Fokker D-III, the Albatros D-II, the
Halberstadt D-III.

On November 23, 1917, on a cold clear afternoon—after tiffin—
a patrol went out. Leading the flight of three was Lieutenant
John Oliver Andrews. Hawker was in number-two position, and
Lieutenant R. R. S. Saundby in number-three position. At two
o'clock Andrews pointed out two German machines in the crystal
sky near Bapaume, two-seaters. They were droning along at 6,000
feet. The patrol attacked them and the enemy planes fled. But
from ambush about half a dozen German one-seaters came down
for the kill. Andrews had his gas tanks ripped open and his engine
went dead at 5,000 feet. He tried to glide home. Saundby also ran
for it, but Hawker decided to stay on to fight. Andrews, seeing
this, turned back to get off one burst of fire and then was hit
again himself. He glided toward home, followed by a German
who got several bursts into his plane; Andrews landed un-
wounded, however.

The attacking Germans consisted of Manfred von Richthofen
himself and his best Jasta 2 fliers. Hawker and von Richthofen
went at each other tail after tail—like cat and dog in a circle—each
trying for some advantage. The rest of the flight drew aside to let
the couple fight it out.

The two fliers turned and twisted at least two dozen times around each other in a move the Germans called *Kurvenkampf*—a fast-whirling twist. All the time they were losing height. At 2,000 feet the wind was brisk and both were drifting into the German lines. They were flying in steep banks, wings at right angles to the earth; often the two men could stare at one another, only a couple of dozen feet apart. Hawker even waved to the Red Baron, who did not, however, acknowledge the greeting.

Then Hawker made his bold move, going into a loop, and got off a burst from his Lewis gun; but it was wild shooting. Still in the loop, he headed for the ground, but pulled back in time at a bare 100 feet. Now he was at tree-top level, running for home. A half mile would see him safe. The German, however, had the faster machine and he was on Hawker's tail, had him in his sights for a burst at 50 yards. Then his gun jammed. A cocking lever usually existed to clear this, and the jam gave way. Von Richthofen pressed his advantage and at 100 feet drilled Hawker through the head. The British plane and its dead pilot began to turn shattering somersaults, bouncing hard into the muck and filthy water of the shellholes of No-Man's-Land, a complete wreck.

Von Richthofen was given Hawker's machine gun, dug out from the ruin, as a victory trophy; one does not kill a VC every day. (The gun was hung over the door of the von Richthofen house at Schweidnitz.) His account of the killing of Major Hawker reads like that of a big-game hunter on safari, gloating over the size of horns or tusks. He wrote for the press:

> I must confess that it was a matter of great pride to me to learn that the Englishman I shot down . . . was the English equivalent of our great Immelmann. Of course, I did not know who he was during the fight, but I did know from the masterly manner in which he handled his plane and the pluck with which he flew, that he was a wonderful fellow. . . .
>
> I was in the best of spirits and keen for the hunt. Flying at an altitude of about ten thousand feet, I observed three English planes. I saw that they saw me, and from their maneuvers I gathered that our hopes for the day's fun were mutual. They

were hunting bent, the same as I. I was spoiling for a fight, and they impressed me much the same. They were above me, but I accepted the challenge. Being underneath and in no position to attack, I had to wait till the fellow dived on me. It was not long to wait. Soon he started down in a steep gliding dive, trying to catch me from behind.

He opens fire with his machine gun. Five shots rip out, and I change my course quickly by a sharp turn to the left. He follows and the mad circle starts. He is trying to get behind me, and I am trying to get behind him. Round and round we go in circles, like two madmen playing ring-o'-roses almost two miles above the earth. Both our motors are speeded to the utmost; still neither seems to gain on the other. We are exactly opposite each other on the circumference of the circle, and in this position neither one of us can train our single forward-shooting machine guns on the other.

First, we would go twenty times around to the right, and then swing into another circle going around twenty times to the left. We continued the mad race, neither gaining an advantage. I knew at once I was dealing with no beginner, because he didn't appear to dream of trying to break off the fight and get out of the circling. His plane was excellent for maneuvering and speed, but my machine gave me an advantage by being able to climb better and faster. This enabled me at last to break the circle and maneuver into a position behind and above him.

But in the circling fight, both of us had lost height. We must have come down at least six thousand feet, as now we were little more than three thousand feet above the ground. The wind was in my favor. I saw that now we were even behind the German lines in front of Bapaume.

But he was a plucky devil. With me behind and above him, he even turned and waved his arm at me, as though to say, "*Wie gehts?*" We went into circles again—fast and furious and as small as we could drive them. Sometimes I estimated the diameter of the circles as being eighty and a hundred yards. But always I kept above him and at times I could look down almost vertically into his cockpit and watch every movement of his head. If it had not been for his helmet and goggles, I could have seen what sort of face he had.

He was a fine sportsman, but I knew that in time my close

presence behind and above him would be too much for him.
. . . Apparently the idea of landing and surrender never occurred to this sportsman, because suddenly he revealed his plans
to escape by going into several loops and other maneuvers of
equal folly. As he came out of them, heading for his own lines,
my first bullets began whistling around his ears, for up to now,
with the exception of his opening shots, neither one of us had
been able to range on the other. . . .

Our speed is terrific. He starts back for his front. He knows
my gun barrel is trained on him. He starts to zigzag, making
sudden darts right and left, right and left, confusing my aim and
making it difficult to train my gun on him. But the moment is
coming. I am fifty yards behind him. My machine gun is firing
incessantly. We are hardly fifty yards above the ground—just
skimming it.

Now I am within thirty yards of him. He must fall. The gun
pours out its stream of lead. Then it jams. Then it reopens fire.
That jam almost saved his life. One bullet goes home. He is
struck through the back of the head. His plane jumps and
crashes down. It strikes the ground just as I swoop over. His
machine gun rammed itself into the earth, and now it decorates
the entrance over my door. He was a brave man, a sportsman
and a fighter.

There followed, inevitably, a letter to his mother:

Liebe Mamma,
Accept my most sincere congratulations for your birthday.
I trust this will be your last birthday in wartime . . .

My eleventh Englishman was Major Hawkes [sic], twenty-
six years old and commander of an English squadron. According to prisoners' accounts, he was the English Boelcke . . .
Manfred

CHAPTER 6

AND THEIR RIVALS

1. | Max Immelmann—*Der Adler von Lille*
(1890–1916)

> *"We Germans fear God. We fear nothing or no one on this earth."*
>
> —BISMARCK

The first of the German aces was Max Immelmann, whose name survives in aviation history as the innovator of the famous "Immelmann turn" in the air. When the war loomed up on the horizon, Immelmann was in the army with a railroad battalion near Berlin. This was dull, hard work, and finding that he couldn't get into the infantry of footsloggers—he was small, lean, and not impressive-looking—he put in for aviation. In November 1914 he was taking flying lessons at Johannesthal Airfield, learning how to handle the Rumpler Taube, the Albatros, and the L.V.G. By the end of January 1915, Immelmann soloed after about fifty-five flights. He passed his tests and wrote home on how it was done: "You . . . go up, fly five figure eights, land on the spot where the teacher stood with his red flag, go up again, fly another five figure eights, land as I did before. Lastly, I had to climb to about one hundred meters and land in a glide . . ."

A show-off in his final tests for his military certificate, Immelmann went up 2,600 meters instead of the required 2,000, and for gliding 80 meters he went on to 2,200. Told to stay up an hour, he stayed up nearly an hour and a half. Always there was the small man's urge to show that he was better. In advanced training at Aldershof, his overconfidence led to a smallish crash. Immelmann passed the rest of the test flights and cross-country flights, however, and was ready for service.

Immelmann was not popular. He was fussy as an old maid about details. He was deeply introvert, and being small, he looked weak, though he was muscled and hard with that speed and catlike movement that small lean men often have. He feared and avoided women, and among the lusty oversexed young fliers he stood out as a sort of frightened prude. No *schottische*, *polka*, or *valse* for him, no girl resting lightly in his arms.

Max Immelmann's only close friend was his dog Tyras, who hardly left his side when the flier was off duty. Immelmann proved a puritan of a high order. To his mother he wrote, "For us airmen abstinence from alcohol is the basic requirement, if we are to gain success without having to complain of nerves overstrained."

It is very easy for an observer to read Freudian overtones into Immelmann's relationship with his mother. Certainly, it was not a healthy one. He wrote her nearly every day, with a kind of compulsion to keep her informed of how dangerous flying was for her son; torture of the love-hate object is very clear in his letters. He did not smoke, of course, and as a vegetarian his feeding was a military problem. His fellow fliers mocked him for that, as well as for having his nose always in his books, and for his classroom brilliance. These virtues in any group mark one as a softie, but more so among male pilots in the prime of life.

Initially, Immelmann flew mail and plane parts to airdromes; then he was promoted to aerial scout and was shot at twice by French planes. But he came into his full glory when the Fokker-synchronized machine gun was put into German planes by Oswald Boelcke. Immelmann, emerging from the shadow of his mother, became friendly with Boelcke. He was given a Fokker E-I, and armed and wily, went up to knock down Allied planes with such skill and directness that he was glorified by the press as "The Eagle of Lille."

Captain Boelcke himself recorded a description of Immelmann's first air victory:

So all unwashed, with my nightshirt still on, but no puttees, I shoved along to the airfield on my motor bike and came just in time to see those chaps—there was not one but four of them—amusing themselves by dropping bombs on our airfield. I jumped into my machine and took off. But as the Englishmen flew home as soon as they had dropped their bombs and had very fast machines, I did not manage to get within range of them. I turned back sadly.

When I got over the airfield again—I could scarcely believe my eyes—there were another five machines that had come to pay us a visit with their bombs. So I went for the nearest, a monoplane. I got to grips with him nicely and peppered him well, but when I was close enough up to think that the next shot must send him crashing—Lord, my gun jammed! Oh, I was wild. I tried to remove the jam up there, and used so much force in my rage that the obstructing cartridge broke in half. So there was nothing for it but to land and get a fresh supply of ammunition.

As I went down I saw our other monoplane coming up and felt pleased that those English machines would at least get their tails twisted by it. While I was loading with new cartridges down below, I saw Lieutenant Immelmann attack an Englishman in grand style and send him bolting. I climbed up again quickly to help Immelmann against the others. But they cleared off again as soon as they saw me arrive on the scene the second time, and I only had disappointment for my trouble. Meanwhile Immelmann had forced his Englishman to land; he put a bullet through his elbow, so he had to come down as quickly as he could.

Immelmann was extraordinarily lucky over the whole business; I only gave him his first lesson on a Fokker three days before, i.e., I went up with him in his machine and let him help handle the controls. The day before he did his first solo and had great difficulty in pulling off his landing. He had never flown against the enemy in a Fokker and had never fired his machine gun before—and then he had the luck to catch a defenseless biplane over our airfield, because the Englishman had left his observer at home to save weight for his bombs. All the same, Immelmann did his job beautifully, and I congratulate him sincerely on his success. But I am really annoyed at my own bad luck. . . .

The "invention" of the Immelmann turn arose from Immelmann's close study of every type of plane and his consequent knowledge of what could and could not be done with them. The famous turn is nothing more than a short swift climb, which at the same time becomes a half roll. The maneuver helped him make record kills when he flew in battle against Allied pusher planes with machine guns mounted in their noses.

Death came quickly to most of the men of that Fokker group, who are remembered now only by their records. Ernst Hess, 17 victories; Hohndorf, a fine flier, 12. Victories by von Athaus, Wintgens, Parschau. All got the Ordre pour le Mérite, dead or alive; in all 81 German fliers were awarded this chest decoration, signalling the highest honor. Indeed, Immelmann's 15 kills sound rather unimpressive against von Richthofen's 80 (?), Ernst Udet's 62. He was a bad shot, but a fine flier, which accounts for his low killing score; although in the air he could be savage and determined, he never handled his guns well. His skill was that he got the most out of a plane. He piloted a Fokker over the front lines, unarmed, in a test with a 80-horsepower engine at 70 miles an hour, up to 6,000 feet, and stayed in the air two hours; a remarkable performance for those early ships. It was foolhardy, but he was lucky and no Allied machine ran into him. His turn, he proudly agreed, gave a pilot the chance to "sew the enemy fliers in a shroud of bullets."

One of Immelmann's most famous air fights was with Captain O'Hara Wood, a professional tennis champion from Australia. Wood was flying with Ira Jones as gunner and observer. They had been briefed that Max Immelmann was up with a Fokker squadron near Lille. "There's a chance you might get a crack at Immelmann. Good hunting . . ." Immelmann was much respected by the British. By December 1915 he had already shot down seven French and British machines and the German press was building him up as its first great air hero.

The British gunner, Jones, had a problem. The Lewis gun at

that time had to be manhandled. It could be lifted and pushed into any of four mountings on the plane, each of which allowed it to cover only specific areas of the sky. At 100 miles an hour, with the plane twisting, turning, and diving, the gunner had an almost impossible task. The BE-2C they were flying was also a hazard, since its cockpit was tight and awkward for moving about.

They took the plane high up over Lille, wisps of scudding clouds whipping by the wrecked landscape torn into almost abstract forms. Suddenly Jones saw a fast German machine rushing in from the rear. Wood banked the plane hard so that the gunner could get his gun pointed at the enemy closing in on them. He fired, and the enemy plane went at once into an evasive spin. Coming back just under the blind spot—the belly of the English machine—the German fired, ripping through the fabric. It was hard to outguess the German and to lug the Lewis gun from mount to mount. Jones made a desperate choice. "I would hold the gun in my arms, lean over the cockpit and fire down at him. I did, but unfortunately I had not allowed for the sudden and sharp vibration of the gun and the rush of air, and a cold sweat ran down my back as the gun jerked itself out of my grasp and fell earthward."

That tore it. The damn fancy Fokker would come in for the kill against an unarmed ship. They could see it moving around in the thin air so as to cross ahead of their path and pour the deadly bursts into them.

But nothing happened. The enemy had exhausted his ammunition and could not reload in the air. The British plane escaped. It was only later that the Australian said to Jones: "I didn't tell you at the time . . . over Lille we were up against a body rather important. I recognized his plane and his tactics."

"Who was it?"

"Max Immelmann himself."

Immelmann's letters to his mother continued to point out the danger to his life. His dog and he cherished one another as faithfully as ever. He chewed the tasteless vegetables of the mess, frowned on the drunken fliers in their cups unwinding after the tension of battle; their thick cigars made him cough. And he stayed clear of women. Most likely he was celibate and died a virgin.

To Immelmann only flying mattered; for him it was almost a revealed religion. We sense a deep alienation from society and a desperate need of the mother because of his size, and his fears of sex, meat, alcohol, tobacco; yet paradoxically he was constantly chafed by the tug of the silver cord that tied him to *liebe Mamma*. In society he felt *them*—the big ones—to be always insensitive. He considered the vast universe indifferent toward him; certainly he lacked the attitude of some fliers to God as a helpful classmate.

Immelmann's death on June 28, 1916, remains a mystery. The British say he was penetrated by a Lewis gun handled by a Corporal John Waller from the nose of a FE-2 plane, and the Allies accept this cause of his death. But Max's older brother, Franz, gives another version. He claims Max had been having trouble with his gun synchronizer; a few weeks before his death, he had shot away both propellers of his Eindekker plane and had come down in a hard landing. Franz claims that on the day of his death Max shot off a propeller blade and the wild-running engine broke loose, crashing the plane.

An Official Board of Inquiry was hastily convened to whitewash any idea of accident or sabotage to Max Immelmann's plane. It resulted in the report: "Loss of plane due to antiaircraft fire collapsing the machine." Anthony Fokker welcomed this verdict, for his welded steel-pipe Eindekker was currently under attack as being weak in structure. *Der Adler von Lille* could not have been killed by a stupid accident, he felt. Here is Fokker's official report:

> It was first given out that his Fokker fighter had failed in midair. This explanation did not satisfy me, and I insisted on examining the remains of the wreck, and establishing the facts of his death.
>
> What I saw convinced me and others that the fuselage had been shot in two by shrapnel fire. The control wires were cut as by shrapnel, severed ends bent in, not stretched as they would have been in an ordinary crash. The tail of the fuselage was found a considerable distance from the plane itself. As he was

flying over the German lines there was a strong opinion in the air force that his comparatively unknown [sic] monoplane type —which somewhat resembled a Morane-Solnier—had been mistaken for a French plane.

However, the evidence in fact seems clear that on the fatal day the propeller had just been replaced, and being needed before the crew could check the connections between prop and gun, it was locked into the wrong alignment, so that on firing the weapon, Max Immelmann did shoot off his propeller—as his brother claimed —and died (in a way) by his own hand.

2. | Oswald Boelcke (1891–1916)

*Was mich nicht umbringt, macht mich
starker*—What does not destroy me
makes me stronger.
        —MILITARY PROVERB

To historians of air wars Oswald Boelcke is the greatest of the German fliers and Jagdstaffel administrators. Yet except to the specialists he is virtually unknown. He came not from the nobility or the military caste. He was the son of a Saxon professor, from one of those pedantic families where everything—clothes, toys—does duty twice; and where some of the children begin to dislike the academic life, hoping for wider horizons with a more colorful experience and richer material rewards. Oswald refused to become a scholar. For all his brightness and intellect, he had seen enough of the professor's way of life. Instead, he took wildly and with much energy to tennis, swimming, diving, rowing streams and rivers; to tossing himself about in gymnastic patterns, climbing mountains and yodeling from the top. Some aberration drove him to excel in worlds far away from the classroom.

Boelcke as a schoolboy saved a French boy from drowning, and got the usual medals for his deed. While still a youth his thoughts turned to flying, and just before the war when he saw

Adolph Pégoud and his flying machine dash through the skies, bank, and turn, he decided this was living more dangerously even than mountain climbing (he was, of course, a follower of Nietzsche). With war talk rising in pitch, Boelcke got into the air service, and soloed after short training in the most dismal kind of aircraft. But the engine died on him and he ended up in a plowed field, with a damaged plane.

Nevertheless, he found his way to the Champagne front; indeed, by some disregard of orders he managed to fly over the front and get shelled, a fragment hitting his armor-plated seat. He carried no machine guns, and when two Allied planes came at him, he fled. His airdrome was bombed, killing some Uhlan guards.

Oswald and his brother Wilhelm flew an Albatros together, and Oswald began to pile up a good record. Just two months after the outbreak of war he was awarded the Iron Cross (October 12). When they separated him from Wilhelm, he protested so violently that there was talk that if he didn't simmer down he'd end up in the trenches with "the cannon fodder" (a popular phrase at the time).

However, the army doctor decided Boelcke could use three weeks' convalescent leave to remedy a "severe bronchial infection." Most likely it was a cooling-off period for a hot-tempered youth. It served in any case to change Boelcke from a mere flier into a man who from then on kept his own thoughts, a man who sternly disciplined not only his men but also himself. He had come up against the blind, unreasoning power of authority, and knew it for its rigid hold on precise molds of conduct, glorified as "discipline" and "tradition." He also began to see that in a war the rights of the individual mean nothing, that all must conform or be destroyed. He realized that the unique wonder of the human being shaping his own destiny, as when climbing mountains, bore little relation to the way wars are fought. Old soldiers said: "There are two ways to do things—the right way and the Army way . . ."

As Boelcke's reputation grew, he was bothered by young fliers, by civilian questioners, by newspaper men. To avoid this he produced a printed sheet with the title: *The Airman's Defense Against Troublesome Question Askers.*

PLEASE!!! Do not ask me anything about flying. You will find the usual questions answered below: Sometimes it is dangerous, sometimes it is not. Yes, the higher we fly, the colder it is. Yes, we notice the fact by freezing when it is colder. Flying height, 2,000–2,500 meters. Yes, we can see things at that height, although not so well as at 100 meters. We cannot see well through a telescope because it shakes. Yes, we have dropped bombs. Yes, an old woman was supposed to have been injured, and we put the wind up some transport columns. The observer sits in front and can see a hit. We cannot talk to each other because the engine makes too much noise. We have not got a telephone in the machine, but we are provided with electric light. No, we do not live in caves . . .

The tone suggests he was still the professor's son.

Boelcke had flown nearly fifty missions before he was summoned to test the new Fokker-synchronized gun capable of firing through the propeller. As we have seen, it was Boelcke who proved it was the needed weapon.

But it wasn't until July 1915 that he rang up an early victory with a machine gun. He was flying an Albatros C-1 with Leutnant von Wuehlish as observer when they sighted a Morane-Parasol plane near Lietard. The planes circled each other and moved around looking for a spot to attack. The leutnant got his gun firing and at once killed the two Frenchmen in the Morane, one of whom was the Comte de Beauvicourt. The French plane heeled steeply and dived into a wood; the count had come home in a strange way. The wood was part of his estate.

Soon Boelcke and Max Immelmann had eight kills each, and both wore around their necks the Ordre pour le Mérite (named in French from the time of Frederick the Great, who insisted on a French-speaking court).

But Boelcke was far more than a fighter. He was a student of planes, a teacher of fliers. It was he who convinced Fokker to improve his E-IV, which had too delicate an engine and was not trustworthy under changes in air pressure when going from high to low flying, and vice versa. This was replaced by the 100-horse-power Oberursel engine. Boelcke also disliked the rotary engine then in use on both sides. In time, both the Allies and the Germans replaced it with radical and in-line engines; these could work at their best with high compression ratios and improved speed and power for faster planes.

During the dismal long-drawn-out agony at Verdun that began in February 1916, Boelcke realized that although the Germans had the bigger, better air force, they could not control the air space. The French, by playing to the German mistakes, flew like bloodthirsty hawks and held complete command of the air over Verdun. Boelcke began to talk of unit organizing for the air force, tighter controls, better, more scientific methods of attack and defense. He had been behind the front, detailed with other fliers to keep the French from taking pictures of the Verdun area. The German planes behind the lines fought the French, so that very few French planes could get through, and without detailed information from the air the ground forces took staggering losses.

General Erich von Falkenhayn, commander at Verdun under Crown Prince Willie, was able to confuse the French in the opening days of the Verdun battle by using his air arm to prevent the French from scouting. In the below-zero weather of February, the Germans were thus able to form a 30-mile siege line against the fortress city, backed by 12-inch cannon and 420-mm mortars. For nearly a year the most monstrous battle of the war dragged on. In the end the Germans lost it, and Falkenhayn his career. (The new star who replaced him was Paul von Hindenburg.)

Fliers moving over the ruins of Verdun saw only the gutted earth, the reeking, churned bogs and rubble. The dead were everywhere; three-quarters of a million men had died or been wounded here. Coming in low, the fliers could see the glistening bones of those who had died early, still putrefying in muck. The French soldier often went into an attack with his name and address pinned to his jacket, aware he was going to certain death for no good reason. Few now believed the slogans of the war leaders.

The French plane loss had been 20 per cent of their strength. The Fokkers did not do well either, and messages came from the front, "Where are *our* airplanes?" In the German trenches soldiers began to sing a song mocking the Crown Prince:

> *Goddam England, France*
> *And Uncle Willie's*
> *Air Force!*

But three men were picked out for making such remarks and received two to four years at hard labor.

The new French plane, the Nieuport 17, was hard to beat. Boelcke objected to the way the Fokkers were sent out on dawn-to-dark patrols. What did favor the German pilots, however, was a prevailing west wind which drifted battling Allied planes over behind the German lines, often before they were aware of it. A sure proof, some claimed, that God had chosen sides.

Boelcke took a great interest in captured enemy fliers and entertained them in the officers' mess, talked earnestly and long with them, listening to their ideas of air warfare, and outlining some of his own. He was remembered by several prisoners as "a jolly good host."

In 1916 Boelcke set off on a tour of the Eastern Front to pick up fliers for a new unit. He netted von Richthofen, Max Muller, and Max Böhme, all future aces, to form a fighter squadron, the famous Royal Prussian Jagdstaffel 2.* While he trained his men, Boelcke himself still flew. And he in turn was hunted through the skies by Captain G. L. Cruikshank, who led the RFC 70th Squadron. Early in the war the captain had worked at landing spies behind the German lines. Meeting Boelcke in the air, Cruikshank had exchanged bullets but neither had been in a position to fight to a fiinish. Now the captain was in pursuit again.

One morning Cruikshank took off after dawn, with the sun behind him, in his trim, purring Sopwith. Over the front he zigzagged through antiaircraft fire; the Allied shells burst white, the German black, so it was easy to know which side was firing at you. Cruikshank was joined by six Sopwiths of his squadron. Flying in a tight V, they saw a formation of enemy planes coming their way. Both sides began to peel off and split apart to make

---

* There never was a Jagdstaffel 1.

elbow room for a dogfight. The captain went high to view the developing fight. Boelcke, who had been waiting for the right moment to attack the bold *Englander*, came in with a sharp angle rush, firing a burst that was too far off to reach the Sopwith. The captain banked to get the German in front of his guns. The German expertly banked away and the English bullets hit only air. Using low clouds as cover, Cruikshank began making bull-like rushes at the enemy plane. Taking a quick look, Boelcke took to guessing where the enemy would be at the moment he broke cloud cover, both firing, sending off bursts of slugs. The Sopwith shook, one of its wings tore itself loose and fell away into space. It still flew but its controls were messed up. Cruikshank took aim again, but was seconds late as bullets tore into his cockpit and his engine, destroying the tail section on their way out. By that time Captain Cruikshank was presumably dead. The plane disintegrated as it fell in flames near a place called Havrincourt Wood; Boelcke flew thoughtfully back for breakfast, no elation in his heart. These short, somehow mean durations of actual combat were not exhilarating to him.

In September 1916, Boelcke led his group into rain-scrubbed skies under a lead-bowl ceiling. There were no cloud formations low enough to hide in, or to use for ambushing the enemy. Over Quéant they bumbled into the enemy. Boelcke was in no mood for a fight, but there they were, a squadron of FE's returning from some mission. He led the attack from above, the British firing as they passed over. He banked and turned to see a fast Morane coming boldly at him. He kept up a running fight until he shot it down in flames. Below he saw a British plane making an emergency landing and a wounded man being helped out. Boelcke flew back home, reporting the enemy as "the toughest lot of British we ever met."

The Germans had suffered too. Flier Reimann had run into a Morane or been run into. Pilot Graffe was also dead. In revenge for their casualties, the British sent over a half-dozen Martinsydes to bomb the German airfield. No German planes could get up to meet the attack as the runway was being heavily bombarded.

Oddly enough, no enemy was to kill Oswald Boelcke. Death

came about in a strange way for this decorated winner of forty air battles. On October 26, 1916, he was flying with his group next to Leutnant Erwin Böhme, both on the tail of a British fighter. Baron von Richthofen went on ahead, recklessly chasing another enemy machine, cutting sharply in front of the two planes. Reacting too quickly, Böhme's wheels went tearing into one of Boelcke's wings. In the speed of their movement the wing tore loose, and Boelcke, unable to control the badly crippled plane, spun down to his death.

That night Böhme begged for a Luger; full of guilt and remorse he tried to kill himself, but was restrained.

That month, just before his last flight, Boelcke had grown thin, almost morose. After one hard fight he had told his orderly, Fischer, "I found an opponent who was for me today a match. But no bullet will ever hit me." The night before that last mission there had been a wild drinking, cigar-smoking songfest. It made Boelcke's head ache and he went to his quarters. Erwin Böhme joined him there and they sat talking quietly. Böhme was actually too old to be flying fighters (he was thirty-seven; senility for a front-line fighter pilot) but Boelcke felt a warmth for the older man and presumably could not bring himself to order him out of the air.

A few days after Boelcke's death a British plane dropped the now ritual wreath with the message: *To the Memory of Captain Boelcke, Our Brave and Chivalrous Opponent.*

Oswald Boelcke lacked von Richthofen's dashing flair, so that, although considered a better flier, he never sustained the heroic image of the Red Baron. On the contrary, he was steady, solid, under strain most of the time, with no neurotic outbursts in his maturity. In some ways he was a sad man, suggesting to one observer that Spanish saying *Nada y pues nada*—Nothing and after that nothing. As that fatal October day drew near, he seemed to hint in his talks with his orderly that he was conscious that one has limited, blunted powers of determination. Many of the fliers who flew too much developed an awareness of being pawns in a game where the rules work only until they prove that one's life is settled often by insignificant accident.

CHAPTER 7

THE RED BARON

*Clear as an unflawed crystal remains the Splendor
of the Name . . .*

—RICHTHOFEN FAMILY ESCUTCHEON

Legendary heroes become fixed in the mind of posterity so that harm can no longer be done to their image either by research or by presenting the actual, verified facts. The popular pictures of George Washington, General Grant, Buffalo Bill, or John F. Kennedy can never be replaced by historical truths that would dent the established portraits. Manfred von Richthofen, the Red Baron of Snoopy's fantasies in the comic strip about Charlie Brown and his friends, is pretty much the image most of us accept, if we accept him at all. The actual man is a fascinating study of tradition, Prussian pride in family, in discipline, skills in hunting beast and man, and dedication to the *Vaterland*.

Manfred von Richthofen was born on May 2, 1892, born well, supplied with some noble ancestors. The Prussian junker stock that bred him went back to claims of nobility in the seventeenth century, admittedly hardly on a par with those who could claim crusaders, sainthood, the seed of pagan chiefs from Viking keels harrying the Baltic coasts. But the baronage was solid, if not exciting. The Richthofens were landholders, country squires, great drinkers, feeders, and fornicators, skilled hunters of deer and wolves (with the help of their huge and savage dogs). They rode on war stallions; walking was for peasants. Their armor-carrying warhorses in time were bred down to jumpers and military mounts. The Richthofen estates were orderly, pfennig-pinching, efficient. They lived in rather tasteless, solid houses, grim but clean. The decor sported elk and deer horns in the hallways, and portraits of solid thick faces, stern and unsmiling, turning black under old varnish; not one masterpiece among them.

The Schickfuss folk, Manfred's mother's family, were of the same kind of stock; rigid, conservative, getting the most out of their land, worshipful of order and the expected rights of small-county nobility. They too hunted and rode as the major way of life. The protected game forests of Silesia echoed to the sounds of the killing of animals, large and small. Manfred's father was a ramrod-stiff Uhlan career officer, half centaur, half godhead to the family, who respected his code as a lover of order in the Schweidnitz Manor in which they lived, Manfred and his two brothers, Lothar and Bolko.

Their uncle, Alexander Schickfuss, however, broke the pattern of staying close to the land, the local hunting fields and forests. He became a notorious worldwide killer of big game, in the days before the commercial safari, whose specially made guns destroyed tigers, lions, wild buffalo, and elephants by the score in Africa and Asia.

These Richthofens were Teutonic primitives, given to strength in muscle, keenness of eye, with no doubt about their skill or their proper place as barons. Manfred as a small boy was already a stalker of game spoors, a killer of any animal seen in his rifle sights. He hunted with ardor, and while the shotgun might recoil, even knock him down, he usually got his game. Even before puberty he liked to show off what he had killed, stuffed, and mounted; he collected his trophies and displayed them with pride.

The game of the hunt was the thing, and the kill was the prize of skill and knowledge. The contest was between two life styles, winning or losing. There was no hatred in this, and no vulgar necessity to kill. So, too, in his future air combats there was no hatred of the enemy at first, beyond being a symbol of those who would harm the *Vaterland*. In the air it was once more a grand game of hunting, matching wits; of knowing the proper way to approach, fire, and see the victim of one's manhood, breeding, power go to his death. Pure love of the hunt, the only genuine long-held emotion Manfred von Richthofen was to experience. The love of victory over some other living thing, whether human or animal.

Even in the worst years of the war, when von Richthofen was home on leave, he would hunt the wild boar, the elk, any bird within range of his collection of hunting weapons—the etched rifles, the silver-mounted shotguns. Back he would bring the dead game to the manor house to be processed and kept—memories of yet another gallant hunt.

Manfred had no fears. His nerves seemed set in some inhuman fluid that kept them immune. He could write of dead comrades: "Death comes to each of us." He had no nuances, no subtle emotions. He was one with the words on the family coat-of-arms: CLEAR LIKE AN UNSHADED CRYSTAL REMAINS THE SPLENDOR OF THE NAME.

A wound, decorations when they came, merely fulfilled the dreams of glory of the boy hunter. Actually, we know little of von Richthofen's personal life beyond the gossip of fellow officers behind the lines with the girls and the brandy. He did want to marry, but he said he wished no widow left to mourn him. Like Hemingway, whom he resembles closely, he expected death, and there is a sense in his letters that he would welcome it. Again like Hemingway, he feared it only as a natural event resulting from decay and senility. As the eldest son the manor would eventually come to Manfred, but some claim he had no desire to survive. His brother Lothar, wild, reckless, rather stupid, would in time be an ace himself. Only Bolko, the youngest brother, remained too young to enjoy the war.

As the son of a professional military man, and heir to the Richthofen tradition, Manfred naturally entered the Prussian cadet corps. He was proper, reserved, a good soldier. In time, as called for, he became a leutnant in the Uhlan Regiment Number 1. For von Richthofens rode to war, did not foot-slog with peasant- or merchant-raised infantry.

He fought in 1914 on the Eastern Front against the Russians, then rode to war in Alsace, when the infantry's spiked headgear had not yet been replaced by the coalscuttle helmet. But as a skilled hunter, Manfred was aware that this would not be a horseman's war. He asked to be put with the clerks and students in the infantry, but was ordered to quartermaster's duty behind the lines. This would not do. His comment on counting hams and herring kegs, issuing boots and bullets, went directly to his commanding officer. It opened:

> My dear Excellency: I have not gone to war to collect cheese and eggs, but for much another reason . . .

His request to be transferred to a flying unit was granted, and in May of 1915 he was in Cologne training as an aerial observer. He served with a reconnaissance flier on the Eastern Front, observing the blue lakes, the ghostly white birches, the scattered farm huts, and the gigantic size of the Slavic land mass. Then the Ostend Carrier Pigeons were formed, but the big twin-engined bombers didn't excite von Richthofen. He called them "apple barges." The youth was becoming hard to please. Bombing blindly was no fun; the clumsy airships held no excitement for him. Again he took to pen and ink, another letter to another commander. Soon he was flying as an observer with a reconnaissance unit, but this time on the Western Front, over the cadences of battle.

With a pilot, a Leutnant Osteroth, he went after a Farman enemy plane in the skies and shot it down in flames. It fell behind the French line of trenches, and von Richthofen was hopping mad he could not get credit for the kill. But there *had* been a kill, and he had felt again in his loins the same glow as when he got a deer in his rifle sights, or broke the charge of a wild boar with the massive blast of a heavy rifle. When about a week later he met Oswald Boelcke, who had downed four enemy planes in air combat, the young flier could only wonder how it felt to have so many on one's record, and, damn it, *all* verified.

Von Richthofen asked Boelcke, "Just how do you manage to shoot them down?"

"Elementary and simple. I fly close to my man, take good aim. Then, well, down he goes, falls away."

The young baron hadn't found it that easy. He'd have to find a better plane than a scouting job, and be a pilot, not an observer. Boelcke had had a synchronized machine gun fixed so it could fire right past the propeller without knocking it to bits. He also flew the darling of the air force, the light Fokker monoplane. As an observer in a biplane, von Richthofen had had to use a ring-mounted weapon. There was nothing for it; he would just have to learn to fly one of those things himself. Perhaps after centuries of horsemanship it was a comedown to handle a machine. But it had to be done if he was to kill more of the enemy in the sky than Boelcke.

It was clear among the people he flew with and trained with that Baron Manfred wanted to win, wanted to be leader. He took two dozen training flights and then soloed. He crashed on landing. Back to training, more examinations, he coolly learned to slow down properly for a landing and not come banging in. His instructors didn't much care for his flying. But fliers were badly needed, so after Christmas 1915 he got his certificate as a pilot; he wasn't considered good enough to go into actual combat at the front, however.

Von Richthofen raged and sulked, grew taut and surly. He didn't write to any generals this time—not with his poor flying record—but to Mamma went a letter in January complaining. Since New Year's holiday, "I have not flown, not even once. The rains are incessant here. I seem to be making no progress. I should love to be at the front and right now. I think there is so much going on there . . ." (he never showed any compassion for the ground soldier and his dreadful agonies).

When the weather improved, von Richthofen was permitted more practice flights. To Breslau, Luben, home to Schweidnitz, then more lessons at Schwerin to get to know more about plane engines. Driven by a desire for action, ever ready to seek the man in control, he approached Anthony Fokker and tried to get an E-plane to the front. But Fokker was unimpressed by his flying.

Yet in some way von Richthofen sensed he was on the threshold of a new phase of his life, as his letters home show. He was in search of strong challenges, battle and fulfillment, something that would truly test the abilities he knew he had. One catches glimpses in his letters of the young man who dreaded growing old, saw no future in senility. In the air, for all his inability to please his teachers (perhaps because he was too eager, too wound up to show his true skills), he felt at ease and in his proper place.

Von Richthofen was sent back to the front to observe in a two-seater Albatros. It was the Verdun front where the French and the Germans were battering themselves to fragments in useless, ghastly battle. Men drowning in mud by platoons, whole generations being brutally destroyed. The baron saw that men died in hopeless agony in a land laid waste, the shell craters giving it the dismal image of a moon landscape. From the air it seemed "one of the lower circles of Dante's hell," as one flier remembered it.

It is doubtful if von Richthofen ever held any such literary images in his mind, though. He was thinking as a pilot now, mounting a machine gun on the top wing so that he could fire directly ahead over his propeller. The observer's machine gun he considered merely a back-up weapon. It was his first innovation and when the other pilots mocked him, he merely smiled.

Flying in April, his Albatros sighted a French Nieuport. Both machines seemed wary of each other, but von Richthofen flew forward to engage. The Frenchman, thinking the German had only a rear gun with the observer, made a turn to avoid combat, knowing the rear gunner could not reach his vitals.

The Albatros came on until it was about 60 yards away. Setting his wing sights on the Nieuport, von Richthofen pressed off a burst of stuttering bullets. The Frenchman's plane leapt upward as if stung and side-slipped downward. Was it a trick? Had the burst done any damage? Von Richthofen thought perhaps it was a dodge, the way a hunted-down bird would act wounded to lead one away from its nest, and then become lost in wild brush. As a hunter he knew the techniques. He was not falling for such a stunt. (He was to say later that these Allied fliers were so damn unmindful of the respect one owed to the conduct of war combat.)

As he watched, the stricken plane headed for Fort Douaumont, gaining speed in its dive; then it smacked with deadly impact into the woods behind the fort. The observer cheered and beat on the baron's shoulder. Von Richthofen had tasted a kill in the air. He wrote that it was a splendid feeling.

The official German war communiqué listed the day's victories as "two hostile flying machines shot down in aerial fighting above Fleury, south and west of Douaumont." And one of them was his, von Richthofen's; if the score keepers accepted his claim.

Home went a letter. "In haste, some joyful news. Look at yesterday's communiqué. My gun dropped one of those planes." He did not mention that again he would get no official credit for the kill: the rules then did not count planes brought down behind enemy lines.

Now he knew his destiny, the satisfaction of his special skill, the direct action of combat logic. He knew he had the instinctive assertiveness, the accelerating intensity that makes a fine hunter. Let them send him where they willed, he'd fly any kind of plane. He would do combat in the air, one man in a plane against another. He had a keen sense of individualism, and the psychological toughness to remain immune from the problems, the doubts, that plagued men with more involved and puzzled minds.

Back he went to the Russian Front again in a two-seater. He was unhappy at the situation and showed it. Then the great chance came. At Kovel he was called in to see the air inspector of the Eastern Front, the already fabulous Oswald Boelcke. Things were going badly in the air for the Germans on the Western Front and Boelcke was on his recruiting trip to put together a Jagdstaffel to take back to the west. General Karl von Bülow was worried. "The state of affairs is much aggravated by the enemy's superiority in the air . . . enemy fliers direct artillery fire . . . day and night they harass our infantry men with bombs, machine guns . . . a decided lowering of effect on our troops' morale . . ."

Dressed up for the meeting, von Richthofen found a long line of pilots outside the railroad carriage where the interviews with Boelcke were to take place. Although near the head of the line, von Richthofen became tense, jumpy. He had suffered so many setbacks in trying to become a fighter pilot.

Boelcke was looking splendid in his dress uniform, on which

gleamed the Ordre pour le Mérite. Von Richthofen remembered
the interview was short and to the point.

"For some real fighting, Baron, would you care to come with
me to the Somme?"

"Yes, sir."

"All right, you will."

It was that simple, that brief. On the train carrying him to the
Somme, the flier glowed with pride and hope. The Somme. Already that fearful battle was talked of as one long journey to hell.
"The stubborn, mutton-headed British generals" were destroying
the youth of England in the usual headlong attacks launched directly into the German machine guns. Thousands died for a few
yards, for some broken section of a trench. Back and forth
swayed the two weary armies. Nothing much was gained; only
the staggering casualty lists mounted. "The women stand staring
at the long lists pasted up—then a cry breaks out, a sob—very little
else—it's been expected . . ."

Only the Allied air arm had prevented the Germans from making stronger gains. Bombing, strafing, they managed to control
the air with the DH-2 and the Nieuports. The Fokkers seemed
helpless against the French and British fliers. The Germans still
lacked both organization and inspiration. As one prisoner put it
to his Allied captors: ". . . the English planes fly low; it's a
wonder they don't just pull us up out of the trenches. Our German air heroes, you don't see them around . . ."

But on a train moving west to the Somme slaughter Manfred
von Richthofen was thinking, as he remembered it: "From *now*
on began the finest time of my life."

Liebe Mamma:
In the last six weeks we have had, of our twelve pilots, six dead
and one wounded, while two have suffered a complete nervous
collapse. Yesterday I brought down my seventh shortly after
I had accounted for my sixth. The ill luck of all the others has
not yet affected my nerves.

Manfred

Of all the recruits Boelcke brought back from his trip to the

Eastern Front to form the Royal Prussian Jagdstaffel 2, von Richthofen turned out to be the prize.

On September 17, 1916, the baron got his first confirmed combat victory, shooting down two British fliers in their FE-2 in the first outing of the new German group, Jasta 2. From then on he seemed to be able to knock down almost anything he met.

By November 9 he had a confirmed ten enemy planes to his credit, and on the twenty-third he got number eleven, the well-respected flier Major Hawker, within range of his fire.

By victory sixteen von Richthofen got the Ordre pour le Mérite. Suddenly, after being ignored for so long, he was the rising German star, glowing and exploding into fame. Victory eighteen came near to closing his career at its rise, when the wing of his Albatros D-III was fragmented in part and he crashed, destroying the plane.

His only rival had been his discoverer, Boelcke. Early in November he had written home:

Liebe Mamma:
. . . Boelcke's death came about in this way: Boelcke, some of the men of the squadron and myself were involved in a fight with British planes. While attacking the enemy, I suddenly saw Boelcke being rammed by one of our own fliers, to whom, poor boy, nothing else happened. I followed Boelcke at once. But then one of his wings broke off and he crashed. His head was smashed by the impact; death came at once.

During the funeral services, in the procession, I carried his decorations on a pillow. The funeral was like that of a reigning prince.

Manfred

Leutnant Kirmaier took over Jagdstaffel 2 after Boelcke's death and the group was renamed the Jasta Boelcke; but they had a hard time of it as the British appeared in new planes, the Bristol Fighter and the SE-5.

Soon Baron von Richthofen was busy getting his own Jagdstaffel into shape, in time to be labeled by journalists von Richthofen's Flying Circus. The Germans badly needed heroes in the grand style, brave Teutons modeled on Wagner's operatic supermen. Two early heroes, Boelcke and Immelmann, had gone to unheroic, rather foolish deaths, neither in combat. But in Manfred von Richthofen the propaganda machine found a live hero, master of the rolling, plunging dogfight in the clouds, expert gunner whose echoing machine guns blasted enemy ships from the air in regular procession. He avoided air crashes with his own or enemy planes. He brought back his ship, usually with some confirmed or unconfirmed kill or kills.

He was known as a brainy flier, who figured all odds, objectively using the mathematics of angle, fire control, and position to stalk his prey. He was always ahead of his flight, plunging first into the maneuvering, crisscrossing planes of a dogfight. He was neither shy of his rising fame, nor indifferent to being recognized by the enemy. It was at this point that he had his plane painted a bright scarlet. Soon his own men and the enemy knew him equally well as the Red Baron.

There were personal rewards for many of the German fliers. Oswald Boelcke had presented victorious fliers with fancy beer steins, which were always filled and drained in toasts when a new stein-giving event took place. Von Richthofen compiled a silver cup collection—one for each kill—with such lettering as *I. Vickers 2. 17, 9, '16*. He was very careful to instruct his Berlin silversmith as to the kind and size of cup he wanted. Just a plain cup, small because of his many'victories; not too ostentatious: "5 centimeters high, 3 centimeters diameter across the top, sloping sides, a base smaller than the top, all in sterling silver, the plating inside of dull gold . . ." After every victory he would write, "One more cup, please, just like the last ordered. Engraved as follows . . ."

Von Richthofen was no romantic, no scatterbrained Bohemian, as so many fatalistic fliers became. He remained the cool Prussian aristocrat, demanding order and discipline, daily meetings to talk over flying tactics, ordering his fliers to follow the methods he approved of, not their own versions of air combat. And his ideas were sound.

Just under two weeks after he took over command, he and his men engaged in one of the great air battles of the war. The dismal Battle of the Somme, four months of unbelievable horror, had just ended. It was November 9, 1916, a clear sky, fine visibility. The baron told his men it looked like "a fine day's sport." He was as calm as if starting out on a boar hunt or some long-planned chase after forest wolves. The pilots at attention received his orders, then took to their planes, the scarlet leader ahead. There were to be eighty German planes up that day. At this point the baron led six, and after fifteen minutes in the air, over Vraucourt, he sighted sixteen big Allied bombers. (Vraucourt was the home of a German army operational headquarters; also of a sugar factory busy trying to meet the needs of a starved, blockaded Germany.) Von Richthofen gave the hand signals for his flight to engage. But from all sides planes were crowding in, both friend and foe.

"The sky was as blue as a Dutchman's pants." The British bombers did not know that they had been sighted; in fact they were betrayed, for someone had given away the secret of the bombing raid.

Now commanding a growing collection of Albatroses, the baron signalled the long dive down onto the unsuspecting bombers. Struts and wires sang like harps—as the fliers recalled it—and the wind tore at goggled and helmeted heads. The scarlet plane led the V-formed attack at an air speed of 100 miles an hour.

But it was not to be an easy fight. Coming up fast were fourteen British fighters from RFC Squadrons Nos. 11 and 60, sent along as escorts to the bombers. They, too, went into a steep dive to divert and meet the Germans before they could open up the deadly fire of machine guns on the heavily loaded bombers. The scarlet plane of the Red Baron was recognized, and the British were eager to take him on.

It must have been a magnificent scene as the two V's of planes converged, moving over the expanse of sky against that crayon-blue day to the stutter of raced motors, the twanging of strained wires.

The bombers finally became aware of what was happening, and gunners began to fire test bursts. The war fell in fury upon them. Both sides held on course toward their target area, the Germans to attack, the British fighters to protect.

Planes fell vertically in steep dives that could tear off wings, for no one yet knew for sure how much strain these flimsy planes could take. The red plane was diving now at 115 miles an hour. Von Richthofen held steady; he could do little else, for to try to pull out of this dive too quickly would pluck off his wings and leave him with only a fuselage for that long ride down to death. His followers began to seek out enemies to engage.

The Germans started to pass the bombers, firing as they did so. Von Richthofen had a bad position and held his fire. Then the Germans led by the baron banked steeply, for they were now below the bombers in their dive and above were the vulnerable bellies of the enemy. They came in and up, meeting a shower of fire from the bomber's gunners. Somehow none were hit. The baron led his men into a *Kurvenkampf* (a fast twist), and they were onto the tails of the British fighters. Now it was a matter of seconds, motors screaming, propellers flashing in the sun, the rattle of machine guns. Amid the apparent confusion, German planes attacked the bombers, while the scarlet plane and its escorts tangled with the enemy fighters. A cousin of the famous Max Immelmann was pouring blasts into a bomber, while two British planes hung on his tail. He got a bomber to fall away, burning red with long plumes of black smoke.

Von Richthofen turned to give help, chasing a second bomber young Immelmann was after. As he came in, the British bomber—carrying Lieutenant G. K. Knight as pilot and observer Lieutenant J. G. Cameron—let go with a Lewis gun on the scarlet machine. A volley of tracers came too close; death was buzzing in the baron's ears. Something flashed in his mind. He twisted his ship and poured a withering fire. The young English gunner died at once at his controls. Then the baron pulled away to get a better view of his victory; his close brush with death had unbalanced his cool mathematical sense of air combat, and the unaccustomed fury still held him.

He shattered the British engine with several blasts and began skillfully to part wires, spars, ailerons. He wanted to pound the plane into a thousand fragments. Knight, still alive, found the control loose to the touch. There came to him that dreadful, stomach-tensing approach to the last deadly dive. The failed control could not lessen the increasing speed of the fall.

Like a wolf the Red Baron circled the falling bomber, its bombs showing clearly in their racks. Now his rage settled into a worried calm. If the crippled bomber could release its bombs, it would destroy the greater part of Vraucourt.

Knight tried to reach the bomb release, but his dead comrade lay across the mechanism. The fall continued at a great speed. The bomber swerved and passed the town. It crashed down into treetops and fell broken and smoking into a field. Von Richthofen came down to a couple of hundred of feet and was amazed to see Knight leap from the wreckage. The Englishman stood looking about him, dazed but unharmed. Not a bomb had gone off.

The other British bombers had managed to drop seventy-two of their bombs on the town, but in the haste and bad aiming as a result of the dust that rose all around there had been little damage.

The most amazing sight that day was Manfred von Richthofen. He had given way to some savage fury and even after the air battle, when he went to inspect the town, he wasn't the neat, cool Prussian. His face was streaked black by the backfire from his weapons. His clothes were drenched with oil which his overheated engine spewed out thickly from a leak. This was no medieval knight of the air. The lethal horror of what could have happened to him had come closer than ever before. To Manfred Freiherr von Richthofen, challenge in the air had almost brought dark and final fulfillment.

We see clearly that on that dangerous day von Richthofen was badly shaken, his murderous fury showing a crack in what had been his self-discipline and more than superior ability. Even the faith in his own unique quality of leadership, that too he had lost in the moment of wanting to take that British plane apart, bit by bit, even when there was no longer further need.

Later he was to be ruthless, but in a calculated, grim way; machine-gunning enemy fliers as they dangled helpless in parachutes, gunning them on the ground as they escaped or crawled from burning, crashed planes. That was war, cruel war, but he shot then coolly, not in a mad uncontrolled tremor of rage.

Now as he stood in Vraucourt after the great air battle, he was eager to look over the wrecks of the bombers. Brushing aside the introduction to some high official figure who was congratulating him, he went to see the downed remains. He was told later that the official had been His Royal Highness Grand Duke of Saxe-Coburg Gotha. Two days after the battle, at His Highness's headquarters, the baron was decorated by the grand duke. By that time von Richthofen was properly stiff and formal and once again in full control of his reactions . . .

CHAPTER 8

"THE BLOODY ZEPPS"

Zeppelin, flieg,
Hilf uns im Krieg,
Fliege nach England,
England wird abgebrannt,
Zeppelin, flieg!

All told, German airplanes, aside from Zeppelins, were to raid England fifty-two times, dropping a total of nearly 3,000 bombs (somebody at the War Office in London kept count)—a weight of 73 tons of high explosives. Number of deaths, 857. But the real menace so far as the Englishman in the street and his wife were concerned, were "the bloody Zepps."

The dirigible, a hydrogen-filled airship pushed by hanging attached motors, intended for use in peace or war, seemed to have been jinxed from the first. Count Ferdinand von Zeppelin got his first model up in the air in July of 1900. It rose, the LZ-1, from its floating hangar on Lake Constance; but at 1,300 feet, the aluminum frame that held its canvas hide stretched tight, buckled, and affected its steering. There it was, twisted to ruin, drifting uncontrollably. In 1905, the count got his LZ-2 up twice, and then disaster again. The following year the LZ-3 managed a 208-mile flight, and the German War Ministry showed interest. The Kaiser was not impressed by the count, however. "Of all Swabians, he's the biggest jackass."

England was warned of the military progress of the new air monster by the *Daily Mail:*

Out upon the glassy surface of Lake Constance the giant craft lies hidden in the floating corrugated-iron shed. Count Zeppelin's crew are at work inside, making various changes suggested by the successful trials. Count Zeppelin is confident he will be able to sail for an unbroken period of twenty-four hours. German military experts were exultant over the Count's recent achievements, and are bringing their utmost influence to bear to induce the government to purchase the ship without waiting for further experiments.

The German army bought two Zeppelins. LZ-4 plummeted from a height as a result of engine trouble, then a storm came up and the ship exploded. The Kaiser watched the LZ-3 being tested and gave Count "Jackass" the Order of the Black Eagle, reversing his old opinion. "I thank God, with all Germans, that He has deemed our people worthy of you. May it be permitted to each of us, as it has to you, to be able to say in the twilight of our lives, that we have served our dear Fatherland so beneficially."

LZ-5 was destroyed by fire. The firm of Deutsche Luftschiffahrt Aktien-Gesellschaft (it was easier to say as Delag) began to build passenger dirigibles with such names as *Viktoria, Luise, Hanse, Sachsen, Deutschland* (the last-named and one called the *Schwaben* both crashed and burned).

The ships could make 45 miles an hour in the air with three motors combining to 450 horsepower. Hydrogen was the only gas available, but it was dangerous and deadly in an explosion.*

In 1912, Germany was preparing for war, and the crews of Delag were made military reservists. Oddly enough, orders for new Zeppelins were placed first with a rival firm, Schutte-Lanz, that used laminated wooden frames. When war did come, the Zeppelins were first used for scouting. In the second week, on August 7, one was sent over the German advance into France. The day before, a Zeppelin had bombed Liège. (The "bombs" were artillery shells to which kite tails made of strips of horse blanket were attached, so that they would hit nose first.)

Actually, the French had been the first to acquire a dirigible as

---

*Helium, the inert gas, was tightly held under monopoly by the U.S.A., and still is.

a military weapon. In 1905 they put the *Lebaudy*, a gift to the nation, in service. It was the brainchild of the Lebaudy brothers, Pierre and Jean, aided by the engineer, Henri Julliot. By 1914, the French had twelve small semi-rigid dirigibles. But they were more excited by airplanes, and their dirigibles remained using up back hangar space, never brought to full service as a military weapon. Only four were actually fit for use in 1914, and they were small and underpowered.

The British built the nonrigid *Nulli Secundus*, which took three flights before being junked. The next one was called *Baby* (English humor is not to be scorned). After this the British passed.

Early in August, the captains of the Delag Zeppelins were ordered to ground their ships while wireless, machine guns, and bomb racks were installed. The hulls were made longer simply by inserting new 25-foot sections, and military numbers were painted on the sides. The Zeppelin had officially gone to war.

Germany began the war with no idea of just what to expect from its airplanes. But it took high pride in the terror and destructive potential of its Zeppelins. Fleets of them, some predicted, were expected to fly over English cities and bomb the nation into submission. Ascot Race Week, Bank Holiday or no, bomb.

The Allies worried, not knowing the capabilities of Count Zeppelin's cigar-shaped ships or the smaller Schutte-Lanz dirigibles. They were naturally apprehensive, for Zeppelins had the cruising range and the lifting power to carry huge bombloads.

The weapon, on sight, was impressive, and in the days before effective bombing by planes, it seemed the natural method of inflicting dreadful destruction from the air. And only Germany had fleets of the big dirigibles ready. The *Wacht am Rhein* could become the *Wacht am Thames*.

They were tried out with proper bombs on the Eastern Front, where on September 11, 1914, a fleet of Zeppelins dropped bombs on the railroad center of Viljka, near Vilna. Minsk, too, saw the hydrogen-filled shapes and the Germans claimed great damage there.

The ships were found to be a dangerous weapon, even to their owners, however. The Z-18, the biggest, costing the most, blew up in its new hangar at Tönder, Schleswig. A court of inquiry brushed aside the usual talk of sabotage. They assigned the cause to some *schweinhund* dropping off live cigar ash while the ship was being filled with gas. It had gone up with a tremendous explosion, a red glow, blowing off the hangar roof, puffing down walls, destroying the buildings surrounding it. A dozen personnel were killed or fearfully injured. The disaster was to be kept secret, but the American press somehow got hold of the details a week later and printed them.

The first Zeppelin attacks on England were agreed to by the Kaiser in January of 1915. The German fleet of airships had now been given additional new power: six new Zeppelins for the navy and four for the army. On the nineteenth, the attack on England began with three ships, two from Fuhlsbuttel close to Hamburg, and one from Nordholtz near Cuxhaven on the Elbe River. *"Gott strafe England!"* One Zeppelin turned back with a balky engine; the second killed two people in Yarmouth with its bombs; and the third made drops on King's Lynn, also killing two people, but managing to wound thirteen. (Both these Zeppelins were lost in a storm a month later while over the North Sea.)

Zeppelin hangars and sheds were built near the Channel on the Belgium coast for shorter runs to England by the big ships. Kapitanleutnant Heinrich Mathy, who was to make over 100 air raids in Zeppelins, went out to bomb London in June. Strong headwinds drove him to Hull, where he killed twenty-four people.

In another raid, just as the cry of *"Klar für zum Werfen!"* was passed from ship to ship (the moment approaching to drop the eggs), angry red spots appeared on the ground, and the continued glare showed that England was aware of Mathy and was firing antiaircraft shells at him. The captain gave the order to tilt rudder and seek height, so fast that the Zeppelins rose at dangerous angles. At what he felt was a safe altitude, Mathy ordered the engines to a quicker speed.

He was disappointed. He had hoped to sneak in quietly, but the English gunnery observers were able to pick up a Zeppelin's motor hum at nearly 10,000 feet, if there was no wind and the night was still.

The bomb-release men were at their posts and below lay the inviting spread of the countryside. But the gun flashes were still active. And now the searchlights would seek them out behind the scudding clouds, pinpoint them sharply against the backdrop of night. Soon they were within range of the City:

> . . . Our eyes and minds are concentrated on our work, for at any moment we may be plunged below, a shapeless mass of wreckage and human bodies shattered beyond recognition. . . . Balfour said London was not a fortified city, and that its defenses against aerial attacks were poor. We know, however, there are several forts and batteries around the city and outside, and had he stood by my side and looked into those flashing guns, all over, he wouldn't say London was not a militarily defended city, and perhaps not think so poorly of its aerial defense.

At midnight Mathy radioed: "Place, North Hinder Lightship. London attacked."

English civilians died, men, women, and children. But the Zeppelins had taken hard punishment from the guns below. They were holed, parts shattered, men wounded. The ships limped back, moved slowly on across the sea, landing at Evere near Brussels where the wounded were removed.

The commander looked over his battered fleet. So far, on all the raids over England, the English gunners had found it impossible to down a Zeppelin from the ground. It was like shooting at an elephant with a .22 rifle.

In one raid in June 1915 the huge LZ-39, after bombing Ramsgate, drifted off from her escorting Zeppelins and appeared near Dunkirk, going easily on her way. The British Naval Flying Group at Dunkirk took up the challenge as she passed. Three fliers took off, Spenser Grey, Reggie Warneford, and A. W. Bigsworth. Warneford felt that 20-pound bombs dropped on the damn Hun cigar might do the trick. Maybe.

At over 10,000 feet, Bigsworth had the first try. The Zeppelin was 200 feet below him. He dropped bombs and thought he had missed, though black smoke started escaping from the tail: there had been no hit, but the shock waves had done damage. The

Zeppelin crews were busy firing at the other two planes and had been surprised at Bigsworth's attack from above. Meanwhile the planes below were pouring machine-gun fire into the gondola where the dead were piling up. Wounded men rolled from side to side helplessly as the huge bag shook and shivered. The crew's machine guns grew too hot to fire for long; men yelled in pain, in fear, at the horror of their wounds and what could happen to them.

The LZ-39 staggered on, as if drunk, to Evere. The crew was in no condition to handle the ship; she bumped down heavily. When the doctors got on board, the scene was like a slaughterhouse.

Back at Dunkirk, Warneford, still excited by the attack on the LZ-39, now sighted her sister ship, the LZ-37, approaching in the air lane over Ostend. The Englishman's Morane could not seem to catch up with the Zeppelin, no matter how much he opened throttle; but by the time both were over Bruges, he felt he was within sufficient range to do some damage. The LZ-37 gun crews fired first and he had to climb to 11,000 feet to avoid their fusillade. He still had his six 20-pounds bombs.

Warneford decided to dive. He was wind-whipping by, the whole force of gravity pulling him down at an incredible speed. He kept one hand on the stick, while with the other he reached for the bomb-lever release. It was hard to keep the plane under control. The fast, steep dive was bringing him close to a blackout.

At 150 feet above the LZ-37, he got the bombs off one after the other, like drops of water from a faucet.

There was a tremendous explosion, a roar like a volcanic mountain blowing itself up. Fires at once began to outline the huge ship. The blast reached Warneford and his plane was pitched upside down. Now he went under into the blackout, sucking air, breathing his own powder fumes. He came to to find himself in a steep vertical dive. The moments left to level off were evaporating fast. He pulled back and came level with the horizon, jolted alert by tormented nerves and his agonizing experience. Then he leaned over to watch the death throes of the Zeppelin spread out on the earth, smoke and fire streaming upward.

Some heavy sections of the ship were scattered over a convent, where heavy machinery fell in on two of the nuns and took them to God's mercy. Through the convent roof with part of the control car fell Helmsman Muller, right into a nun's bed (she had just left it!). The helmsman later told his story of how he got there from the moment the Zeppelin was stricken:

The ship lurched and began to quake, and my helm spun wildly. It found no more resistance, a sign that our steering system had become useless. The gondola was swaying so violently that I lost my footing. I went skidding across the deck. My head glanced against a metal upright and I was momentarily stunned. By the time my wits returned, there was nobody in the gondola but me. Everyone else had either jumped or had been pitched overboard. . . . The whole ship above me was a roaring, hissing inferno. Instinctively, I pressed myself flat to the deck and began clawing at the rails, trying to elude the tongues of flame. The heat was unbearable. I was being roasted alive. I wondered how long it would take to fall three thousand feet. It seemed an eternity to hell. I knew the end was close at hand, but I welcomed the oncoming collision as preferable to the slow torture of incineration. At last the gondola slammed into something. I was vaguely aware of the crash. I felt myself somersaulting through the air just before I blacked out. When I regained consciousness, the pain was excruciating. The flesh of my arms, legs and torso was frightfully singed.

Warneford sat in the sky circling his kill, then headed for his base. Night was coming on, and his motor was beginning to shake and cough. He still had oil pressure, but his fuel-pressure needle was dancing up and down. He had a broken fuel line and was pouring out gasoline into the air. There was a good chance that when the free-flowing fuel hit a red-hot part of his engine, he'd follow the LZ-37 down in another explosion.

The engine died, the prop went still, feathered. The night was inky dark. He had no visibility at all. Warneford came down in a glide in a meadow. By touch of hand alone—a match would explode his leaking plane—he hunted out the leak. It was small, but the gasoline was dripping out. He found rags and tape and bound up the cracked fuel line. It still leaked a bit, and remained hazardous for flying.

Starting the motor was a problem, since there were enemy guards on duty nearby. The motor came alive. He took off after a mere 30 seconds of maximum throttle, and leveled off at 11,000 feet. The mist made landing another guess, and he was lucky to come down at Cape Gris Nez.

Warneford was awarded the Victoria Cross. But it came posthumously, for he was killed ten days later testing a Farman plane that came apart in the air near Paris, the result of shoddy workmanship.

The Germans shrugged off the kill of the LZ-37 as a lucky accident on the Britishers' part. They still had faith in the gas bags, and predicted they would still do great damage. They changed the shapes of the Zeppelins a little, trying for a more symmetrical form. The bulk was put ahead and the behind made slimmer. An extra gondola was added. Bomb crews and pilots had more room. Gun platforms were put up on top of the ship, reached by a long ladder going through the ship.

In August 1915, the L-12 was hit by British guns at Dover, began to give up her gas, and came down into the sea at Zeebrugge.

In one famous 1915 raid with a party of eight Zeppelins, the L-19 vanished from sight and both British and Germans hunted her. A few months later, a bottle with messages inside written by the L-19's commander, Loewe, was found on the Norwegian coast. The first message was dated three days after her disappearance:

> With fifteen men on the platform of L-19. The envelope is floating without any car. We had three engine breakdowns. A very high headwind on the homeward flight hampered progress and drove us in the fog over Holland when we came under rifle fire. Now, about one o'clock in the afternoon, our last hour is approaching.

A second message in the bottle read: "My greeting to my wife and child. An English trawler was here and refused to take us on board. She was the *King Stephen* and hailed from Grimsby."

Yet another message in a bottle was found by the Swedish yacht *Stell Smogen:*

With fifteen men on the upper platform, roof and body of the L-19, minus cars, drifting at about longitude three degrees east, I am trying to write a final report. With three engine breakdowns and a light headwind on the homeward leg, my return was delayed, and I got into fog over Holland, where we met heavy rifle fire. Ship became unwieldy and three of our engines stopped running simultaneously. February 2, 1916, about noon, probably our last hour. Loewe . . .

The *King Stephen* captain, summoned to defend his action in not picking up the Germans before an investigatory board appointed by the Admiralty, testified as follows:

"The commander of the airship hailed the skipper of the *King Stephen* with a request that the airship crew be taken on board. The skipper replied: 'No, if I take you on board you will take charge,' for it was his conviction that his few hands could, and would, be easily overpowered by the Germans, even if they were unarmed. He therefore steamed off to find and report to a patrol boat, but it was not until he had put into the Humber, on the morning of February 3, that he found a vessel to receive his report. Then it was too late. A search failed to locate the airship, which is presumed to have gone under with no survivors . . ." Later, the Germans sank the *King Stephen*, and took the captain and crew prisoner instead of turning them loose to the mercy of the sea.

On the afternoon of September 9, 1915, Heinrich Mathy was again on his way to England with four Zeppelins. Mathy, blond hair close cut, a short man, wide and plump, had led many raids. Zeppelins were mostly under the command of the Royal German Navy; Mathy was a seaman rather than an airman, and had been happiest as commander of a destroyer. But he was attracted to Zeppelins as to a new toy. In the air, as at sea, he was a sort of Captain Bligh. No drinking, no hot food; those who were gluttons could bring their own sandwiches. Smoking was of course forbidden under those thousands of cubic feet of deadly dangerous gas.

The commander sat comfortably in his cabin as they moved high over the North Sea. Dusk was falling fast. The crew were at their various tasks; the air screws were spinning, those damn screws that sometimes broke free and tore the ship's fabric, endangering them all. But so far all had gone well. In the last of the day's light, they sighted the Essex coast. Behind Mathy his three other Zeppelins followed like cumbersome circus sea lions.

The *New York World* reported that over the Thames estuary, Mathy had but to follow the river shining silver in the night straight to London, and bomb the sleeping city. Slowing down, they changed to battle formation, no longer tail to tail.

"My instructions," Mathy said,

were to attack certain points to the south of the City of London, such as railway stations, bridges, industrial establishments; strict orders to do everything possible to avoid hitting St. Paul's and other churches, museums, the Palace, Westminster Abbey, Parliament, and, of course, residential districts . . .

. . . The English can darken London as much as they want; they can never eradicate or cover up the Thames. It is our great orientation point from which we can always get our bearings. That doesn't mean that we always come up along the Thames, by any means. London was darkened, but sufficiently lighted on this night so that I saw the reflected glow on the sky 60 kilometers away shortly before 10 o'clock.

Soon the city was outlined, still and silent below in the distance. Dark spots stood out from blue lights in well-lit portions. The residence sections were not much darkened. It was the dark spots I was after, and bore down on them, as they marked the city. There was no sign of life, except in the distance—the movement and the light of what were probably railroad trains. All seemed very quiet, no noises ascended from below to penetrate the sputtering motors and whirring propellers.

Then in the twinkling of an eye, all this changed. A sudden flash and a narrow band of brilliant light reached out from below and began to feel around the sky; then a second, third, fourth, fifth, and soon more than a score of criss-crossing ribbons ascended. From the Zeppelin it looked as if the city had suddenly come to life and was waving its arms around the sky, handing out feelers for the danger that threatened it, but our deeper impression was that they were tentacles seeking to drag us to destruction. First one, then another and another of those ribbons, shooting out from glaring search-lights picked us up and then from below came an ominous sound that deadened the noise of motors and propellers, little red flashes and short bursts of fire, which stood out prominently against the black background. From north and south, from right and left, they appeared and following the flashes rolled up from below the sound of guns.

It was a beautiful and impressive but fleeting picture as seen from above, and probably no less interesting from below, with the grayish dim outlines of the Zeppelins gliding through, wavering ribbons of light and shrapnel cloudlets which hung in the sky, with constant red flashes of many guns from coal-black sections. At any moment we might be plunged below in a shapeless mass of wreckage. When the first search-lights pick you up and you see the first flash of guns from below, your nerves get a little shock, but then you steady down and put your mind on what you are there for. I picked out St. Paul's and, with that as a point of orientation, laid a course for the Bank of England. There was a big search-light in the immediate vicinity of St. Paul's and a battery of guns under cover of the church, as I could plainly see from the flashes as they belched shrapnel at us. Although we had been fired upon from all sides, we had not yet dropped a bomb.

When we were above the Bank of England, I shouted through the speaking tube connecting me with my lieutenant at the firing apparatus: "Fire slowly."

Mingling with the dim thunder and the vivid flash of guns below, came explosions and bursting flames from our bombs. I soon observed flames bursting forth in several places. Over Holborn Viaduct and the vicinity of Holborn Station we dropped several bombs. From the Bank of England to the Tower is a short distance. I tried to hit London Bridge, and believe I was successful—to what extent in damage I could not determine. Flashes from the Tower showed that the guns placed there were keeping up a lively fire. Maneuvering and arriving directly over Liverpool Street Station, I shouted, "Rapid fire!" through the tube and the bombs rained down. There was a succession of detonations and bursts of fire, and I could see that we had hit well, and apparently caused great damage. Flames burst forth in several places in that vicinity.

Having dropped all the bombs, I turned for a dash home. We had not been hit. Several times I leaned out and looked up and back at the dark outlines of my Zeppelin, but she had no holes in her gray sides. Ascending and then descending until we found a favorable wind current, we made a quick return. The main attack was made from 10:50 to 11 p.m. It lasted just ten minutes. Zeppelin tactics in attack require you to make a dash to the points to be bombarded and then make a quick getaway.

Heinrich Mathy went on his last raid early in October of 1916. The sound of his LZ-31 motors was picked up by the English on amplifiers. It was a cold damp night, the usual London autumn weather. At North Weald Airfield, the phone got the fliers out into the cold still buttoning up their heavy flying suits, their plane motors coughing into life.

Lieutenant W. J. Tempest jumped into his BE-2C and the big four-bladed prop was spun and yanked at. But the machine was dead. A new spin and the motor came to life and the plane went off roughly across the grass field, lit by oil lamps set on empty petrol drums.

At 14,500 feet, Tempest was over London. Big Ben would strike midnight in a few minutes. It was cold up there in the freezing wet weather. Tempest's teeth chattered as he huddled in his cockpit. Fifteen miles ahead he saw the searchlights crisscrossing to focus on a long silver shape. Then they held it in their white sights. The Zeppelin was heading directly for him. Tempest was getting airsick from the bouncing around his machine was taking as a result of the concussion of antiaircraft fire being aimed at the German ship. None of the shells was coming anywhere near the enemy.

The Zeppelin dropped its bombs and began to rise, considerably lighter. It was now level with him, and turning away as if it had seen him. The plane began to tremble; the pressure in the gasoline tank was going. The motor-driven pump had failed. Tempest would have to keep the tank pressure up by pumping with one hand, the other on the stick. If he wanted to fire his machine gun, he'd have to leave the controls to take care of themselves.

The Zeppelin was clearly on the run and moving away from

him. Giving chase, he hand-pumped, taking one hand off the stick to fire a burst from time to time. He raked the big ship from end to end, then turned and got back behind her rudder. He was being fired at from the ship's car and gondolas. Tracer bullets sang and glowed around him. Tempest kept firing. Then, as he wrote in his report, the Zeppelin began "to get red inside like a Chinese lantern . . . flames shot out of the front part of her, she shot up about 200 feet, paused, and came roaring down straight onto me, before I had time to get out of the way . . ."

It was a strange and fearful situation, the plane diving—an entire furious funeral pyre chasing him like some Viking burial in the sky. Tempest made a hard bank; the plane obeyed and pulled. The German ship "went past roaring like a furnace."

The great glare made a torch by which other Zeppelins, as far away as Lincolnshire, saw the signal of the disaster. In the flames of the LZ-31 died the veteran of over 100 raids, Kapitanleutnant Heinrich Mathy.

It seemed the Zeppelins were failing to break the spirit of the British. There was little about the disasters in the *Neue Freie Presse* or the *Neues Wiener Tageblatt*. Readers were spared most of such bad news.

How did other raiding commanders feel? Karl Linnarz, who led some of the early raids on London, describes one glorious success:

At full speed we steer for their capital city, the jewel of their civilization. I am standing at my command station, every fibre of my body taut. "Let go!" I cry. The first bomb has been hurled at London! We wait with baited breath, listening. We lean over the side, watching. What a damned long interval between release and impact, the bomb falling those thousands of feet. "It's a dud," someone mutters, voicing the anxiety of us all—and then the quick flash, the faintly audible thud of the explosion, a chorus of hurrahs in the cabin. Already we have frightened them below. Away goes the second, an incendiary bomb thrown out by hand, a pin being removed to activate its percussion cap. Suddenly the searchlights come alive, right, left and all about us, stabbing the night, reaching after us like the legs of gigantic spiders. Soon the gleaming hull of the airships

lies athwart two dazzling rays of light and others are con-
verging. . . .

Paris suffered a few raids—but not of the same intensity. Gertrude Stein recalls:

> . . . there was a loud boom, then several more. It was a soft
> noise and then there was the sound of horns blowing in the
> streets and then we knew it was all over. . . . The next time
> there was a Zeppelin raid and it was not very long after the first
> one, Picasso and Eve were dining with us. . . . Picasso and
> Gertrude Stein talked until two in the morning when the "all
> clear" sounded and they went home. . . .

The Germans still felt the Zeppelin was the magic weapon to
bomb the enemy cities into such devastation there would have to
be a peace plea. New ships came with five engines that could
develop 200 horsepower each (through six vertical cylinders) and
were water-cooled.

In mid-1916, there were forty Zeppelins in the war, mostly in
sea-patrol duty over the North Sea and the Baltic. Leipzig was
the big Zeppelin center for building, training, and organizing
crews. Zeiss made the gear and fittings; Chemnitz produced the
lifting power, the hydrogen.

Undoubtedly the most skilled fanatic commanding the Zeppelin
forces for the German navy was Kapitan Peter Strasser. No losses,
no failures could move him from the fixed, stubborn idea that the
Zeppelin was the ultimate weapon. Peter Strasser was a hard man
to serve under. What he wanted for his Zeppelins, he announced,
was volunteers who not only were mad about flying, but for
whom duty came above everything. He demanded German will
power and self-control in action. But also "the mental alertness
to form proper decisions quickly, good eyesight, physical dex-
terity, sound general health, especially heart and nerves, no tendency to dizziness or seasickness; a well-coordinated sense of
direction; appreciation of basic principles of warfare, understanding of tactical, strategical conditions; familiarity with science of
ballistics, practical skill at gunnery, ability to operate aerial camera
and interpret resultant photographs; working knowledge of in-

ternal combustion engines, meteorology, telephony, wireless telegraphy, signaling lamps, the use of carrier pigeons. . . . Your sacred obligation, the demolishment of London. Be prepared to make the supreme sacrifice for the Fatherland, which is the crowning glory for any loyal son of Germany . . ."

Here is Strasser's so-called "Appraisal of Army Zeppelin Procedures":

> Army crews carry parachutes instead of additional bombs. A crew of twenty-three taking parachutes weighing 30 pounds each amounts to 690 pounds, which is a considerable quantity of ammunition to leave behind. Parachutes are *verboten* on Navy zeppelins. . . . Vials of poison are distributed to crews as a means of instant merciful death in the event you are trapped by fire and escape is not available. . . .

There was no humor—except gallows humor—in Strasser. He was a man of combat and total dedication, who made it clear that his intention was nothing less than to destroy, to raze London. He had fully absorbed Nietzsche's will to power. New Zeppelins were coming off the German production lines each month, and he sent them in squads against the city of London. But he was also encountering stronger antiaircraft fire. He must hit hard while he could. "*Hassgesang gegen England.*" He had to move quickly before the British planes grew so skilled they could climb all over his ships. Perhaps he had access to information on a deadly new British secret of Royal Navy ammunition: powerful incendiary bullets, the "Pomeroy" and the "Brock," designed to plow through a Zeppelin's skin and explode when they hit or penetrated the walls of the gas bags inside.

The Germans needed something to be proud of by late 1916. Verdun had been sheer butchery and blood-letting on both sides. The French had held out, against appalling losses from which France never recovered. The Germans had been killed by hundreds of thousands. Result: Stalemate.

Like so many fliers, Strasser frequently wrote letters home to his mother:

> We are enjoying pleasant weather here, and we are marching against England. . . . We who strike the enemy where his heart

beats have been slandered as "baby killers" and "murderers of women." Such name-calling is to be expected from enemy quarters. It is maddening to learn, however, that even in Germany there are simple fools and deluded altruists who condemn us. What we do is . . . but necessary. Very necessary. Nowadays there is no such animal as a noncombatant; modern warfare is total warfare. A soldier cannot function at the front without the factory worker, the farmer, and all the other providers behind him at home. You and I, Mother, have discussed this subject, and I know you understand what I say. My men are brave. . . . Their cause is holy, so how can they sin while doing their duty? . . . If what we do is frightful, then may frightfulness be Germany's salvation.

In this particular argument he was backed up by some of the nation's intellectuals. Wrote Professor von Bernhardi: "Weak nations do not deserve to exist and should be absorbed by powerful ones . . ."

On one raid, of the twelve Zeppelins Strasser sent against London, only one got through, only four managed to cross the Channel, the fog was that thick. Nine civilians died, forty were wounded. Next, he sent over twenty Zeppelins, having borrowed some spares from the German army, whose Zeppelin handling he had once found cowardly because they carried parachutes. He went along this time, on the L-16. On his visiting list in London were the British Admiralty and the Bank of England. Strasser was naïve enough to think that burning the Bank would bankrupt the English war effort and break the pound sterling.

When they arrived, the Zeppelin raiders found the English city and countryside blacked out. The British had picked up German radio messages, so that the element of surprise was gone. A wireless listening service called Room 40 held British codebreakers taking down radio messages. The weather was foul, the full fighter air patrols had not gone up. But a handful of the RFC made it into the air through the pea-souper when the Zeppelins got close. Among them was 2nd Lieutenant W. Leefe-Robinson, who had never flown as an air fighter in actual combat. To look older, he had affected one of those flowing yellow mustaches so favored by British officers. He was an excellent pilot, given to stunting over the farms and getting cursed for it by the natives.

The antiaircraft guns went into action but tracer bullets and exploding shells all seemed to miss the Zeppelins. The SL-11 was picked up by crisscrossing searchlights. Hauptmann Schramm continued on his set route.

In the dark sky, Leefe-Robinson held steady in his BE-12, which had been made into a single-seater and carried a machine gun armed with the new incendiary bullets. Finally, he came diving out of the mist toward the Zeppelins, and found the exploding antiaircraft shells were shaking his plane with their concussion. He got down to 800 feet below the SL-11, and flying along beneath her, got off a full drum of ammunition into her fabric bulk. It didn't seem to bother the huge ship; it was like an elephant being molested by a flea. The antiaircraft stopped their firing, the searchlights fell away. Lieutenant Robinson was alone, playing, as many were to say, David to this gas-filled Goliath. He pressed in on the stern of the ship and began to fire, concentrating on one spot. Nothing. By the time he had gotten his third drum of bullets off in bursts, he was so excited he shot off part of his own plane. Why hadn't he damaged the Zeppelin? Or had he?

The silver painted stern of the big ship was turning chrome yellow, then old rose, then a quivering scarlet. After that came explosions and long tongues of flames. It was nearly 12,000 feet down to earth, and the long ship fell stern first, a glowing Roman candle in the night. After it crashed, the SL-11 burned for two hours, being a Schutte-Lanz built with a wooden frame, not with the aluminum girders of the larger Zeppelins. It was like a scene from *Gulliver's Travels*, tiny people watching the whale of a ship burning.

The ship had fallen near the village of Cuffley in Hertfordshire. Crashed in bush and tall grass. By morning, some fires still burned, and smoked all day. People filled the roads making for the pillar of smoke. The bodies of the crew were scattered around and incinerated in the ruin; baked, battered, torn, singed, and fearful to look at. The ground was wet and soon the fields were mud as thousand came on to see the enemy in ruins. Souvenirs of the wreck were being hawked about. People even picnicked within sight and smell of the downed remains.

A reporter from a London newspaper, viewing the wreck, took a high moral stand (a fair sample, incidentally, of the kind of writing the war journalists often produced):

> I wish some cruel Fate might have taken the Kaiser by his trembling hand yesterday morning and led him to that rain-soaked meadow in Hertfordshire, and bade him look, as I looked, at the charred residuum which a few hours before was the crew of an Imperial German airship. I wish Count Zeppelin, the creator of the particular brand of Kultur which sent the baby-killers to their doom, might have been in the Supreme War Lord's entourage. I wondered, standing there by the side of that miserable heap of exposed skulls, stumps of arms and legs, shattered bones and scorched flesh, whether the Kaiser would have revoked the vow he spoke in the Black Forest eight years ago, when he christened the inventor of airship frightfulness, "the greatest German of the twentieth century." . . .

At the empty hangar back at the German base the usual band welcome to a returning ship, "See What Comes There from On High," went unplayed.

Second Lieutenant Leefe-Robinson was awarded the Victoria Cross "for most conspicuous bravery. . . . He attacked an enemy airship under circumstances of great hardship and danger, and sent it crashing to the ground as a blazing wreck." *

The victory weapon that failed; a dream that never came true. Neither the Zeppelin, nor any other lighter-than-air craft, ever

---

* Leefe-Robinson became the consequent victim of headquarters stupidity, that desire to use his VC as publicity to boost the RFC. In April of 1917, with no training in air battle, no skills in handling the fast new Bristol fighter, he went to the Western Front. Promoted to major, he was sent out to lead a formation of fighters to attack von Richthofen's airdrome at Douai near Arras. He had never fired a gun in battle in France; it was plainly a suicide mission. The British were met by five Albatroses led by the scarlet plane of the baron himself. Only two British planes escaped the execution. A German sergeant named Festner sent Leefe-Robinson down into a crash landing. Robinson spent the rest of the war in a prison camp, where he went into a deep depression. The prison fare and miserable conditions destroyed his body. Returning to England, pneumonia killed him the day before New Year, 1919.

came up to the hopes of the dreamers. The ships were dreadfully costly. They were hard to handle in anything over a 12-mile wind and, in such a breeze, could not leave a hangar. They were murderously dangerous, as any leaking of the gas could set off an explosion to wreck the ship.

By the end of 1916, it was clear they would not do the job. The total record of that year shows only twelve people killed, forty-one wounded by Zeppelin raids.

The last big Zeppelin raid on England was in September 1917. Of eleven Zeppelins, only seven came back. A little later, five blew themselves up at Ahlhorn Zeppelin Base. Naval fliers from *HMS Furious* got two more on the ground at Tönder. Totaling all the Zeppelins, including the Schutte-Lanz wooden-framed ships, 150 German dirigibles were active in the war. Of these, nearly 70 per cent were wrecked, either by storm, bad handling, or enemy fire. England took the brunt of the attacks. The records show forty raids on the British Isles. About 225 tons of bombs fell, nearly 600 people were killed, and close to 1,600 injured (many by British antiaircraft fire). Ten million dollars worth of damage was done to London, twenty million to the rest of England. But the Germans did not get their money's worth.

Count Zeppelin himself deplored the waste of money and men that went into the Zeppelin as a war weapon. Indeed, he confessed to a strong doubt about the ships as military aids. His *Luftschiffe* was a dream not intended for killing English women and children.

Admiral Alfred von Tirpitz, too, worried at the slaughter of civilians by airships. He wrote his wife:

> I contend . . . for the standpoint of "an eye for an eye," but I am not in favor of the evil policy which is lately gaining vogue, I mean the policy of "frightfulness." The indiscriminate dropping of bombs is wrong; they are repulsive when they kill and maim children and old women, and one can too soon grow callous to such wanton cruelty. We should not be so opportunistic as to stoop to our baser instincts.

But the German newspapers perhaps give a closer insight into the wartime German mentality.

Cried the Leipzig *Neueste Nachrichten:*

> London, the heart which pumps lifeblood into the arteries of the degenerate huckster nation, has been mauled and mutilated with bombs by brave German fighting men in German airships. . . . At last, the long yearned-for punishment has befallen England, this people of liars, cynics and hypocrites, a punishment for the countless sins of ages past. It is neither blind hatred nor raging anger that inspires our airship heroes, but a religious humility at being chosen the instrument of God's wrath. In that moment when they saw London being consumed in smoke and flame, just as Sodom was burned by fire from heaven to requite the wickedness of its people. . . .

As Count Zeppelin told General von Hindenburg, and the general remembered it well, "Even then, early in 1917, he regarded his airships as an antique weapon in warfare. In his judgment, the airplane, and not the airship will, in the future, dominate the sky. The Count died soon after his visit . . . so he was spared the misfortune of his *Vaterland* . . . fortunate man . . ."

But the *Führer der Luftschiffe*, Strasser, never lost his faith. Toward the end of the war, Strasser went to see Admiral Reinhard Scheer at his headquarters in Berlin. He had a new airship, the L-70, and his plans were as grandiose as ever. While the admiral listened, Strasser pulled some papers from a briefcase and laid them on the desk. Here, he told the old seadog, were the plans to "attack the United States by Zeppelins!" He pinpointed the first target: New York City.

The admiral showed his surprise and some wonder at this wild scheme, but Kapitan Strasser went on talking. The L-59, he explained, had flown nonstop from Bulgaria to the Sudan in Africa and back. A newer ship, the L-70 had a larger range, could go even further. Two more L-70's were under construction. With the three ships, Strasser said, he could drop bombs on New York City, ruin it as a port, strike the terror of German might in American hearts.

The admiral sighed and told Strasser to leave the papers. He sent them back a day later, marked in pencil *R.S. Nein.*

In August 1918, Strasser led a mere five ships over England. His flagship was the LZ-70, just completed, that could speed at 82 miles an hour. The British were waiting. A DH-4 went out to meet the LZ-70 and the ship roared down in flames, crumpling as she fell into the sea, taking her commander with her. With this last fiery effort and disaster, there was no more talk of the Zeppelin as an important weapon of war. Its major advocate, Peter Strasser, lay at rest amid the sea-rusted girders of his beloved flagship.

PART III:
The Middle Years

CHAPTER 9

LIFE ON THE AIRDROMES

Keep your bowels open and never volunteer.
—FLIERS' CODE

As the fury of the air war grew, and more and more planes flew and fought and bombed, only a cynic would have pointed out (and one did) that in 1890 forty nations had signed an agreement to outlaw the dropping of projectiles or explosives from balloons or "other aerial vessels." The words "aerial vessels" had not been defined, however, for while there were gliders, and crank inventors trying to get motorized wings into the air, no one in his right mind contemplated true flying machines. Still, it seemed diplomatically practical to put the two words in. (It is significant that by 1895, only twenty-seven of the original signatories re-signed at the Hague Convention outlawing the dropping of destructives from the air.)

In Europe now it was clear that airpower was moving in new military directions; at least it *was* moving, which was more than could be said for the scene on the ground where, from the Channel to Switzerland, the deadly stalemate continued.

To the folks at home, the hero was the British or French fighter pilot, the single-seater fighter commander, or a wild man like Ernst Udet or the Belgian Balloon Killer, Willy Coppens de Houthulst.

The young fliers now openly mocked the vast bureaucracy of a war, traditional ways, respect for age. Service under the generals had created no respect for the way the war was going. They saw the same parochialism that had initially held back aviation. But while the war below was frozen, plane production rose, and more and more fliers went into training in flimsy ships.

However, the British were at last ordering better planes, aircraft that could outfly and outfight the Fokkers, such as the FE-2B and the DH-2, the de Havilland Scout. The first had the 120-horsepower Beardmore engine and a cockpit with enough room for the fliers to observe the sky from all angles; a great improvement over the crowded, half-blind space in other craft. (Except for some enclosed bomber cockpits all other planes had no weather protection, and no fighter pilot would have accepted the prison of an enclosed cockpit.)

The DH-2 that Geoffrey de Havilland turned out was the British hope of beating the Fokker, forcing it to yield its place in the sky. The DH-2 was a one-seater. It could go at 86 miles an hour at 6,500 feet, and its 100-horsepower Monosoupape engine could get it up to 10,000 feet in under a half hour. Its ceiling was 14,000 feet. The problem for the British was not planes but pilots. Five weeks was often the mortality rate of a front-line flier, and replacements were young and raw.

German engines didn't catch up right away, but by 1916 they had the 160-horsepower water-cooled Mercedes, and Fokker found his planes being replaced by rival aircraft more and more. His 80-horsepower Gnomes were fuel eaters, and their mechanical parts developed strange illnesses if the flier switched off without pulling back the throttle. Men with better or improved ideas were now treading on his heels. When Fokker was still in his twenties he was already past his peak, and would see himself equaled, even surpassed, by men with new ideas and designs that wrested from him the top position.

In 1916 a really extraordinary plane was produced by the Germans: the Albatros D-I from the Albatros Works of Johannesthal, Berlin (not from Fokker). First of all, it was explained to the fliers, the engine itself was very special, being made by Daimler of Stuttgart-Unterturkheim, a water-cooled 160-horsepower six-cylinder job. The body of the plane used plywood and the fuselage did away with inner braces. The wings still kept the fabric cover of the planes of the period, but the plywood strips and solid wooden sides made it a plane that could take a great deal more punishing firepower. It also mounted *two* machine guns in fixed positions, instead of the usual one. It was fast and could outspeed anything it would meet in the air.

The Halberstadt Aeroplane Works at Halberstadt had produced a Doppeldekker, a two-winger, the D-II with a 120-horsepower Mercedes engine, and the D-III with a 120-horsepower Argus power plant. A fixed Spandau gun gave these firepower, but the day was not far off when twin guns rather than a single weapon would become mandatory.

Fokker built a model specially for Max Immelmann, the German ace, a plane with a 160-horsepower Le Rhône engine, and added *three* machine guns. But it was now a hard-fought race. No matter how well Fokker designed, other plane makers were his equal or ahead. He felt it was a plot. He cried out in self-pity that he was "craftily jockeyed into the ragbag end of mediocre manufacturers after making a flying start to supply the Germans with their first fighter planes."

But the dubious affection of the War Department dwindled; Fokker was losing favor with the Germans because he did not choose to become a German citizen. He was to find that an order for four trainers given to his factories was not for Fokker planes but for one designed by the General Electric Company (of Germany). He himself worked on a plane made of welded-steel framing, with a strange top wing and a midget lower wing. He tested it at Schwerin before the government committee, but they turned away uninterested.

The truth was that the Germans no longer trusted Fokker. Their secret service filed a report that their rival, the British Intelligence, had been trying to contact Fokker with an offer of £2 million to return to Holland. (Of course, it may have been a cool British game to discredit him.)

Fokker was being watched day and night to prevent his escape. The folk logic of the Germans was that if they forced him to become a German national, he would be loyal, and a true enemy of the Allies. When the official order went out that he was to receive no more orders, he sent back an answer that he was selling his factory and going back to Holland. The next move was up to the Germans. The War Office officially notified him that he had been listed as a naturalized German citizen. He was also sent notice to register at once as a soldier in the army reserves. The trenches loomed ahead for Anthony Fokker unless he played ball with the forces of oligarchic politics.

He gave in—as an honorary German—and designed a new plane, beating out Pfalz, Aviatik, and Rumpler to get an order for 400 planes at the cost of 10 million marks . . . Better tyranny and profits than catastrophe.

Meanwhile, the Lewis gun had proved too light and was going out of favor with the British and French. The Vickers .303-caliber was the one found to do the air job best. It had a much higher rate of fire than the Lewis; it took to the interrupter gear with mechanical ease. The Lewis was drum-fired and ninety-seven rounds was the best it could carry at the time. The Vickers, once the belt-fed jamming problem had been solved by Captain Lanoe Hawker and a dentist friend, was able to fire as long as there were ammunition belts of any length at hand.

The connection of firepower to the engine for control made for the problem of slow firing when the flier throttled back his engine. Also the Allied gear was designed for one gun only while the Pfalz and Halberstadt machines they met in air combat had twin guns, giving them double firepower.

Not until May 1917 would the Allies have a perfected new system, the C. C. gear, introduced on the Sopwith Camel. It worked on oil pressure—by hydraulic principles—and was invented by a Roumanian named George Constantinesco and a Major George C. Colley. The firing impulses were transmitted by oil pressure and nothing the engine did could affect it. One drawback, however, was that the oil pressure was kept up by a hand pump. If during an air battle the pressure went down, the flier had to pump like mad by hand to get it up again so that the firing gear would function properly.

Each nation's fliers at the front (though generalizations are always dangerous) lived their own way. The British often had a Church of England parade, but only the upper classes attended—

for to them God was chiefly a state function. The British had a certain air as fliers; the swagger stick, often an eyeglass, and of course a caste system—made up of the various grades of accents: Oxford and Cambridge on top, then stage actor's diction, Cockney "H"-droppers, Liverpool-Lancashire drone, the Scots burr, the Australian twang; always accents decided one's social standing.

The food in the English officers' mess was still poor, unless they had a French cook and scrounged the countryside. One Frenchman remembered the British cuisine as "everything boiled to death in live steam, then covered with a white sauce made of wall paper paste. Tea and tiffin are sacred."

The French ate best, somehow managing always to enjoy *la soupe* with true body and a herb flavor, a bit of salad, then fish if possible, a leg of mutton. Only in hard times did canned "monkey meat"—a slimy corned beef sometimes left over from old colonial wars at the turn of the century—reappear. The French fliers on dress parade were impressive, but in the main were given to slumpy ease, over-casual, clothes none too well cleaned. Their fighting spirit was excellent, but their view of events, in the main, was ironic, cynical: "We know who are making a good thing out of it all back home, getting all the fine plump girls, drinking up the best wine." For their generals (*fatres*), they had contempt, for their political leaders, obscene suggestions. Most French fliers were Catholics, yet while often pious, they were very anti-clerical. They attended Mass, made confession; but it was a political class approach to the Godhead rather than a full spiritual one. However, obviously this did not hold true for all: "Fat priest, broken ruin of a church, smell of soup cooking, church candles. A long line for confession—tomorrow we move up to the line."

The Germans, to judge from their letters, have been the most misunderstood, perhaps because our chief impressions of the Great War have come from the skilled British propaganda machine that slanted information and details for the world. There were, of course, the cartoonist-type young German fliers: shaved neck, faces duel-scarred. Humorless, rigid, we see them always stiffly at attention, saluting crisply. Mechanical killers, dedicated to *Volk und Vaterland.*

But there were others, just as skilled in war, who shared that strained romanticism, that blood cult of *Kultur,* of seeing themselves as somehow better, wiser, more artistic, more musical: "We are above the peasants and materialists of other nations." They lived in gardens of fantasy, wept easily, sang a great deal; they banged steins on oak tables and embraced each other as *Brüder* in a great cause. They were ribald, callow, often too young to have much more than a gallant idea of dying, or at least a smartly bandaged wound. "I dream of a soft rumped blonde and willing nurse, a baroness if one is available, say a freshly made widow in need of release of her healthy yearnings . . ."

These men made excellent fliers, and were certainly not mere disciplined robots in the air. They improvised, they thought out the art of battle; and they died by the hundreds. Most never penetrated to any real idea of the world beyond Germany, or of events after the war. Part of their minds did respond to certain sounds, to slogans, to mottoes. They were nobles, upper middle class, some of merchant stock; the mechanics and field crews often peasants. "All of us are revolting at times in our acceptance of a brutality toward other populations . . ." German self-pity in defeat was a national cult remarked on by many trained observers. In defeat sullen, in victory unbearable, in peace sweating to classical music. (Again this is clearly not to be taken as speaking for all individuals in the German air force.)

They ate well when France provided it, "great eaters of pork and sausage, lung soup, stuffed entrails . . ." When the blockade meant a shortage of food, they lived on what there was, detesting most the *ersatz* coffee made of acorns or parched corn.

Many observers seem to agree that the most reckless, innocent, spendthrift with life were the Americans, those who joined the British and the French air forces. They were conditioned victims of Buffalo Bill's Wild West Shows, the early Bronco Billy films, the tradition that as a frontier people, they were "half hoss, half alligator." A stomping, loud-mouthed folk, tall in the saddle and able to wrestle wildcats. They flew ignoring science and advice, and their casualties were fearful until they simmered down. They were often college men, or students living abroad, or upper-middle-class spoiled sons full of pictures of planes, sure that it would be fun and romantic to fly in a war. Some were racing-car drivers; a few had flown soon after the Wrights. It took time, and tragedy, before they became as good as any fliers in the war. They were gallant; and they were actually fighting while people wondered how soon America would come to the aid of the Allies.

In all the nations' air forces, the main requirement was youth. Usually the manpower consisted of the hastily trained, survivors of training crashes, along with the misfits, the unlucky, often weeded out by early death. Young men (some not yet shaving), with nothing but good coordination and a burning desire to fly. Taking any sampling of them, they might have included student, clerk, wastrel, cuckold, mechanic, actor, idler, cowboy, singer, shopkeeper, homosexual, lawyer, virgin; transferred from cavalry, infantry, sports, and a few from the Church.

Missing from reports is any special mention of Jews and Negroes. All air forces had Jewish fliers, or men of Jewish descent, but in minute numbers. They were kept out if possible. The writer knows of several Jews who were in the RFC. One was decorated personally by George V in hospital (he has refused to recall his flying days for this book, so there must still be some residue of bitterness as to how he was treated). I have not been able to find any record of American Negro fliers in any of the air forces, except for one legendary French sergeant. This is of course no evidence that none flew; surviving records, too, can be very selective.

The English flier on leave or invalided home, recovering from a wound, watched his society changing, changing. So little like it had been when he was cheered and sent off to train in a flying machine. Lord Norwich had expressed it well: "It was . . . felt that war was a glorious effort and the British always won . . . in those days society . . . still appeared to live in the atmosphere of the Boer War. There had been tragic losses . . . but it had not been war . . ."

The flier on leave found much to drink, a great many partners for fornication available. Always some fine-feathered lady giving a party for "the dear lads, poor chaps starved for the sight of a

refined English woman." For most fliers there was a glimpse of
home and family. But it was not calming to many—brooding of
the front, of the dead fellow airman. It made them yearn for
wilder ideas of pleasure, to go through the act of reproduction
endlessly while still alive and kicking. With the right introduc-
tions plus one's rank, one danced and made love in the houses of
William Waldorf, Viscount Astor, Lady Anson ("Air raids like
thunderstorms are a frightful nuisance . . .").

The rank-and-file enlisted men of the airfield ground crew, on
the other hand, had to make do with fish and chips fried in horse
fat, weak beer, and (when they were on rare leave for wounds)
the tarts around Covent Garden or in Whitechapel; or a bag of
French spuds for Mum, and the sight of the ugly way of life, the
kids so thin from that blue-white milk when they could get it,
after standing two hours in line.

Duff Cooper wrote of the men on leave:

> . . . over them all was hanging the shadow of death. How
> splendidly our youthful spirits resisted the gloom and terror
> which that shadow is wont to cast! It may well be that the near
> presence of death enables us to form a truer estimate of its im-
> portance. The nineteenth century had been, especially in
> England, a period of great security, and sudden death was so
> rare that it came to be regarded as the greatest of all calamities.
> These four years of war, with casualties more numerous than
> ever before or since, familiarized us with the spectre. We did
> not feel our losses the less because we wore our mourning more
> lightly. Among my own friends it became a point of honour
> never to show a sad face at the feast . . . we wept in secret.

The first airdromes, flying fields (as we've seen), consisted
merely of huts, tents, and hangars resting on mud. The shoddy
construction of everything that housed men and planes has left
an indelible picture in some minds:

> Cubby holes, sleeping quarters cluttered with maps, binocu-
> lars, dogs, a few cats, even several monkeys shivering with cold.
> Everywhere smelly clothes, busted up mementos of the war,
> shattered propellers, patches of enemy wing insignia cut from

downed planes, parts of burned out motors used as paper-weights.

On walls group photographs of fliers, a goodly percentage dead, ghost arms around survivors, ugly pictures of dead enemy fliers, or friends mutilated by exploding dum dums. Broken kids in charred twisted death. . . . A scattering of magazines, pipes, tobacco jars, yellow bound novels, little boxes of stomach pills, tailor bills from London, letters, singly or tied in bundles, a few silver-backed hair brushes, splintered floors . . .

Airdromes on the Western Front were all more or less at first a haphazard collection of tents and vans, and delicate canvas and wooden planes were even at times kept on the grass of some meadow. Indeed, most airfields were pasture and meadow, but semi-permanent fields were graded and rolled. The Allies favored a tarmac cover—tar and macadam rolled and pressed for a fairly smooth airstrip. Bomb craters could be quickly patched. Night lighting was poor—usually kerosene oil flares on oil barrels. Some planes carried klaxons—early but loud primitive auto horns; and air-to-ground sound signals—simple ones—were worked out. (Wireless came in very late in the war, and worked poorly in the trenches; it was not officially in use in fighter planes.) Machine shops were little else but collections of tools; gasoline and oil were brought in by barrel.

But as the war progressed there was an attempt at planning, and airfields and their buildings took on a semi-permanent condition. By 1916–17, an English airdrome was usually set down near some town with one or two major roads passing through it. The flying area was a smoothed-out field, generally of sod with bare patches worn in it. It was square or rectangular in shape, its four sides each about half to three-quarters of a mile long. Dugouts, topped by heavy timbers and sandbags, served as raid shelters.

Four squadrons of planes, fighters, would find this room enough for from eighty to ninety-five machines fit to fly, plus a junk pile of wrecked planes used for parts. Overnight the planes were kept in ten to a dozen hangars, actually large sheds, sometimes of canvas over wooden frames, sometimes wooden structures, often with corrugated iron roofs. Each hangar had room for a dozen machines and a mechanics' section for repairs and servicing.

Three mechanics were assigned to each plane, responsible for its health, grooming, and mechanical being. These mechanics were usually filthy sights with their oil stains, their garments glossy with grease, their hands ingrained with worked-in grime. Near the hangars were the buildings that housed the flying officers, and the mess halls. Each squadron had twenty to twenty-four pilots, and as there were usually four squadrons to the kind of airdrome we are describing, two squadrons usually ate together.

The enlisted men led a life of their own, the field having separate sleeping and eating quarters for telephone crews, lighting-plant men, searchlight crews, mechanics, lorry drivers, office personnel, and pilots' orderlies, called "batmen" in the British units. Cooks, machine-gun loaders, chute-folders, and other assorted help, some hard to define, made up a small village. A squadron needs 200 enlisted men to be up to its quota, so 800 enlisted men hardly ever got into the air but serviced the planes, fliers, ground, and guns.

Also on the field was the Red Cross, giving some vague service, and the Americans usually had a YMCA unit. Medical officers ran a hospital unit, and there were stacks of raw-lumber coffins behind some building to bury the remains of recovered fliers. The infantry were buried where they fell—fliers usually got a ceremony in a real graveyard.

None of this ran smoothly. The cook and his staff often sold off part of the food supply. Alcohol, cigarettes, bedding, medical supplies, spare parts, dead fliers' gear, all at times had a way of being transformed into money or barter. Pilots' orderlies had the best of it, being boodle grabbers, often all too close to the officers' food and whiskey. It was in most ways just like society back home.

Some small effort was made to camouflage airdromes, but it hardly paid. Both sides knew where the major enemy airfields were. Their only protection was antiaircraft fire from the guns that rimmed the field. Dugout shelters were handy. An alarm sent fighters into the air when enemy planes were reported approaching. (Neither the antiaircraft nor the warning systems compared to the specialized gear of later wars when electronics and radar became perfected.)

Living was often primitive. Hot water was in constant demand, baths and showers improvised. There was an officers' lounge for the fliers, a bar in most messes; the bar orderly was usually a wise, sly fellow who knew a great deal, held bets, pimped, and often loaned money at the going rate of interest.

The decor of the average officers' lounge was simple: flags; the remnants of enemy planes, such as propellers and insignia cut from wings; group photographs of fliers invalided home or dead; pictures of George V, the Kaiser, Woodrow Wilson, Mary Pickford, Fairbanks, and Chaplin. Notice boards and blackboards for flight orders, lots of ribald verse, a few graffiti of nude or seminude women. Limericks, the best always indecent, were penciled or inked on latrine walls. In the main room there were tattered old magazines and newspapers and usually a collection of novels, light or romantic.

Space was given to religious tracts, Church publications, texts on national pride, glory, the nobility of the causes the fliers were dying for; and newspapers printed specifically for the armed forces existed. Music was sometimes obtainable on a stolen or rented piano, but mostly the old hand-wound gramophone and its scratchy, whining records was music. "Coon songs," ragtime favorites, vaudeville entertainers, early Irving Berlin, George M. Cohan, Chauncey Olcott, Al Jolson. The English preferred music-hall entertainers. A favorite was Harry Tate, a comic of slow and hilarious delivery. (The British fliers named the RE-8 reconnaissance biplane, one of the worst planes of the war, the " 'Arry Tate.") German gramophones issued popular love songs (sad), Strauss waltzes, scores of operettas, some Wagner, and singers of the Richard Tauber type. No genius had yet thought of putting comic strips into book form.

All the airfields and buildings were surprisingly overrun by dogs—barking, mating, birthing litters. There were cats for ratting and mousing, some pet monkeys, often a goat. A stern commander of an airdrome could keep some kind of order and a surface cleanliness; a slack one often had a roaring distress area on his hands. From a military standpoint, much in the conduct of fliers was deliberately overlooked. Their lives as active fighters was short, and there seemed little sense in bringing them before a military court when they might be dead or prisoner before it sat; decorated national heroes were hardly likely to be tried for being drunk, abusing a superior officer, attempting rape, or commandeering an official car or truck. The Americans would ask an unpopular flier, like Bert Hall, to transfer out.

Drink was the big moral problem. Whether legally or through connections, brandy, whiskey, and cognac were available. Many pilots went to bed drunk and usually returned from leaves in a very shaky condition. Battle fatigue, war nerves, light mental breakdowns were treated casually as "the shakes," "jollies," "the wind up," or just plain "bugs," unless violent or dangerous to limb or property. The medical staff available did little beyond body-patching; the theories of Freud, Jung, and Adler had not yet penetrated the army medical service; indeed, they have made only a few dents since.

Gambling was another outlet from the tension of being on patrol duty, flying over the front. A few Americans who joined the RFC introduced poker and crap shooting. But for those who had been raised on whist and bridge, roulette at Monte, the royal flush or the rattling dice seemed vulgar. Reading seemed a sedative and an escape from immediate reality. While some read deeply of philosophers and historians, translated Horace and Virgil, in the main the escape was to the novels. Arnold Bennett, Galsworthy, Conan Doyle, Edgar Wallace, Edgar Rice Burroughs, Zane Grey. These were the novels often found in a dead airman's luggage sent to his next of kin.

For the flier who was no hero, no national figure, there was a grim, depressing mood. He was a number, an item, nothing less. As the long years of slaughter continued, the airmen and soldiers could only look back with wonder on so much that had been lost and would never be brought back again. Not just the millions dead, the millions crippled and mutilated, the churches and libraries burned. Those on the fighting fronts sensed that a whole social system was already gone, as they found out when they went back on leave. The old madman Nietzsche might be right after all: "The twentieth century will be essentially a century of war." It looked that way as the German lines still held firm and the Allies still pushed and struggled and tried vainly to break through. In the air the men, younger and younger, could hardly remember "how it had been once in peace time."

The narrators of air battles, usually writers who were not there themselves, have a tendency to load their stories with a sense of ecstatic triumph, trying to intensify an already dramatic scene. The writers at second hand also fail, usually, to understand that air warfare often meant a matter of mere seconds between contact and kill. Only to the pilot does the moment prolong itself into an eternity in which his paramount thought is, If I have to die, let it not be lightly.

The fliers, themselves, on the other hand, often wrote remarkably clean and fine narrations of their fights. One hunts them out in letters, in texts produced during the war or just after it. Here is how some of them—names often unknown—recounted their air battles.

First, Edward Mannock, the famous British flier, reports on a tight spot:

> . . . I tried my gun before going over the German lines, only to find that it was jammed, so I went over with a revolver only. A Hun in a beautiful yellow and green bus attacked me from behind. I could hear his machine gun cracking away. I wheeled round on him and howled like a dervish (although, of course, he could not hear me) whereat he made off toward old Parry and attacked him, with me following, for the moral effect! Another one (a brown-speckled one) attacked a Sopwith and Keen blew the pilot to pieces and the Hun went spinning down from 12,000 feet to earth. Unfortunately the Sopwith had been hit, and went down too, and there was I, a passenger, absolutely helpless not having a gun, an easy prey to any of them, and they hadn't the grit to close. Eventually they broke away, and then their Archie gunners got on the job and we had a hell of a time. At times I wondered if I had a tail-plane or not, they

came so near. We came back over the Arras with two vacant chairs at the Sopwith mess! What is the good of it all?

A week ago the Germans posted a notice up in their trenches which read: "For God's sake, give your pilots a rest."

And on another occasion:

E.A. attempted to attack our balloon, descended to low altitudes for that purpose. Nieuport engaged E.A. at approximately 1,000 feet over Neuville St. Vaast and fired 70 rounds during the course of a close combat. The hostile aircraft was observed to be hit, a glow of fire appearing in the nacelle, and glided down under reasonably capable control south and east of Petit Vimy, landing downwind and turning over on touching the ground. Prisoner: Lieut. von Bartrap, sustained fracture of left arm and flesh wounds in right arm and leg, and was taken to hospital immediately on landing. Machine was in very good condition, although upside down . . .

Went over to Petit Vimy and Thelus in a sidecar this morning in an endeavor to pick up some relics of the last victims, downed yesterday afternoon in flames. Regret that nothing remained of the machine. I met this unfortunate DFW at about 10,000 over Avion coming southwest, and I was traveling southeast. I couldn't recognize the black crosses readily (he was about 300 yards away and about 500 feet above me), so I turned my tail toward him and went in the same direction, thinking that if he were British he wouldn't take any notice of me, and if a Hun I felt sure he would put his nose down and have a shot (thinking I hadn't seen him). The ruse worked beautifully. His nose went (pointing at me), and I immediately whipped around, dived and zoomed up behind him, before you could say "knife." He tried to turn, but he was much too slow for the Nieuport. I got in about 50 rounds in short bursts while on the turn and he went down in flames, pieces of wing and tail, etc., dropping away from the wreck. It was a horrible sight. . . ."

Coppens, the Belgian Balloon Killer, was an excellent reporter:

I can only lay claim to five or six night flights. The first, of which I can remember witnessing the start, was on April 5, 1917. The village, outwardly asleep in the pale light of the moon, was in reality agog, for it was one of those ideal air-raid nights when hostile airplanes might be expected at any moment. Those villagers who had not sought refuge in the few isolated farms in the neighborhood, stood in groups on their thresholds, ready to flee—the Lord knows whither. In the Flying Corps mess, where dinner was cheerily drawing to its close, an indefinable excitement was observable, as pilot after pilot rose from the table, beckoned or called to his observer, and slipped out into the velvety shadow of the streets—a velvet backed with silver, wherein human figures passed at once into oblivion. On the airfield, other figures, ghostly figures these, moved about among the motionless fleet of wings and struts standing outside the sheds. The blackout had been absolute, and not a single light could be seen anywhere; it was indeed an ideal air-raid night. Ears strained to catch the slightest murmur from the skies—the murmur of aircraft that one could not hope to see, steady and monotonous, filling space with its rhythm, converting the moonlit heavens into a fount of sound.

The bombs had been hooked on to their racks under the wings, and the mechanics were swinging the propellers. One by one, as the engines started, the exhaust pipes spat out long tongues of blue flame, intermingled with red sparks that spun eddying into the darkness. Then, with a roar that grew, each machine lurched forward, gathered itself together and drove full tilt into the night, away and upward, a compact contrivance of all that was dangerous—an engine vomiting fire, tanks containing gallons of the most inflammable of any known liquid, and fabric-covered wings draped with explosives.

As they returned from their expeditions, the machines fired a prearranged color light, calling for the landing ground to be lit up. An answering light fired from the ground was provided for, to warn pilots should it not be safe for them to land.

On this night Lieutenant Louis de Burlet had just signaled his return when Captain Gallez buckled a wheel of his airplane while landing in the center of the airfield. The following machine was therefore warned not to land. De Burlet had circled the airfield once or twice and had asked a second time to be allowed to land, when a third light signal of a different color attracted our attention. Strange though this unforeseen signal appeared, no precautions were taken, and a few seconds later we clearly made out the silhouette of a German machine diving toward us. It passed us not more than fifty feet away, with a machine gun spitting fire at us as it came and went. By a miracle no one was hit . . .

Flying at night at 10,000 feet on a bombing raid had its share of extra danger:

Near the front, colored lights rose in curves, their momentary reflections visible in the flood waters. Other flares, attached to silken parachutes, threw patches of the sky into dazzling light, making the stars appear pale by contrast.

Soon we entered the danger zone. As we droned our way across the lines, clusters of incendiary balls of fire came winding up to meet us for all the world like the bubbles breaking on the surface of a glass of champagne. Searchlight beams, giant's fingers groping sinisterly for us, cut the firmament into so many wedges of blackness, and, now and then, like a moth crossing in front of a headlight, an airplane would emerge into a beam from one of these wedges and turn into a thing of silver, while the giant's finger, trembling with excitement, essayed to hold it, and other beams converged to assist, and the guns below concentrated their fury on the target, filling the sky with detonating high explosive; until the airplane, diving and twisting this way and that, plunged back into the obscurity whence it had come.

In the pattern of the carpet moving in beneath me, I could see our objective. As we drew near, the enemy's fire became fiercer and the fanlike glow from our bombs, bursting at the end of their unseen fall, added itself to the pyrotechnic display. I could visualize the stir being caused down there; the gunners and the machine-gun crews sweating at their weapons, fleeing for their lives.

The first time I released my load of bombs, I was astonished at the extremely slight movement imparted to my machine, which went on its way undisturbed. I had expected the sudden release of a hundredweight or more of cargo to have more effect on an airplane.

On the homeward journey I switched on my instrument lights at intervals in order to read my compass, and in the calmer regions of our own lines my pistol rocket of prearranged color turned away our searchlights and quietened our anti-aircraft guns. The landing searchlight was lighted in answer to our request, and I went down into an artificial daylight, my shadow preceding me—running along over the grass of the airfield, growing longer and longer, until my engine stopped and my wheels kissed the ground. The next instant my machine was trundling toward the sheds under its own inertia, to the accompaniment of the hollow rumble of its undercarriage.

The taut excitement of the start of a raid was also vividly pictured by Coppens:

One by one the engines are started by the mechanics, and one by one they are run full out for a few seconds to the accompaniment of a deafening din. They then subside into a leisurely purr, ticking over as regular as clockwork with that indescribable hollow cough now and then escaping from the twin exhaust pipes that run back along each side of the fat-bellied fuselage. The airscrews trace twinkling cockades in the air and flatten down the oil-soaked grass behind the machines in shining ripples.

Fifteen airplanes are lined up there, fifteen rockets fitted with wings, all ready to take their departure. Fifteen pilots have lowered their goggles over their eyes and fifteen pairs of eyes —round eyes that stare fixedly—are focused upon infinity. The next instant, with a roar that sets the ground trembling, first one and then another of the line of machines lurches forward, gathers momentum and is gone. The whole sky slowly fills with their noise, as machine after machine leaves the ground and climbs upward. The first to leave circle while waiting for the remainder to take up station behind them and on either side, and almost before one has realized that the last has left, the whole formation is in V, heading for the lines and rapidly growing smaller and smaller, a compact, disciplined entity composed of specks, now being greeted with full military honors above the horizon. The sky becomes blotched with the dark clusters of shell smoke that spring up in front of and all around the invaders. Thirty machine guns aim their barrels into the depths of the enemy's lines, and before them the enemy's scouts disperse and dive. . . .

Bishop, the Canadian ace, tells of the nearness of the touch of death:

> I heard the rattle of machine-guns . . . and saw bullet holes appear as if by magic in the wings of my machine. I pulled back as if to loop, sending the nose of my machine straight up in the air. As I did so the enemy scout shot by underneath me. I stood up on my tail for a moment or two, then let the machine drop back, put her nose down, and dived after the Hun, opening fire straight behind him at very close range. He continued to dive away with increasing speed, and later was reported to have crashed. . . .

Baron Manfred von Richthofen wrote on the subject of aerial warfare; indeed, his official report to the commander of the Sixth Army Corps on enemy tactics is a detailed text:

> . . . The adversary often slips downward over one wing or lets himself fall like a dead leaf in order to shake off an attack. In order to stick to one adversary, one must on no account follow his tactics, as one has no control over the machine when falling like a dead leaf. Should the adversary, however, attempt to evade attack by such tricks, one must dash down without losing sight of the enemy plane. When falling like a dead leaf, or intentionally falling wing over wing, the best pilot loses control of his machine for a second or two, therefore it is a maneuver to be avoided.
>
> Looping the loop is worse than worthless in air fighting. Each loop is a great mistake. If one has approached an adversary too close, a loop only offers a big advantage to the adversary. Change of speed should be relied on to maintain the position desired, and this is best effected by giving more or less gas. The best method of flying against the enemy is as follows: The officer commanding the group, no matter how large, should fly lowest, and should keep all machines under observation by turning and curving.
>
> No machine should be allowed either to advance or to keep back. More or less, the whole squadron should advance curving. Flying straight or above the front is dangerous, as even machines of the same type of plane develop different speeds. Surprises can be avoided only when flying in close order. The

commanding officer is responsible [for seeing] that neither he nor any of his pilots are surprised by the enemy. If he cannot see to that, he is no good as a leader. . . .

The English single-seater pilots always fly in squad formation when on pursuit work. Reconnoitering and artillery fire is also now carried on by squads of two-seater machines, sometimes containing as many as twenty machines. Many English airmen try to win advantages by flying tricks while engaged in fighting but, as a rule, it is just these reckless and useless stunts that lead them to their deaths.

When flying in large squads, the English planes keep close together in order to be able to come to one another's assistance at any given moment. When attacked, they maintain even closer formation. When an English plane which has fallen behind is attacked, the first planes of the enemy formation make left and right turns and hurry to its assistance. After the rest of the formation has passed them, they close up the rear as the last planes.

Von Richthofen's logbook records an unsuccessful encounter with a British squad, despite his perspicacity.

I watched whether one of the Englishmen would take leave of his colleagues, and soon I saw that one of them was stupid enough to do this. I could reach him, and I said to myself, That man is lost!

I started after him, and when I got near, he started shooting prematurely, which showed he was nervous, so I said, "Go on shooting, you won't hit me." He shot with a kind of ammunition that ignites (tracer bullets containing a phosphorus mixture that leaves a trail of smoke behind and shows the gunner where his bullets are going. These fiery bullets are deadly to fuel tanks).

At that moment I think I laughed aloud, but soon I got my lesson. When within 300 feet of the Englishman, I got ready for firing, aimed, and gave a few trial shots. The machine guns were in order. In my mind's eye I saw my enemy dropping. My excitement was gone. In such a position one thinks quite calmly and collectedly, and weighs the probabilities of hitting and being hit. Altogether, the fight itself is the least exciting part of the business, as a rule. He who gets excited in fighting is sure to make mistakes. He will never get his enemy down. Calmness is, after all, a matter of habit.

At any rate, in this case, I did not make a mistake. I approached within fifty yards of my man. I fired some well-aimed shots, and thought that I was bound to be successful. That was my idea. But suddenly I heard a tremendous bang when I had fired scarcely ten cartridges and something hit my machine. It became clear to me that I had been hit, or, rather, my machine had been hit. At the same time I noticed a fearful stench of gas, and I saw that my motor was running low. The Englishman noticed it too, for he started shooting with redoubled energy, while I had to stop. I went right down. Instinctively, I switched off the engine. I left in the air a thin white cloud of gas. I knew its meaning from previous experience with my enemies. Its appearance is the first sign of a coming explosion. I was at an altitude of 9,000 feet and had to travel a long distance to get down. By the kindness of Providence, my engine stopped running.

I have no idea with what rapidity I went downward. At any rate, the speed was so great that I could not put my head out of the machine without being pressed back by the rush of air. Soon I had lost sight of the enemy plane . . . I had fallen to an altitude of perhaps 1,000 feet, and had to look out for a landing. These are serious occasions. I found a meadow. It was not very large, but it would just suffice if I used due caution. Besides, it was very favorably situated on the high road near Henin-Lietard. There I meant to land, and I did, without accident.

My machine had been hit a number of times. The shot that caused me to give up the fight had gone through both the fuel tanks. I had not a drop left. My engine had also been damaged . . .

In contrast, the Americans were often reckless beyond sense and reason. Wrote one unidentified flier in his diary of a mission:

Nigger leads and McGregor and Cal are on his right, behind and a little above. Springs and I are on the left and Thompson in the center in the space between Cal and me. We fly in the form of a triangle with the back corners high. McGregor is deputy flight commander and takes command in case anything happens to Nigger. We fly pretty close together and have a set of signals. If Nigger is going to turn sharp, he drops his wing on that side. If he is going to dive steep, he holds up his arm. If he wants us to come up close or wants to call our attention to something he shakes both wings. If it's a Hun, he shakes his wings and points and fires his guns. If he means "yes," he bobs his nose up and down and if he means "no," he shakes his wings. If we see a Hun and he doesn't, we fire our guns and fly up front and point. We fly at three-quarters throttle so we can always pull up. If he has trouble and wants us to go on, he fires a red light from his Very pistol. If he wants us to follow him out of a fight, he fires a white light. If he wants to signal the other flights, he fires a green light.

Finally, for the ground view, here is an extract from a German diary, describing French planes:

We cannot fire on them without immediately attracting heavy artillery. . . . The French use nothing but heavy guns, and have been bombarding us all day, their fire control being beyond reproach as the result of the action of their aviators. The French aviators are masters of the air. . . .

The value of our aviators is so small that even far behind the lines they are not masters of the field. Generally our aviators are far from being as good as the French or English and consequently we dare not move a step outside our leaf-covered shelters. Enemy aviators keep circling around the wood we are in and signalling our presence. Whether we like it or not, it is evident from this point of view that we are inferior. We are told that Germany is holding her own in the air, but it is no use telling us that, and that is why we have these enormous losses. There is absolutely no one to drive away these parasites that give us no respite from dawn till night. . . . The situation is the more astonishing because of the large number of French airplanes we bring down. . . . Enemy aviators flying at 100 meters took part in the fighting with machine guns. Some of our men were wounded in the head . . .

No ground soldier ever thought his side had enough planes in the air . . .

CHAPTER 10

FOUR FRENCH ACES—
AND A BELGIAN
BALLOON KILLER

1. | Roland Garros (1888–1918)

Many of the early war fliers were exhibition fliers and stuntmen. One of the most remarkable was Roland Garros, who made a habit of entering almost all flying meets and contests he could reach. In 1911 he had thrilled Americans with his stunt flying, had then been the first man to fly the Mediterranean (1913), winner of the Grand Prix d'Anjou, and of the Paris-to-Rome and Paris-to-Madrid races. He was a typical hero of his time. One finds echoes of these gypsy fliers in Scott Fitzgerald's *Tender Is the Night* (the heroine's lover is a French flier), in the footloose characters of Hemingway's *The Sun Also Rises*, in William Faulkner's *Pylon*. Hard drinkers, womanizers, without a sense of obligation or even tenderness. Most of them drifters from fete to air meet, to bullring, to county fair, to steeplechases, weekend parties, debauchery on the Riviera.

Garros was a handsome fellow, healthy, and, even when drinking heavily, urbane and aware of himself with a sort of baroque conceit. He took music seriously, and as a dancer he was compared to the later Rudolph Valentino.

In August 1914 when war was declared, Roland Garros was in Berlin where he had been doing exhibition flying for nearly a month with a small Morane-Saulnier plane. On the night of August 3 the German officers were toasting the war, cheering *Der Tag, Der Kriegernahut den Krieg!* With them, in a fancy restaurant, was Garros—the Germans handing full glasses to the French flier. It meant internment for him on the morrow. *"Die Zeit bringt Rosen!"* Acting more drunk than he was, Garros excused himself and wove his way to the door marked *Herren.* Out of the lavatory window went the Frenchman to the field where his plane was sheltered under canvas guarded by four policemen to keep people from tearing souvenirs off it.

It was after midnight, and Garros suggested to the police that he would like to take a spin in the night. In fact, no one flew after dark in those days, for there were no instruments to act as an artificial horizon; one could be flying in the dark upside down headed for earth without knowing it until the coins fell upward out of one's pockets.

The field was in bad shape, wires and telegraph poles all around. Also, who would crank up the Le Rhône engine? It was a rotary with the kick of a mule team that usually took eight men to start: three on each side to keep the plane steady, one muscleman to spin the prop, and the eighth to jiggle the priming pump and finger the ignition switch. But once the engine began roaring and spinning at full throttle, it was off and away with no waiting.

The gasoline tank was full. Garros added a couple of extra loose cans to the plane's load. He adjusted controls in the cockpit and then, alone, pointing his plane in a direction he hoped was less cluttered with obstacles than the rest of the field, he grabbed the propeller blade and spun it. He ducked as the engine roared into life and the plane began to move swiftly. As he flung himself onto the wing, it caught him a fearful blow in the gut and he was momentarily staggered. The machine was on the move, heading for flight, and if no one was at the controls it would go into a dangerous ground loop. Seizing the brace wires within reach, Garros somehow managed to get into the cockpit, grab the controls, and take off into the night to fly over a city of lights celebrating the revenge it would shortly take on France.

Somehow, after many hazards, Garros reached Paris. He was assigned to the Escadrille Morane-Saulnier, Squadron 23. It was a stunt flier's heaven, full of old comrades from Garros's exhibition days, men like Maxine Lenoir, Marc Pourpe, Armand Pinsard, and the first man actually to loop the loop, Eugène Gilbert. The army gave them ground drill with the saber of Napoleon's wars, planning defenses against charging cavalry. Wrote Pourpe in disgust: "I think the Boches have no horses that gallop in the air."

The Escadrille was sent out on scout and reconnaissance duty. Garros found this dull, and when a visiting officer at mess one day suggested over the brandy that all fliers, enemy or no, should not try to harm each other in the air, Garros seized a bottle to brain the fool but was hastily restrained. Garros was angered that the German press was accusing him of being a spy who had come to Germany to take pictures of the fortifications. Also the *chronique scandaleuse* of the horrors of German treatment of Belgians made him picture every German as a brutal degenerate.

The story of Garros's ingenuity in devising a method of shooting successfully through his propeller has already been described. But with Garros's capture in April 1915, his plane intact in German hands, the secret was out. Twice Garros was reported dead; the Germans gave out no word on his fate, although his fall had been witnessed. If they were to insist that Garros had been acting as a spy before the war, they could execute him. He was kept first at the prison camp in Magdeburg, then at Cologne, all the time closely watched and forced to check in every half hour when he was not locked into his cell. This remained the routine for three long years of war.

He was joined in captivity by Lieutenant Marchall, who was downed dropping propaganda leaflets over Berlin. Making for the Russian lines less than 50 miles away, Marchall's fuel had given out and he was captured. He and Garros tried out seven complicated escape plans but they were always caught. Finally, in January 1918, they got out again, and via some secret underground escape route (never revealed) reached England.

Garros soon was back at war in the sky. For nine months he was free again to delight in the smells of gasoline, castor-oil lubrication, and the airplane dope used to put patches on torn wings.

One October day he was flying in clear autumn weather when a Fokker D-VII with its banshee scream came at him out of the direct sunlight and let loose with its twin synchronized machine guns, based on some development suggested by Garros's original invention. Garros's plane exploded into flames and began the dreadful screw through the air toward the earth. Garros may have already been dead. If not, it was an end all fliers feared so much that some would jump from flaming planes to die unsinged rather than ride down to the final holocaust.

There is another version given of Garros's death: that it was not a plane but a Zeppelin raiding Nancy that killed him. The story goes that he had gone out to hunt down a reported airship, a raider on the loose. He found it, but knew it was armed to such a point that only an attack from above would give him a chance of success. Garros therefore dived his plane directly into the backbone of the Zeppelin. The steel girders buckled and the Zeppelin began to fall, carrying with it the wreck of the Frenchman's plane and its dead pilot . . .

2. | René Paul Fonck (1894–1953)

René Fonck was born in 1894, at Sauley-sur-Meurthe, nestled among the foothills of the Vosges. His people had no great past. They were ordinary folk in an ordinary village. As a boy, René was fascinated by magazine stories of balloons and flying machines. At twenty he was conscripted, in August 1914, and sent to camp at Dijon. But he was refused service in the air force; instead, he dug trenches and latrines, and helped to set up bridges in an engineer battalion. With losses in the air mounting, however, Fonck was sent to Saint-Cyr early in 1915 for flight training. First came almost three weeks of lectures. Then he was sent on to Le Crotoy for training—in virtually flightless planes. He flew at first in Penguins, short-winged planes that could not get airborne at all. But in two weeks, he was flying in airplanes that took off and had received his brevet as a flier, the silver brocade wings against his deep blue jacket. He went to the front, assigned to Escadrille Caudron 47 at Corcieux. Flying the slow clumsy Caudron as a scout, he did not carry even a rifle. As time went on he took up a carbine and fired at German planes with no results but rage and frustration festering in his heart.

Fonck was a born pilot, a daring flier, and a very skilled handler of planes; but he was a dreadful show-off. He had to prove to everyone how easy it was for him. And it was. Fonck was mentioned in dispatches as a scout of merit, who flew through shots and shells with a damaged plane. He told a remarkable story about his own bravery: that once when he had a loose fuel connection, he landed behind the German lines, did a quick repair job, and took off again. Like so many of his stories, no one knew if this was true or not; most likely it was. Next time, he got his fuel tank holed, so he crash-landed and took out his camera to take a snapshot of his damaged plane as *proof* of this new adventure.

René Paul Fonck got a second mention in dispatches as a skilled air scout. If he had been a show-off before, he now became doubly intolerable. He was always bragging of his skill, his kills, his cool nerves. He pointed out his smartness in outwitting the enemy. Most of this self-praise was true, but highly colored. Needless to say, he was not popular with his less flamboyant comrades.

Fonck was rather like a famous actor who shows charm and grace to his public, one who really doesn't care too much for the spotlight but who, back stage, is a mean, egotistical tyrant and taskmaster. Fonck had this ham-like streak. He made many claims of kills in the air which were disallowed, but he never withdrew them. Yet he was an amazingly fine flier, and a marksman beyond the skill of most. He perfected a special gunsight to set up the true size of an enemy plane and help his aim.

Fonck stated that no German bullet had ever struck a plane he was flying. Pressed on this, he admitted well, *one* bullet maybe. A poseur, a braggart at the airdrome, to the public he was the great hero of the air—one who was getting even, settling old scores for the humbling of France carried over from the defeat of the Franco-Prussian War of 1870. Gaudy, loud, Fonck belittled his rivals in the French air force as he basked in glory. Indeed, he seems to lack the shading, the gradation of tones found in real people. We have no details of his boyhood, his inner emotions—he is historically the victim of caustic generalizations. Certainly he was hard to take, and not a man at ease with other fliers; expressionless at times, even morose, and, outside of his bragging, not talkative. Fonck had a mean wit and often hurt his fellow fliers by his deliberately cruel remarks.

He was a solitary, avoided alcohol. Back from a flight, he would at once take a nap, never joining in the relaxation, the boozy tapering off of his mess mates after a hard patrol. Predictably, he was a body-building addict, given to arm-flinging exercises, body-twisting calisthenics. At a workout, he'd be surrounded by mocking flight crews who offered obscene advice while he exercised; he saw his body as a temple, and these mockers as infidels.

Fonck was an attractive-looking man, with a pencil-like mustache and disciplined face, properly barbered. He was almost over-neat, tightly tailored, pressed, never sloppy or wrinkled no matter how disorganized the war front. On the ground, Fonck lived always in full dress, and he held the cleaning and pressing of his clothes sacred—a hard job at an airdrome. Most fliers on the field dressed any old way. But Fonck, neatly groomed, a handsome figure, stood out, which was what he wanted. He was the victim of jests, of considerable horseplay at his expense; yet he rose above them, convinced of his superior skills. All admitted the bastard could fly—and kill.

In many ways, Fonck was like a great bull fighter who, as he performed his agile and deadly ballet of the matador on the sands, moved around with a strut to show off his marvelously formed buttocks. The matador comparison must have occurred to Fonck when he said, "I put my bullets into the target as if I placed them there by hand."

He did foolish brave things like removing the dead body of a French flier from a wreck after landing, bearing off the corpse. He had a narrow escape when a shell damaged one of his wings. Another time, flying a twin-engined G-4, he mounted a machine gun between the propellers and he and his observer forced down a German two-seater. Fonck landed and captured the unresisting crew. In April 1917 he was flying a Spad for Escadrille

Spad 103—the famous Storks. He met heroes: Guynemer, Alfred Heurteaux, Armand Pinsard; for once, Fonck managed to keep his mouth shut and listen.

One day he reported a kill: "I fired twenty rounds, victim spun out of fight and crashed." No, came back the answer—claim not proved. Flying as part of a unit of three planes, he got into a dog-fight with an enemy plane and destroyed it. Fonck claimed it although no one knew for sure who had shot it down. It was suggested the pilots cut cards, as was the custom. Fonck of course refused. His comrades shrugged, and let him have the victory. The next plane he shot down fell on the French side. He had the proof he needed.

The summer of 1917 was hard on the French fliers. There were losses, wrecks, intense pressure from the enemy. Fonck didn't do too well. He was to write: "I prefer to fly alone . . . when alone, I perform those little coups of audacity which amuse me . . ." (If he hadn't printed it in a book, it would be hard to believe such a statement. Perhaps it translates badly; in French it has some grace, but no dignity.)

But by August, he was hitting his stride, knocking enemy planes out of the sky. He made a friend of Lieutenant Claude Marcel Haegelen, who came from Fonck's neighborhood. Haegelen, a true and a forgiving one, remained loyal to Fonck, the only man ever close to him.

"He is not a truthful man. He is a tiresome braggart," Haegelen admitted of Fonck, "and even a bore, but in the air . . . a slashing rapier, a steel blade tempered with unblemished courage and price-less skill. . . . But afterwards he can't forget how he rescued you, nor let you forget it. He can almost make you wish he hadn't helped you in the first place . . ."

Late in September, Fonck shot down a two-seater Rumpler. The machine turned over, two bodies fell out, a wing came off. From papers on one of the bodies, the pilot was shown as a Leut-nant Kurt Wissemann. A month after Guynemer had been lost (July 1917), Wissemann (as we shall see) was posthumously given the unlikely credit for downing the French ace. Thus Fonck was now the avenger of French honor, victorious over the killer of Guynemer, whom all France mourned. Fonck told a reporter he was "The tool of retribution . . . shooting down the murderer of my good friend Guynemer." A claim of friendship that would have surprised Guynemer and the fliers who knew them both!

So Fonck became the national hero, heir to the dead ace, with an unofficial claim of fifty-three kills to the dead Guynemer's official fifty-three. France needed a flying hero and Fonck, like Barkus, was willing.

Christmas 1917 was cold and dismally wintry. Fonck asked for a long leave to get married. We know little of his love life, his romance, or much about his bride except that she appears to have come from his part of the country. The marriage took place with many official good wishes. He honeymooned, or rather the couple did (Fonck has a way of dominating all stories relating to him), in the south of France, on the Mediterranean. U-boats were operating all round and dead bodies were often washed up on to the shore but the Foncks seem to have avoided them, and had a fine time.

Returning to the front in January 1918, and going straight up, Fonck shot down an Albatros and a "Focker" (his spelling), his first double kill.

The Storks—*Les Cigognes*—were the best of the French air fighting units. Commandant Brocard, who commanded the four squadrons Spa. 3, Spa. 26, Spa. 73, and Spa. 103, kept even René Fonck (who was with Spa. 103) under some sort of control.

René Paul Fonck is very hard to understand. He appears free of any of the demands of normal love for humanity; his demoniac energies were all used to advance himself. Like so many modern-day executives of big military-industrial combines, he had that enormous conceit that he was omnipotent at his job, the orthodox wisdom of a man who knew his talents and never went beyond the limits of his abilities, abilities which were *very* high. It is this care, this wary alertness, smartness, that makes him such an unlikable figure. For he was so often right, so often able to predict what he could do. He lived in a world of possibilities measured by his own yardstick: his robust, resolute, inquiring intellect had no time to spare for life on the ground, for giving, taking, sharing, or for any sense of humanity or humility.

Fonck lacked what so many French have: sophistication, the Gallic ability to be amused at one's own eccentricity. What was actually behind the façade he took such care to build up, we cannot know. The tragedy is that, in many ways, he was what he worked so hard to present. If only people could have agreed that he was a god.

His success only led to more bragging. He claimed that he would bring off an amazing air show he had promised the scoffers: "A kill of five enemy planes, maybe more, in one day." Yet this braggart was also a producer, as some of the critics warned.

On May 9, 1918, the fog was late in clearing over the airdrome. It was already four o'clock, hardly a day to make good his boast. With the mist rising, Fonck took off with two other Spad fighters. Moving toward the din of the trenches, they met two fighters with flared crosses on their wings escorting a camera plane. Fonck dived at once and with the gesture of a knifethrower, hardly looking at his familiar target, shot down first one and then the other enemy fighter in a matter of seconds. The third German tried to get away. Fonck, to use a popular flying expression, "got him up the arse," and the machine fell apart. In a square mile near Grivesnes lay the wrecks of three enemy planes and the broken bodies of the dead airmen. Just a *lever de rideau*—curtain raiser.

Returning to base, Fonck went up again at 5:30, alerted by a phone message that the enemy was in the air. At nearly 6:30, he jumped out of a cloud bank to fly upward on a Montdidier two-seater, and blasted through the blind underbelly of the machine. A formation of nine German airplanes appeared on the scene, all roaring in Fonck's direction. He managed to place himself in their rear and pick off their Tail-End-Hans. The eight remaining planes gave chase to Fonck, trying to shoo him eastward into German territory. This gave him a chance to get off a good burst: down in flames went his sixth German machine of the day. He had added a bonus of one to his boast of five-in-one-day. The six-in-one-day victory was officially verified as the amazing *coup de maître*. (Fonck was careful not to mention that his great feat had been accomplished six weeks before by a British flier, Captain J. L. Trollope. And a short time afterwards, Captain William Claxton and Captain H. W. Woollett also got their half-dozen each in a day.)

It was now an open contest, using living men as pawns in the game. By September Fonck had done the trick again, making him the only *double* six-in-a-day man. Frankly, he admitted when pressed, he could have gotten eight or even more enemy planes, but his machine gun had jammed.

As the war came to a climax and it was clear that the German power to carry on was waning, Fonck continued relentlessly with his kills. He scored six more double kills, and had three triple days. No new areas of sensation seemed open to him.

When, in July 1918, he had received an official fifty-five on his score card, he had passed Guynemer's record. There were periods when he got a kill every time he went up. On August 14, the perfect virtuoso, working for speed, he shot down an enemy flight of three planes in nine or ten seconds with the ease of Annie Oakley hitting a half-dozen glass balls in mid-air. The German planes fell almost on top of one another.

Fonck's last official win (he put in later disallowed claims) came ten days before the final Cease Fire. He shot down a German propaganda plane dropping leaflets about how the Allies had already lost the war.

Like a master surgeon who takes pride in using the fewest stitches, Fonck tried to shoot down his enemies with the least amount of ammunition. He was a scientist of the air, knowing all the mathematical angles, the power of flight in his bullets, the speed and size of whatever enemy plane he wanted to destroy. His eye was perfect. He does not seem to have made a mistake at any dangerous corner in the sky. He was never reckless in the sense of letting emotion, eagerness, or rage lead him to a mindless barreling in to kill. His style was cool, it was studied grace and knowledge, pure as Euclid. His thrift and pride let him kill with a mere five or six rounds, never shooting off his drums aimlessly or pouring on more bursts than were needed to do just the full measure of destruction.

Spa. 103 as a unit got credit for an official 103 downed enemy planes. Fonck's claim of 127 seems ridiculous, even if we add over 60 possibles or probables. There were other fine fliers around. His kills, however, made up 66 per cent of the squadron's confirmed score. In our incomplete picture of this unpleasant man, we must not overlook his amazing skills. He was never wounded, and at his trade, as he would have said, he was merely a genius.

René Fonck was for some time a hero on exhibit, but, as with Charles Lindbergh, the public found strange warped vanities, outrageous opinions, certain disloyalties to popular appeal. Fonck was then scorned by most of the press. His continuous conceit in time dulled his image. But he kept himself in the public view until the start of World War II. In 1939, he retired as the nation's Inspecteur de l'Aviation de Chasse. He died in 1953, aged fifty-nine.

3. | Georges Marie Guynemer (1894–1917)

At the peak of his short career, Georges Guynemer was described by Cecil Lewis, the British pilot, as "a slight, consumptive looking boy with curly black hair and a timid manner." Even when he was one of the three highest ranking aces in the French air force, Guynemer remained a boy; generous, self-effacing, humane in a world of violence; some even said Georges was winsome. He was a kind, good friend, and the fliers knew he was a man to trust and honor.

Georges Marie Ludovic Jules Guynemer; the name rings like sword blows on a fine suit of armor. His armor was family tradition, centuries of it, going back nearly 1,000 years to the Crusades. A family of pride, love of country, rigidly Catholic, living a bit too much in the past, that was the Guynemers. The father was a Saint-Cyr (the French West Point) graduate, who had left the service in 1890 to retire to Compiègne, there to bury himself in historical documents of times gone by. Four years later, on Christmas Eve, his son Georges was born, a sickly baby, and later a sickly child. Always ill of some childhood plague, suspected of being a victim of tuberculosis, his bones seemed to hold no flesh. He was delicate, protected, much beset by a mother and two sisters who oversheltered him to keep him alive.

Like so many frail, over-cared-for children, Georges was wilful, a quarrel picker, and not reliable. Also there was that flashing brightness and vivid imagination one finds in invalids with brain power. Science was becoming a glamorous profession in France, so the boy acquired a smelly chemical set, and often blew up the corner he called his lab with concoctions mixed in test tubes. He adored mechanical toys. All sorts of gadgets found their way to his delicate but skilled fingers. Rigid Catholics, the family was not torn between the Devil and the Holy See.

Came 1914, and Georges, as a soldier's son, volunteered four times. He was twenty years old, not a specimen to impress an army medical doctor. Thin, too thin, flat-chested, hardly any muscle on that white, smooth body.

Somehow at last he was accepted as an apprentice airplane mechanic at the Pau airfield. He did have skill in that direction, and he had charming manners; one saw breeding in his bearing. His captain, impressed, helped the boy to become a pilot in training, and by March of 1915, he was soloing. He received his corporal's chevrons, holy to him as his ancestor's lance. He went to Vauciennes to join the Escadrille M-S3. Six months later, tired of scouting and taking pictures, his observer shot down his first enemy, and earned Guynemer his first medal to place on his thin chest.

As Guynemer tells the story, they sighted a German over Coeuvres.

> I took off with Guerder and was soon in pursuit of the enemy. Shortly afterwards we saw him over Pierrefonds, but he saw us at the same instant and fled. As his machine was faster, there was no chance of catching him. From a great distance, a very great distance, we fired at him . . . without any real expectation of hitting him. We chased him as far as Coucy airfield, where we saw him alight . . . it displeased us enormously.
>
> There we were with these sad thoughts, when suddenly an-

other black point appeared on the horizon. We sped toward it. As we came closer, it grew in size and was soon plain. It was an Aviatik sailing at about 3200 meters. The German pilot was moving toward the French lines, thinking only of what he might find. He did not guess for a moment that an enemy bent upon his destruction was in his wake. . . .

It was not until Soissons was reached that we came up with him, and there the combat took place. During the space of ten minutes, everybody in the city watched the fantastic duel over their heads. I kept about fifteen meters from my Boche, below, back of, and to the left of him. In spite of all his twistings, I managed not to lose touch with him. Guerder fired 115 rounds, but he was having trouble as his gun jammed repeatedly. Conversely, my companion was hit by one bullet in the hand while another "combed" his hair. He answered with his Hotchkiss, shooting more deliberately than before. At the 115th shot fired by Guerder, I had, I will admit, a very sweet feeling at seeing the enemy pilot slump to the floor of his cockpit, while the "lookout" raised his arms in a gesture of despair and the Aviatik swirled down into the abyss in flames. It fell between the trenches. I hastened to land nearby . . . I can vouch that I never felt a keener elation.

The episode was, to lead to fifty-three victories in the air, to more medals than he cared to remember, to fame. Many of the airmen made themselves public heroes, touchy as prima donnas, demanding public exposure like a motion-picture star. Not Guynemer. His life was the public's because they sensed in him something universal and unique. Perhaps because even as a great warrior of France, he had not the look of a killer, or the stance of an actor too aware of his role. *Aucun chemin des fleurs ne conduit à la gloire.*

After that first victory, the colonel asked the plane's observer-gunner who was the skinny kid coming toward them in his flying suit?

"My pilot, *mon Colonel.*"

"That's so . . . And how old are you?" the colonel asked.

The skinny kid said, "Twenty."

"And the gunner?"

"Twenty-two, *mon Colonel.*"

"*Mon Dieu!* Don't we have anything but children left to fight a war with?"

By 1915, flying with the famous Cigognes—the Storks—Guynemer was firing his own gun, and in December of that year, over Chauny near Compiègne, he encountered two Germans in the air. Guynemer began to fire on the nearest at a range of 150 feet, then came in closer to 50 feet, and got in a long burst of bullets. The German went into a tail spin, at which point Guynemer turned his attention to the second enemy plane. But that one had no heart for a fight and fled.

Guynemer was in a hurry to check his kill and went back to look for the downed German. Where the devil was the wreck? It must have crashed, but where? He went round in circles, and more circles. He had to have proof of his victory. His gas was running out, and a glance at his watch showed him it was time to meet his mother and father at the airdrome. As a well-raised Catholic child, he was going to Mass with them. (Even when Georges was on duty, Mama and Papa Guynemer were never far from him if they could help it.)

On landing, Guynemer rushed to his father yelling, "Papa: I've lost him! I've lost my Boche!"

"You've lost *what*—your Boche?"

"An aeroplane I shot down . . . I don't want to lose him."

"No, of course not. But what do you want me to do?"

He looked at his parents. "I have to go and report to the squadron. Go out and find him for me, he's out there some place, Bailly way. Toward Bois Carré."

And Georges went off to report. His father did organize a search and found the body of a German pilot. But no crashed plane. The whole story, in the French text, reads like one of those old-fashioned books of instructive tales.

Guynemer's victories were regular, clean mostly, and he had that flying skill that becomes so legendary it seems also effortless. In March 1917, he sent down two Albatros twin-seaters in smoke

with a trusty Spad he had named *Le Vieux Charles*.* In the afternoon, he went up again and found two Nieuports not able to
handle an evasive Albatros D-II. He moved in to show them how.
He used only ten bullets, wounding the pilot and destroying the
engine. It began to go down for a smash landing. Guynemer following it down like a hired escort. The enemy pilot was Leutnant von Hausen, a nephew of the General von Hausen who
commanded the German Second Army. Guynemer chewed out
the two pilots who had failed to down the Albatros, then began
a long monologue on tactics in the air.

The Groupe de Combat XII (as Guynemer's unit was named)
did a lot of flying almost as a circus group. In May 1917, Guynemer had his best day, shooting down four of the enemy, making
his score to that date forty-five. His reward was the Rosette of
the Legion of Honor. He stands out for us, a *pilote de chasse*, in
a photograph of the period; big-eyed, boyish, frail, with an amazing number of decorations across his chest. The legs, spider-thin,
in high-laced boots. He is not smiling. He has been wounded
several times, and many of his flier friends have died in battle, or
of wounds.

On leave, Papa sounded him out on the idea, because of his
delicate health, of becoming an instructor, an air adviser.

The son shook his head. "It will be said that I ceased to fight
because I have won all the awards."

"Let them say. Later when you come back, stronger, more
ardent, they will understand. There is, after all, a limit to human
strength."

"Yes, Papa, a limit. A limit to be passed. If one has not given
everything, one has given nothing."

When he went back to Les Cigognes, Guynemer found that
his best friend Heurteaux had been seriously wounded the day
before. Everything went wrong. Guynemer's special plane was
under repair, the crock he was given instead was useless. In battle

* Guynemer's standard Spad, one of the best planes in the air at the time,
was a high-compression designed one, with a special 4-pound pom-pom cannon that fired through the propeller shaft, aimed by using a fixed machine
gun as a sight.

his guns jammed, there were forced landings. The weather was rotten. He had to exist grounded, in the drafty dirty living quarters at the airdrome, not able to fly. He lost his temper, friends were insulted. He would pace the room, eyes angry, snarling at his comrades.

It was the same old pattern found in some fliers, a *cafard*, the French called it, when their nerves went, when they were past their prime, when fame and decorations had made them jaded. They had to fly, and the flying was destroying them. Black despair remained when Guynemer flew again but met no Germans.

During the summer of 1917 his scores mounted until he had reached fifty-three victories by August 20. Yet the malaise continued.

In a single day, in September 1917, Guynemer made crash landings with three different planes. The next day, September 11, the weather was chancy; no one could predict how it would turn. Capitaine Guynemer had not slept well, was the mess gossip. Stay out of his way, he's breathing fire. Very jumpy. And the big shots were coming to see him: Commandant du Peuty on the staff of aviation at GHQ, Commandant Brocard, former CO of the Cigognes, now chef de cabinet for the War Ministry. Very important big ones. But at that very hour, Guynemer decided to fly. There were spots of blue to be seen in the overcast, if you looked hard enough. What about the commandants? someone asked. Plenty of time, said Guynemer. He'd take up Underlieutenant Bozon-Verduraz, just the two Spads, to see what was in the air over Poelcapelle.

At 8:30 a.m., up the two Spads went. At 9:00 a.m., there were Commandants du Peuty and Brocard and party. Where was *le Capitaine?* Hunting for blue sky . . . Over the German lines they spotted an enemy plane. Guynemer waved a signal to his comrade, and began to climb toward the wan sun. When he took another look, clouds had cut the sun from view. So, no chance of jumping out from the glare to surprise the enemy. He signalled Bozon-Verduraz to go up under the German, and he'd come in from the side: a two-pronged attack.

The enemy was no novice. He went into a flat sudden spin and evaded them. Guynemer dived after his elusive foe. At this point, Bozon-Verduraz saw a group of Albatros D-III's coming up fast into the developing fight. He decided to try to get them away from Guynemer. So he charged straight at the whole group, gathering speed as fast as he could, throttle wide open. He went right on through the whole formation of Germans, who scattered like ducks in a barnyard. He circled and came back to where he thought they had begun to fight. Amazingly, the whole sky was empty. Nothing but mist, high clouds, and the sun dead in the sky.

Bozon-Verduraz still circled, hoping Guynemer would rejoin him. The light had almost gone. For an hour he circled; just one more, *one* more. His neck was stiff from peering in all directions. Now the fuel was nearly gone, maybe already gone. Finally, he landed with dry tanks at St. Pol-sur-Mer.

"*Capitaine,* Guynemer here?"

"Not yet."

Guynemer never did come in. No more would he land and cry out joyously: "*J'en ai un!* (I have one of them!)"

For twelve days the hunt went on. Was he wounded some place? Was he prisoner? Or so badly shot up he couldn't tell them who he was? Then, at last, came the official communiqué from the War Ministry:

> Captain Guynemer flew off on patrol at 08.25 hours, September 11, with Lieutenant Bozon-Verduraz and disappeared in the vicinity of Poelcapelle, Belgium, during a combat with a German biplane.

The magazine *L'Illustration* ran an editorial, "If a prisoner, he'll escape. He must come back to life." *Le Temps* commented: "Guynemer they say is dead. Guynemer dead! Bah! Those who would believe that don't know him!"

Churches filled, masses were held, rosaries recited. Cathedrals held multitudes of widows, haggard, red-eyed; mutilated soldiers; the blind, limbless, underfed children. It was mass hysteria in some ways, as classes began in school with prayers for Guynemer's safe deliverance from peril: the national hero who could rise from the dead. The political voices spoke out. Said President

Georges Clemenceau: "He was our pride and our protection. His loss is the most cruel of all those, so numerous, alas, which have been visited upon our ranks . . . Our revenge will be hard and inexorable . . . Guynemer was merely a puissant idea in a rather frail body, and I have lived near him with the secret sorrow of knowing that some day the idea would slay the container . . . He will remain the model hero, a living legend, the greatest in all history . . ."

It was four weeks before the Germans got around to deciding just who had killed Guynemer. A Rumpler pilot of a crack Jagd-staffel, Kurt Wissemann, was given the credit for downing the French ace. After the war, the Germans gave out a strange story that Guynemer's plane had crashed into an old burying ground near Poelcapelle. An army doctor and some soldiers found the wreck with the pilot dead in the seat, a slug through his skull. British guns were in action all round and so they had to leave the Spad and the body still seated in the cockpit. The rest was silence. No body was ever produced, no wreckage of the Spad.

Die Woche, the German publication, came out with a mean bit of prose stating that Guynemer attacked only weaker planes, never anyone his size or firepower—and if his first charge failed, he gave up, "having no stomach for fights of long duration, in the course of which there must be a display of real courage." Kurt Wissemann was not mentioned.

Poor Wissemann, who never knew he was supposed to have killed the French ace, was shot down himself by René Fonck nearly a week before the Germans knew they had destroyed Guynemer. Yet someone published a letter from Wissemann in the *Kölnische Zeitung*, in which he claimed that he had shot down the celebrated "flier Guynemer . . . I shall never again meet such a dangerous foe . . ."

The name of Georges Guynemer was cut into a marble plaque in the Panthéon's crypt in Paris where the great of France are usually entombed. The text of the inscription reads:

Dead on the field of honor, September 11, 1917. A legendary hero fallen in glory from the sky after three years of hard and incessant struggle, he will remain the purest symbol of national ideals for his indomitable tenacity of purpose, his ferocious verve and sublime gallantry. Animated by an invincible faith in victory, he has bequeathed to the French soldier an imperishable heritage which consecrates the spirit of sacrifice and will surely inspire the noblest emulation.

4. | Charles Nungesser (1892–1927)

Before the war, Charles Nungesser was a boxer of some reputation. He had lived in Paris until he was ten, when his parents broke up and he was moved to Valenciennes. The psychiatrists tell us that children of broken homes try to excel in outside activities. The young boy went in for sports: boxing, swimming, soccer, bicycle riding. Early in life, Charles decided he wanted to be a racing-car driver or a flying-machine pilot. He had that love of danger that is partly a fear of natural death. He was to say, "A strong heart does not fear death, even in its most terrible aspects." He courted wounds like a drunk piling up saucers at the Bois Charbon Vins. All in all he was to collect a fractured skull, a jaw fractured in several places, a brain concussion, a broken palate, a shattered right arm, and one leg stiffened permanently, so that he walked crabwise. In 1916 both his legs were broken in a takeoff, and he had to walk with the aid of a cane at all times.

But at sixteen, in 1908, Charles was still in one piece. To achieve his dream of driving racing cars, he joined an uncle in Buenos Aires where a local Argentine fast-car buff hired him to race and condition racing cars. A chance encounter with a tramp exhibition flier gave Charles a chance to learn to fly, and soon he, too, was giving exhibitions for a local firm. When he joined his uncle on a plantation, his mind was not on pineapples or coffee trees; instead, Nungesser began to build his own plane, but gave it up when talk of war in Europe reached South America.

Two months before the war started, Nungesser was in France, trying to volunteer in the French flying service. It wasn't easy;

at twenty-two, he looked fourteen. He was rejected. All he could get was a horse with the Second Hussars! He received the Médaille Militaire during the retreat to the Marne. Nungesser and some cavalrymen, stragglers on foot, ran into a loaded German Mors staff car flying the black and white pennant of high staff officers. They killed two officers, then rushed the car, killing the driver and three more officers. Taking over the car under heavy fire in the great French retreat, Nungesser drove at racing speed toward what was left of the Allied lines. He not only got the medal, but was allowed to keep the car. Now his commanding officer could not refuse the hero's request to join the air force.

In March 1915, Nungesser was breveted a pilot at Avord Airfield. He flew for the Escadrille Voisin No. 106 that spring. His plane usually came back bullet-holed, torn, and damaged. His observer, Pichon, spent his free time patching their ship. In April, Nungesser took on a German Albatros carrying a Parabellum machine gun. (The French plane's observer was armed with a carbine.) The German didn't fight, however, but led Nungesser into an ambush over an enemy antiaircraft battery. Shrapnel nearly tore the plane apart, the engine went dead. By sheer determination, and some gliding power, Nungesser made a dead-stick landing behind his own lines and crashed. He and the observer Pichon walked away, limping, feeling themselves *avoir du guignon* —unlucky.

Later he broke both legs and fractured his jaw by crashing a Morane plane. But after only a month in bed, walking with two sticks, Nungesser was back in a plane—a battered and patched-up one, of course.

Near Nancy, he was appointed a stand-by pilot, and as he stood by, he began to hunt women. He became a notorious womanizer, a compulsive Don Juan, when not at the airfield always either in a bedroom or a bar. His airfield was still being fitted out. As a duty pilot, the sight of a new Voisin plane just uncrated, with a swivel-mounted Hotchkiss gun in the cockpit nacelle, proved irresistible. Nungesser grabbed a duty gunner and took off. Unfortunately, back at the airdrome an air-raid alert sounded, with a report that four enemy craft were winging toward Nancy. It was the duty of the pilot on call to go up and intercept; but Pilot Nungesser was no place to be found. The CO was wondering where he could be when a phone message came in stating that one of his planes had just shot down an enemy ship. Then it was discovered that the new Voisin was with the missing flier. Nungesser received no hero's welcome, just eight days' arrest for leaving his duty post.

"Was that punishment so unfair?" he was asked.

"For shooting down an Albatros," he replied, "what was fair would have been the Croix de Guerre." He got it, and gifts of fruit and love letters from the citizens of Nancy (and their wives and daughters) viewing the fallen German plane. Nungesser was also rewarded by a single-seated fighter plane of his own.

Near the end of January 1916, Nungesser crashed on takeoff and came out of hospital with a permanently atrophied leg, a half-paralyzed limb which, however, did not curtail either his gay life or his flying. Like so many aces, he does not appear to have been a really top-rank flier. After shooting down a balloon and two enemy planes, his ship was beaded with bullet holes. He usually came back from a fight with his patched plane in worse condition. Either twenty-eight slugs (by count) in the frame of his plane, or forty bullet marks on his cowling. He was injured so many times that one suspects a sort of madness and recklessness beyond mere courage. Either he was the bravest of men, or he took a perverse delight in injury. He flew bandaged, splintered, in plaster of paris. He seems to have escaped from the shakes, the bad nerves of other aces. He never vomited up his raw egg, brandy, and milk breakfast on a jumpy stomach as did so many good fliers. Most likely, Nungesser ate a good solid breakfast and kept it down.

In May 1916, he was assigned to Escadrille No. 65 and at once painted on the sides of his plane his personal coat of arms: a black heart on which were set a skull and bones, a coffin, and on either side candles. He then went stunting, and was reprimanded and reminded there was a war on. Nungesser took off again and stunted over a German airfield. Result, another eight days' arrest. Evidently a rather loose arrest, for a day later he shot down an

Albatros over the Moselle. Result, remission of the rest of the sentence, and the Légion d'Honneur!

It was now clear to all that this was no mere flier, but a character out of Alexandre Dumas the elder. A soldier of the skies, reckless, without respect for his superiors or even perhaps for war. In some ways he resembled too Tolstoy's Vronsky, enjoying all from good society to the demi-monde, from generals to café habitués.

Ernest Hemingway used to claim he had been Mata Hari's lover, one of his many sexual yarns to bolster his own shaky inner male image. As Mata Hari was shot by the French in 1917, and Hemingway didn't get to Europe until 1918, it was like Shaw's love affair with Ellen Terry, a passion done by long distance. However, Nungesser was close friend and bed companion to Mata Hari when he was in Paris. They were seen at the cafés, at dinner, and in and out of certain discreet hotels. He was to say he knew quite well that Mata Hari was a spy, and added that she was "clumsy at it," spying, that is. It was no secret, he said, that she was a poor sort of double agent, working for both the British and German Intelligence. Nungesser, his humor wild, told her the French had a new secret plane powered by eight huge new super-engines. It may have been this kind of "secret" passed on to the Germans that was the cause, as some say, of their betraying her to the French to get rid of her. (The legend is that she was shot while clad only in a fur coat.)

In Paris, too, Nungesser moved in the world of Colette's grand courtesans, as well as among the women of the better brothels near the Ritz. He might have met the Cubist critic and poet, Apollinaire, on leave from the front, soon to receive a head wound that would ultimately kill him. But mostly his leaves were spent in the bars jesting with American fliers, now and then meeting a society woman whose husband was at the front or busy making war millions. The last was cause of certain whispered scandals.

Nungesser had no respect for GHQ, and this also was to harm his reputation officially. Once in the air, his behavior was abstracted from the dull reality and morality he disliked below. He flew above the miserable incessant rhythms of the failed ground attacks, at his best in the eye of the hurricane of battle, where mind and body must move as one, by instinct, quickly.

On the ground, he reverted to a sly, gay insouciance. Politics meant little to him; it was all greed, expediency, and voices uttering cant and pious slogans.

By New Year's, 1917, Nungesser had twenty-one kills to his credit. After many more wins he was made to take a vacation in March 1918 at the seashore resort of St. Pol. But from there, he still flew every day looking for action and found six German navy planes. He got one, wrecked another.

Then back again, back to the real war at the front, and here he was attacked one day by a British plane and hit fourteen times. The Englishman kept firing, so that Nungesser, suspecting it was a Hun pilot in a captured plane (the enemy had played this game a few times) shot the British-marked plane down. On landing, he discovered it was actually a new young English flier who probably had taken Nungesser's black heart, skull and bones, coffin, and candles insignia for a Teutonic symbol. Nungesser shrugged and at once had broad stripes, red, white, and blue, painted on his wings until his plane looked like an old-fashioned peppermint candy stick.

But the symbols got him into a real duel in May of 1917 through a challenge dropped by an Albatros on his airdrome, addressed TO MY WORTHY OPPONENT, MONSIEUR SKULL AND BONES. It asked him to come up and fight at four o'clock. Nungesser brooded. He was warned it was a German trap yet that only added spice. After going over his gun and plane with care, Nungesser took off at 2:30 and paused to shoot up an enemy airfield, wasting petrol and bullets he might need later in the duel.

He came to the dueling place in the sky as set down in the German note a little early, and was at once jumped by six Albatroses hiding above him in cloud banks. German honor, as usual, was nothing but a scrap of paper. It was a trap and it was being sprung on him with deadly skill.

The Frenchman banked into a dive at once, and built up speed in a wide loop. Then, at the climax of the loop, he went into an Immelmann turn which put him right up on the tails of the enemy planes. He got two of them, loosing off a whole case of bullets. He had little ammunition left and the gas-tank needle told him it was already time to scoot for home. Astonishingly the Albatroses, presumably shocked at the poor results of their ambush, let him go.

By this time Nungesser's body was a mass of scar tissue, rebuilt bones. The bad leg had grown worse; it was unbearable pain to kick at the rudder pedal, and stabs of pain ran up his leg like electric shocks every time he moved. He had to be carried into the plane, and out again, every flight.

To add to the physical pain came the news that the great Guynemer, whose score was fifty-three kills, was missing, most likely lost. Nungesser was the leading ace now. But René Fonck, a rather "revolting glory hunter," had himself officially proclaimed the top French ace. They didn't like Nungesser much around GHQ. He was almost *too* French, the caricature of the gay man about town, the boisterous Bohemian of fiction. A rogue, they said, with too much wit, a teller of ribald adventures, wrecker of homes. All that bonhomie, and those broken bones. There were also scandals over ladies in high places. So René Fonck became the pet of the country, the idol of the French air force.

Nungesser was in no shape to carry on. Under orders to take it easy, he refused to slow down. Driving to Paris for a spree one night with his pet mechanic, Pochon, at the wheel, there was a serious accident. Pochon was killed, Nungesser again broke his jaw. On recovery, back in action, he shot down several German planes too far behind their own lines to count.

Then began a race for top position. First Fonck led, then Nungesser. Fonck, in perfect health, began to pull ahead, 45 to 40. Nungesser after a few more wins and two more spells in hospital, brought his score up to 45. The official score at the end of the war gives him 45, ranking third to Fonck, who was number one with 75.

For Nungesser there were consolation prizes—the highest awards from the American, French, Belgian, and Portuguese; and the Serbian Cross of Karageorgevitch, the last a pawnshop favorite.

Nungesser had the great quality of irreverence. He wanted no grandeur, but he wore it with an easy grace, as if it held little value for him. Unlike René Fonck—of whom someone once said, "He acts as if waiting for a vacancy in the Holy Trinity"—Nungesser wanted to live fully, physically, as if he knew that most of the platitudes offered to a flier sounded too much like an eulogy.

In May of 1927, still flamboyant, still living to the hilt, Charles Nungesser came back to public attention when a series of air races across the Atlantic (either solo or by partners) was set up. A hotel owner with an eye for publicity, Raymond Orteig of New York, pledged a standing offer of $25,000 for "the first aviator who will cross the Atlantic in a land or water aircraft (heavier-than-air) from Paris or the shores of France to New York, or from New York to Paris, or the shores of France, without stop." The race was won by an "unpleasant young man," Charles Lindbergh, who later accepted from Hermann Goering the Nazi Eagle decoration. A week before Lindbergh's crossing, Charles Nungesser and François Coli took off for an east-west crossing. They and their plane disappeared over the Atlantic, never to be seen again.

5. | William Coppens de Houthulst

All nations, large or small, involved in the war had some kind of air force, even if only of half a dozen planes. Little Belgium, much put upon, brutalized by German *Kultur*, occupied, had at least five aces, outstanding among whom was Lieutenant William Coppens de Houthulst, with thirty-six accredited victories over German objects in the air. He began to fly in Septmber 1915 and was known as the great observation-balloon killer. Balloon killing was very dangerous since each balloon was usually ringed with anti-aircraft batteries, and a flier must come in low and close to set the gas bags on fire.

Coppens hardly fitted the role in appearance. Slight, short, not at all handsome; almost colorless, not talkative. In a crowd, he would have passed for just another cipher. In the air, he was a hawk, a creature part plane, part human engine of destruction. Coppens would attack a balloon at 3,000 feet, as the ack-ack fire grew closer and the cable crews reeled about sweating in their sausages. Coppens would follow the balloon down until it fell in flames, the crew jumping with their chutes if they were lucky. Once he rode and rolled his plane's wheels right across the top of a balloon. "I had to do something and I was out of bullets, and if I didn't get in close . . . what would the Boche have said?"

Early in the war, Coppens attracted world attention by his bravery. The Germans had loaded a balloon with high explosives deliberately to bait him to his death over Zarren, in occupied Brussels. One shot, and it would explode. And as Coppens often shot balloons at a distance of fifty feet, that would be the end of the balloon buster.

Allied agents discovered the scheme, and Coppens was warned. But, against orders, he decided to inspect the air bomb anyway; he couldn't resist it. The balloon was only halfway up to its final height when he came buzzing along. Below were German staff officers out on holiday to see the end of the damn Belgian ace. Coppens didn't hesitate. In seconds he had the balloon in his sights and let go a burst. The explosion was much greater than expected, a blooming red expansion of gas, and the deadly stuff went up and off in all directions. Coppens's plane was caught and tossed about like matchwood; how the patched wreck held together no one knew. The burning balloon, overloaded, fell swift as doom on the watching staff officers, killing many and injuring the rest. Coppens controlled his plane and flew off, unhurt.

The Germans began to put smaller balloons on cables all around their fat Hildas (as they called their balloons) to entangle any flier trying to come in on the central observation balloon. Coppens decided to go up with another flier named Gallez: they would fly high, then drop down in a dive right onto a big balloon among the nest of small ones. Here is his description of events after they had gone high:

. . . Gallez steering southeast and I northeast. I kept him in sight, and as his machine stood out clearly against the blue sky, this was easy. But why did he not dive? Surely he must have reached a point, as I had done, just in front of the target. We were wasting time, and I began to fear that they would pull the balloons down; for the noise of our engines must have been audible beneath the clouds. Finally, he dived, and from then on I thought no more about him. I dived, too, and as, owing to my earlier preoccupation with the fortunes of my partner, I had not been able to watch my own course as carefully as I should have liked, I found myself, on emerging from the clouds over Stampkot, exactly above the balloon; that is to say, too literally above it—so much so that I had to dive absolutely vertically on it, and my speed became enormous. The balloon appeared to fly at my face, increasing in size at an extraordinary rate. I had time to fire one round and no more, and then had to pull out of my dive with a jerk, narrowly missing a collision. With my engine full on, I shot away to the north, toward my second balloon, followed by the shells, whose black bursts leaped into existence all around me, and the 20-mm "flaming onions" with their snaking milky trails curving away behind them. To my ears came the intermittent crackling of the small-caliber machine guns, whose invisible bullets whistled about me, accompanied by the angry woof! of the shells. . . .

Three minutes later, I set the second balloon on fire, over Wercken. But, chancing to look toward the south in search of Gallez, I saw my first balloon, and his, both intact!

What could have happened? Gallez told me later that he had drifted and come out of the clouds too far from the balloon. As for me, I had come out too much on top of mine, and my solitary bullet, although an 11-mm one, fired vertically downward, had not succeeded in setting it on fire. Or, perhaps, in my anxiety to avoid colliding with the gasbag, I had pulled my machine out of its dive as I fired. In which case I had missed the balloon altogether. But it was not too late to retrace my steps and cover once more the five or six miles separating me from it, and "roast" the wretched thing before they hauled it right down! I might even be able to set Gallez's balloon off!

I swung around to the south, and suddenly saw a strange object, apparently bearing down upon me at high speed, which

I almost immediately recognized as a kite covered in white silk. It was, of course, stationary, supported by the wind, and its apparent forward movement was due to the fact that I was approaching it at a speed of over 120 mph. I immediately pulled my nose around and up, and began a spiral climb to avoid the apron of steel cables that I guessed must be stretched between the kites surrounding the balloon I had just sent down in flames. The enemy must have been bitterly disappointed not to have caught me in this practically invisible snare, that a pilot, flying at full speed, could not hope to avoid or detect. . . .

The Boche cursed that Belgian courage. Coppens had got twenty-eight balloons, despite the fact that he and his fellow Belgians had to fly in lousy planes, whatever lemons the French and English were discarding; rebuilt jobs, patched wrecks. Not until 1918 did they get a few Sopwith Camels, when the war was nearly over. Mostly they flew Nieuports no longer fast enough for actual warfare and consequently phased out by the Allies. Coppens himself got hold of a plane no one in his senses ever wanted to fly, the dismal Hanriot HD-1, a biplane; he painted it an electric blue to resemble a toy snake he had owned as a child. He received twenty incendiary bullets a month from the stingy French; a serious handicap as he needed inflammatory bullets for balloon hunting.

Coppens had some odd habits. He had an aversion to being decorated, for one. He held off accepting his awards, saying, "other pilots deserve them more." He was told the military brass never made errors; he should keep his mouth shut and take the awards. He also had no ear for music but liked to whistle shrilly off key, and several buckets of water were poured over his head by more sensitive comrades. It didn't cure him. They fetched a chipped teacup from an English railroad station, and made a mock presentation to Coppens of the "Paddington Whistlers' Cup." When he got married, the other fliers noticed he stopped whistling. No bride would have stood for his blasting off-key notes in the bedroom!

On September 7, 1918, he was forced finally to accept his awards. Coppens took a fancy ride to headquarters, a castle at

La Panne. A whole battalion of infantry was lined up to honor him. He was invested against his will with the Cross of the Legion of Honor, and the Croix de Guerre. Standing before the King and Queen of the Belgians, and the Tiger of France, Clemenceau, Coppens's helmet, which fitted badly, began to wobble alarmingly. After accepting the honors, he went around to the generals' kitchen and bummed a gallon of salad oil; his air pals had been eating their salad without dressing! He also found a small cannon that had been made to fire through the hub of the propeller with a Bowden cable trigger. This delighted him, although the invention was never used as an official weapon.

Coppens' last and most dangerous mission was to lead an attack on Thourout, in northwest Belgium, where a cluster of Praet-Bosh balloons hung swaying at 1,000 feet. As he puts it:

I was about 450 feet away, when I felt a terrible blow on the left leg. An incendiary bullet, after passing through the thin planking of the floor, had struck my shinbone, smashing everything in its passage and inflicting a wound all the more painful for the fact that the bullet, being hollow, had flattened, becoming in effect a dumdum bullet. The muscles were torn apart, the bone shattered, and the artery cut in half.

So great was the pain that my right leg became rigid, stretched out to its full extent with the result that my rudder bar was kicked violently forward on that side (my left leg being without say in the matter, limply inert) and my machine swung around and went into a spin. Simultaneously, my hand clutched the trigger control on the control lever (for I had been on the point of opening fire), and for several seconds my gun spat bullets in every direction, hose-fashion, until at last my grip relaxed. The first of these bullets, at least, hit the balloon, which burst into flames.

My only thought at the time was of how to get back to our lines. I could have landed at once, in enemy territory, but that was a thing no one worth his salt would have dreamt of doing, a pilot's only thought in such a case was to get back—to recross the lines.

My rudder bar was fitted with straps at each extremity, and my feet passed under these straps. This prevented my left leg from jamming the bar, and allowed me to work the rudder with the right foot alone. I was in this way able to bring my machine out of its spin after it had described two or three turns. . . .

One inlet pipe on my engine had been perforated by another bullet, and my revolutions had fallen slightly, but Houthulst Forest was gradually drawing nearer. I still had five miles to cover before reaching our lines—call it six, before I should be clear of the enemy's fire. At the speed at which my engine was turning this occupied three minutes, during which I could feel the severed artery beating furiously. A sweat on my forehead made me snatch down my goggles, so that they remained hanging around my neck, and pulled off my fur-lined cap, and nothing would have parted me from it; with an effort, I stuffed it under my coat. I tore off and shed my silk muffler protecting my face from the cold. I wanted air, ice-cold air, to bathe my face and keep me from fainting. I felt my strength forsaking me and fought against it desperately. I wanted at all cost to avoid falling into the hands of the enemy.

At last the firing died out, I was home. . . . At the end of my strength, unable to go any further, I landed near Essen, to the east of Dixmude. I chose a small field by the side of the road, on which a fair amount of traffic told me that I should soon obtain help. The field, all too small, was hemmed in with hedges, and I had to put my machine down rather heavily in order to arrest its progress. My undercarriage, which had been badly weakened by the machine-gun fire, collapsed on contact with the ground. The machine had, indeed, been pretty badly shot about all over.

As soon as my machine came to rest, I saw stretcher-bearers forcing their way through the hedge, hurrying to my rescue. They at once started ripping open the fuselage of my airplane, which caused me some concern. The feelings of a pilot are very much those of a horseman toward his mount. They experienced some trouble disengaging my left foot from the strap that held it to the rudder bar, and the pain was acute. I heard one man say that I had lost a tremendous amount of blood.

They cut off his leg and a brave man was out of the war.

CHAPTER 11

THE BRITISH AGAIN

1. | Edward Corringham Mannock (1887–1918)

Edward "Mick" Mannock was born on May 24, 1887, of a
Scots father and an English mother, at the army training grounds
at Aldershot.* His father was a corporal in the Greys, a figure
out of Kipling's *Soldiers Three*, crafty, drunk, a professional soldier for the Queen's shilling. The family toured the Empire military posts. Mick grew up in the married men's quarters of the
lower ranks. Grew up catch-as-catch-can, with beery voices,
blows given and taken by married couples, the children included
in many a lick to the chops; "the back-of-me-hand to the lug-
hole." With five children and a complaining wife, one day Corporal Mannock was declared time-expired, out of the army. Deserting wife and children, he was off and gone with the morning
bugle call. Mick was twelve, and they were destitute.

He had been one of those shy boys who read anything he could
lay hands on, despite a congenital defect in his left eye. Hungry,
undernourished, people were amazed at how thin his legs were in
their worn, patched breeks. He was serious, never smiling. Mick
had to leave school to help an older brother and sister keep the
family going. It was before the days of the welfare state, and
what little private charity came in was thin and overlarded with
the smug cant of Victorian hypocrisy.

Mick lugged groceries, was a barber's helper (lathering chins,
going out for a customer's pint, sweeping and blacking boots).
He did some work for the Army Ambulance Corps, but in the

* Many historians have mistakenly called him Irish.

end joined the telephone service, stringing wires for more and more people who were beginning to see the value of Alexander Graham Bell's invention.

Working in Wellingborough, Northants, the boy boarded with the Eyles, a couple who had no child of their own. They helped him pull himself out of the despairingly hopeless condition of the have-nots of England. A sense of social injustice burned high in Mick Mannock by the time he was twenty. The Fabian Society was at its height, and Messrs. Shaw and Wells were planning to do over the world. The Webbs were going to explain it with charts, how the toffs had exploited the worthy poor in a cruel class society. And Karl Marx had been hard at work in the British Museum.

Mick joined the Labour Party, found he had a good voice, could think on his feet, and make interesting the formula of the misuse of wealth, the sham of social position, the degrading of women—all the unfair sexual taboos of the time. Most of all he hated Germans and their *Kultur*, their boorish stance in shiny armor. His hatred of anything German was close to being pathological, and the Germans in those years before the war did nothing to mitigate a thinking man's contempt. The fallacy of believing that the British were much better, Mick, as a young man, overlooked. He banged away at the *laissez-faire* business ethics of commercial life and industry, yet he was a patriot for all that, having as an army child been to India, Ireland, and South Africa. For him it was an insult to say the sun never set on the British Empire "because God didn't trust it in the dark."

At the end of 1913, Mick—virtually blind in one eye—went to Constantinople as an inspector for an English telephone firm. When Turkey joined Germany as one of the central powers against the Allies, he was interned and put to work—dirty, hard work. Attempting to escape, he found out how hard Turkish punishment could be. In solitary confinement he became ill, developed sores and rashes, was plainly dying. The Turks rushed him into repatriation to save themselves from burying a corpse. Besides, a one-eyed man would never become an enemy soldier.

In 1915 he returned, recovered, to England and joined the

Royal Army Medical Corps. From there he went to the Royal
Engineers and, in April 1916, the ex-army corporal's son was being saluted as a fresh-made lieutenant. His good eye was on the
skies, on flying, and the victories of Alfred Ball.

At twenty-nine, middle-aged for a flier, Mick Mannock was
anything but a dashing eager youth in the RFC. He was too tall,
too lean, his face too seamed by his illnesses and hard life. Grim,
yes; sad, too. Not a talker, but his stare showed some resentment
of a world he had not made.

At his medical examination he wore boots and spurs and held a
riding crop, which baffled the doctor, perhaps so much so that
he passed Mick as fit for pilot training. The story goes that his
good eye snuck a glimpse of the whole eye chart, and he memo-
rized it all in a fleeting second so that he could recite it when
his left eye was tested.

In February 1917, accepted at last as a flying officer, Mick was
in the Joyce Green Reserve Squadron. Here he made friends with
James McCudden and Meredith Thomas. The latter remembers
Mick in training on a new ship. "That was his first solo flight on
a DH-2, when he was told, as all were told in those days, 'Don't
turn below two thousand; if you do, you will spin and kill yourself.' "

Mick proved this wrong early one Sunday morning when he
accidentally got into a spin at about 1,000 feet over a munitions
factory—then just across the creek on the edge of the airfield.
He came out extremely near both the ground and the factory,
landing successfully in a small field which was too small to fly
out from. He was accused of spinning intentionally, and a rather
unpleasant scene in the mess and later in the CO's office followed.
However, he made a friend later of the CO, New Zealander Major
Keith Caldwell, who describes Mannock thus:

> We were great friends at Joyce Green and had many both
> amusing and serious talks when waiting in the cold on a fuel
> drum—at one period for a whole three weeks—for a flight, but
> I cannot recall anything definite beyond our mutual disgust
> because of the manner in which the staff threatened the pupils,
> many of whom had seen pretty severe war service before trans-

ferring or being seconded to the R.F.C., while the staff had seen very, very little, and in some cases, none.

My first impression of Mick was: he was very reserved, inclined toward a strong temper, but very patient and somewhat difficult to arouse. On short acquaintance he became a very good conversationalist and was fond of discussions or arguments. He was prepared to be generous to everyone in thought and deed, but had strong likes and dislikes. . . .

From a letter to the Eyles at Wellingborough, we get an impression of Mannock's style in the air:

Got the M.C. . . . made captain on probation. Had some more luck, only bad this time. Busted two buses in the past three days. Engines broke in midair. Got down all right. Some pilot! The CO congratulated me. Hurt myself a little bit on the second occasion, but not much. . . . Last week I had five bouts of my own and fired off 470 rounds of ammunition. . . . Lost some fellows during the last week. One was hit by Archie direct. Went down in a spin from seven thousand feet . . .

April 1917 was the cruelest month indeed for the Allies at Arras. Mick got to the RFC's 40th Squadron. They were flying Nieuports and were commanded by a well-known stage actor, Robert Loraine. Mick Mannock seemed cold to the men and his looks were against him. He seemed not "our kind," perhaps because he ignored some of the usual schoolboy fetishes the fliers held sacred. Coming in for dinner his first night with the 40th, he sat down in an empty chair. The room went still, the men looking at him with frowns of disapproval.

As a working bloke, he wasn't having any of that. "Have I done something sinful?"

"That's Pell's seat."

"Sorry." He rose to find another seat.

"Might as well stay there . . . Pell, poor chap, didn't come back today."

Mick sat down, knowing now it wasn't cricket to sit in the chair of a fallen flier, not right away. Mick shared none of the nonsense about the old school tie or a Church of England God who watched even a sparrow fall. Mick was fatalistic, didn't knock on wood or blow out three on a match. He knew his chances of being killed were good. His philosophy was simple; he loved the Crown, hated the Germans, and believed that some day the Labour Party would bring heaven down to earth for everyone. To be a good flier, to win in the air, a man had to be sure, cool, and not let a bit of temper get the best of him. He ate his dinner in silence.

Mick took it slowly in the air, too, held himself back. He learned the ways of the ships, the guns, the enemy. It was felt that Mannock was showing "a bit of yellow up his back." His one defender at mess was "Zulu," Captain G. L. Lloyd from Africa, a seasoned flier. Zulu predicted they'd all be damned proud of Mick yet. He might even knock a few Huns out of the air for them. All he needed was to get a few kinks out of his system.

On May 7, Mannock shot down an observation balloon, feeling sure that now the chaps would accept him. It was dark when he came down at the airdrome. The mess was so thickly gloomy, you could have cut the atmosphere with a knife. Mick asked why the long faces?

Albert Ball had not returned from a tangle with von Richthofen's Jasta. He was dead. Mick turned away and wept.

Shortly thereafter he was nearly killed himself in a training exercise. He was firing at a ground target when his bottom right wing fell away and his plane crashed. Mannock walked away damning whoever had grown bloody rich putting in faulty wing struts.

He hid the fact of his blind eye, which made a doubtful marksman of him. Despite the handicap, he kept practicing flying and gunnery, and had shot down enough German planes to get the Military Cross in July 1917.

Mannock was among the few fliers who were interested in the hell of the infantrymen; to him, these men were the workers. They fought, died, carrying Bangalore torpedoes to the Hun wire, died so easily down there while he flew in good clear air. They were scroungers, rum drinkers, hard lots, but to Mick the Royal Welch Fusiliers, the Argyles, the Middlesex, and the Sutherland Highlanders would take over the exploiters' world, one day, for a socialist state.

Mick was determined to try to wipe out the German Empire single-handed with airplane and machine gun. Basically he was a fine leader, and his enthusiasm was felt and needed by the younger men he flew with. He wanted no individual heroes, but saw the squadron as a team always prepared, always ready to counter some enemy flier's sudden move. Remembering his own green flying days, new pilots were aided by him when he became a patrol leader, made to stand tall on their own. He cared nothing for credit and would let a new lad finish off one of his kills to get the honor and have a record. Mick kept score, but in a mocking way, as when he wrote that he had downed forty-one of the enemy. "If I have any luck I think I may beat old Mac's [his friend, Major James McCudden] fifty-seven victories. Then I shall try and oust old Richthofen . . ."

At the end of the year, the squadron got SE-5's with the stationary water-cooled Hispano-Suiza engines. Mick felt fine having an engine that didn't revolve with the propeller like the Le Rhônes.

Sent back to England for leave in January 1918, he found that he could not accept life at home while others flew and fought. By the end of March he was back in France as flight commander of the just-formed 74th Squadron. In his group was Captain Ira Jones, who deserves mention for the fact that on his instrument panel he pasted a note: HE MUST FALL. REMEMBER BALL. A grim *memento mori.**

Mannock went on shooting down the enemy relentlessly, keeping bad records, making too few claims. He became obsessed with the dreadful image that he would be burned alive. It was a terror he tried to hide, but it brought him close to a mental breakdown. He saw his end: screaming, drenched in gasoline and oil from his burning craft, and baked alive, smelling himself cooking as the fire lapped at his vital parts. Mannock carried a pistol, always checked

---

* Jones shot down forty enemy planes in six months, and survived to fight in World War II. In 1934, he wrote a book about Edward Mick Mannock at war entitled *King of the Air Fighters*.

to be sure it was loaded and in working order, every time he took off. To those who asked, he said, "I'll put a bullet through my head if the machine catches fire . . . they'll *never* burn me."

It was odd that a man so sensitive to terror saw nothing frightening about all the deaths he had been responsible for. The truth was, he had reached such a pitch in his madness against the Hun that he no longer saw Germans as human beings. "I sent one of them to hell in flames today . . . I wish Kaiser Bill could have seen him sizzle." Mick Mannock, like Kipling, reacted strongly to his father's desertion of the family, the brutal life he led as a child. But Mick, not being a writer, turned his acid images of his childhood world into a revenge on the visible enemy provided him by the war.

A South African, Van Ira, and the CO, Keith Caldwell, have given us some of the best close-ups of Mick Mannock in his growing fury, his rage against the enemy. He would follow a dying plane to the ground and grind it to bits with his guns as it lay there in ruin, smashing up the flier alive, wounded, or dead. Van Ira tells of one particular dogfight:

> . . . going on between a number of machines east of Merville at about 14,000 feet, so I went along to join in the fun, although I was at a lower altitude. As I was climbing toward the scrap, I suddenly saw a machine falling away from the whirling mob and come tumbling down in my direction. I awaited its approach with a considerable amount of anxiety, as I suspected a ruse, and that he was going to attack me. However, as he approached my level, the Pfalz, which was highly colored with a black body, white-tipped tail, silver and black checkered top surfaces, suddenly assumed a position on its back, and I noticed that the propeller was stopped. I flew close up to it, and to my horror, I saw the body of the pilot partially dangling out of the cockpit as if he were dead . . .

Another time, Mannock and Dolan were up, "and on seeing British Archie bursting on our side of the lines," they chased along to see what could be done. They spotted a Hun two-seater beetling back toward the lines, and got down just in time to prevent this.

The Hun crashed, but not badly, and most people would have been content with this—but not Mick Mannock, who dived half a dozen times at the machine, spraying bullets at the pilot and the observer, who were still showing signs of life. I witnessed this business, and flew alongside of Mick, yelling at the top of my voice (which was rather useless) and warning him to stop. On being questioned as to his wild behaviour, after we had landed, he heatedly replied: "The swines are better dead—no prisoners!"

Says Major Caldwell:

I can remember Mannock got a Hun when alone . . . when he attacked a Fokker scout just east of Ypres one afternoon in June. He attacked at short range, did a climbing turn to keep height in case the Hun zoomed, and never saw the Hun again. When he landed on the airfield he told me that he thought he could not very well have missed from such close range. . . . I rang up the Archie battery near Ypres and asked for a description of any combats between 7,000 feet and 10,000 feet just east of Ypres between 3 p.m. and 4 p.m. The reply came straight back that an SE-5 had shot down a Fokker. . . .

Van Ira describes an amazing feat at 12,000 feet:

. . . six Pfalz scouts flying east from Kemmel Hill direction. One he shot to pieces after firing a long burst from directly behind and above; another he crashed; it spun into the ground after it had been hit by a deflection shot; the other, a silver bird, he had a fine set-to with, while his patrol watched the Master at work. . . . First, they waltzed around one another like a couple of turkey cocks, Mick being tight on his adversary's tail. Then the Pfalz half rolled and fell a few hundred feet beneath him. Mick followed, firing as soon as he got in position. The Hun then looped—Mick looped too, coming out behind and above his opponent and firing short bursts. The Pfalz then spun—Mick spun also, firing as he spun. The Hun eventually pulled out; Mick was fast on his tail—they were now down to 4,000 feet. The Pfalz now started twisting and turning, which was a sure sign of "wind-up!" After a sharp burst close up, Mick administered the coup de grace, and the poor fellow went down headlong and crashed . . . a really remarkable exhibition of cruel, cool, calculated Hun-strafing. A marvelous show.

I asked Mick after he landed why he fired during the spin. He replied, "Just to intensify his wind-up." This was the first occasion that I have ever seen a machine loop during a fight. It was obvious to us, watching, that to loop under such circumstances is foolish. Mick managed, however, to keep behind him, and did not lose contact with him, although it was obvious by his maneuvers after he came out of the loop that the Pfalz pilot was all at sea, for he twisted and turned his machine in a series of erratic jerks, just as if he was a dog stung on his tail. Mick says he only looped as well for a bit of fun, as he felt his opponent was "cold meat." He says what he should have done instead of looping was to have made a zooming climbing turn as the Pfalz looped, then half-rolled and come back on his tail as he came out of the loop. By this means he would have been able to keep the Hun in sight all the time, while he would not have lost control of his machine as the Hun did while coming out of the loop.

Mick's other Hun was a two-seater, which he shot down after a burst at right angles. The old boy crashed into a tree near La Couranne, south of Vieux.

Four in one day! What is the secret? Undoubtedly the gift of accurate shooting, combined with the determination to get to close quarters before firing. It's an amazing gift, for no pilot in France goes nearer to a Hun before firing than the CO, but he only gets one down here and there, in spite of the fact that his tracer bullets appear to be going through his opponent's body!

Mick flattered us with his praises of our fighting efforts, but I have suspicions that he did not approve of either the cleanliness or the mode of our dress . . . we are not particular about our dress . . . believe in being comfortable today, as tomorrow we may be dead.

Mick, who had just landed, was the most disreputable of all . . . he was hatless, without a collar, his tunic open, his hair ruffled. . . .

The General said, "Which is Mannock?" Mick was duly pointed out to him. When he set eyes on him, I really thought he was going to pass right out. By a masterly effort, however, he pulled himself together and literally seemed to stagger up to Mick with his arm outstretched. Mick's dirty paw clutched the gloved hand and squeezed it in his usual hearty manner. [General] Plummer's face twitched, and for a second, I thought he was going to give a shout. "Mannock," he stammered, "let me congratulate you on your DSO."

This was the first intimation of Mick's well-deserved award which we've been expecting for some days. . . .

But by now Mick Mannock, the iron man, was breaking up. The death on July 9, 1918, of his old friend McCudden had affected him more than he knew. Yet he still flew, and almost every day—as if part of a ritual—brought down an enemy plane. Days of four or five kills came together. There was a time he was bedded with influenza, a bad case aggravated by nerves. When he went on his third tour of duty at the front, he passed along word to some friends he had had premonitions of his death. The number 3, he was sure, was unlucky. When he had leave from the 74th Squadron in June 1918 for another command, he wept openly in public before his comrades. He explained it by saying the influenza had weakened him, but it was clear there was more to his sadness, a true melancholy. He was malleable now, with soft spots in the metal.

Mannock began to doubt if he could kill a German just like *that*, coolly. A preoccupation with neatness, the fussiness of an old maid wanting everything in its proper place, overcame him. He took care to comb his hair in the tight larded fashion of tango dancers—he had his uniforms cleaned, even pressed. He sewed on that row of decorations most fliers literally died for. The once-dusty boots gleamed with polish. On his gramophone he played over and over "The Londonderry Air." He quietly told visitors he was approaching something final. He grew gallant with some nurses, joining them for tea, and met a young New Zealand flier, Donald Inglis, there. "Have you got a Hun, Inglis?" Inglis, flushed, admitted he hadn't, "Not yet, sir." Mannock set down his teacup. "Well, come on out, we'll get one . . . excuse us, ladies, for a few minutes."

However, Inglis's plane had a sick motor and Mannock flew alone. But it was clear he was hunting a close male friend—to replace the one he had lost. Life had become an intolerable malaise. The great cause, the revolution, would come, *if* it came, after he was gone. He sensed some failure, some flaw in his rationalist past.

Mannock swore to make a great many more kills for his dead friend, McCudden, as if offering up some pagan rite, human sacrifices to a dead comrade. Donald Inglis became his new friend.

On July 26, 1918, Mick let Lieutenant Inglis finish off a German plane for him; a ghastly game. But after Inglis had destroyed the doomed sacrifice and was following on Mannock's heels in the air as ordered, there was a swift change in the drama.

As Inglis told it,

Suddenly, he turned toward home, full out and climbing. A Hun, thought I, but I'm damned if I could find one; then a quick turn and a dive, and there was Mick shooting up a two-seater. He must have pegged the observer, as when he pulled up and I came in underneath him I didn't see the Hun shooting. I flushed the Hun's fuel tank and just missed ramming his tail as I came up, when the Hun's nose dropped. Falling in behind Mick again we did a couple of circles around the burning wreck and then made for home. I saw Mick start to kick his rudder and realized we were fairly low, then I saw a flame come out of the side of his machine; it grew bigger and bigger. Mick was no longer kicking his rudder; his nose dropped slightly and he went into a slow right-hand turn around about twice, and hit the ground in a burst of flame. I circled at about twenty feet but could not see him, and as things were getting hot, made for home and managed to reach our outposts with a punctured fuel tank. Poor Mick . . . the bloody bastards had shot my major down in flames . . .

Was he killed by a stray shot from a German soldier firing blindly upward? Or did Mick use that pistol for a last act of mercy on himself? Did he die inhaling fire, baking alive as he fell, that nightmarish final act he so dreaded and yet expected? We shall never know. The fire was so consuming there was almost nothing left to bury.

In July 1919, someone thought of awarding the Victoria Cross to Mannock, dead a year, credited with seventy-three victories. The citation—"This highly distinguished officer . . . an outstanding example of fearless courage . . . devotion to duty and self-sacrifice, which has never been surpassed . . ."—was the usual heroic cant, pious phrasings that were empty of the man's angry zeal, his strange hatreds, his vision of some better world where the dispossessed and the have-nots would make a garden of the world and there would be fish and chips for everybody.

2. | Albert Ball (1896–1917)

> *Blow out you bugles over the rich dead;*
> *There's none of these so lonely and poor of old,*
> *But dying has not made us rarer gifts than gold . . .*
> —RUPERT BROOKE

Albert Ball was one of those people whom the cynical slogan, "Die young and leave a beautiful body," might have fitted. But he did not at all fit that flip, gay young man one finds in the stylish tales by Saki—the knut, the lounge lizard of the period just before the Great War. Albert Ball was properly elated to be one of God's creatures, and he prayed in church with his head down and no shame at public worship. His father, Sir Albert Ball, was an alderman, and later mayor of Nottingham.

In 1914, at eighteen, young Albert joined up in the ranks of what was to become the first 100,000 victims of "the Donkey Generals." Stationed in Nottingham as one of the Sherwood Foresters, he was soon a sergeant. Then he requested a commission, and as a second lieutenant was sent to the North Midland Cyclist Corps. Using his spare time and the government-issue motorbike, he paid for flying lessons at Hendon Field. He didn't fly too well, but by January of 1916 he was with the RFC's 13th Squadron at the controls of a BE-2. In May he shifted over to fighters, flying a Nieuport Scout, and that month Ball downed his first enemy planes in the air.

Albert Ball was young, he was complex, he felt the all-seeing eye of God upon him. Yet he had a killer's instinct. He came early to the use of weapons: as a small boy he became a dead shot, training with tin cans as targets. In an odd way death was always with him; at the front he talked to soldiers of dying and sold land to them back home; something to leave their loved ones when they themselves were gone. It is a macabre story. At home he prayed for victory and grace and the hope of forgiveness for sin or wandered to the church at Shenley (a village in Hertfordshire).

Ball was one of those people who dream away their fantasies to the sound of music, for him the classics. He always carried his violin to the airdromes, to the flying fields; and on a sad night, after some bitter loss of personnel in the air, Ball's violin would be heard among the windy, dusty set of hangers and rusty tin huts that made up the flying unit. Schubert's *Unfinished Symphony* was his favorite.

In the air he flew with care, for he had not been a good flying student. He wore no helmet and loved to feel the wind whipping through his hair. He flew with a feeling that every Englishman indeed had to do his duty. He addressed himself to his stern God, declaring it was not hatred on his part but rather the need to keep the Hun out of England that kept him in the air. He did not see himself as engaged in a sport, as so many fliers did at the beginning of the war. He flew to kill Germans, and made no great fuss about it. He flew alone, the hunter. (Later, solo flying at the front was forbidden. Orders were that fliers should go in groups of three.)

He flew a Nieuport Scout which was fast, full of grace, with ease of control. It had speed, visibility, and could climb high to 10,000 feet in just over ten minutes. A Lewis gun was mounted over the pilot's head, fired by a Bowden release held in his hand.

Ball never became a great pilot; some lack of coordination or of mechanical sense prevented that. He had wrecked seven planes in training, and his landings were bad. Yet in his prime he spent as much as four hours a day flying.

He was intransigent and humorless; he made himself a kind of tent hut where he played his violin endlessly when not flying. If the night was warm enough, he could sometimes be seen in his pajamas, lighting a red flare stuck in the ground around which he would march as he played. There is no doubt that between his music, his ardent, almost bigoted hold on a Godhead, and his views of the rightness of England's war against the Hun, he had little contact with reality; even when he pressed off his Bowden button and the Lewis gun barked in his ear, and an enemy plane spun and whirled its pilot away in flames. He sensed death destroys man but gives him the last true perspective of existence.

But the oddest thing about Albert Ball emerges when one is trying to piece together a true picture of the facts of his battle record: Was he in fact a false hero, created deliberately by the press and the RFC? Or was he a true knight of the air? He hardly tried to record all his kills, as if this were bad luck. Others say he never actually shot down many German fighters. Officially, the score is forty-four victims.

His mother sent Albert packets of home-baked cake, and he would sit in the tall grass eating cake and practicing shooting with a Lewis gun. He was a remarkable shot. When not playing the violin, or shooting, he was planting cucumbers and peas from seeds he had asked his father to send out to him. The other pilots raged at Ball, claiming his vegetables were rot and scabs, but all ate them in the mess house.

During the dreadful Somme disaster of 1916, in the muck and rain, men dying in layers on the ground, he and his flight went up after enemy observation balloons. Ball downed one of the six his fellow pilots had gotten out of a field of twenty-three German gas sausages. Ball, unhappy at his low score, went up again and took some enemy shrapnel in his plane, which damaged it badly. But he did knock down one more balloon. The problem was getting back, for his ship was a flying wreck. Controls and fuel line were done in. His main top wing seemed ready to fly off and away. The machine shook like an animal about to die; fuel pressure was gone, and there was a mist over the home airdrome. Somehow he made it down and onto the field—by inches. He was awarded the Military Cross.

There is no doubt he was picked out to be made a national hero; special reports were ordered written of Albert Ball, and the strange road to the status of wartime folk hero was ready paved for him. He had been in France just over four months.

It should be said, however, that he himself ignored all this; he seemed more interested in trying to talk a French peasant out of manure for his vegetable patch.

German machine gunners were slaughtering the rows on rows of English youth marching into their crossfire. Ball heard that 80 per cent of his old friends in the Sherwood Foresters were gone. British air attacks were ordered on Bapaume, Cambrai, Busigny. Ball improved his battle skills by training himself to replace an ammunition drum and reload in the air, thus avoiding having to come down to earth to reload. As he killed, he tried to remain a Christian, unaware of the contradiction in terms. He was to say: "Nothing makes me feel more rotten than to see them go down . . . the Hun is a good chap with very little guts, trying to do his best."

Such a remark is the sign of a man not in tune with reality: the Germans at their best were superb fliers and fighters. His remark also showed a threatened breakdown of his nervous system. He asked for leave but was moved on to the RFC's 8th Squadron to fly a 90-horsepower BE-2C. He wrote home: "I am feeling in the dumps." The business of survival from minute to minute was fraying his nerves.

One day he attacked a German observation balloon, sending a few bursts into it, and the balloon observer jumped out to float down in a parachute rig. Ball did not fire at the man swaying below him. On the way home, his machine was badly damaged by enemy ground fire. One wing was gone, the main spar of the plane just holding on. Ball landed singing lustily. He remained damaged but not diminished.

The war produced its full share of spy stories, most of them invented or built up beyond the facts. The spies were not in fact much help to either the Allies or the Germans. Yet they existed. "M. Victor" was a spy the English planned to land behind the German lines. No one knows at this date just who "M. Victor" was; most likely a Frenchman or a Belgian attached to the RFC to ferret out enemy air secrets. We have to rely on what scanty facts there are. Anyway, three landing attempts had been bungled. Weather and poor flying were the excuses given around the airdrome. Albert Ball said, "I'd like to give it a go." "M. Victor" appeared and Ball took him up and headed for the drop point.

Here is Ball's own version of what happened next:

> We got over the lines and three Fokkers came after us. We had no gun, for the machine could not carry his luggage, etc., and guns, so we had to dodge the beasts. At last it was so dark they would not see us, so they went down. The Archie guns started, also rockets were sent up to try and set us on fire. Oh! It was nice. I really did think that the end had come. The planes were lit up with the flashes. However, at last we found a landing place and we started down. Naturally everything had to be done quickly or we would have been caught. But we got down! Picture my temper when we landed. The damned spy would not get out. The Fokkers had frightened him and he would not risk it. There was nothing to do but get off again before the Huns came along and stopped us, so off we went. I went down three times again after this, but the rotter refused to do his part . . .

By August 1916, Albert Ball was acting flight commander. He flew a great deal in mist, in foul gusts of cold rain. One evening, at the end of a bad day, he went up again after tea to protect bombers heading for a raid on Warlencourt Valley. The day was dank, the watery sun just setting when he sighted seven German machines, shark-nosed Rolands, flying in geeselike formation. Ball slid in behind them as part of their formation. The Germans had no idea he was there. He got the rear machine in his sights and poured in a deadly burst as the formation scattered. Ball pressed closer, still shooting. Holding the stick between his legs, he changed ammunition drums. With new bursts he saw another German crumple and fall. The gray sky was deepening and he could dodge about trying to avoid the remaining German gunners from getting a clear shot at him. He got away successfully, but ran into a new formation of Germans, five of them at 6,000 feet, south of Vaux. Ball never hesitated. His motto was: If it's there, kill it, or give it the old school try! Again he joined an unsuspecting enemy formation. He got the rear plane in the gas tank and it exploded like a rose of fire. The Germans now came at Ball from three directions. In the speeded-up confusion and the gathering dusk they all missed. But not Ball. He put five good rounds into a machine which went down to land on a house.

The three remaining Germans came in, losing all sense in their rage at this lone Englander. Ball dropped like a stone to 2,000 feet. The Germans gave it up as a bad job and Ball rode his machine home. It had one bullet hole in it; his timing had been assiduously accurate.

Some strange acid was in his veins that day. He asked for fresh drums of bullets and, with heated engine, heat-colored exhaust, went back into the air. Dusk had fallen like black pollen. From eight until nearly nine Ball moved over Vaux, seeing the bombers return—those he had started with as an escort. And *there*, suddenly, were three more German planes. A chase took place, a dozen Rolands after him. He dived, coming down nearly into the ground, the wind almost tearing him from the cockpit. But up he went again, firing as he came.

It was now time tò make sense of the odds piling up against him. He headed back to his base in his overheated, strained machine. The windscreen had taken four shots, the main plane spar was splintered. In all, eleven bullets had hit the machine. He landed with a dry tank.

It was suggested that a billboard be put up facing the Germans, lettered: ALBERT BALL. It would scare the bloody beggars into messing their trousers with fear. Ball, however, didn't see the humor of the suggestion. He continued to shoot down Germans, keeping no true record; and the habit grew of landing and going up again if he was not satisfied with the day's action. Home on leave in September 1916 he got the DSO with a bar. We don't know what music he played at home, what he spoke about to God in the village church. He was not yet twenty.

Back in France he went into fireworks, delivering to the enemy the deadly Le Prieur rockets, six to a batch, fixed onto a plane wing and fired by an electric connection. It was an early form of napalm, a deadly weapon, and Ball brought down many planes and balloons with it. If it failed, he ran them down to the ground with his Lewis gun. But he reached a breaking point. He told the medical officer he "had the shakes," and wrote home: "I do want to leave this beastly killing . . ." Yet he fought down his rebelling nerves and went on killing.

The Russians awarded him the Order of St. George, for no reason he could figure out, unless they were all in this cruel war together. He went on with those fantastic larger-than-life crusades of killing for England in the air—a kind of bitter persistence. He appeared vulnerable in his innocence to the murderer in man. War remained for him a merciless demand, and a hugging to himself of his eccentricities: his violin music, his gardening, his views of God as an Englishman.

Did he still parade around a flare in his pajamas, playing Schubert? Did he still recite Kipling? As his nerves gave out, his letters home began to show some grace of human pity. While he shot ceaselessly at balloons—the *drachens*—with the Le Prieur incendiary rockets, he worked out an over-simple and dreadful explanation of our plight here on earth: beside German fighters and *Der Rote Kampfflieger* in the skies there was also always his God.

Albert Ball was a God-filled man. He could be muddled and evasive, but never facetious. Yet he could never throw off the comfort of myths. He could write of the English as superior to all others; the Germans were "chaps whose brains had been pickled by all that sauerkraut." As for special graces, "Am indeed looked after by God . . . feeling very old just now." And schoolboy slang, "Terrifically topping."

Alone in his hut, nicknamed by the other fliers "Ball's Hermitage," he was still a snub-nosed adolescent with brown curly hair and the face of a boy going taut for all the fact of his being a hero (George V himself had pinned the DSO on his uniform jacket). Ball's confusion, as he saw it, was caused by the unpredictability of life. He hunted for some assurance that there was a relationship between life and order, beyond his fellow fliers posing for a picture in a picturesque grouping.

When in October 1916, in order to preserve the life of a popular hero, he was ordered to become a trainer of pilots, he objected and fought his transfer. But he was appointed a fighting instructor, and early in January 1917 his name was in the *London Gazette* section: "Mentioned in Dispatches."

He was offered £1,000 to resign from the RFC and become a director in a new airplane company. Nottingham presented him with "the freedom of the city." He became curt with people, even sullen. The death wish was pressing in on him. He wanted to get back to the front. He told his father no fighter pilot who "fought seriously could hope to escape from the war alive."

In a moment of lucid evocation he fell in love with a girl of seventeen and took her flying. The press wrote of "The Flying Romeo." There are hints that the affair was consummated. He gave her his identification disk and a copy of "Prayers" by Robert Louis Stevenson and sang for her "Thank God for a Garden."

Ball was posted to France and told the girl he hoped to get the Victoria Cross for her. She said she'd rather have Albert as a husband if he was promising gifts. Early in April 1917 he was in France with the 56th Squadron. He hated the SE-5 planes and got permission to fly his favorite, a Nieuport. He made more kills. But he tired again and a numbness came over him; the shaking spread to his limbs. He avoided everyone if he could and yawned with no control over his sleepy grimaces. He became short-tempered. His sense of fantasy grew; he appeared to be expecting the release of death at any moment. "I never met but one German aviator who really had courage."

On May 7, 1917, he led out a flight of SE-5's on a mean day. They flew in a gray-green drizzle. At 7,000 feet, visibility was blurred and runny like a dissolving world in a child's watercolor. Over Bourlon Wood, the headquarters of General von Bülow, they ran through a cloud bank. As they came out of it again, they saw that von Richthofen had his gaudy painted circus out. Both sides at once flew to engage, racing their motors to reach 100 miles an hour. A British plane fell from the terrible sky. Ball and a flier named Knaggs teamed up to charge into the German circus, firing their guns. But Ball, as if suddenly changing his mind, banked away from a German machine. The fight now spread out for miles in the darkling weather; guns sounded, plane wings dipped in the rain-scrubbed sky. There were running fights. Then as the night became opaque and thickened, each side began to gather its flying shapes and head for airdromes. The British made for Arras.

Ball's plane was dogged by one lone German over Fresnoy. Ball fired his gun at the persistent machine. Then both were swallowed up in a giant sea of clouds. Albert Ball vanished from the sight of his comrades at that moment, vanished forever.

A surviving British pilot, who last saw and searched for him, wrote: "The height was 4,000 feet . . . I knew my fuel must be running low. I reluctantly made for our lines . . ."

The rest we must put together from fragments of reports, newspapers, what may or may not be eyewitness accounts. Was he taken prisoner? Had he died and been so charred that his corpse could not be identified? (His identification disk hung between the breasts of an English girl.)

The French press headlined: *Ball Est Prisonnier . . . Un Anglais Disparu . . . La Chute de l'Aigle.*

It was claimed that one of the Germans shot down in the battle had been Lothar von Richthofen (brother of the baron), whose red Albatros was shot down by a triplane. But he landed with punctured petrol tanks. Near him was the wreck of an English plane, a tangle of smoking ruins, and from it was dragged the body of a young flier. The pockets contained clippings about a Captain Albert Ball and a well-worn cigarette case. However, the records show that Lothar at this time was in Berlin on sick leave!

Weeks later a Royal Navy flier who had been shot down was brought to Douai by the Germans and asked if he knew a Captain Ball. He said he had met the man once in his home town of Nottingham. Shown a much broken and badly preserved body, he said that was Ball, sure enough.

The Germans told him they had suspected as much. Actually, no one had reported this kill or claimed it. The credit was officially given to Lothar von Richthofen, but as he had only claimed a triplane (shot down from Berlin?) it is doubtful if the true killer of Albert Ball ever knew he had gotten the famous British ace.

Another version is that of a Captain Hunter. After he had been shot down and put into a German hospital, he was told that Ball had been killed. "On the following day the German brought Ball's identity disk [the duplicate?] and showed it to Hunter as proof . . . stating Ball was brought down by antiaircraft fire, and his machine was badly smashed up . . ."

One more version exists: "That's the end of your great Captain Ball . . . shot down by a lowly soldier hiding in a church tower . . ."

In the end the Germans sents over a scarlet Albatros to toss down a message onto a British flying field. It read: *RFC Captain Ball was brought down in an air fight on May 7 by a pilot of the same order as himself. He was buried at Annoeulin.* (A further contradiction.)

Whatever way Albert Ball died, his brief career was to symbolize a national hero for the British.

The Victoria Cross came posthumously—on June 3, 1917. Official record: forty-four kills.

CHAPTER 12

BATTLES OF EAGLES

In November 1916 the baron had won that great air fight with Major Hawker, VC. A fight between two deadly killers, witnessed by thousands of soldiers on both sides of No-Man's-Land between Bapaume and Albert. It was dubbed The Battle of Eagles.

The baron was a great scavenger. He had his men hunt out souvenirs—he treasured what could be found of Major Hawker's plane: cloth, wooden struts, fragments of engine parts. Hawker's machine gun he carried off proudly to hang over the doorway at home. *Liebe Mamma* hated the ugly thing, tried to talk him into removing it, but it hung there for many years.

There was something childish about this relish over the remains of Hawker's plane. For the Germans, hard-pressed in the war, the baron's glory was always kept fresh. He received the Austrian War Cross from the hands of the tottering Emperor Franz Josef (the café wits said, "*that* and a silver coin will get you a cup of coffee"). Women chased the baron, wrote baskets of letters, demanded his time, his body, offered devotion, or any release his Wagnerian passions might desire. Yet he did not lose control at this heady dosage of fame. At fetes, balls, celebrations, he felt flushed, in a state of embarrassment at all the adoration the nation bestowed on him. He knew his worth and wanted to be recognized; but not by this mass of staring, cheering faces, these people, starved, blockaded, a million losses across the nation, worndown folk, thin, wide-eyed children with pallid skins.

Von Richthofen had no philosophy to explain why horror on the civilian front had to be a part of war. He hated the fat and the new rich, growing ever fatter and richer on the profits of war; smuggling, black-marketing, controlling contraband, hoarding food, coal, supplies. George Grosz and Otto Dix, two rebel artists, were already beginning to draw the dreadful contrast between the top, middle, and bottom of the nation, all trapped in a war that was seemingly unending. But the baron lived protected in his vacuum of glory, his skilled moments of warfare. There is no evidence that he knew more than the stern test of duty and loyalty and survival, the attrition of spirit and flesh facing daily death in the ludicrous horror of air battles. He was safe, bedded in the absoluteness of his beliefs.

Then came love—as in a second-rate film or novel. A love at long distance. We know something about it, but historians have not yet discovered the name or station of the woman. It was all done by letters, or so it seems. But it was passion-filled. (George Bernard Shaw, when he too was involved in a love affair only by letter with the actress Ellen Terry, said: "Why not? Most fine moments, philosophies, ideas, beauties and satisfactions exist as yet only on paper.")

The baron in love went to great lengths to be sure his orderly got her letters to him as quickly as he could. Her handwriting was known to his batman, and when von Richthofen's scarlet plane was sighted over the airfield, the orderly was there, waiting, with a packet of letters from the lady. So eager was the lover that he would leap out, seize and open the letters, indifferent to the other pilots and airfield staff. There he stood, grimy from battle, often fresh from some sudden death, avidly reading the letters from the woman of his desires.

Very little else is known. He took few leaves, and when he did, he still went home to *Liebe Mamma*. There is no record he ever brought the woman home to meet his family. Certainly, love made him no tenderer in the air.

The English flier William Ivamy vividly remembers his meeting with von Richthofen in the air around this time:

> German planes were in position on four sides of us and above. Directly the DH-4's had dropped their bombs, they turned for home, and this evidently was the signal for the Germans to attack, and the lot of them came down on us with a bang. Their

plan of attack was to get anyone with streamers on. As deputy flight commander, I flew these streamers from my wing struts, and being in the rear of the flight and highest up, I can't say that I had much of a fight with his highness the baron, as I was slightly handicapped almost from the start, having an explosive bullet in the petrol tank and the emergency tank being punctured.

I was saturated and blinded with petrol and sitting up there with a dead engine. There was nothing to do but descend, which I did in a veering nosedive. I have a faint recollection of the speed indicator going off the scale, but the old Sopwith hung together, and I made the best landing I ever made—up the side of a hill among a bunch of German infantry who were training for the big push. They appeared none too friendly with their rifles. By the time I could get out of the bus, three German planes were buzzing around over it, and the scrap up above seemed to be over.

I looked up and saw that the SE-5's had pulled away a bit to the north, so that we were rather in the soup. We lost five of our nine; the flight leader, two deputy flight leaders, and two new fellows, three of them prisoners and two killed. The SE-5's lost two and the bombers one, and I don't know what the German casualties were. . . .

The Canadian flier, Wilfred May, also met the Red Baron, but was unaware of it. Describing the end of a fight,

. . . one of my guns jammed and then the other. I could not clear them, so I spun out of the mess and headed west by the sun. When I leveled off, I looked around, but nobody was after me—or so I thought. Feeling pretty good at having extricated myself, the next thing I knew I was being fired at from behind! All I could do was try and dodge my assailant, which was a red triplane. Had I known it was Richthofen, I probably would have fainted . . .

Perhaps the baron was in a hurry to get back to his mail.

The wounding of von Richthofen took place in July 1917, when, as Commander A. E. Woodbridge remembers it, six British FE-2's ran into eight enemy planes.

Cunnell handled the old FE for all she was worth, banking her from one side to the other, ducking dives from above and missing head-on collisions by bare margins of feet. The air was full of whizzing machines, and the noise from the full-out motors and the crackling machine guns was more than deafening. The Jerries showed more spirit than usual. . . . This enabled us to fire from the closest range and was really to our advantage. Cunnell and I fired into four of the Albatroses from as close as thirty yards, and I saw my tracers go right into their bodies. Those four went down. . . . Some of them were on fire —just balls of flame and smoke, you know—a nasty sight to see, but there was no time to think about it at the moment.

Two of them came at us head-on, and I think the first one was Richthofen. I recall there wasn't a thing on that machine that wasn't red, and gosh, how he could fly! I opened fire with the front Lewis, and so did Cunnell with the side gun. Cunnell held the FE on her course, and so did the pilot of the all-red scout. Gad! With our combined speeds, we must have been approaching each other at somewhere around 250 miles an hour. . . . I kept a steady stream of lead pouring into the nose of that machine. He was firing also. I could see my tracers splashing along the barrels of his Spandaus and I knew the pilot was sitting right behind them. His lead came whistling past my head and ripping holes in the bathtub [cockpit].

Then something happened. We could hardly have been twenty yards apart' when the Albatros pointed her nose down suddenly and passed under us. Cunnell banked and turned. We saw the all-red plane slip into a spin. It turned over and over and round and round. It was no maneuver. He was completely out of control. His motor was going full on, so I figured I had at least wounded him. As his head was the only part of him that wasn't protected from my fire by his motor, I thought that was where he was hit. . . .

This was the scalp wound from which von Richthofen developed, for a time, very bad headaches.

Being attacked and shot down by von Richthofen gave little chance of survival. One who did live to tell the tale was Second Lieutenant F. J. Kirkham of the RFC's 13th Squadron, who was flying with Lieutenant Follet as pilot:

Flying along, observing for artillery, suddenly . . . a burst of machine gun fire came to my ear directly behind me. I turned quickly and stood up to man the rear gun. I was too late. The red Albatros had continued its dive downward just in back of our tail and was way out of range. He must have been doing 150 miles an hour. He was away in the flash of an eye. I saw two others swing by. . . . They had taken us quite by surprise. . . . Poor old Follet had crumpled up and fallen forward on the stick. I couldn't see his face, but I knew that some of that first burst had hit him. His body on the stick sent the plane down in a steep dive. He must have rolled off it, however, because we seemed to straighten out once or twice.

We were going down at a frightful rate. There was a dual control stick in my seat which I might have rigged and pulled her out of the dive, but that would have meant turning my back to the Hun's scouting machine, and I should have got it the same as Follet. I thought everything was over but the finale, so I just stuck to the rear gun and fired away at him in the hope that I might get him also . . . I emptied the entire drum without effect. The red scout stuck close on the tail, and his two machines were pumping lead all the time.

I had a number of bullet splashes on my face and hands. The sleeves and shoulders of my flying jacket had several dozen holes through them and then one bullet hit the barrel of the machine gun right under my nose. I remember looking over my shoulder, and the ground didn't seem over ten feet away. I closed my eyes and said good night. . . .

But luck was with me. The plane hit a clump of small trees in the German big-gun positions. I woke up while German gunners were cutting me out of the wreckage. The first thing I heard was Follet's voice: "God, we're on fire!" he shouted weakly. I think he must have been unconscious and raving. The tanks had split wide open and gasoline was over us and everything, but no fire started. . . .

Another survivor who lived to tell of it was a Lieutenant Heagerty. The von Richthofen squadron had been lying in ambush,

. . . and they dived down on us from out the sun. They seemed to drop down in all directions, pumping lead as they came.

Cantle was working the aft Lewis, and I heard him let out a good blast at someone at the back of us. At the same time, a spray of lead whipped past my head, and several bullets tore through the woodwork beside me. I kicked over the rudder just in time to see the red plane passing below. He swerved at the same time, and round and round we went, each trying to get on the other's tail.

With six or seven planes all mixed up and diving around, it took all my attention to avoid collisions, but I managed to rip out several bursts from the forward-firing Vickers. . . . Cantle's gun was rattling away, when suddenly he ceased firing, and at the same time the pressure on the joystick was suddenly released. It was useless. My controls had been shot away. They must have gone in the same burst that killed Cantle. . . .

All the way down the red machine, or some machine, kept right at the back of me, ripping burst after burst of machine gun bullets into the plane from the rear. I remember seeing the windshield in front of my face fly away in small pieces, and then the propeller stopped. Our speed was terrific . . . I could only hope to get her out of that dive. I recall putting my weight on one foot on the rudder and seeing one wing tip swing towards the ground, which was coming up at a fearful rate. That was my last recollection . . . crash . . .

Heagerty recovered with a fractured jaw.

The baron showed no such British casualness when he re-counted an air adventure of April 1917. To von Richthofen any-one attacking him was "impertinent" or "prey," as he put it.

I was still in bed when my orderly rushed into the room and exclaimed, "Sir, the English are here!" Sleepy as I was, I looked out . . . and there were my dear friends circling over the air-field. I jumped out of bed and into my clothes in a hurry. My red bird had been pulled out of the hangars and was ready to go. My mechanics knew that I would probably not allow such a favorable moment to go by unused. . . . I snatched my furs and went up.

I was last to start. My comrades had started earlier and were much nearer to the enemy. I feared that my prey would escape me and that I should have to look on from a distance while the others were still fighting.

Suddenly, one of the impertinent Englishmen tried to drop down upon me. I allowed him to approach me quite near, and then we started a merry quadrille. Sometimes my opponent flew on his back and sometimes he did other tricks. He was flying a two-seater fighter. I realized very soon that I was his master and that he could not escape me. During an interval in the fighting, I assured myself that we were alone. It followed that the victory would belong to him who was calmest, who shot best, and who had the cleverest brain in a moment of danger.

Soon I had got him beneath me without having seriously hurt him with my gun. . . . Suddenly, when he was only a few yards above the ground, I noticed how he once more went off on a straight course. He tried to escape me. That was too bad.

I attacked him again, and to do so I had to go so low that I was afraid of touching the roofs of the houses in the village beneath me. The Englishman defended himself up to the last moment. At the very end I felt that my engine had been hit. Still I did not let go. He had to fall. He flew at full speed right into a block of houses. . . .

However, in my opinion, he showed, after all, more stupid foolhardiness than courage. It was again one of the cases where one must differentiate between energy and idiocy. . . . He paid for his stupidity with his life.

The baron never changed the flaming scarlet color of his plane; the leader could not go into hiding. His reports of kills remained stark and direct: "The plane I had singled out, caught fire after I had sent 150 shots into it from 50 yards. . . . The plane fell burning. . . . The occupant of the plane fell out of it at the height of 500 yards. . . . Baron von Richthofen."

The fallen flier in this particular case was an untried pilot, John Hay, flying an FE-8, escorting two camera planes. The Red Baron had almost torn Hay's plane to bits with his fire. Hay, dead or alive, dropped 1,000 feet and thudded to death in the middle of a Canadian regiment. They buried him near Aix-Moulette, in a grave marked for the War Graves Commission only as R30, a.92.

Ironically, John Hay was so new to the RFC at the front that there is no record, officially, of his flying at all that day. It took the bureaucrats some time to accept the grave as conclusive evidence that there was a dead flier in it.

The baron did not like to hunt British camera planes. He preferred to rush on ahead and engage in combat with his equals, the Allied fighter pilots. But under orders, he did go after the camera planes, in a foul temper. They were slow ducks in the air, with their pusher propellers and 160-horsepower Beardmore engines; they carried two Lewis guns, one forward, one in the rear. Because of their mountings, they could not fire toward the earth, nor much behind them. Flying against these camera planes was the new B.U. Albatros, a shiny sharklike machine driven by a 200-horsepower Mercedes engine. It could climb into the sky three times faster than anything the Allies sent against it, and two heavy machine guns were synchronized to fire through the propeller.

It was against such power that the 25th Squadron of the RFC sent out a camera plane to fly over Vimy Ridge on January 23, 1917. Captain O. Grieg was pilot, Second Lieutenant J. E. MacLenan observer. (It is hard, as we've said, to find first names spelled out in many official records.) Their job was to take a whole series of pictures which would be tacked together later to give a full picture of that sector of the front. The plane, with a companion machine, had to fly at a certain speed and height in order to get the proper pictures. There was an escort of three fighters for the two camera carriers.

Out of some place in the sky, the Richthofen Circus suddenly attacked. Bullets began to stream into the slow ship, and Captain Grieg grunted as he looked down and saw his leg torn to fragments, blood pouring over everything. Trying to regain control, he found that either shock of battle or the dreadful wounds had tied him immovably. His nerveless dead feet, or what was left of them, could not shift the controls.

Falling to one side, he forced himself to grab the joystick and tried to pull the plane out of its dive. The Red Baron was still firing at him; no mercy from that quarter. Bursts hit the gasoline tank. Oil lines were severed, the pressure fell; oil spurted and everything it touched turned to black glacé kid.

MacLenan discarded his camera, turned toward his Lewis gun,

and began firing. The baron, making a turn to bank, was back, his guns blazing, doing great damage. The British shook their fists at him, schoolboy gesture. Grieg was nearly blinded by the blood from his face wounds blurring his vision.

MacLenan kept firing his Lewis gun. The Red Baron seemed no more affected by it than by the buzzing of gnats. The British plane was falling, but slowly. The scarlet machine came in closer to look over the situation and finish it off with his two guns blazing. The British, however, were still in action. A burst from the Lewis caught the machine's plane surface, tearing and breaking. Like a new raw cadet, the baron had let down his guard, been too sure of his kill. Now his Albatros, mortally wounded somewhere, was not properly responding to the controls.

The battered British machine crash-landed and the humiliated baron made a quick, jolting, and undignified landing a quarter mile beyond them.

MacLenan pulled the badly injured Grieg to safety. As German land forces came up on the run, he calmly went back to the camera plane, found a flare pistol, and fired into the cockpit, starting an immediate blaze.

Von Richthofen, however, was badly shaken up by his near escape from death. He had become careless; his Prussian pride was irked at how slack he had been there, for that one slim moment. His report was sober:

> After a long fight, I forced my enemy to make a landing near Vimy. The occupants burned the plane when they landed. I myself had to land, having cracked one wing when at an altitude of 900 feet. I was flying the Albatros D-III.
>
> According to the English fliers, my red painted plane was known to them, for on being asked, "Who brought you down?" they said, "*Le petit rouge.*"
>
> Freiherr v. Richthofen

The baron was now entering his final phase as a killer. It had become more than duty to the Luftstreikrafte, more than the thrill of the hunt. A strong streak of sadism appeared: such cruelty for the sake of cruelty that even his comrades noticed. He calmly shot at men lying badly wounded on the ground after escaping from crashed planes. He shot men in desperate straits trying to turtle their way out of the cockpit of a doomed ship. He was not a good companion, not talkative, not known to smile at table jests quoted from the *Frankfurter Zeitung*. He was only seen to smile when he had done some daring in the skies.

His men were rigidly disciplined, and von Richthofen himself tried to show them—by example—how an officer of a Jagdstaffel and a German should act. Another strange manifestation of his change was an unhealthy interest in the men he had killed; men immolated in a sky-borne pyre. It was as if he were the high priest of some sacrificial altar he maintained in the sky and supplied with bodies. He talked of his kills and those he would make with a morbid compulsion that grew more and more macabre.

His strange omen of fortune, a sort of potent charm, was a clear photograph of a dreadfully shot apart pilot's body.* It had been a gift to von Richthofen from "An Admirer." On the back, the person had written:

> Sir, I witnessed on March 17, 1917, your air battle and took this photograph which I send you with hearty congratulations, because you so seldom see your prey. *Vivat sequens.* [Here's to the next.] With fraternal greetings, Baron von Riezenstein, Colonel, Commander, 87th Reserve Infantry Regiment.

It held the baron, this horrible image, and he grew to enjoy inflicting the sight of it on many people.

The baron's reports grew simpler and more direct. "After a short fight, my opponent's plane lost both wings and fell. The machine crashed into No-Man's-Land and was fired upon by our infantry." He still celebrated each kill with a silver cup, engraving on it the date and other data. By March 26, 1917, thirty-one of these little silver cups were on show in his quarters.

In one month over his sector, the Allies lost 151 airplanes. The German war effort was in desperate condition, however, and the United States of America had entered the war. Could they fight? When the Americans came, flying Allied models, they were met with Albatros and Halberstadt fighters; better climbers, faster

---

* The victim in the picture was Lieutenant A. E. Boultbee, whose body was found in a trench at Oppy.

The Red Baron (in the cockpit of the Albatros) and some of his pilots

Reed Chambers, 94th Squadron, U.S. Air Force, and his Spad   U.S. Air Force

Oswald Boekke

Baron von Richthofen

Max Immelmann

W. Leefe Robinson, recipient of the
Victoria Cross

James McCudden, recipient of the
Victoria Cross

L. G. Hawker, recipient of the
Victoria Cross

Rene Fonck, French ace

Charles Nungesser, French ace

Mata Hari became the mistress of the French ace Nungesser to gather French Air Force secrets.

Count Zeppelin, inventor

Eddie Rickenbacker, American ace

Eddie Rickenbacker and Douglas Campbell in front of a Nieuport 28

Frank Luke, Jr., American ace   U.S. Air Force

U.S. Air Force DH-4 with Liberty motor   U.S. Air Force

Nieuport 17

De Havilland DH-4

Americans on their way to France pose (badly) for sexiest picture of the war

Albatros D-III

English SE-5

Ypres—July 1918. RAF Squadron No. 1

Model of Sopwith Camel

Model of Spad XIII

Model of the Red Baron's Fokker triplane

Nieuport 28

Revell

Fokker DR-I

Revell

Sopwith triplane

Albert Ball in an SE-5

Reconnaissance bomber, BE-2C

Sopwith Snipe

German Rumpler

Sopwith Camel

Sopwith Pup

Fokker D-VIII

Spad VII

The horse lovers—General Kitchener and aides, in spurs, mistrusted the warplane

Anthony Fokker and
Hermann Goering.
Both survived the war.

Ernst Udet and Fokker D-VII

Gotha gunner breathing oxygen

British two-crew RE-8

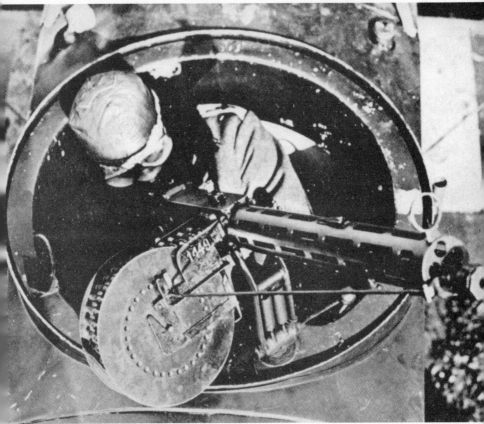

Rear gunner with German Parabellum machine gun

Curtiss Jenny—U.S.A. training plane

Von Richthofen, the day he died   Imperial War Museum

The British bury the Red Baron   Imperial War Museum

ones too, than any they usually flew—and with an ease of handling, carrying powerful twin guns.

The Allied fliers had to improvise air procedures; such skills as Ring-o'-Roses, which was to circle a German until slightly above him and on his tail, then fire into him. While slower British machines could dive at speeds to amaze anyone watching, these fantastic dives had to be pulled out of at 500 feet, or the machine would screw itself into the earth and explode. At such low altitudes, the Allied planes could then escape to their airdrome, hedge-hopping toward a home base.

In the so-called "Bloody April" of 1917 the German ground forces were retreating toward the Hindenburg Line. The Americans were indeed the fresh blood and bodies needed to revitalize the Allies, the worn-down mutinous French, the casualty-haunted British with their hundreds of thousands of dead.*

Supplies were coming across the Atlantic in greater and greater strength. Now the Jagdstaffel 2 and other units were sent into the sky to cover the pullback to the Hindenburg Line—to damage and blunt as much of the enemy advance as they could. The baron and his brother Lothar engaged in violent, prolonged warfare in the air.

After one kill, the Richthofens got into a car and drove out to see their victims, the broken British planes, the bloody mess that was all that remained of its fliers. The baron took pictures. Someone later quoted the old German proverb, "Birds of prey do not sing."

The day turned to snow. On their return, the baron went up into an air fight and shot down an enemy plane. But the pilot landed with enough strength left to set fire to his machine, and von Richthofen flew low enough to see what was on the ground. Commented the baron on sparing the flier's life: "He was one of the few lucky fellows who escaped with their lives. I felt very merry as I flew home, my thirty-third plane downing to celebrate."

---

*In the first major war of the twentieth century, the casualties shocked the world. Since then, talks of 75 million dead, on either side, at a first atomic strike are shrugged off.

In the official report he stated that he had killed the flier on the ground. "I once more attacked him already on the ground and killed . . ." On one dead flier a book of poems was found, with a line of Pope's underscored: "A mighty hunter, and his prey was Man . . ."

The baron continued victorious on his hunting grounds, the skies over Lembras, southwest of Douai, and over Quincy. The base of the Jagdstaffel was at Douai, and the Red Baron had become the obsession of the British air force. They decided to destroy Douai Airdrome on April 5, 1917, to pulverize it and its planes on the ground. But someone talked, or else German Intelligence was deeply imbedded in the RAF, for the plan came as no secret to the Germans. The baron was told he could do what he liked: evacuate the field, or stay and fight off the raiders.

He chose to order a splendid dinner for his senior pilots, and stay put. They sat down a few hours before the raid was due. It was a good rich meal under the Teutonic eagle. The wine was from the best French cellars; there was even coffee. (In an army where parched acorns were the normal brew, real coffee was a constant dream.) The fliers, however, were ill at ease, sucking their cigars a bit too hard. Heads were turned toward the baron, who was explaining to his *Korpsbruder* with professional pleasure some of the fighting tactics of the British in the air. He dissected the Sopwith machine, explained just where were the blind spots in the plane for a sure cool kill. He talked of his victories in aerial combat. The pilots swallowed hard and listened. But it was a strain. Then, as one eyewitness remembers the evening, a phone rang. The message was: "English bombers are on their way."

The baron smiled, picked up a bottle of wine and some glasses, and said calmly, "Gentlemen, come."

They went down into a deep dugout shelter, and the baron later wrote home that they had a very merry time of it. He kept the wine flowing, told jokes, made ribald jests, commenting on life, sex, and other topics of men at war. Would the damn English never find the field? Von Richthofen had no great respect for British methods of air navigation. He brooded, smiled, suggested it would be a lark to get above ground and climb into their machines and make a good fight of it. Yes . . . but it would be best to wait until they heard the British motors. No use wasting petrol sitting in the sky.

Impatient, the baron came above ground. There was a gathering dusk. The air was still; not a sound. Nothing. Then a low humming, which meant a single plane. A low-flying plane finally appeared, but its motor went silent.

Oberleutnant Wolff at the baron's side said, "Well now, we're for it."

It was foolish to try to reach the lone flier with carbines, but two men did fire off a few shots. The antiaircraft batteries held their fire. Then, all at once, the searchlights went on and the lone plane was clearly outlined overhead pronged by forks of criss-crossed lights. A half mile away, it was still coming toward them in a steady glide, motor off. Then the motor came on with a roar. The plane flew directly overhead, dropping its deadly load of phosphorus bombs, trying for hangars and machine shops. All cursed as the shops were hit and badly damaged.

Above the lone Englishman—somewhere—were thirty-six English pilots who had come from Izel-le-Hammeau with more bombs: 22-pounders that could do enormous damage. Seventeen of the planes had now found the airfield, lit by searchlights and phosphorus fires, and began circling and dropping their bombs. The sound of their engines was deafening as it accompanied the bomb bursts. Hangars caught fire, fuel tanks, ammunition dumps, administration buildings. The antiaircraft gunners went on pumping shells into the sky. They would explode like red roses opening, someone noticed, only to be clouded out by their own smoke and the night.

Not one British plane was put out of action, and they even went home to reload and return for more bombing. The fires on the ground were doing great damage; shell explosions, gasoline roaring up in tongues of flame. Von Richthofen himself acted as a fire-fighting director. Some captured French water pumpers helped a bit, but not much. The second run of British raiders with fresh bombs hit two major hangars.

So the havoc of the night wore on. The danger above ground was considerable and the German fliers went back to their deep shelters.

They drank the rest of the wine. The baron explained that there was no way of fighting back on such a dark night. Planes and major fuel dumps were burning. "It will be perhaps half a day before the fires will die down, gentlemen, and make it possible to assess our losses. Drink up!"

Daylight amidst smoke and stubborn fires showed that the damage was indeed great, and the runways full of craters. The British came back again the next night and the baron set up machine guns and armed everyone on the airfield with rifles and pistols. The firepower aimed at the first raiding plane was huge, but ineffective. The Englishmen came so low over von Richthofen that he had to duck into the shelter. When he came above ground again, there were thirteen British bombers dropping deadly high explosives on the remaining hangars, fuel and ammunition dumps, and hitting them. After which they attacked the antiaircraft positions and searchlight crews. Diving directly into the lights, the British machines did fearful damage among the field crews, then dropped bombs to complete the ruin of the defense system. It was sheer carnage.

Only one British plane was lost.

The Red Baron was outraged at the damn islanders' skill and courage. When he could again take to the air, he killed and killed in revenge. On one particularly good day, the Richthofen Jagdstaffel scored thirteen enemy kills.

When the baron had made his forty-fifth kill, he was invited to have lunch with the Kaiser, and also found time to do some game-bird shooting. Back to the war, he found that his group now held the record of twenty-three Allied planes shot down in one week as reported in the *Neueste Nachrichten*, the German army newspaper . . . The success of Richthofen's fliers continued for almost a year to delight the German population.

CHAPTER 13

TWO LIVES

1. | Ernst Udet (1896–1941)

"All mythology opens with demigods . . ."
—RALPH WALDO EMERSON

Most of the fliers carried into the war some ghost out of their past. Young as they were, many had been warped, pernickety, and querulous in childhood. Some damage had gnawed at them. These considerations have hardly been gone into in accounts of that period of war flying. Ernst Udet, who had sixty-two accredited victories, and who survived into World War II (to commit suicide with his pearl-handled Luger when wrongly blamed for the failure of the Battle of Britain) was one of these cursed children.

His father was the typical German *hausherr*, the dominating, cruel, insensitive male of fiction. Ernst, as a small boy, was fully brutalized. The father wanted a tough son, and the boy showed instead a talent for art, an interest in music. He was forced into wild rough sports. He was made to see—with the aid of blows— that a good German was one who studied the sciences that would give the *Vaterland* a place in the sun by its strength, cunning, and fury. Udet was small, delicate, thoughtful, sad, not *ein lustiger bruder* (a jolly guy) at all. But he had to prove his manhood; he had to show the coarseness that was Teutonic pride. His sensibilities were rubbed raw. In order to survive, he became sly—a doubter of all virtues.

Ernst never gave up the drawing he loved. During the war he made some fine pictures of planes and men; but he hated the physical side of wartime life—and so he was sidetracked into a life of drink ("Alcohol makes sharp the artist's perception"), a seeking of rich food, a hedonism that ended in orgies, a libertine's way with too many women. Udet's is such a perfect case history that we often overlook his charm, his true artistic side, and his skill as a flier.

His father approved of his learning to fly in 1913. That was a dangerous game, a male world. The father even put up money to keep the flying club active. Udet, however, had at that time no true interest in flying and drifted away to more voluptuous games, a jaunty figure once out of his father's sight.

As a boy he had tried other forms of air travel. From the family's first balcony, he had dropped himself into space with an open umbrella, wearing roller skates as shock absorbers. The head of a passing policeman broke his fall. Nothing daunted, he then made a small Zeppelin out of one of his mother's ample dresses. He filled it with house gas, and, unaware of the explosive power of the gas, set a lighted candle under it. The resulting blast was not enough to kill him, but it cured his interest in experiments through space.

His interests as he grew up shifted to the pleasures of food, of drink, and his first awareness of the undulant movement of girls, the pleasures of the female body. It was the kind of life his father disapproved of, which only gave it more spice. In his first letters home as a soldier, at eighteen, he was already taunting his father about the frivolous life he led.

When war came, he had gone into the 26th Württemberg Reserves as a motorcyclist. To his father he wrote bitterly: "You have often accused me of being a coward. I think you are wrong. I am off to the front tomorrow, and I hope soon to win the Iron Cross. . . . Should I be killed, it will be a worthy end to my frivolous life . . ."

He was soon waylaid and wounded by a French patrol and ended up in the hospital at Strasbourg. Losing his regiment on his recovery, he became an army mailman. The dull safe life was spiced by Udet's constant seeking out of fine food and women. Meeting another lover of good food, Oberleutnant Waxheim of a flying scout unit, the two shared the joys of rare French dishes and the flesh triumphant. The war seemed on another planet.

Then Udet applied for transfer to a flying group. Waxheim was killed by one of the first French planes to have gear enabling it to fire through its propeller, but the awareness of danger didn't dampen Udet's desire to fly. He completed his training, got his wings, and was soon flying out of Heilenkrenz, near Colmar. It was scout work, not fighting, however.

One day, Udet and his observer came across a French plane shooting up a railroad station and dropping exploding darts. They saw the French plane go dead in the air: its propeller stopped spinning, and the ship began a glide toward the earth.

They followed it down and saw a group of German horsemen capture both plane and its pilot. It was Roland Garros, and the capture (as we have seen) was to prove a very significant one.

Udet soon showed himself a remarkable flier and fighter, piling up amazing kills. He had begun with the Fliegerabteilung 206, flying Aviatik planes with an observer. In airfield slang, the pilot was *"Emil"* and the observer *"Franz"*; the first adventure of this *Emil und Franz* was nearly their last. A bracing wire on a wing snapped and the wing began to wave recklessly in the breeze. The ship went into a sliding dive to the left; the right wing being on the rise drove the left one down. It was impossible to keep the plane on the level. They kept falling. Franz got out on the wing to try to balance the plane with his weight. Still Udet couldn't move the stick to right the ship properly. The observer climbed back in, kicked out the panel separating him from the cockpit, and added his own muscle power to Udet's.

This helped. But they were now over Switzerland. They steered slowly for Germany, and just made it across the border to come down in a hay field. There had been a defect in the batch of planes delivered (two other fliers were killed the same day in the same kind of accident). Both men received the Iron Cross, Udet the Second Class, the observer the First Class.

Udet had two more crashes before he went up in single-seater fighters.

By the end of 1915, he was flying over the Vosges front in cold clear weather. Coming on a French Caudron in his superior Fokker E-I, he had a clear shot, but suddenly got buck fever. He couldn't press the trigger. The French flier pressed off a burst that riddled Udet's plane, shattering his flying goggles. Udet could have been killed or blinded but miraculously escaped both fates. He dived and went home painfully picking glass slivers out of his eyes.

He had, it was clear, no desire to kill, so he trained himself deliberately to overcome this. It was not manly at nineteen, in time of war, to have no desire to commit legal murder in the air. It was an irrevocable decision—he may have been aware of Kafka's advice: "In your battle with the world, always bet on the world."

In March 1916, Udet found himself involved with a group of French Farmans on a bombing raid over Mulhouse. Udet went into a dive right into the middle of the group, and at 100 feet began firing. The French gunners spattered his plane with bullets but he went on calmly firing at the target he had picked. Finally, it took a hit in the engine and coughed fire. Udet dived past the burning plane and leveled off after a fall of 1,000 feet. The stricken Farman was burning like a torch and spinning head over tail toward the earth. One of its fliers, still alive, fell out and went down spinning his arms about as if attempting to steer himself down for a landing.

By August of 1917, Ernst Udet was commanding Jasta 37 in Flanders, at Wynghene near the North Sea. Still boyish, his flying uniform often too large for him, he continued to clock up spectacular air victories.

In March 1918, Udet was stationed at Le Cateau, in very rainy weather, watching the Jasta settle into its new quarters. There was mud on the airfield, that special glue of northern Europe in bad weather. In *Ace of the Black Cross*, Udet tells what happened next.

We set to work erecting the big marquees for airplanes by the side of the road leading to Le Cateau. It was raining, a penetrating drizzle that was slowly and surely coating everything in liquid mire.

I had pulled on a leather jacket and was helping my mechanics to drive in the tent pegs, when a motor car came by. So many cars passed us that we took no notice of it. We continued our work, silently and doggedly.

Then I felt a tap on the shoulder and, turning around, I saw Richthofen. Rain trickled from the peak of his cap and ran down his face.

"How d'you do, Udet," he said, negligently acknowledging my salute. "Nice weather we're having today."

I looked at him and noted the calm expression and the cold eyes, half-shaded by heavy lids. He looked older than I had imagined, older than a man of his age ought to look. But he was the fighter who had already brought down no fewer than sixty-eight enemy aircraft—our best ace.

His car was waiting alongside the road, and he had climbed down the embankment to speak to me. I waited.

"Udet," he asked me, "how many have you shot down to date?"

"Nineteen recognized, one waiting for confirmation," I replied.

He raked the mud with the tip of his walking stick.

"Hmm, twenty," he commented. Then he raised his eyes and scrutinized me for a while. "That about qualifies you to join us. Would you care to?"

Would I care to? It was the most attractive suggestion anybody had ever put to me. If it had rested with me, I would have packed up and gone with him at that very moment. There were many good outfits in the German air service, and Jasta 37 was by no means the worst of them. But there was only one Richthofen *geschwader*.

"Jawohl, Herr Rittmeister," I said, scarcely able to contain my elation.

We shook hands and he left.

I watched him—a slender, fragile-looking fellow—as he climbed back up the slippery embankment. . . .

Ten days later, Udet was a member of the famous von Richthofen Circus, flying in Jasta 2. At noon he joined the baron and his squadron on a patrol. Flying at 1,500 feet in the direction of Avesnes-le-Sec, they met a British RE-8 spotter plane. A signal sent Udet after the enemy. He passed in front of the Britisher and shot at the engine, which caught fire almost within hand reach of him. The plane fell and Udet moved back into formation like a good hound rejoining the pack.

They came over a road with old trees, wrecked and battered. Below, the color and movement of troops were animated under the tree limbs. The baron led them down to near tree-top level and began gunning at the men flinging themselves into any kind of shelter. The planes leveled off and went roaring up the road, firing. The soldiers began to shoot their rifles and many of the planes took bullet holes. The Germans made a turn and swept the road again, then headed for home. A day's work done.

After they landed, the Red Baron went to ask Udet a question. "Do you always, Udet, attack your man from the front?"

"It works well sometimes."

"Hmmm . . . By the way, you take over Jasta 2 tomorrow."

Udet, in a state of shock, could not reply.

As acting commander of Jasta 2, he continued to be a deadly killer in the air. Early in April 1918, one of his ears became infected. The cold, the wet, the open cockpit flying, and the rapid changes from warm indoors to freezing outdoors; all this made throat and ear infections an occupational hazard. The pain grew; it was unbelievable how much he could endure. There were times when it was so great that Udet had periods of blindness. Yet, by some strange code of duty, he kept himself flying. One didn't let the baron down. It was that way often on both sides of the line. Love of country, honor, and duty to the nation's war efforts might all pale at times. But one didn't let one's own unit down.

So, his head on fire, spurs of pain digging into his brain, Udet came back from his twenty-fourth victory, hardly able to walk away from his plane. He stumbled right past von Richthofen without seeing him as he headed for the field dispensary, seeking a painkiller.

The first-aid orderly who poked at the inflamed ear showed little skill or knowledge. Von Richthofen came in and stood there, frowning sternly.

"Udet, what's wrong with you?" The orderly stiffened to attention. Then, seeing Udet didn't answer, he said: "Very serious infection, sir, that should have immediate medical attention."

"You're going on leave, Udet, and *now*."

So Udet went, and the ear infection passed. Back with the circus, he set out to become the Udet of fame.* His victories ultimately totaled sixty-two confirmed kills. In one six-month period in 1918, his score was forty-two. But in September of that year he was seriously wounded after destroying two American DH-4's. That put him out of the final stages of the war.

In the postwar years, Udet continued to live high, eat well, and chase women, earning his way by exhibiting himself as a stunt flier. His acrobatic shows became world-famous and he toured all over the globe.

He was remembered in his war days as ebullient, jolly, full of fun, always ready to try a new dish or drink. The limits of existence blurred for him during the war; the idea of an individual settling down to a normal life was lost. He knew "the morning after that debauchery never pays back what it costs," but no one is absurd when he is in agony. Udet was a man fitted chiefly for war. His life brutalized as a teen-age soldier, given a deadly toy to play games with, he never was able to climb back in the peace. In his circle, hope remained the major sin.

With the start of World War II, Udet joined Hitler's Luftwaffe and, as a result of his fame, was soon high in the power echelons as a general in charge of plane production. He was not very good at his job; he wasn't even a very sincere Nazi. And his orgies continued to shock unshockable Berlin. Hermann Goering, an old flying comrade of Udet's, did nothing to save Udet (his own reputation at stake) when a plot was created to blame him for the failure of the Luftwaffe over England during the Battle of Britain. Before Udet died by his own hand, he left a note. "You will see, they'll say I died of a heart attack, and will give me a State funeral." He got it; "died while testing a secret weapon . . . the noblest of Aryan heroes . . ." Goering added a typically insincere "Farewell, my best friend."

* Ernst Udet's flying style can be seen today in such motion pictures as *The White Hell of Pitz Palu*, a classic of flying scenes caught on film.

2. | Werner Voss (1898–1917)

"Life is dead, long live life . . ."
—JEAN COCTEAU

Werner Voss was the son of a rich dye factory owner of Krefeld. The house on Blemenstrasse was well furnished, comfortable, full of Gothic *sicherheit*. Voss was the heir, cherished as the future head of the family factory. Instead, he was to become the fourth-ranking German ace (following von Richthofen, Udet, and Lowenhardt), with a total of forty-eight victories. Curiously enough, Voss was also one of the few fliers to become really friendly with the Red Baron—and his dog, Moritz. The aristocratic von Richthofen visited Voss's family on their leave together. Yet it was a friendship complicated by rivalry. Voss was just too good an air fighter for the baron's own reputation. Some said they were aware of a strain, a growing intensity between the two heroes.

When Voss was just nine kills behind the baron, there were times when he felt von Richthofen to be the slower man. Their styles were different. Voss improvised a battle, like a jazzman playing with a chord, letting things happen, testing his abilities. He moved in on an enemy plane with an open mind, adjusting to the fight as the event took place. The baron was a man with a method, a mathematical, preconceived plan of battle; and as his plans were based on skill and experience, he did well. But there were times in the air when the baron was confused if things did not fall into place. Then he would withdraw from the fight. It was the opinion of those who observed them both in battle that Voss was the better fighter in close combat, with a sauciness, and a lack of *angst*, that stood him in good stead.

Like so many fighters, Voss made the jump from horse to plane, having been with the 2nd Westphalian Hussars, fighting on the Eastern Front. Also like so many of the fliers, he was slim, and not too large a man; the flimsy planes were no place for heavyweights. Voss, blue-eyed, fair-haired, cheerful, made an effervescent contrast to von Richthofen. He had flown as an observer at the Battle of Verdun, but by the time of the Somme, he was pilot of an Aviatik fighter.

Flying with Boelcke's famous squadron, he began to pile up victory after victory and was soon appointed commander of Jasta 5. When the four groups merged into Richthofen's Circus, with its own lorries, railroad cars, baggage, tools, machine parts, and planes, it was a splendid sight on the move.

Voss gave his silver-painted Pfalz D-III a red nose and a striped body. He was at his best in the air, preferring to leave the running of things on the ground to others. He had no ostentation or ambition to become an office flier in a command post.

As the war dragged on into 1917, after many victories, Voss the boy suddenly began to grow old. The pace was telling, and he was still trying to outkill von Richthofen. By this time he was flying the new Fokker triplane, the remarkable Dreidekker. It was his pet, his darling. He had it painted sky blue, all but the red nose spinner. The whole front became a face as he painted on eyes and nose and a regal mustache that some said was meant to be the Kaiser. No boy ever decorated his Model-T flivver with more joy.

Once Voss went up with von Richthofen in the famous scarlet machine as a guest. As von Richthofen told of that flight, they were flying in the direction of Arras when they spotted an English patrol close by. The baron saw a chance to impress his guest and add to his string of victories.

Immediately the thought occurred to me, "Now comes number thirty-three." Although there were nine Englishmen, and although they were on their own territory, they preferred to avoid battle. I began to think that it might be better for me to repaint my machine. Nevertheless, we caught up with them. The important thing in airplanes is that they should be speedy.

I was nearest to the enemy and attacked the man at the rear of the formation. To my great delight, I noticed that he accepted battle, and my pleasure increased when I discovered that his comrades deserted him, so I had once more a single fight.

It was a fight similar to the one I had had several hours earlier. My opponent did not make matters easy for me. He knew the fight business, and it was particularly awkward for me that he was a good shot. To my great regret, that became quite clear to me.

A favorable wind came to my aid, and it drove both of us over the German lines. My opponent discovered that the matter was not as simple as he had imagined. So he plunged and disappeared in a cloud. He had nearly saved himself.

I plunged after him, and dropped out of the cloud, and as luck would have it, found myself quite close behind him. I fired and he fired, without any tangible result. At last I hit him. I noticed a ribbon of white vapor. He would have to land, for his engine had stopped.

But he was a stubborn fellow. He would not recognize that he was bound to lose the game. If he continued shooting, I could kill him, for meanwhile we had dropped to an altitude of about nine hundred feet.

However, the Englishman continued to defend himself by shooting at me exactly as his countryman had done in the morning. He fought on until he landed. When he reached the ground, I flew over him at about thirty feet in order to ascertain whether I had killed him or not, and what did the rascal do? He leveled his machine gun and shot holes into my machine.

Afterward Voss told me that if that had happened to him, he would have shot the aviator on the ground. As a matter of fact, I ought to have done so, for he had not surrendered. He was one of the few fortunate fellows who escaped with their lives. I felt very merry as I flew home to celebrate . . .

Voss continued to chase the baron's record. In three weeks he accumulated ten victories; forty-eight planes in all during one year and two months of flying. On September 23, 1917, he was visited by two of his brothers attached to the lowly infantry. It was the Sunday morning after his last kill. Like good Christians the three attended church services and had a fine lunch. Then they took each other's pictures.

Late afternoon, back to duty, Voss took off, alone. Ypres in ruins lay below him at 17,000 feet. Under him he saw twelve British planes, six Bristols convoyed by six DE-6 fighters. He had reached that point in his career where he felt he was immortal. He dived down, even as on the far horizon he spotted four flights of scout planes and Sopwith Camels.

He attacked a plane which dived, and followed it down with gun bursts. But at his back were seven SE-5's. Voss broke the chase to take care of the new foes. What followed was fast and furious, and in no sense an orderly battle. Voss kept dodging and trying to fight the gathering of British as more and more joined in, hemming the lone enemy into the friendless sky.

Captain James McCudden, of RFC Squadron 56, remembered the battle well. As they closed in, he says, Voss flew

... in a most disconcertingly quick manner, not a climbing or an Immelmann turn, but a sort of half-flat spin. By now the German triplane was in the middle of our formation, and its handling was wonderful to behold. The pilot seemed to be firing at all of us simultaneously, and although I got behind for a second time, I could hardly stay there for a second. His movements were so quick and uncertain that none of us could hold him in sight at all for any decisive time ... he was coming towards me nose on, and slightly underneath, and apparently had not seen me. I dropped my nose and got him well in my sights, and pressed both triggers. As soon as I fired, up came his nose at me, and I heard clack-clack-clack-clack, as his bullets passed close to me and through my wings. I distinctly noticed the red-yellow flashes from his parallel Spandau guns. As he flashed by me, I caught a glimpse of a black head in the triplane with no hat on at all.

By this time, a red-nosed Albatros had arrived and was apparently doing its best to guard the triplane's tail, and it was well handled, too. The formation of six Albatroses which we were going to attack at first stayed above us and were prevented from diving on us by the arrival of a formation of Spads, whose leader apparently appreciated our position and kept the six Albatroses otherwise engaged.

The triplane was still circling round in the midst of seven SE-5's, who were all firing at it as opportunity offered, and at one time I noted the triplane in the apex of a cone of tracer bullets from at least five machines simultaneously. . . .

Few fliers could have escaped from the ring of fire spewing from the twin guns on each enemy plane. Voss did not flee. He attacked and hit an enemy plane. In return he took several hits himself. But the fight went on; the red Albatros that had gone to his rescue went down in flames. Voss's plane was badly shot up. He was flying strangely now and may have been wounded.

The Englishman, Erwin Rhys-Davids, was closest, and he began to fire the Lewis gun on his upper wing into the oddly acting plane, using up his full drum. Then, moving into a more favorable position, he let go with his twin Vickers guns, raking Voss's plane without mercy.

Voss's machine began to slide downhill, veering toward the sunset. Reloading, Rhys-Davids again began slicing bursts into the falling plane. If Voss was still alive, he made no effort to control his ship. At 500 feet the German plane shook itself like an animal from a blow, stalled, and fell with the force of a rock behind the Allied front lines. He "hit the ground and disappeared into a thousand fragments, for it seemed to me that it went literally to powder . . . as long as I live I shall never forget my admiration for that German pilot [McCudden did not know until the next day that it was Voss], who, singlehanded, fought seven of us for ten minutes and . . . put some bullets through all our machines . . ." *

* It was at the British celebration for Rhys-Davids that Edward Mannock, at the call to drink a toast to von Richthofen, said, "I won't drink a toast to that sonofabitch."

PART IV:
They Were Americans

CHAPTER 14

THE ESCADRILLE
LAFAYETTE

By 1916, there were enough hearty or foolish volunteer American fliers around for the French to form, in April, the so-called *Escadrille Américaine* at Luxeuil-les-Bains, with French officers and ground crew. German officials in Washington protested at neutrals by name fighting for France, so the name *Escadrille des Volontaires* was suggested; in the end, the title became *Escadrille Lafayette*. The first unit contained thirty-eight Americans. Those who couldn't get in joined the French as members of the Lafayette Flying Corps. In the two units (combined), over 200 Americans went to war. (In February 1918, the Escadrille Lafayette was absorbed into the U.S. air force to become the 103rd Pursuit Squadron.)

It was Norman Prince, an American expatriate, who got the plan rolling, backed by Dr. Edmund L. Gros, the organizer of the American Ambulance Service. The problem was objections from Washington. And the obvious answer was, Don't tell them until we are organized. The Americans were not asked to swear allegiance to France, any more than Americans with the French Foreign Legion. In fact, they were privateers.

Some Americans in the Legion were transferred to the Escadrille. They were a strange and in some ways amazingly romantic bunch. The cynical, depressed outlook on the war was to come later. William Thaw had a wacky knee, poor vision, feeble hearing. Others of the founding group were Prince himself, Elliot Cowdin, James McConnell, Laurence Rumsey, Kiffin Rockwell, Victor Chapman. None had ever fought in the air, but most could somehow—more or less—fly a plane. They were given Nieuports.

They settled in at the Grand Hotel in Luxeuil, and began to make life hell for their French officers, Capitaine Georges Thénault and Lieutenant de Laage de Meux. The flight instructor was Capitaine Haape. He showed them first where there were emergency landing spots in case the planes proved too balky for them. From French flying groups, Dr. Gros lured over such Americans as Paul Pavelka, Didier Masson, Chouteau Johnson, Raoul Lufbery—names that hardly sound like old Yankee stock—and Dudley Hill and Clyde Balsley. They were war-blooded men and able.

Over all, in command, was Capitaine Thénault. He watched silently as the boys wrecked planes by bad landings and running into hangars. The French public cried out that the damn Americans were living it up in the lap of luxury. Then the Americans were moved into battle areas around Verdun, where the Germans commanded the air. They took as their insignia a feathered, yelling Indian chief copied from a powder company's trademark; it looked fine painted on the fuselage.

The boys were unlucky, or perhaps as yet unskilled. Thaw nearly bled to death from a bullet wound to a main artery but, spurting blood, managed to get back to Bar-le-Duc before passing out. Rockwell had his windshield smashed in air battle, which tore his face to bits. Nearly blind, and in agony, he too got back home. Next day, his head in a cocoon of bandages, he forced himself back into the air. Victor Chapman was waylaid by four Germans in the clouds, and got his scalp split. The wound dug a canyon in his skull and he could not stop the flow of blood. The stabilizing controls of the plane had also been shot away. Chapman just made it to Bar-le-Duc. He was a terrible sight, but refused to go to hospital, permitting only emergency bandaging of his serious wound. The French shrugged their shoulders. Perhaps all this fighting spirit was "*de bon augure.*"

Going up as a group under Thénault, Balsley, Rockwell, Clyde, and Prince ran smack into fourteen enemy planes. The Germans circled them like an Indian raiding party, firing all the time. The *capitaine* led them in a dash for home, but Balsley failed to make his escape and took on all fourteen Germans. He dived and he banked, trying to give them the slip. They continued to rack him, and one of his legs was torn open. The enemy was using exploding dum-dum bullets—in theory, outlawed for war. Finally, Balsley got clear, and came down at the airdrome. He could not lift himself from the cockpit. Put in hospital nearby, however, he was soon on the road to recovery.

Balsley's comrades, Chapman, Lufbery, and Prince, getting hold of some fruit, decided to fly to visit Balsley in hospital. In the air, an entire flight of Fokkers jumped them. Victor Chapman's plane went into a burning dive, and hit the earth with fearful impact: the first American flier to be killed in battle. The earnest, worried French decided at this point that the Americans were "inexperienced and brash." They were withdrawn from the front and returned to Luxeuil. Here, they found fifty Royal Air Force pilots in residence. The Yanks and the Limeys hit it off and bottles passed around, with much group singing. Except for taking wounds, the Americans had not been impressive.

On leave in Paris, Lufbery, Hall, and Thaw acquired a snarling lion cub who was promoted to squad's mascot and named "Whiskey." It became a ritual for the Americans to go to Paris on leave, to meet French fliers and to get rid of any remaining puritan obsessions by means of the fleshly pleasures available there. A few were said to have visited Gertrude Stein. The madam and her life-long friend, Alice Toklas, were driving a Model-T ambulance as their contribution to the war effort.

But the real business of war went on. Rockwell went out of formation in the air to try to get himself a Fokker. The German, diving at over 100 miles an hour, riddled him with the illegal exploding bullets, tearing open Rockwell's throat and mutilating the body fearfully. Photographs of the grim cadaver were sent in protest to Geneva, which did nothing about it, not even appoint the usual committee.

The French decided to put the reckless Americans to escorting bombers. Prince, returning from a flight on a dark night, ran into a high-tension wire. His machine spun head-over-teakettle, broke up with tearing sounds, and Prince was thrown hard onto the ground. He tried to stand, failed, and discovered both legs were broken. Also there was something wrong with his entrails. He died of internal injuries (and French army surgery, some claimed) three days later.

The Americans began to need replacements. Dr. Gros sent out the call for volunteers: fifty men showed up. There were those who had been close enough to a plane to touch it, and many who had never seen the inside of a cockpit. The Americans never settled down, but they flew.

The planes they had were now Spads, with Hispano-Suiza engines that vibrated badly and went weak in power in extreme cold. Landings on icy fields were a further problem. Yet, in January 1917, Raoul Lufbery—who was turning out to be the ace of the group—scored his seventh German victory, in wind and snow.

There were also personalities who posed problems. Bert Hall was soon to be sent away to one of the Stork Squadrons. He didn't wear well; his mean and boorish habits, snide grudges, and overwhelming sense of ego meant that he was always trying to outbrag the rest of the group. Sent to Coventry, he was to ask for transfer, noting in his diary: "Moved with as little excitement as possible. I hate goodbyes . . . glad to get rid of me. I don't blame them . . ."

It was the tradition—and still is to some historians—to present the air heroes as sterling characters, dedicated to duty, liberty, and country, almost without fault, and modest in their behavior. Perhaps a little local color thrown in at times, carousing on leave, the lifting of a skirt, or a bottle drained to release tensions. But above all, outstanding individuals. And many were; but not all.

Bert Hall was a drifter, what used to be called "a soldier of fortune." Of Hall it may be said that almost anything can be made of his life, according to whatever version of his past one wants to believe. He bragged, he slurred his speech, suggesting a dozen settings for birth, for background.

Our information on his past, based on what he himself said, is quite vague. He would claim to have been born in Kentucky sometime around 1880. Or he would say the place of his birth was Higginsville, Missouri. He might have flown and fought in the Turkish-Bulgarian War in 1912; on either side, as the stories shifted. Next night, he could relate that he had been at the bloody Battle of Mons with Kitchener's army, which, with his help, saved England. Yet at the same time, if one compared dates, he was also in the French Foreign Legion, having been in supposedly from the start of the war, from August to December 1914!

He wrote of his adventures as a soldier and flier, but no account is trustworthy. If one began to like him, and wonder perhaps whether some of all this yarning could be true, he would come up with the information that he had guided Dr. Cook, the notorious imposter, to the North Pole. As Cook was proved never to have reached the Pole, Hall must have done it alone.

His collection of medals was amazing. Many were of orders rare and hardly known. He did shoot down three Germans while with the Americans, for which he was awarded the Médaille Militaire and Croix de Guerre. Yet before that, when this war-tested flier transferred from the Legion to the French air force, it was discovered he hardly knew one end of a plane from the other. He did become a flier after training, and in time was taken in by the Escadrille Américaine (in April 1916). However, his past, either the fiction or the true facts, was catching up with him. The French secret service kept close surveillance on him, being sure he was a German spy. Two French army Intelligence men, posing as student fliers, slept in beds on either side of Bert Hall, in case he went out at night to signal the enemy or perhaps gave away secrets in his sleep. Intelligence services, as we know, are none too wise at times, and there was never any evidence that Hall was anything but a blowhard sponger and a liar on the grand scale.

In appearance, Hall was not impressive. His pictures show a short, skinny bantam of a man, bowlegged, a life-worn face. Without social graces, poorly raised, not well educated, set down among this group of mostly college men, even intellectuals, he struck back with sardonic vulgar wit. The Americans with whom Hall flew found him a bit too "lucky" shooting craps or handling a deck of poker cards, and it was almost impossible to get him to sign for bar or mess chits. The usual explanation given of his departure is that he was "invited" to leave the squadron, with hints that that was better than being booted out on his well-traveled arse. In any case, Hall, as we've noted, was transferred. He came to the French Nieuport Chasse Squadron 103, where he lasted a month, even after getting a citation as a "clever, energetic, courageous pilot, spirited, attacking daily at close range enemy planes." Bert Hall was evidently a man who wore out his welcomes swiftly.

Of his two books, *One Man's War* and *En L'Air*, it can be said that they lack the charm and verbal ability that he could show at times, and owe more to imagination than to fact. But one cannot overlook his record before he left the Americans, nor his sense of style. Flying a Spad with Escadrille 103, he got his fourth victory over a German plane. When his commanding officer congratulated him with a *"Vive le Spad!"*, the flier could not resist an acid, *"Non, vive Bert Hall!"*

From the French squadron, Hall went off on some undefined "diplomatic aviation mission" to Russia.*

The old gang was breaking up fast. Laurence Rumsey was discharged because of ill health. Paul Pavelka volunteered for service at Salonika and died, not in a plane, but in a fall from a horse.

A new recruit was Edmond Genêt, descended from that Citizen Genêt sent to America by the French Revolutionary government who never came home again. Young Genêt went AWOL from the U.S. navy, joined the Foreign Legion, and then got into the air force. He wrote to his mother:

> . . . if anything does happen to me, you all surely can feel better satisfied with the end than if I was sent to pieces by a shell or put out by a bullet in the infantry, where there are seventy-five out of a hundred possibilities of your never hearing of it. The glory is well worth the loss. I'd rather die as an aviator over the enemy's lines than find a nameless, shallow grave in the infantry. . . .

* When the Russian Revolution came, Hall returned to the United States and wrote the French that he wanted a release to enter the United States army. Released, he became a civilian. (The French military records still list him as a deserter.) Later, while training fliers for the Sun Yat-sen government in China, Hall embezzled $34,000. He was tried by a U.S. tribunal and sent to McNeil Island Penitentiary on a two-and-a-half-year sentence. In 1948, he died in an auto accident in Ohio.

Enemy antiaircraft guns killed him, the first American killed after America entered the war. (U.S. army red tape listed Genêt as a deserter; but after the war, his name was cleared.)

In photographs the Americans pose usually smiling. There was an official uniform, but the Escadrille Lafayette always were snappy dressers, quick to renew their pink Bedford breeches, shipboard tunic, Sam Browne belt, Savile Row boots. Some carried swagger sticks. All wore pilot's wings, insignia of rank, decorations over the heart. They were well known in Paris, where they gathered at times at the Café Maxwell, or were welcomed at the brothels near the Gare du Nord. They sweated in summer; in winter watched their mechanics, with balaclavas pulled down over freezing ears, condition their planes. In the air, with fogged goggles, they pressed the trigger of the Lewis or Vickers guns, warming the oil with a burst of shots. And when the gun jammed, they cursed, pulled at the cocking lug to clear it.

Eleven Escadrille Lafayette fliers became aces. Among the dead were: Lufbery, Bayliss, and Putnam. Baer got nine enemy planes, Cassady nine, Larner eight, Parsons eight, Biddle seven, Ponder seven, Conneley six, and Thaw five.

To be able to join the U.S. air force, the Americans were discharged by the French. But U.S. red tape and delay, a two-month wait for commissions, caused them to fly and do battle as outlaw civilians. The Escadrille Lafayette officially ceased to exist on February 18, 1918. (It became Escadrille Jeanne d'Arc, and was staffed by French fliers.)

CHAPTER 15

AMERICANS AT WAR

"The great object of life is sensation—to feel that
we exist, even though in pain."

—LORD BYRON

The United States went into the Great War with a whoop and a holler. The young men with no strong apprehensions who were fliers or would-be fliers rushed into uniforms. There were advertisements that officers' uniforms could be got at bargain prices for $16. But those who could ordered their uniforms from Brooks Brothers or the better tailors, whipcord breeches, the Sam Browne belt, and even, for a time, boots and spurs.

The fliers saw themselves as members of "the most dangerous, the better service"; they were the chosen, the anointed. No matter if the *Congressional Record* printed some sour protests against the war: "We shall Prussianize America . . ." "It will destroy democracy at home, while fighting for it in France . . ." "Conscripts are not worth considering . . ."

The young men in uniform, training for their wings, dreamed of shooting the Red Baron from the sky in the exaltation of their youth. It was the last romantic war. Women and young girls in summer dresses adored them. They flocked onto country-club porches—the boys being treated as men by elders who had been to Cuba with Teddy—and oldsters stood the drinks while gossiping of Shiloh and J. E. B. Stuart and the way the Shenandoah Valley looked when Sheridan had passed through it: "Why, if a crow flew over it, he had to carry his own provisions."

It was good to be young and train to fly, to see the country rally to the glorious, just war. Yet a bit of it, to a young man dreaming of planes in the sky, seemed foolish, even sinister. Wagner and Bach—"Hun music"—were no longer played; children stoned dachshunds, sauerkraut became "liberty cabbage," and hamburger had a dozen other names. Sentiment sank to a sugary low as Al Jolson sang "A Baby's Prayer at Twilight" (the cover of the score showed Baby and Mommy staring at a photograph of Daddy in uniform). Another favorite song was "My Beautiful Alsace-Lorraine." The young flier in training had heard of the place, but didn't know whether it was beautiful; all he knew was that it had been raped by the predatory lust of the Germans.

The French sent over some maimed fliers to America, and a few English RFC men also came over, somewhat mutilated, to stand up at public rallies and ask all good citizens to join in the fun of paying for war. And there were the slogans: LIBERTY BONDS OR GERMAN BONDAGE; COME ACROSS OR THE KAISER WILL; HE BUYS TWICE WHO BUYS QUICKLY. (No one could explain the last one too well.)

It was fine to go to rallies, to kiss and be kissed, to see young matrons in their Red Cross headcloths, like warrior nuns. To have actual sexual intercourse with an older woman, nearly thirty, "doing her bit in the ecstasy of a patriotic orgasm."

If the flier was the symbol of the best and the most romantic side of America, the symbol of hate became the Kaiser. He was the popular comic villain; cruel, a bit of a beast (*The Beast of Berlin*—six reels). There was no end to the slogans against him. A BOND SLACKER IS A KAISER BACKER . . . LEND A HAND TO UNCLE SAM OR BEND A KNEE TO THE KAISER . . . WE'LL HANG THE KAISER TO A SOUR APPLE TREE.

After getting their wings, the young men in uniform were usually entertained in New York City. The embarkation point was either Hoboken or Jersey City. They escorted worshipping girls to Mr. Ziegfeld's new *Follies*, and ignored Will Rogers and W. C. Fields for the sight of Ann Pennington's knees. Eddie Cantor did a stage skit about a nervous young man facing his test as an aviation student.

What else could a fresh flier do while waiting for the crazy-patch-painted troopship to sail but go to the flickers to see *The Claws of the Hun* or *Outwitting the Hun*? These films always had one scene in which the snarling, leering Prussian in his pointed helmet (neck shaven) raped the beautiful Anglo-Saxon blond virgin, forcing his foul will upon her plump body, while her eyes, huge and staring in dishonor, turned directly toward the young men in the audience.

Casualty lists started to come in, and new words like "*Minnen-werfer,*" "Stokes mortars," "Mill bombs." But the old American spirit would not fail. Cried the colonel of the 102nd Infantry to his men: "Men of Connecticut—you blue-bellied, shad-eating Nutmeg Yanks . . . we're going to fight!"

When the names of the first three Americans to die in France appeared, Christopher Morley produced a verse:

> *Gresham, Enright and Hay!*
> *There are no words to say*
> *Our love, our noble pride*
> *For these our first who died.*

Stern's department store—always practical—ran an ad offering WOMEN'S CORRECT ATTIRE FOR MOURNING WEAR. Posters showed heroic males in stylish uniforms. The Americans alone, by 1917, still retained a romantic, exalted idea of the war. As one example, we have the text of Elsie Janis's *The Big Show*. She is now forgotten as an entertainer, singer, song writer, and poetess, but she was very popular in France at American airdromes and among the soldiers.

One verse of a war poem shows her mood:

> *Where are you, God,*
> *In whose hands this great world*
> *Is like a tiny ball,*
> *That can be turned and twirled?*
> *I can't believe that you have seen*
> *The things that they have done.*
> *With poison gas and crucifixions*
> *Battles have been won,*

And yet upon this earth of yours
There still exists the Hun.
Where are you, God?

With cheerful innocence, the United States announced that it would build 40,000 military planes in one year—and these were "on order." But no American-designed plane flew in combat in World War I although $640 million were voted and spent, and a more feasible monthly quota of 200 planes and 4,000 engines was later set as the target. The rights to the British DH-4's and the JN-4D trainers were licensed to the United States. Orville Wright came to the Dayton Wright Company as a consultant engineer but war-plane styling was out of his range (and perhaps desires). A plane engine of 300 horsepower was developed, but the army decided no human being could fly anything that powerful and survive for long. The Signal Corps had an aviation section: records show that it bungled things badly. The Americans were eager as bird dogs to fly and fight. But always present were the human elements; greed, political dishonesty, the rigid army protocol, the vast untrained raw material. It all made for confusion, waste, graft, and the sluffing off of needed skills. The American war effort was amazing in its size, its determination; it was also too big, and run by too many greedy or stupid officials safely seated behind their desks.

But 15,000 small American fliers *did* get to France—as carrier pigeons. Five thousand disappeared, mostly into French cooking pots. The survivors carried many messages. One message which is best remembered reads: "I'm tired of carrying this god-damn bird."

Colonel Billy Mitchell (later to be court-martialed for his efforts to prove that planes could sink battleships) did a great deal to clear the way for training American fliers. It was soon evident that the misfits training the Americans would never make combat pilots. The cadets were shipped to England for advanced flying lessons.

An unidentified American wrote of his fellow students beginning training, and his own flying:

He ran all the way across the field, and it was a big one, and then pulled the stick right back into his stomach. . . . The next one did better. He got off and zigzagged a bit, but instead of making a circuit he went straight on. His instructor remarked that he would probably land in Scotland, because he didn't know how to turn.

I got off in a Pup yesterday. Gosh, what a thrill! They are not so different, but they are so quick and sensitive that they will crash taking off or landing before you know what they are going to do. I didn't bust anything but I pancaked like the devil landing. . . .

Flew a Spad today. Easy to fly but dangerous as hell. Just like flying the famous barn door . . . and it has the gliding angle of a brick. I've always laughed at the regulars wearing spurs to fly in, but I needed a pair in this Spad. . . .

The American fliers' training camps were primitive as outhouses. Only 250 planes were available for training initially and some of them not in good shape. A plane company rented out acres for a training center near San Diego in California. And there was another among the duck farms on Long Island. Kelly Field in Texas was new, and sheer hell. The weather consisted of blue northers, winter blizzards, and hot winds. Camp life struggled against rotten food, the dreadful living conditions in contractors' plank slums, and rattlesnakes. Scorpions and tarantulas had to be shaken out of boots every morning.

In the air a garden hose and tin cider-funnel was used as intercom between teacher and trainee. One careless student killed a British instructor sent over to train Americans.* The JN-4 trainer, the notorious Jenny, was no delight to learn in, certainly no guarantee one would make old bones.

Over in France, after delays and problems, squadrons like the 95th, which had a kicking mule as its insignia (*Maude the Mule*, from the comic strip by cartoonist Fred Opper), were formed. They had a song in the 95th, "Hurrah for the Next Man to Die," and for a victory in the air, the winner had to treat the company:

---

* The student was Vernon Castle who, with his wife Irene Castle, had put America on its dancing toes.

downing an enemy plane rated five bottles of champagne; getting downed yourself, three bottles; cracking up on landing, one bottle. That and learning to say "*Mercy boo-coo*" and "*vin rouge,*" and a few direct obscene questions were the first lessons. Wrote one flier home, "It's fine to hear the French girls yelling *Vivent les Américains! Vive Pershing! Vivent les États-Unis!*"

American infantry went by to the trenches in camions and the young fliers yelled out, "Give the squareheads hell!" One dough-boy group yelled back, "Fuck you!" in true democratic fashion.

There was entertainment—besides Elsie Janis—for fliers and infantrymen alike. Not all the doughnuts and coffee were free. Some organizations made a good cash balance out of entertaining the boys; but the runners who carried doughnuts up to the front would be proud to report: "We never lost a doughnut." From an old scrapbook comes one program—which it is hoped was not typical entertainment for the American boys far from home:

OVERTURE, BATTLE SONG OF FREEDOM—
  The Orchestra
DUSTIN FARNUM IN FIVE REELS—
  Davy Crockett
SELECTION, "MY SUNSHINE JANE"—
  The Orchestra
CONJURER . . .
SINGING BY ALL HANDS
  Busting into Society—One Reel
NATIONAL ANTHEMS—The Orchestra.

There was still training in the Penguin land-hopper that could not get into the air. A seat belt and a helmet were issued to pro-tect the head. As one trainee wrote back home ". . . it weighed just short of a ton, it came in two sizes, too small and too large . . ."

The nation suffered bitter-sweet twinges of glory and sacrifice when Teddy Roosevelt's son, Quentin, green and badly trained, was shot down on July 14, 1918, and his grave marked by a broken propeller, photographed for the rotogravure section of the Sunday newspapers.

There were stories to be told of the American Escadrille,

where the first boys in had been shocked to find "an American nigger who was a French sergeant and trained Americans for the Lafayette Escadrille . . ." *

James McConnell, who had been flying with the Escadrille, left a letter at his airdrome to be opened in case of death.

> My burial is of no import. Make it as easy as possible for yourselves. I have no religion and do not care for any service. If the omission would embarrass you, I presume I could stand the performance. Good luck to the rest of you. God damn Germany and Vive la France . . .

As more young Americans went over to England to complete their training, it became clear that being English and being American meant two very different things. Letters home and journals provide us with some complaints. "Down to London to hunt a bit of ass. The hurrs all have bad teeth and want you to get it off standing up in a doorway . . ." "Once a week we had rabbit . . . cold storage rabbits, packed in Australia in 1911, few of us ate them . . ."

The beer wasn't the same, nor the sausage-and-veg in the shops; and the fish and chips were certainly not hot dogs or apple pie. "Damn beer is drunk warm as horsepiss, and they try to pony off stout and ale on you . . ."

Meanwhile morals, health, and dogma were not forgotten.

All kinds of preachers and do-gooders arrived and left again. A medical staff dental officer sent the boys off with the proper advice: "Men, I'm about to address you for the last time. I want you to promise me—in fact I'm putting you on your honor—you will keep your teeth clean . . . You are to brush your teeth night and morning like *this* . . . up and down, *not* sideways!"

The 95th Squadron set up a saloon on the Marne, "The Chateau 95." Nearby was a hospital with live American female nurses. Only officers were allowed to date them. Of course the aviators, from "the most dangerous branch of the service," vied for the nurses' virtue and bodies. However, army nurses were not all like

---

* I have been unable to identify this Negro by name, but he is mentioned by several people.

the willing Miss Barkley in *A Farewell to Arms*. Neither was the original on which the character was based. That Miss Barkley who gave her thighs with such lovelike zeal.

Those squadrons not finding such willing females began to impregnate French country girls in the vicinity of the flying fields. Babies appeared in time with names like Foch, Woodrow Wilson, Pershing; there is even record of a Charlot (Chaplin). One pilot was reported shot down and mourned by his friends:

Granville was elected to pack his effects and to console and stifle the sobs of the blacksmith's daughter who was distraught with sorrow. *"Si brave, si gentil,"* she wailed. Charlie has just divided the most popular of Jim's belongings . . . the blacksmith's family was beginning to get dry-eyed again, when the prodigal son returned. . . .

The Americans did not use parachutes, and none were issued. The young fliers, for some reason, felt it was sissy, and the pack unwieldy. Unofficially, desk officers decided that with a parachute handy a flier might be tempted to leave his plane too easily when he should have stuck to his gun and machine and gone down fighting. This, of course, was one of those things that made the Americans seem so foolhardy and careless of their lives to Euorpean observers.*

The task most hated by the fliers was dropping leaflets. "The charming picture of the deserter's reception in France made me feel like deserting myself . . . the bundles built up and the cook started breakfast fires with them." Of another drop to the "Lost Battalion," 1st Battalion 308th Infantry, Billy Mitchell wrote that he ordered:

chocolate and concentrated food and ammunition dropped. . . . Our pilots thought they had located it from the panel that it showed, and dropped off considerable supplies, but later I found out they had received none of the supplies we had dropped off. The Germans had made up a panel like theirs and our men had calmly dropped off the nice food to the Germans who undoubtedly ate it with great thanksgiving. . . .

* The parachute only became standard plane equipment in the U.S. air force in 1919. The ruling was made compulsory in 1922, a less heroic era.

With or without chocolate, to the Americans the war was often a kind of bitter picnic. They never got over the romantic concept of their new strong nation helping tottering Europe—like an old lady across a street. F. Scott Fitzgerald, who was to become to some the voice of the postwar young, looked back at what the war had meant to so many: "This western-front business couldn't be done again, not for a long time."

Fitzgerald never fell into the schoolboy emotionalism of Rupert Brooke, who could write a wartime letter to a friend saying: "Come and die. It'll be great fun . . ." (The friend didn't think so, and lived.) Fitzgerald sensed that a whole generation of the young was done in by the war, the living as well as the dead. "I was certain that all the young people were going to be killed in the war, and I wanted to put on paper a record of the strange life they had lived in their time . . ."

He came to regret that he never got to France, and in conversation after his crackup expressed a wish to have died young in battle.

Few Americans ever knew the truth of the failure of their government and the big industries to arm their air force and the AEF properly in World War I. It was a shabby series of performances.* The great armadas of the air—more than "20,000 planes . . . to darken the skies of Europe . . . bridge the Atlantic . . . crush the Hun . . ."—were newspaper talk and very rewarding factory contracts. As we've said, not one plane of American design ever fought in the air over Europe. The English de Havilland licensed its DH-4 to be made in the U.S.A., but it was engined by a shoddy item called the Liberty motor that the Detroit auto kings knocked together. It was not worthy of their skills. In the main, the American war orders made millionaires, but hardly equipment fit to use overseas. Take the word of General Halsey

---

* The record in World War I is not good for American industry as a whole. The U.S. army fired 9 million shells; only 208,000 came from American war plants. Of the 2,250 artillery units, just 130 came from American steel and processing plants. There were 23,000 tanks on order; records show about 20 were manufactured and accepted.

Dunwoody, in charge of aviation procurement, "We never had a single plane that was fit to use . . ."

Altogether, 3,225 Liberty DH-4's were put together. They were worthless as fighters and were changed for use as scouting and bombing planes. Of the 1,885 that got to Europe, almost all were found to be defective. They had to be refitted and rebuilt at Romorantin, the U.S.A. airplane repair base in France. Then 665 were moved up to the front, but their gas tanks were not fireproof; they were suitably dubbed "Flaming Coffins."

Except for the fine fighting quality of the American soldier, who at his best proved himself the equal of any fighting in the war, the American war effort, from the manufacturing end, was a national disgrace. It is perhaps worth analyzing this a little further.

It took nearly a year from the time Woodrow Wilson brought the nation into the war before American fliers saw action in the air. There were 7,000 flying cadets in training soon after war came to America; 500 had finished ground training; 1,800 went to France to continue flying the Curtiss Jenny in training at the U.S. air base at Issoudun. It was a waste of time, for they had to begin all over again (as we've seen) when they got the speedy French war planes; there was not one type, but six.

General Pershing had many problems with the French and English as to how to use his manpower (beyond getting it killed). Four million Americans were in the army; 2 million would get to France, and 116,000 of them would die there. The air force was a headache to that fine old horse soldier "Blackjack" Pershing. He himself would never fly in an airplane, and avoided any commitment that would have gotten him into the air. Pershing was an old-line West Pointer, a lifetime loyal career soldier. He did things by the book. And it was his firmness that held the Americans together as a unit in France, not permitting them to be scattered and lost among the Allied forces. They would fight, he made it clear, as Americans, or not at all.

But his mind was rigidly set, and as a military man, he was no Grant or Stonewall Jackson. Early on, Billy Mitchell realized that if there wasn't a separate service for the air, it would become a mere stepchild. Pershing saw the U.S. air force as part of the army: like the Missouri mules, the rolling field kitchen, but not important enough for a branch of its own.

Mitchell had spunk—and little tact. He told the general it was nonsense to keep the air force buttoned up as part of the army. Pershing, in anger, demoted Mitchell and replaced him. But Mitchell fought on, to become in 1917 chief of air service of the 1st Army Corps. Pershing's stiffish notes and letters to Mitchell didn't break his spirit; he enlisted the help of General Hunter Liggett, another believer in air force skills; Liggett, too, had ideas of how to get the best out of the war plane. In his 1917 journal, Mitchell wrote: "The general staff is now trying to run the Air Service, with just as much knowledge of it as a hog knows about skating. It's terrible to have to fight with an organization like this."

Billy Mitchell is worth remembering for more than his famous court-martial.* He had a habit of rubbing the U.S. High Command the wrong way that was to cost him his career in the end. In 1913, he was a captain (at thirty-two), telling a congressional committee that the nation was way behind in military aviation. He learned to fly late in 1915. Commissioned a major, he headed a small flying section for the Signal Corps. He was in Europe when the United States entered the war. He offered his services to General Pétain, and was the first American officer to fly over enemy lines and receive the Croix de Guerre (admittedly an award that seemed to be given out as regularly as flea powder; "Every street cleaner in Paris has one . . .").

In May of 1918, Pershing turned over the job of chief of the air service to General Mason M. Patrick, his former classmate at West Point, who, in shock, admitted, "I have never before seen

---

* Mitchell was mocked for his ideas on future air warfare. He believed "The only real defense against aircraft is other aircraft." Army and navy brass fought him and broke him, calling his ideas "ridiculous heresies . . . romantic fiction." Court-martialed in 1925 for his criticism of the War and Navy Departments in their mismanagement of the aviation service, he was sentenced to suspension for five years. In 1926 he resigned from the army. Dying in 1936, his last words to Colonel Homer Berry were: "Homer, the American people will regret the day I was crucified by politics and bureaucracy."

an airplane, except maybe casually . . ." However, Patrick turned out to be a forceful manager, who got the limping service off the ground. He tried hard to have an air arm, but most pilots, when they got their planes at the front, found someone had forgotten to order machine guns, or to deliver them if on order. The foul-up was so bad that some American pilots flew over the front without guns. The pilots, eager to fly, did not make a big fuss over this because they feared they would be grounded if it was discovered that they were flying unarmed war planes. Captain James Miller was actually shot down with nothing to defend himself with.

As one flier put it: "We can't shoot the Heinies, but there's nothing in the rules says we can't thumb our noses at 'em!" Pershing was not their favorite. The men, by an act of Congress, expected extra pay and rank for serving in a hazardous air branch; but the general negated the idea that service in the air was any more hazardous than shouldering a gun. He put pressure on Congress to revise the law (changing the flying orders so as to drop out the words "on duty" as meaning more pay).

In the usual service ball-up, desk officers and groundlings were paid triple the salaries of the men fighting, and soon to die, in the air. The entire service was mostly run by regular army sweats who never flew and never learned. It must be admitted there was no one else around. One gristle-heel general, seeing a pile of wrecked planes, was told they were "the result of rough landings." He had an order sent out forbidding "any more rough landings . . ." Another general who found fliers training on the outdated Caudron plane objected to the wing-warping method of control, not yet replaced by the more modern ailerons. He, too, issued an order that from now on, no "machine be allowed to sit in the sun where their wings may warp . . ." (Truth outfantasies fiction. Who could invent such stories?)

It was only three months before the war's end (in August 1918) that Mitchell became all-over commander of the American flying forces in France. With French help, he controlled forty-nine squadrons in three wings made up of chase planes, observation machines, and bombers. On paper he had 1,500 planes, most of which he kept as show or in fair repair. He proved their great value in the fighting in the Saint-Mihiel sector, and later in the Meuse-Argonne blood-letting. Only 200 of his crocks, the Liberty DH-4's (of 600 then shipped over) were fit to fly. In October he sent up over 250 bombers and 110 fighters to drop 35 tons of bombs on enemy staging areas.

Billy Mitchell wrote frankly of one American bombing group:

> Our bombardment group was not in good condition . . . was poorly commanded, the morale was weak, and it would take some time to get on its feet. This was largely due to the fact that when I was away, the 96th Squadron was left behind in the Toul area. The officer who was then in command of the 96th flew over into Germany with what ships he had available for duty. He lost his way in the fog and landed in Germany with every ship intact. Not *one* single plane was burned or destroyed, and the Germans captured the whole outfit complete. This was the most glaring exhibition of worthlessness we had had on the front. The Germans sent back a humorous message which was dropped at one of our airdromes. It said, "We thank you for the fine airplanes and equipment which you have sent us, but what shall we do with the major [Harry K. Brown]?"
>
> I know of no other performance in any air force in the war that was as reprehensible as this. Needless to say, we did not reply about the major, as he was better off in Germany. . . .

Mitchell was a delightfully original character. In the leaflets he dropped to American troops from his planes, he gave some advice:

> Whenever a Boche plane is brought down in your sector, do not collect souvenirs from it; you may remove an article or marking that would have given valuable information to us. If Boche aviators are not dead when they land, wait ten minutes before approaching within one hundred feet of the plane after they have left it; sometimes they start a time bomb. DO NOT TOUCH ANYTHING IN A BOCHE PLANE—they sometimes carry innocent-looking infernal machines. . . . Use us to the limit, show your panels, burn signal lights, wave a cloth; anything to tell

us where you are and what you need. After reading this, pass it along to your buddy, and remember to show your signals.

One letter home from a thankful flier said: "Its all right now we have guns. This Billy Mitchell is a Buster Brown for getting things done . . ."

In Mitchell's first raid, a dozen enemy planes were knocked from the air to the loss of one American machine. Mitchell, it was soon clear to some, was a remarkable commander and organizer. What had begun as a Signal Corps project of 65 officers and 1,000 enlisted men ended up with 20,000 officers, 170,000 enlisted men; always at least 800 fliers available at the front, and nearly that many fairly flyable planes. The score for the forty-five American squadrons was 780 enemy planes downed, 73 balloons. They dropped 140 tons of bombs in 150 bombing runs.

Mitchell soon saw the value of aerial bombing, and like all advocates of it, perhaps overvalued it. But he did sense the pattern of the air war of the future. For all his gaucherie, he was valid and bright; precociously eager, despite the wild aberrations that made him unpopular with the conservative military and congressional higher-ups. It would be hard to imagine the American war effort in World War I in the air without him. He succeeded in rising above the abstruse technicalities that make military minds so often their country's worst enemies, and went through great tribulation to serve his country well.

CHAPTER 16

SOME AMERICAN ACES

1. | Edward Vernon Rickenbacker (1890–   )

In every branch of the service there is one man who becomes the symbol of that arm, taking on folk-hero status and, by some eccentric behavior or grim inhuman devotion to duty, retaining that position—often long after the war is over. Eddie (the "Edward" was for formal documents) Rickenbacker is the best-remembered name in the American air force of World War I. Perhaps the only one. He earned that reward by determination, by skill in killing, and by a flying ability that was nearly inhuman, driven by an almost inexhaustible determination. He may well be the only flier of that period and that branch of service whose name, for the average citizen, still has a familiar ring. His career has lasted well into contemporary life and commercial aviation.

The son of William and Elizabeth Reichenbacher of Columbus, Ohio, Eddie was born in 1890. His father soon died and the boy left school at twelve to support his mother. The new horseless carriage business attracted him. It was a happy time for a boy who was mechanically inclined, the age of Thomas Edison, the Wrights, and Ford. Eddie went to work for the Frayer Miller Aircooled Car Company. In those early days (someone has figured out) there were at least 6,000 different companies trying to make auto cars; today there are three and a half firms. So for the young Rickenbacker (in 1917, the Reichenbacher was anglicized to Rickenbacker), this was a main chance and he took it. Racing fast cars became his trade. By the time America came into the war, he was one of the famous racers of the world, making $40,-000 a year.

He was in England in 1917, organizing racers for the Sunbeam Motor Company. With America's entry into the headlines, he rushed back home to propose an air flight squadron made up of crack racing drivers. In Washington he cooled his rump in official waiting-room chairs, and the War Department (today euphemized as the Defense Department) hardly took Rickenbacker seriously. Their minds were on mules, corned beef, puttees, and the closing of the sporting houses in New Orleans's Storyville.

However, it was in the War Department that Rickenbacker met General Pershing and accepted a job as one of his chauffeurs. Meanwhile, the truculent Secret Service investigated him as "a possible enemy agent." (In England, Scotland Yard held Eddie Rickenbacker while his credentials were checked with the United States Embassy.)

Driving the general brought Rickenbacker close to the ultimate military power; he could, he felt, perhaps wangle the position in the air force which was what he yearned for. Some said Rickenbacker resented being a chauffeur. Certainly Pershing, for all his façade of cool formality, was amused at the idea of being driven by the famous racing driver. Rickenbacker did have the advantage of meeting high staff brass who knew of his racing records. One of these was Billy Mitchell, who hardly hid his dislike of stuffed-shirt Pershing. It was Mitchell who managed, with all the skill of army infighting and jockeying for position, to get Rickenbacker transferred to the 94th Squadron, the First Pursuit Group.

Rickenbacker's rise as a flier was amazing. Perhaps the initial impetus came because of his racing prestige; but it was backed by knowledge of motors and engineering, a cold courage, and a will of steel. His advancement, while helped by his fame in public life, had under it the solid qualities of a man who was to become a great ace. The will, the drive, the inherent cunning as to how to get along in the world of competition.

Soon he was a flight commander, with a group under his control. He flew the way he drove a geared-up, overpowered racing car, knowing all the odds in his favor—never going soft. He was no foolhardy reckless show-off; that was never part of his character. What he did looked dangerous and it was. He depended on speed and skill and Eddie Rickenbacker. He was a Spartan who wanted fame, reward, power.

His first flights were not good. He had still to learn air fighting and to know his machine. Sometimes, at first, this cool man lost control in the air. One of his kills, a Fokker, he downed by sheer accident, firing his guns from excitement, not from aim, and getting a bull's-eye.

He admitted: ". . . whenever you're over the lines you have to keep twisting your neck in all directions every minute, or you're sure to be surprised . . ."

Oddly enough, in private Rickenbacker was a conservative who wanted the world of the past to continue unchanged, without any sudden unpleasant shifts from the old values he had set up. Only in the area of flying did he prove to be a progressive radical.

He thought out this business of being an ace. As a racing driver, he knew the value of being in the public eye and had retained this sense of publicity, self-publicity. To be an ace was his avowed ambition. As he flew and learned and made progress in shooting down enemy planes, it was clear to his superiors that Eddie Rickenbacker was just what they needed—splendid ace material. Even so, they resented the fact when he was given command of the 94th. The upper echelons felt that a racing driver might be a great pilot, but could he run men? operate a unit? handle all that administration? Hardly likely. There was then a repellent snobbery among career men in the army and navy. But they were wrong in this case. Rickenbacker was a born manager, the type that *Fortune* magazine was to worship years later: the solid, firm-jawed, hard-eyed corporation head. He drove the men, expected results. No sleeping late for Rickenbacker's Hat-in-the-Ring fliers, as they were called. Up and at the physical jerks in the cold morning breeze. Every spot on the airfield inspected again and again. Things *had* to be right, *had* to be in place. No oily discarded parts, no waste. Rickenbacker hated waste. Not martinet discipline, but expecting his best from every man.

"Every plane must be ready to take-off any moment, day or night, guns loaded, gassed, engine tuned." And he added, in all seriousness, that if all was not correct, "the war could be lost."

Often Rickenbacker went up himself to battle in the sky. He failed to see the humor, or the danger, of luring enemy fliers into a fight over his own U.S.A.-marked hangars simply in order that his men could see how a proper air fight should be conducted. He always knew the odds, figured the percentages, and won.

Billy Mitchell rubbed headquarters staff noses in the success of his boy. His reports told not only of Eddie Rickenbacker the ace, but of his methods in keeping his flight on its toes:

> A squadron commander who sits in his tent and gives orders and does not fly, though he may have the brains of Solomon, will never get the results that a man will, who, day in and day out, leads his patrols over the line and infuses in his pilots the esprit de corps, which is so necessary in aviation and which, so far, has been so lightly considered by the authorities. . . .

Rickenbacker soon had the five enemy kills that made him officially an American ace. There had been some bad luck before he got all his honors. He had to go to the hospital to have his mastoids operated on when he developed an infection from open cockpit flying. With every promotion, Rickenbacker decided to become more perfect. His diary shows such items as: "I must work harder now than ever before."

His fliers were inspired, driven to victories. By the war's end, his group had confirmed sixty-nine air kills, over a third shot down by their commander, Rickenbacker himself. He had that strong male desire for the buddy system amongst his men. They were all his pals, and they all said so. In return, he said "I shall never ask a pilot . . . to go on a mission that I wouldn't go on."

At meals there were roundtable conferences of methods, blackboard talks, and ideas for air-battle tactics. It resembled a big-time coach and the football team boning up for the season ahead; but it was deadly serious, and, like big-time football, it paid off in results in the air. Rickenbacker wanted teamwork. He led his men more often than any other American commander.

Active in the American sectors of the front was Captain Merian C. Cooper, a motion-picture camera man (later to become famous for the classic film, *King Kong*). He was impressed by Rickenbacker, who agreed to star in a staged motion-picture sequence to inspire the folks back home by his deadly skill in the air.

Rickenbacker's airdrome had a captured German Hanover machine, which had been forced down intact. Pilots often took the enemy ship up and let others practice flying around in it, studying its movements and aiming their (unloaded) guns. But Captain Cooper found filming all this from the ground was neither exciting nor close enough. It was decided to send him up to see the mock battle from a DH-9A, which had an American Liberty motor, never too trustworthy and known to balk at the wrong time. Taking off with Jimmy Miessner piloting, the DH-9A rose a bit, then the motor died and the plane tangled in a row of wires and bounced around, ending up a wreck, tail in the air. Neither the pilot nor Captain Cooper was hurt in the smashup. Captain Cooper loudly demanded another chance to get into the air for pictures.

A new Liberty-motored plane was brought into the airdrome and Miessner was again to fly the camera man. Reed Chambers had the part of the villainous German pilot in the Hanover. The two guns carried only tracers and flame-out bullets, but it would look real when he fired. In the rear of the Hanover was an even more villainous-looking Hun, played by Thorn Taylor. He, too, handled a gun. Out of sight was a dummy dressed as a German flier—it would play the part of the enemy gunner falling or leaping from the diving plane when "shot down."

The dashing young American here was, of course, Eddie Rickenbacker, flying a Spad with the Hat-in-the-Ring insignia painted large on the fuselage. The Hanover plane was to play about a dozen parts, being cast as an entire Jagdstaffel of German war planes that Rickenbacker would shoot down one by one, again and again. When Rickenbacker closed in for a kill the last time, Taylor was to duck down and throw out the dummy. Captain Cooper in the air gleefully kept grinding his camera, often only 20 feet from the action. Rickenbacker made his last attack on the Hanover, loose lampblack powder was thrown out of the German plane to make "smoke," and it began to dive. Flares were lit under the wings, guarded by sheets of tin from actually setting the plane on fire. The dummy fell to its doom and Rickenbacker circled his falling prey.

But suddenly the staged melodrama shifted to reality. The filmed "fight" had been drifting in the wind and there was an explosion in the air as an antiaircraft battery below began to fire. Actors and camera man were over a French airfield, and the French were firing dutifully at the German plane's Iron Cross markings. Then they sent up several Bréguets to help Rickenbacker take on the lone German. Rickenbacker moved his plane between the French and the mock German, and by hand signals convinced them he had the German coming down to surrender. After landing, everyone was amused except the two "German fliers" who might have been killed.*

Both sides made a practice of trying to capture intact the other's best fighter planes. The Americans, after capturing the Hanover (which ended up being exhibited at Orly, near Paris, and in America), also got their hands on a Fokker when a pilot set down in a U.S.A. airdrome. The German flier had become confused and thought he was landing at Metz!

Two naturalized Americans of German extraction had been unlucky enough to be caught in Germany at the start of the war, and were forced into the German army. They worked their way into the air force, and planned one day to take their plane over to the Allied side. A few days before the Armistice, they were permitted to fly their Halberstadt plane over the lines and at once came down at the American station at Columbey-les-Belées. Rickenbacker describes the fliers as "two Yiddish gentlemen who for some years had been in business in New York, and now offered a perfectly good machine at no less than ten thousand dollars in exchange for their freedom, and a pass back to the Bronx. . . ."

In fact, no evidence is available to prove that they were either Jews or from the Bronx, or that they set a price of "no less than ten thousand dollars." The Halberstadt plane they brought over,

---

* In time, the film was processed and passed by the American authorities as fit to show. Many Americans were convinced they were watching actual shots of Eddie Rickenbacker downing an entire flight of German planes.

in time, joined the Hanover and the Fokker in making the trip to the United States for exhibition purposes.

Even on Armistice Day, Rickenbacker could not slow down, feel the war was over. He wrote years later that he thought he was the only flier up in the air at eleven o'clock that morning . . .

> We'd all been ordered to stay on the ground the night before. But I wanted to see the war end, and you could only do that by getting out to the front. I was only up about a hundred feet over no-man's land. I got out to see what I went out to see and went back home. . . .

Rickenbacker was never one to clutch at complex definitions. In a way, he was the last of the Alger heroes who could boast he had done it all on his own; anyone could do so if they worked at it hard enough. It was a nineteenth-century morality, and some felt void of forbearance, compassion, or humility in a modern world enduring a malaise bordering on despair. A world fast unhinging the cherished belief that God would, somehow, provide.

Rickenbacker was a moral man who wanted the buddy system carried over into civilian life. With each victory, he wrote, "comes renewal and recementing of ties that bind together these brothers in arms. No closer fraternity exists in the world . . ." He had totaled twenty-six kills, but he grew dour when he saw the world was not the air force.

In later life, Rickenbacker founded and ran a major airline, in which men and planes performed to his high standards, while the food served—some thought—was poor and the seats not of much comfort to the average human frame. In late middle age, Rickenbacker served gallantly and expertly in World War II as an adviser and troubleshooter. Forced to crash his plane into the shark-infested, enemy-ridden Pacific, he and his crew endured twenty-four days of drifting on a rubber raft until rescued. After World War II, Rickenbacker visited the Heroes' Veteran Cemetery in East Berlin, to pay homage to the graves of Oswald Boelcke, Manfred von Richthofen, and Ernst Udet. He wanted to be photographed by the gravesides, but the Soviets refused permission.

2. | Frank Luke, Jr.

Frank Luke, Jr., with twenty-one victories was second man on the list of American aces, just under Eddie Rickenbacker's twenty-six. Luke was a natural flier. He was a reticent type from Arizona, a shy sort of toe-in-the-dust boy. Meeting General Mitchell one day, Frank was quite flabbergasted, caught in his untidy uniform and slack puttees. He was bashful and silent. He and Joseph Wehner became noted as balloon killers just before the Meuse-Argonne battle of autumn 1918. In eight days, Luke shot down eight enemy *drachen*, two in one day. It was mean work, for the balloons had better and better antiaircraft protection and could send up a deadly net of fire at an attacker. "After one air battle on seeing Luke's plane, Mitchell took his swagger stick and with a zip, pulled huge chunks of fabric off Luke's left wing . . ."

On one mission, Luke was jumped by half a dozen Fokkers. Joe Wehner died trying to come to his aid. Luke escaped, grew sorrowful over the loss of his partner, and was sent to Paris on leave. Going up, on his return, with a Lieutenant Ivan Robins, Luke gained a victory but Robins was killed. He was dubbed "Hard-Luck Luke" by his partners, and felt he was a jinx. Finally he broke up, and went AWOL. Reprimanded, on his return, he took off without orders and sent a balloon down in flames to settle his nerves. He was grounded. But he got to his Spad and took off again.

He dropped a note: "Watch three Hun balloons on the Meuse. Luke." At dusk, he got his first balloon, then moved through the dreadful Archie fire to kill his second. Wounded, bleeding, under deadly fire, he set flames to the third. In real Western style, to calm down, he shot up troops on Murvaux's main street. Next, he crash-landed on the edge of the town. Crawling from his plane, he sat with his back against a tree, waiting for the enemy to come and get him—as in the painting he loved by Frederick Remington, *The Last Stand*. When the enemy surrounded him he went to work with his pistol, getting eleven as if they were Geronimo's Apaches. He died with a Mauser slug through his heart.

The fate of Frank Luke was testified to in a strange document produced after the war:

We the undersigned, living in Murvaux, Department of Meuse, certify to have seen on 19 September 1918 toward evening an American aviator, followed by an escadrille of Germans in the direction of Liny, descend suddenly, vertically toward the earth, then straighten out close to the ground, and fly in the direction of Briers Farm, where he found a German captive balloon he burned. He flew toward Milly where he found another balloon which he also burned in spite of incessant fire directed toward his plane. He shot down a third balloon and two planes. He apparently was wounded by a shot from rapid-fire cannon. He came back over Murvaux and with his guns killed six German soldiers and wounded as many more. Following he landed and got out of his machine to quench his thirst at the stream. He had gone fifty yards when, seeing the Germans come toward him, he had the strength to draw his revolver to defend himself. A moment after, he fell dead from a serious wound he received in the chest. The undersigned placed the body of the aviator on a wagon and conducted it to the cemetery.

Murvaux, 15 January 1919   Voliner Nicholas
                                Cortine Delbart
                                Mayor Auguste Garre

Luke received the Congressional Medal of Honor posthumously.

3. | Raoul Gervais Lufbery (1885–1918)

The third-ranking American ace, famous for his exploits with the Lafayette Escadrille, was not an American by birth. Raoul Lufbery was born in 1885, of a French father and mother, in France. When his mother died, his father remarried and moved to America to become a dealer in rare stamps, leaving the boy with his grandmother in Blois.

At fourteen, Raoul was working in a chocolate factory, sending money to his father overseas, lend-lease in reverse. They never met again. Lufbery himself became a wanderer when he was seventeen. He drifted through Tunis, Algiers, Egypt, the Balkans, Turkey, Germany. He lived as he could, with what work he was able to pick up. He seemed to lack any specific qualities for settling down. He came on to the United States. But his father was away on a trip to Europe, stamp hunting. Raoul, the father tie unresolved, drifted on: Cuba, New Orleans, San Francisco. He lacked funds to get to China but enlisted instead in the U.S. army and served in the steam heat of the Philippines for over two years. This made him an American citizen. Enlistment over, the lonely wanderer saw Japan, China; then still without roots, India.

It was in Calcutta, in 1912, that he helped a French exhibition flier, Marc Pourpe, to erect his hangar tent for his Blériot flying machine. The drifter had finally found something—and someone—to attach himself to: he became Pourpe's mechanic and close friend. The two Frenchmen moved around Asia for a year, flying and showing the natives their strange winged bird. A kite maker in China made a replica of their monoplane and flew it on a string, with a beehive attached to make the motor sounds.

Pourpe remains something of an enigma to us, but we know that he did a stunt flight from Cairo to Khartoum. In the summer of 1914, the two friends were in France buying a Morane-Saulnier plane for a new tour. Then came war. Lufbery claimed U.S. citizenship, but the French pooh-poohed this and he was forced to join the Foreign Legion. Pourpe, who had joined the French air force, was killed scouting behind the enemy lines. But not before he had gotten Lufbery into the flying corps. Lufbery, for his part, never recovered from the death of his friend.

He flew with the Escadrille Voison 106 until the Escadrille Américaine was formed, then transferred to that. His final destiny was set. He had returned to men in whose army he had served, whose nation had made him a citizen.

There is something tragic about Raoul Lufbery's life, but we lack the necessary details to fill it out. As one of the Americans flying for France, certainly he received more than his share of glory, fame, newspaper space, and magazine prose on his life and flying. Both in Europe and America, he became the hero of the moment in the air. Babies were named for him, and dishes were concocted: *Faisan Lufbery, Aubergines Lufbery.* He had the glamour of being both French by birth and a naturalized American citizen by inclination. Many women offered themselves to him either in free love or in marriage. In the cafés and bars of Paris, when on leave, he was greeted and admired, offered drinks and advice.

James Norman Hall, who flew with him, remembered:

How we unheroic and unknown airmen envied him the greetings he had from such men as Guynemer, Fonck, Nungesser and others who had achieved greatly: *"Tiens, Luf! Comment ça va, mon vieux!"* He never boasted or took credit to himself. He counted his success as three-fourths luck, and was always surprised that so much of it should come his way. When foolish people tried to flatter him, he used to say to us after they had gone: "Well, you know, it's funny what things people will say to a man's face. I wonder if they think we like it?" He had to take a lot of it whether he liked it or not.

In time, all this flattery bored Lufbery. He refused to give interviews, and withdrew from the public eye. He retired to his airfield and hardly ever left it. He began to turn against civilians, those back-slappers, some of them growing grossly fat on war profiteering, sellers of shoddy and ill-made plane parts that sacrificed the lives of their own countrymen, while mouthing chauvinistic slogans as far from the front as they could get.

Even while remaining on good terms with his fellow fliers, Lufbery preferred to be alone. He would go to the forests to pick wild mushrooms, walking endlessly through sodden woods. In rainy weather when flying was out of the question, Lufbery would usually don a waterproof and go mushroom-hunting and the airdrome chef grew to expect his supply of mushrooms. The lion cub mascot, Whiskey, had been joined by another lion cub, Soda; they reminded Lufbery of tropical countries he had toured with Pourpe.

There was a gulf between him and these young cheerful Americans, most with homes, families, someone to love. The Americans, at first, didn't know what to make of the world wanderer. To them Lufbery was French—French as Joan of Arc—not American. They called him "the inscrutable guy."

Lufbery had come to Bar-le-Duc from Le Plessis Belleville after training in a Nieuport. His earlier record had not been good; he had wrecked a few planes in poor landings (it is virtually a formula for many great aces to have been slow learners and bad landers). At one time he was almost sent back to remain a *pilote de bombardement*.

As it happened, he came to the Americans on the day that Bert Hall—another wanderer—shot down a plane. Hall was loaded with superstitions. When he saw Lufbery, he wrote in his journal: "Raoul Lufbery joined us today . . . had my first luck against the Heinies . . . took Luf in with open arms. He looks lucky, the boys love him . . ." As the new good-luck charm, Lufbery drank his part of the two gallons of booze mixed by Hall, bartender *extraordinaire*, in a metal bucket.

Lufbery, like other Americans, went through a period of getting bloodied and shot at before he settled down to the business of killing. One day on a dusk patrol, he took on a German plane. They circled and shot at each other. Neither could kill off the other. They drifted in the west wind that always favored the Germans, over the enemy lines. Lufbery broke off the fruitless fight, to help a French machine in trouble. But he was waylaid by a Fokker he hadn't noticed in the sky, and took German bullets in his engine; two tore through his fur-lined flying suit, just missing flesh. Another tore a boot to shreds and a spent slug bounced off his flying helmet. Lufbery's plane also had an elevator fin shot away. Altogether it looked like a piece of Swiss cheese, but he managed to land: the wreck was marked as "beyond repair," and stripped for parts.

An important air raid was set up for October 12, 1916; the target, the Mauser Works in Oberndorf. Short bombers would carry the deadly loads. Among the fighter escorts were four Americans, Lufbery, Masson, Prince, and de Laage de Meux. It was a heavy and dangerous raid on a vital war industry. Oberndorf produced rifles, ammunition, bayonets, shell casings, and the famous Mauser automatic weapons; and of course it was well protected. The attack succeeded in inflicting great damage on the factories, however. After the light bombers had set fires, the Short bombers came over and added their load to the flames. It was a fantastic fire. The earth shook for miles around; stocks of gunpowder and ammunition went off in a vast Fourth of July spectacle. Smoke rose into the sky in a black pillar like a Doomsday finger. Six of the Allied bombers were lost, but they got two German planes. Each American got a kill; Lufbery, de Laage de Meux, and Masson each got a Fokker, and Prince an Aviatik two-seater trying to act like a fighter.

Lufbery's Fokker kill had been his fifth and in the communiqués he became the first official American ace. Landing after the Mauser raid had not been easy in the suddenly dying day. Like most returning raiders, Lufbery had to fly by instruments and what he could remember of the landscape in the gathering dark. He made out the kerosene flares set up at Corcieux (in the Vosges), cut his speed—he didn't trust either his speed indicator or altimeter—and began his glide down. He was still poor at landings, it would seem. He hit the ground hard and bounced up again; set down his wheels, skidded, and finally came to a halt.

Some of the French he had escorted gave him cheers. They were leading him to the mess for a meal and lots of wine and cognac when the whine of a Nieuport engine was heard. The plane circled twice trying to study the murky field and its smoky flares. Then it came down for a landing but never made it. A banging, jolting sound ensued. The plane had snagged its wheels on a high-tension cable, slingshooting the machine onto the turf, smashing it down on its nose, then somersaulting it across the field. In horror, they all ran toward the wreck, wondering who was the pilot. It turned out to be Norman Prince, who had been rocketed from the cockpit, the safety belt tearing loose. The flier's legs were broken and he had fearful internal injuries. Lufbery and the others reached Prince. He was still conscious. In great pain, he heard another plane overhead and muttered to Lufbery, who was helping to carry him, "If that fellow gets down all right, he can thank me for taking the goddam wire out of his way . . ."

Lufbery rode with Prince in the ambulance to Gérardmer. They sang favorite songs as the pain grew worse. The hospital doctors did not think the injuries were too serious, but by morning Prince was in a coma and the doctors had changed their views, saying it was a blood clot in the brain. Unconscious, Prince was never to come out of his coma. Captain Thénault and a group of Prince's fellow fliers stood by as the dying man was given the rank of second lieutenant, and the Légion d'Honneur to add to his Médaille Militaire and Croix de Guerre. Prince died on October 15. He received the full military dress parade burial at Luxeuil, with the firing squad, the bugle dirge.

Lufbery continued to amass air victories. As the leading American ace of the time, he also continued to receive further glory in the press. It was clear that he was being built up by both the American section and the French. He had nothing to do with this, but there it was and he had to live with it. He never got over the loss of his friend Pourpe. One who knew them both wrote, "their friendship was a veritable cult . . ."

There was little he could turn to but walks in the woods, picking mushrooms. If he found wartime flying a stupefying, restrictive life, Lufbery had no other. He could but fly and kill.

At the beginning of 1918, Lufbery became a major in the U.S. air force. With typical military imagination, this skilled flier was sent to a desk at Issoudun, where he had no duties at all. He sharpened pencils and sat. Sent to the VS 94th Pursuit Squadron in the Champagne sector, he found the fliers all had planes. But again, in a not unusual army screwup, no machine guns! Major Lufbery led them—gunless—in practice flights while waiting for weapons. James Norman Hall tells that in visits to the Lafayette Escadrille, Lufbery let off steam about what was wrong.

"It's nearly a year since the United States declared war, and what do you suppose the 94th is doing? Waiting for machine guns! Six hundred million dollars appropriated for the United States Air Service, and we're loafing . . . we can't get enough guns to equip a dozen planes!"

In March 1918 came six miserable Vickers guns, so that three planes could now mount twin guns! The French had called the Americans "impatient virgins," but at last three were flying. For the record, Major Lufbery, Lieutenant Eddie Rickenbacker, and Lieutenant Doug Campbell went up on that first uneventful flight. By April 10, at Toul, the whole squadron was fully armed. Lieutenants Winslow and Campbell got their first kills, the first U.S. air victories for the 94th. After that, for some time, nothing. Eddie Rickenbacker made his first kill over Ponte Mousson, downing a single-seater Albatros. Lufbery got his sixteenth and seventeenth kills.

On May 19, in the morning, Lufbery received a report that a German plane was over Mont Mihiel; very high, above the Archies trying to reach it. When it got within range and was hit by anti-aircraft fire, it went spiraling down. It looked like a goner, but it recovered and like a wounded goose, began to labor back to its base. Lufbery, like a good sportsman, decided to go up and put the wounded creature out of its misery. His own ship was in repair. He asked if a plane on the field was ready, fueled, and armed. He was told by a mechanic it was, and set off in the Nieuport.

It was a seven-mile chase, Lufbery going up to 2,000 feet. He began firing at the enemy photo-reconnaissance plane. Some observers on the ground said they sensed that his guns jammed, and that he circled while he cleared them. Then he came in on the German plane again, from the rear. The enemy gunner got off one quick burst at Lufbery. The Nieuport exploded into bubbles of flame, and went into a shallow dive straight ahead and down. At about 250 feet from the earth, they saw Lufbery jump from the burning plane. Perhaps he was aiming for a nearby canal of a little village close to Nancy. If so, he missed and landed hard enough in a flower bed to die. Rickenbacker wrote that when found, "the charred figure [was] entirely covered with flowers from nearby gardens."

No one knows the name of the man who shot down Lufbery. The German records do not record the kill. Most likely the gunner of the German ship—leaving the scene in a hurry—never saw Lufbery's plane fall.

4. | And A Handful More

Another American of the air—and a wild one—was Sergeant Frank Bayliss from the old whaling port of New Bedford, who had twelve air victories. He favored the bushy mustache of an early bartender or Western sheriff. He had come over to Europe to drive ambulances (like John Dos Passos, Ernest Hemingway, and e.e. cummings). But that proved too tame, so he joined the Lafayette Flying Corps. He was a go-after-'em and shoot-'em flier, taking great chances. He was a dead shot, and when in air battle gave a damn about nothing, including his own life. He had that flair without which no artist in any field can raise his work to a higher level. Shot down while trying to check on one of his kills, he landed in No-Man's-Land, having jumped from the still rolling plane. He ducked some Germans in Keystone Cop style, and as they gave chase got away in a loping run to the French lines, bullets biting the dust all around him.

A friend said of Baylies that he was modest to a fault, full of charm. "No amount of success could turn his head or alter his simple statement that his victories were due to luck. In a crowd he did not often speak seriously, but his close friends knew that beneath his jovial manner ran a vein of thoughtfulness and genuine idealism; it was not for pure love of adventure . . ."

Baylies's end is something of a mystery. Flying on June 17, 1918, between Crèvecoeur and Lassigny, another pilot reported he saw Baylies jumped by four monoplanes and sent down to his death in flames. German records show no such planes in the air at that place or time. Another account tells of three Spads chasing Fokker triplanes and a Spad falling on fire. This may have been Baylies's ship.

Another name is that of David Putnam, from Brookline: a Harvard man, tall, well made, serious, almost pedantic. After training with the French (he was not a particularly good student),

Putnam went not as he desired to the Escadrille Lafayette, but to Escadrille 156. He was bold and at once plunged into a group of eighteen enemy planes. He killed the leader and took a wise withdrawal—swiftly. Putnam became a unit commander and the press began to take notice of him.

On September 13, 1918, he and another fighter flier took on eight Fokkers in battle. Putnam got one enemy but, as he moved to kill a second, two Fokkers on his tail got him with their deadly bursts. His top wing was chewed to bits. His Spad began to dip into a fast vertical dive, tearing off the bottom set of wings so that he fell like a streamlined lead weight. Most likely, Putnam was already dead. He was found with two slugs in his head, wounds in chest and arms. Some fool wrote of his end: "It was a splendid death . . ."

Such is a sampling of the American aces. Others were men like G. A. Vaughn, F. E. Kindley, E. W. Springs, R. Lanis, and J. N. Swaab, all of whom in the short time America was in the war had ten victories each or more. Nearly eighty other American fliers shot down five or more German planes. The Americans in all totaled 750 victories.

They were a special lot, these Americans, in their innocence of European ways. They were overreckless in an already faded frontier tradition of the face-off and the quick draw. They flew with daring and many did not last long in the air. No matter how wild their habits grew, they had a puritanical sense of duty, and only at the end knew the sad impermanence of all actions. They ran to extremes; they were either better, or more keyed up, than the average man under delicate, split-second, deadly conditions. Most had a driving adolescent dependence on the seeking out of action and excitement. In their frenzy, they still retained an American conformist contact with their country, town, city-street upbringings; even if somewhat battered at times, they remained full of American ideals. In the air, as they put on the rudder without banking, or took on a Jagdstaffel of fast interceptors, they often mistook themselves for settlers holding off hostile Indians or riding shotgun on the overland stage. Often short lives, transient joys, were their destiny. Few of them understood the true failure and agony of the disemboweled Europe they fought to save or serve. All lived vaguely in hope of some greater good to come; none could put together with any clarity words that explained their actions or themselves.

CHAPTER 17

A PERSONAL NARRATIVE

This section on the Americans ends with some eyewitness accounts from *A Flier's War*, printed privately for his friends by "W. W. Windstaff" (a pseudonym). "Windstaff" was an American ace, an ironic, clever, hard person whose life was never the same after fighting with the English Royal Flying Corps and catching a bad leg injury in battle in the air over France. *A Flier's War* is remarkable for its vividness and sense of immediacy.

First, a piece on how some Americans joined the RFC early in 1915:

Came the crazy exciting day John B—— and I entrained for Canada with our long underwear, money belts, lice powder and two ivory-handled .45 Colts, a gift from my grandfather. We were off for the war over there and bursting with illusions. Later John said we had screwed our youth. I always felt our youth had screwed us, made us opaque to reality. But that came later.

We found the prosaic system of air training in Canada was to shove everybody into a fast training course with Sopwith Pups and kill off all the awkward chaps. It was simplification—towards the essence of war, speedy and obvious. John and I were scared pissless by the speed, relatively, of those small wire and canvas trainers, but we caught the hang of it. Brooks Brothers made us uniforms; we learned to carry a swagger stick. And once every two weeks, horny as mink, we hired a car for a trip to Toronto where we ate, drank, went to bed with local talent, and later dreamed we were falling in flames. We made friends with a Canadian named Harry Glenn Moore, and saw him mashed to jelly when he ran his trainer into a hillside.

One rainy sleety day "Chunky" M—— from our class at college showed up at our training base with an alligator bag and his guitar. We hugged like lovers, drank warm beer, and sang our alma mater song.

"This is it, fellas—*this* is it!" Chunky said.

"How'd you wrangle it?" John asked.

"Got the old man's sales agent in England to write a letter."

On an over-packed hurtling train one cold winter night near dawn, with a sudden blizzard beating against Mr. Pullman's Palace car windows, we lay in our berths hoping to beat the ice into the St. Lawrence. The telegraph poles went by on a slant, passing the express trains with their roar of red fire, rows of yellow windows and the bong bong of our steel on good ballasted track. Here we were, John said, going far out "over the rounded surface of the globe heading to England, to war over the seas." I remembered my grandfather reading from Homer of "the wine-dark sea" and the "pink-fingered dawn" and was homesick—the way I had been going off to prep school.

The oddly painted Cunarder we boarded, pounding on at a steady series of knots, came with us seasick, tooting into Liverpool, the city all soot and dirt, gray and brown bricks. It was Saturday and we three chums were a bit pale, standing there at the rail, damn lonely, so far from home. The women in uniform were all long of tooth, the officers with pips on their uniforms all very snotty. The dirty sweat-smelling boat train was smaller than any we had ever seen, and its whistle had a shrill, ladylike toot. The people, Chunky insisted, spoke a strange tongue that was nearly related to what we had been taught. "Lousy broad-ass a's," said John. At the hollow glass-roofed London station the fog hung yellow in slowly moving coils, and the smell of coal burning and wet streets and cold pork sandwiches mixed with axle grease and the damp woolen clothes of the pale war-worried Londoners didn't seem a proper welcome.

Chunky said we stood "lonely as survivors of an Indian raid," with our traveling bags, our mufflers tight around our throats as the cold came up through the stone floor and bit into our bodies.

A neat young officer with tired classic features, dressed in an overcreased uniform with an RFC insignia, came over smiling. "You're the Canadians. Follow me."

"Americans," I corrected.

"You're all Americans over there. You mean U.S.A."

Chunky said, "Well, kick my shaggy ass."

"The bloody war will, Yank. This way to a cabbie."

The taxi went slowly along in the pea soup mist and John wondered how people could live in this climate. We were pretty low.

"It isn't always this depressing, chaps. Sometimes it just rains. But we'll not stay here. You're to train in Camels—then on your way to France in a few weeks."

That nearly cheered us up.

"Never been out of the States before?"

I said, "Canada."

"Of course, Canada."

The cab rubbed against a great horse-drawn dray carrying barrels of Royal Crest Stout and Ale.

"Some Americans over here giving you blokes a dinner."

The dinner was dull. We saw our first live English butler. Our hostess, in a low-cut velvet gown, kept swinging her long string of pearls from a plump hand. "Oh, dear, this war—it's unthinkable. Utterly."

I dreamed that night in my too narrow hotel room of the scarlet lobster alive in its mayonnaise dressing crawling over my pillow. I slept till the boy called *Boots* came to knock on the door with the morning paper—GREAT BATTLE ON SOMME. We three Yanks gingerly ate kidneys grilled, and found the coffee dreadful as the weather. We moved out and the next few weeks we flew Camels in Essex, saw more young fliers die, learned how to use the Lewis gun, the Vickers gun, read maps, remember signals, keep our bowels open, drink 'arf and 'arf, fuck standing up against a stone wall. We were so damn earnest and eager to get to France, the gunnery sarge had to keep saying: "Better learn to 'andle yer guns, me young sods, first."

Then we were leaning uncertainly on the rail of a blacked-out Channel steamer, the smoke of the funnel being torn to shreds by a brisk wind from France ("Fair stood the wind for . . ."). Officers were holding their belted stomachs as the steamer dipped and tossed, till someone said that thin bloody line was bloody Calais. "Calais?" Chunky asked, pointing. "Looks like Asbury Park." "Oh, yes, that's hit," said a Cockney batman. "Bloody fucking plice hit is, too. The hures all over fifty and no teef."

The French landscape from the train looked a great deal like being home in New Jersey, only the houses were older and all of solid stone—until we saw some ruins. The first look at Paris came on us with the chatter of what could only be French, and we rode in pale daylight in an open car marked B.E.F. among the bare chestnut trees, and saw the spires of Notre Dame overhead. John, an arts major, said, "It isn't at all like the Pissaros and the Manets."

We stayed at the Hotel Meurice on the Rue de Rivoli and we couldn't even unpack. Chunky asked what was that strange little floor spray in the bathroom? It got to be a very tired joke.

"Too short a day to waste by just resting here in Paris," I said.

John said, "We move to Arras tonight. Let's see the Tuileries Gardens and walk to the Place de la Concorde."

"What about Les Girls?" Chunky asked.

It was a city all very shabby and war-tired. Wide unswept boulevards, ill-dressed people, a smoky sky, the few bits of pale green making it a sad picture all the length of the Champs Elysées. One girl clung to John's arm. She smelled of candied violets and sour wine.

"Uloo, Tommy. Zig-zig wif me?"

"After the war."

"Go 'ump you grandmère!"

That afternoon John was examined by an RFC flight doctor who said John's sense of balance was wrong; we were to leave for Arras without him. He saw us to the train station. There we found the wounded being carried away and lots of dirty drunk French infantry, big mustaches, tin hats, going back to the front from leave, women in dull black weeping, the station smelling of steam, urine, dried butchershop blood. Only it wasn't beef—it was the wounded.

We three had a last drink at a zinc and Chunky gave us a college
song on his guitar.

> *Wild roved an Indian girl, bright Alfarata,*
> *Where sweeps the waters of the blue Juniata.*

We sang in unison.

> *I took my girl to a fancy ball,*
> *It was a social hop.*
> *Then to the restaurant we went,*
> *The best one on the street.*
> *She said she wasn't hungry,*
> *And this is what she'd eat . . .*

Chunky took up the refrain:

> *A dozen raw, a plate of slaw,*
> *A chicken and a roast,*
> *Some sparrow grass with apple sass,*
> *And soft shell crabs on toast.*
> *A big box stew with crackers too,*
> *Her hunger was immense.*
> *When she called for pie, I thought I'd die,*
> *For all I had was fifty cents.*

Then Chunky and I ran to make our train, and I was sure I
would be dead in four to six weeks. . . .

Next, what it was like for an American flying with the RFC in
France in 1917:

That winter we were flying over the front from the Wing
Headquarters aerodrome behind Amiens. It was a bloody, blue-
cold winter; the squadron was using Sopwith Camels nearly as
bad as DH-4's, the goddamn notorious Flaming Coffins. We pilots
lived on milk and brandy, stinking of tension turned to sweat in
our black flying breeks, going over the Hun lines, escorting the
heavy reconnaissance camera planes with the enemy's Archies
exploding high up, bursting in our faces. The legend that nobody
lived beyond the first six weeks was mostly true. In the British
Sixth Wing, actually by count, we lost a third of our flyers, and

it got worse before Cambrai fell, when the Boche began mounting heavier Spandau machine guns in their goddamn Jagdstaffel—hunting packs. They had replaced their older planes with the Fokker triplane, and we were still in the flypaper and canvas and wood Sopwith F.I. Camels. With us, Chunky said, it was the will doing the work of the impossible. We all took to carrying bottles of brandy in our coverall leg pockets.

Flying on patrol, the long-toothed major with the trick pipe got his, trying out over the lines a new Nieuport (as expected, the air valve jammed and the engine conked). He tried to climb vertically, went into a slow roll and a loop. A Hun dipped down out of the sun and began to pour it into him, and I saw the major's face, the Sandhurst mustache standing out. I was flying on his left tip, trying to come up to protect him. He just looked disappointed, mouthed the word *merde,* and the crate began to smoke and flame and slide down discarding wings and parts. He waved. I thought—these buggering British—the willed gesture that becomes a principle.

I didn't follow the major down because I was trying to get the sun between me and the red-streaked Fokker, and when I had him in the sights, I prayed that the rotten mechanical device that synchronized my two Lewis guns to fire through the propeller would work. A week before I had shot off my own prop and landed in the middle of an Anzac battalion in the lines. I had been sweating it out, for the wind was always blowing to the east and there was the danger of coming down behind the German lines.

I fired a burst to clear the barrels and the blur of the spinning prop was all right. Oh, the Hun was good. He tried to keep the sun behind him, but my petrol was clean that morning in my tanks and I circled and got on his tail, he twisting, me after him, the Teutonic crosses on his wings black against the dark canvas. I pressed off half a drum right into him, and the sonofabitch didn't seem to hurt at all. I could see wood and canvas splintering off and falling away. We had become a deadly tight duet, stuck close, to the death.

He lifted away to climb and I throttled back and thought fuck-youkraut, when I sensed something on my right, and there I was jumped by a staffel of Albatros who were laying for me. My pigeon had been a decoy. I kicked the stick over and went into a long, fast dive, wires screaming, did an evasion spin that began to strain the wings, and I cursed the profiteers who cheated on aeroplane specifications. There was a wisp of cloud nearby, looking no bigger than a bathtowel, and I started for that and it was bigger than it looked. I was very young and didn't want to die. Not before I sent my grandmother a picture of myself in my London-tailored uniform.

I went through the cloud and found myself with just one Hun. He had a skull and bones painted on his canvas side and I automatically pressed the Lewis button and a staccato burst caught him in the belly of his machine. I was just under him—in his blind spot—and he fell, all black smoke, flames redder than any paint job. I could see the flier's protuberant bloodshot eyes as he screamed. Nobody carried parachutes in those days, and his right wing just touched mine—a kiss—as he fell away in a big gray world.

I scooted for our lines, sticky with fear. I vomited brandy-and-milk and bile all over my instrument panel. Yes, it was very romantic flying, people said later, like a knight errant in the clean blue sky of personal combat, in whipcord breeches and a British tunic with long Bond Street cut tails. *So* romantic . . . oh shit and piss. I remembered an old Sunday School lesson: "Man is full of misery and all earthly beauty is corrupt because of the untiring abjuration of the Devil . . ."

I was sobbing and my mouth, throat, sour-tasting like acid when I came over our dusty aerodrome and set the plane down with a hard bounce—a bad show of nerves. The ack emma warrant officer came out in the windy cold among the trampled weeds, the Lewis gunnery sergeant at his side.

"The major bought one," I said, climbing out, covered with my own slime.

"We heard. One of the Handley Page chaps saw it."

"Major was due for leave, too," said the gunnery sergeant, examining my guns. "You 'ad 'ardly anything left in the Lewis drums."

I wanted to smoke, I didn't want to smoke. I walked towards the tin hut where the flight officer would want to hear it officially. It was too warm in the hut, a small stove ate coke, gave up gas, and used up the air. Captain H——, M.C., D.S.M., sat at a desk, a gray scarf wound around his neck, his Savile Row boots scuffed. He looked like a proper advertisement for the paraphernalia of war, only his eyes were bloodshot, and he had a small tic on his right cheek.

"Phone call just came in. Your kill confirmed. Your third?"

I poured myself a brandy from the desk bottle, knocked it back . . . "I want to go to Arras on leave. I've shot my load."

"Arras? All right."

"I'll take a bath."

"Saved you a steak. We killed a Frenchie's cow, by accident. Envy you the cossie in Arras." He made an obscene thumb jabbing gesture. I went to the bathhouse and fell asleep standing under the hot shower and nearly scalded myself. I left the flying jacket and the gear for the batman to take to the laundress. I must have slept open-mouthed for some time because when I woke up the sun was on the dirty window pane and my mouth was the Black Hole of Calcutta. The colonel with the A.D.M. had his gramophone going: "It's a Long Long Trail Awinding" . . . I felt poisoned. I had come out of sleep as if from a cave. My throat was raw. The forms of the world's patterns were dim. All dimensions and echoes had lost their outer reality for me. A sure sign a flier is nerve-taut.

I got up and took a pick-me-up brandy and I wished I had a couple of raw eggs to go with it, the way my grandfather used to drink and wink: "Billy, man is the creature of obligations and betrayals, but a good toot of whisky never did a soul harm."

There was a tap on the door and I mumbled something . . . A tall handsome man came in—one of the most handsome dark rabbinical men I've ever seen. Certainly this must be the Jewboy replacement.

"Hello, Lieutenant, I'm Tony P——."

"That's right."

We shook hands. He had that soft curly hair and those big dark eyes, very big ones, violet pupils that women fall right into bed for when they see them. There was a tight caul on my skull.

"Have a drink. How many hours you solo?" He looked very smart, puttees, ordnance belt, all the brass and expensive leather of a fresh replacement. He held out a tin of Papastratos cigarettes, a gold lighter.

"Enough, enough. This looks like a crackerjack outfit."

"We've what's left of other squadrons. The remains are put in here." We smoked slowly. "Tony, the planes are not too good, but the mechanics are wonders, and the C.O. a decent sort of prick, doesn't care what you do so long as you salute and go up when your squadron leader says, 'Let's go, chaps.'"

"Yes."

"What have you been flying?" I asked.

"The Martinsyde, some Nieuports."

"What guns you train with?"

"Vickers."

"We use Lewis—usual airforce ballsup."

My batman Hughie came in with a tray. He wore the Mons Star and some lower award that was given to the rank and file. He lifted the tin lid of some poached eggs. "Stole these, Lieutenant, and the coffee is the real thing. Too bad about the major. One of the best, as they say."

"The very best. This is Lieutenant P——. Get a batman who knows the gear. Tony, Hughie Green—a marvelous thief."

"Right as rain, sir," said Hughie.

He went out and I stared at the eggs and swallowed the very black coffee with the four spoons of sugar in it.

"What's there in Arras?"

"Tail, booze."

He looked at a fragment of a Boche wing with a cross on it, a splintered prop off an Albatros D-III that killed our last squadron leader. "I'm a Jew, you know."

"I wouldn't have guessed," I said.

"I don't want anybody saying the goddamn Heeb, he's got a streak of yellow crap up his back."

"Look, Tony. The trick is, figure the odds. One third of the fliers go west on a front like this, two thirds of the fliers survive. Half of them crap out—mental. It's very quiet just now. Too cold."

Outside they were starting up the afternoon patrol. I could smell the burning castor oil they were mixing with the lubrication, hear the young carnivores in flying suits chattering—most of them celibate, pink-cheeked, earnest. I handed Tony the plate of poached eggs.

"Eat this. In a couple of weeks you may not like solid food." I went out to see about transportation to Arras. The patrol was in the air, trying to get over the trees. . . .

A fighter pilot's view of life on the ground:

The lie was the Germans in the air or on the ground weren't as good as we were, weren't fighting up to snuff any more. Of course the generals, sitting snug on their prostates in their big Rolls-Royces with an aide carefully putting the woolen rug over their legs and paunches, insisted in interviews: *Sacrifice was Glory*. It was for Civilization, for Mankind. We fliers were pretty sick of abstractions. Vaterland, Freedom, Democracy, The King, The Prince of Wales (poor creepy young bastard in his tight little uniform, his sleepy eyes half open, moving down a safe trench and shaking hands with little undernourished Cockneys). It was a war for no reason. We didn't see much hope of surviving. It was all a bloody sell-out, and we fliers now were aware of it.

And as I flew I wasn't buying Father O'Bein, or Church of England's Cecil, or Rabbi Haukfliesh and all their fine moral promises and splendid dogmas. Because there were O'Beins and Cecils and Haukflieshs on the other side, too. God in that war was divided from his crotch to his eyebrows. He promised victory through O'Bein, etc., to those who had the faith. I didn't have faith, only a hatred of official cant. I was becoming an alcoholic, I had crabs, two cavities in my back teeth. I couldn't at times control the twitch on my face. My hands had a tremor. I had murdered half a dozen Germans or Austrians or Roumanians who were out to murder me. And almost everything I and John and Chunky had believed in as boys was *merde*—plain shit. Fortunately for me I went raving, flaming mad when it got too much. But that came later. I always thought I faked it beautifully. The grimaces, the twitching, the filthy language. But several doctors told me, "No, old boy, you had really gone off your rocker."

But back to the day I got leave. I had on a clean uniform, my best unpaid tailored one. The poor London bugger waited years for payment. I had my swagger stick ("Phallic?" Chunky once asked. "Like the English, prick in hand, public exhibitionists?"). I had a nice alcohol glow, I was shaved, cap over one eye; was standing in the flight officers' hut, waiting for the grease monkey to change a tire on the officers'-mess car, a beat-up Bentley. Free for two days from the laws of inevitability.

A muddy Renault came up the wreck of a muddy road from the main highway and under the camouflage nets. Four officers in RAF dress were singing "The Bastard Kings of England." They were all young, very Anglo-Saxon; you could almost use them as as a poster. One waved. It was John B——.

I hadn't seen John since 1916 when we had come over on a boat from Canada and he had flunked the coordination tests (they claimed his sense of balance had been damaged as a boy in some sport accident). He looked very solid, and there were flying wings on his tunic and French and English chicken-shit of gold and silver and bronze.

Chunky was by his side, opening the twisted wires on a cork of a wine bottle. The two officers in the back I didn't know. Chunky got out and slapped me on the back. "See who I found?" John got out and slapped me on the back, and I met the two other officers. They didn't slap. Oxford kids, pink-cheeked, foul-mouthed, very friendly but numb as if anesthetized at some rites.

John smiled, showing the even row of good teeth and the capped one he had shattered. "Imagine, Bill, you still alive. We were running low on petrol and Chunky said let's run in here and steal some. Bill's here."

"I'll get the gunnery sergeant, that's his swindle. Where you stationed?"

"With the Air Group some place near Ypres. It's a bitched-up war, isn't it?"

"It's no damn good. How'd you get to fly?"

Chunky said, as the cork came out, "They took him when they'd killed off all the young folk with good balance." He sucked up champagne and put his arms around me and hugged me. "You don't see any of our strong stern breed out here. But soon, eh, soon? The whole American Army."

One of the Oxford boys nodded. "You'll win the whole bloody thing for us, you Yanks."

"That we will. Want to fight?" asked John. He needed a haircut, his nose had been broken, he was too lean. "Never stick it into an alley, old chap."

"Where you all going?" I asked. I wanted to tell John how pleased I was to see him.

"Some *estaminet*, the Cloche-Clos. Kevin has an old uncle there in the Engineers. We want to borrow a few hundred nickers. Maybe go to Paris."

Only we didn't. The big push to try and capture Cambrai came and all squadrons went up to take on the Jagdstaffels. Both of the English boys were killed first time up. When Chunky packed their things he found one boy had marked a book:

> *By my troth, I care not; a man can die but once;*
> *we owe God a death . . . and let it go which way it will,*
> *he that dies this year is quit for the next . . .*

What leave in Paris meant to the airmen:

The weather had been a great gray bowl of sky, so bad we couldn't fly any sorties over the front at our sector based beyond Arras. The war lay under a lashing rain and the morning mists lasted all day, and below us men drowned in putrefying mud. Chunky, from his squadron, drove up to the airdrome one morning gay as a grig, in a 12.5 horsepower Sizaire that had one big headlight over its radiator like the Cyclops's eye from Greek legend. Chunky, in a long clipped sheepskin coat, pink whipcord breeches, splendid Savile Row boots, looked the tight-assed proper ace. He had the M.C. and I was now a Captain and had the D.S.M., and solid gold insignia on my cap. Oh, we were the fancy stuff to feed the folks back home in newspaper stories and interviews and photos. If you didn't notice the twitch in our cheeks and the stylish tremor in the nicotined fingers.

"Paris, for our Major's wedding?"

"Same girl?"

"Of course, the same girl."

I noticed a huge shaggy dog on the front seat of the auto. "What the hell is that?"

"Wedding gift for the Major. Genuine Boche dog, survived a crash when our group shot down a Heinie ace, his master, in his Albatros. You'd have loved it, Bill. I'm flying at three thousand feet, see, and out of a cloud comes this prick above me, sun in my eyes, I nearly shat, but took a fast wing roll to the left and . . ."

"I've got to wangle leave from the C.O. Three days enough?"

"More than. Bring any buddy you have. *Très* gash, *très* likker, *comprenez-vous?*"

The group major was sitting at his desk under the signed photograph of Guynemer and his Spad, and a small model of the DH-4 in which the major lost his left foot flying over Ypres in the early days. His overbred face—like a racehorse—tired.

"We want to bomb Bissege aerodrome soon as this muck clears. H.Q. is chewing out my arse why we're not flying right now . . . Out of the question. Fearfully sorry."

"Must be at the wedding. Both of us likely to crap out on any flight. Odds against us ever meeting again."

The major did a slow assimilation of my words. "Have the warrant office give you the pass. And pray there's no sunshine for three days."

"I'd like to take Tony P——. He's the only survivor of his replacement group."

"Been lucky, hasn't he? Oh, and steal me a bottle of Hennessy Three Star, like a good chap."

Tony wasn't half pleased to be getting away to Paris. He had turned out to be a marvelous flier, but I couldn't see how he'd live much longer. He had a habit of drifting east across the lines at two thousand feet, and waiting till a group of von Kleinsmit's Fokker triplanes came out at noon, regular as clockwork. Then

Tony would dive in among them, his wings almost tearing out, and pick off one or two before they knew he was there. They'd go into attack and evasion movements thinking it was an R.A.F. group squadron attack. By that time, Tony was either flying low for home over the lines, or cutting off a Hun who had made the wrong move and was alone and vulnerable to the twin Lewis guns pumping tracers into the enemy canvas and wood and living meat. But they were getting wise to Tony and dividing up; some day soon they'd bracket Tony and his damn Camel between them. The Spandau slugs would give us another dead ace. We had plenty of those. The major considered Tony a very *soigné* type.

"The bride pretty?" asked Tony, admiring his dark good looks in a mirror as he buttoned on his London-cut jacket.

"Not as pretty as you are. I never met her."

Outside, Chunky was honking the horn of the car. I had left him in the mess bar drinking doctored Scotch on my slate.

The canvas top of the Sizaire was only fairly waterproof, but we had our trench coats on and between the bottle of brandy and some singing, and the dog Fritz barking, we managed to get stuck only twice in the foul mud the roads had become under four years of horse manure, army traffic, and shelling. It was sad to see the long lines of boys and middle-aged men marching the other way. Wet, muddy, burdened with firearms and war gear. The French were scraping up old men now, ancient farts with whiskers and rounded bony shoulders. The English were mostly mere runty kids, whey-faced and lips blue with rain. The horse-drawn wagons were miserable, everything worn and unpainted till you came across some American equipment, which looked brazen and strange and like a too new toy until the mud covered it.

Chunky bent over the steering wheel of the iron monster. "We Yanks, we'll have to end it for them."

Tony beat his swagger stick on his legs. "Paris. The Louvre, Notre Dame. I wonder if they still have the old bookstalls on the Seine."

Chunky took a suck of the brandy bottle and worked the hand-turned windshield wiper. "*Bien merci, et vous-même!* Jewboy, you out of your rabbinical mind? We're going to Paris to paint it red, marry off our Major, drink, eat, sleep, and get laid. Eh, Fritz, *du swinehund?*"

The dog barked and clawed at Chunky from the back seat. Chunky steered the car around a horse-drawn 75 mired to the wheels. The flogged horses had given up; the Frenchmen, bearded muddy lumps, cursed us out, but with no strength or feeling in it.

"I could open this baby, open to a hundred miles an hour. The power of Niagara under the hood."

Tony said, "Let's try."

"It's a racer with the rear seat built on. After the war I'm going to take it down to Nice and open it up in a road race. After the war."

Tony took the nearly empty bottle. "Nobody, Chunky, unless it's the dog, is going to be around after the war."

Chunky grinned. "All I'm praying for is a nice clean wound, just a flesh wound, see—and a nurse with beautiful tits and some English garden to convalesce in. I'm a Catholic. I believe in prayer. I'll include you guys in when I pray in Paris. What you rather have, a leg wound or an arm wound? Nothing irrational or bizarre. Just a wound."

Tony threw the empty bottle out into the rain beyond the flapping curtains. "Gunnery-Sergeant Peterson got his balls shot off. I'd rather get it between the eyes."

We hit a rut and the car bounced so high we came down on the shoulder of the road. Chunky sang: "*Viens pou-poule*" and Tony offered "*La Petite Tonkinoise.*" The dog and I didn't have any voice.

A Senegalese company of black colonials, blue-green with cold and damp, were huddled over smouldering little fires. They jumped apart as we passed splashing—scattered rifles, knives, miserable little pots of condemned canned stew they were heating, which the regulars wouldn't eat.

Chunky threw some franc notes at them as he plowed back onto the road. "Poor niggers, what are they fighting for?"

Tony said, "The right to eat their grandmothers. What are we fighting for, if it comes to that?"

"To get passes to Paris," I said.

Chunky took his hand off the wheel and beat his gloved fists together. I grabbed the wheel as we passed a mired tank, its crew sitting under a canvas spread like shipwrecked sailors.

"Who the hell has a pass? I just went out over the place the dustbins go."

Tony said cheerfully, "They'll shoot you. Six ack emma in the morning. Twelve rifles, one cigarette, one blindfold, one priest. Officer's *coup de grâce* behind the ear."

"They can't. I'm the only surviving member of the bloody squadron who can get the young squabs up in the air. Oh, it's shameful what we do—the poor little pissers, so game and so scared, rosy-cheeked. They belong on the playing fields of Eton or fagging upper classmen, not going up against Staffel in our old A.K.Ws. Here's a place to piddle and get that brandy."

We slid into a courtyard all manure pile under a grape arbor, leafless and black. Fritz snarled. Several lorries were in the yard lettered U.S.A. The inn was full of deserters and apaches, *maquereaux, mômes* hiding out from the army lists. "*Je prends mon bien où je le trouve.*"

It wasn't raining so hard when we started up again.

Paris in wartime was a sad place. There was little paint, bits of missing glass were replaced by boards and cardboard. The streets were filthy, shutters hung on a slant. The staff cars—Rolls, Pierce Arrows, Fiats, and fancy French jobs, all in battle gray or mustard —moved healthy-looking officers around. Lorries seemed to be passing in never-ending rows. Now and then a Ford ambulance rattled by us and I didn't like the stains around the doors in back. Lots of legless and armless and blind men were available.

We had faked some kind of a paper for Chunky on an old military form for Handley-Page motor parts. I knew it wouldn't fool any English patrol. We detoured around the main gates into Paris and came up past the Gare de Lyon, crowded with returning leave trains, human cargoes going out to die or drown beyond the Marne. We went past hotels looking sodden in the thin green rain.

The major, a rich boy from St. Louis, had taken a suite at the

Ritz for the wedding. There was still a doorman, one empty sleeve pinned across his chest over his medals. We took Fritz in with us and the clerk said we weren't going to be allowed to have the creature along.

Tony said, "This is President Wilson's dog."

The clerk said it was by appearance, Monsieur, a Boche dog.

We went for the lift without waiting to hear any more.

The lobby was full of well-dressed, fine-smelling, meaty women, a few charming in lacy mourning black. There were assorted officers of all nations with that fine smooth look of desk riders, a Jesuit, a man who said he ran the prison of the Santé, staff pips, red-braided caps, fliers. There was a middle-aged French officer, one-legged and on crutches, talking to an Italian major with plucked eyebrows. And there was steam heat, something most hotels were leaving out that season. Ecstasy and excitement seemed on tap. Tony quoted Donne as he sniffed: "And what wind serves to advance an honest mind."

We knew the floor of the Major's suite before we got there. A humming buzzing noise, a breakage of glass, a singing of some sentimental flying-force ballad about taking the engine out of my liver, lift the crankcase from my chest.

Chunky's eyes gleamed. "Hear all that girl-laughter?"

War or not—money was money, and the red carpeted hallway was heavy with waiters and maids pushing little tables of drink and food. The gold and white doors of the suite were open, and there a pattern of officers and well-dressed women mixed together in tobacco smoke, retaining their hold on glasses of wine. The women were, I figured, rapidly taking inventory of haunches, arms, torsos, legs—one-third in uniform of some special headquarters service, Red Cross, Admiralty, War Office; the helpers' sort of wearying desk work that relished the need of pretty girls to keep them alert in the office, warm. Comfortable in bed, and available for dinner or a long distasteful journey to some Legation or H.Q. They, too, fought a splendid war. Basically in war only three things matter (writers lie about it), sexual congress, drunken plenty, and avoidance of death.

Some of the women were in black, and the few men in frock

coats had a sprinkling of mourning bands among them. They had survived their sons and felt pious about it. One learned in three years of war to take death with the proper period of mourning. The black public sign; we, too, have had our loss, and so chin up, drink in hand, carry on, the worst is yet to be. There were American officers looking very Zeta Psi and Skull and Bones from Yale.

Chunky went barging into other rooms. Tony and I grabbed a waiter, cornered him, and before his pleased eyes had three large champagnes each. "It was good," Tony said, "to know the French had lots of vintage wine left."

We went to the buffet, smiled at the suckling pig, at the pink sliced ham, at the spiced animal organs, sea life, tidbits in aspic, caviar on ice, the smoked goose, the *paté* with bay leaves. Tony and I so long alive on bad coffee, brandy, leathery eggs, canned offal from the Chicago packing houses, smiled at each other and fell to, mouths greasy, stomachs at rest now that we didn't have to fly a dawn patrol. We looked about us. Chewing, sipping, eyes on stems at the sight of the clean women. A small band played Victor Herbert waltzes under some palms yellowing in gilt pots. We took it all in with the unanesthetized parts of our brains.

Said Tony with awe and respect, "You ever see so much woman even in your best dreams?"

I lead him over to the seafood buffet. "Stop pawing the ground like a stud stallion."

It was a grand wedding. Three days later—still hung over—I was flying escort to bomb a railroad supply depot.

1917:

By 1917 we tired rummies and crocks were aware of how dreadful a war it was. After all the flying, the Vickers' gun bursts; no flags waving, no gallant charges, no Red Cross nookie; maybe a hairy kiss on the cheeks by a French general.

As we flew we knew below us were five, six million filthy men buried alive underground, living like crazy red-eyed rats in their own shit and piss, decaying comrades' entrails. Years of burrow-

ing, rotting away, dying with silly shocked gestures to gain, re-
tain, fifty yards, a hundred yards. Then back into the crap and
the cootie hells, the stink of unburied dead from 1914 on—all
those rotting horses too. In the air we missed a war that smelled
of horse manure, putrefying generations of dead schoolboys
and fathers. We fliers could only smell it sometimes as we came
in at dusk, back from patrol, flying low over the trenches that
stretched in the earth from the English Channel to the Swiss.
When you went to mess with the line officers, they smelled of
it, their eyes bulging with madness, maybe fear . . .

The young men training to fly wore their polished boots and
danced to ragtime, while Frenchmen in crayon-blue Paris-tailored
uniforms came over with an eye patch or missing an arm or leg to
help the Allied War Drives. In Berlin, we were told, the beer cellars
echoed to the songs of fliers who dreaded to sleep and lived on
brandy and milk and talked. Of what? *Die Todten reiten schnell,*
and *Kurvenkampf* flying.

Jay Gatsby *did* dance with Daisy and dreamed of coming back
from war with a hell of a chestful of medals, and the band played
on. Shot-down German planes—I remember—were hauled through
London. And the districts the Zeppelin burned out, down in
Kent, had to be roped off from picnickers.

One day a German Albatros pilot, his head, I suppose, full of
Wagner and Nietzsche, dropped the boots of a dead Allied ace
over his home airdrome and no one fired a shot. It was in the
beginning the last of the old-fashioned wars—if you didn't have
to live in the trenches, or do the retreat from Mons; lie there, as
I saw it, screaming, your entrails in your hand.

We fliers vomited our cognac and coffee breakfasts over the
instrument panel as we banked our muslin birds, trying to get an
advantage or avoid the machine guns of the Richthofen Circus
blazing into our blind spot. Somehow at home it all came out as
knighthood and tournaments in the stories being written about
us. I still smell the fur-lined leather coats, feel the great goggles
on our eyes (like the look of goldfish in a bowl), a flutter of a
scarf around a cold neck, ends flowing in the wind from the hel-

met top like a bit of Sung drapery. . . . That was how it was flying that war. . . .

After Chunky went down in flames with nothing left to bury, flying became a horror to us old crocks. We were soon, we were told, going to be withdrawn from the advance airdromes. As we drank our café-marc and waited, the war increased in rumor, fury, deadlines. I was leading young English fliers who hardly seemed to understand the theory of it, while the Germans were in as bad a way too, desperately sending staffels of twelve machines out against every patrol, using the Halberstadt fighter to good advantage. A machine that pulled up in a loop so fast we seemed to be walking.

I'd come in from patrol goggled eyes still full of pirouetting burning planes, and the dirty dusty fields of summer where we were stationed still within sound of the front where the Americans were moving up under their tin hats, faces like the ones I once knew at home in high school. I felt like yelling, "What are you stupid bastards doing here?" But I was developing British phlegm and secret grievances.

Tony, who had grown melancholy at missing women, and played all day on a shrill gramophone a recording of Schubert's, taught me a bit of Yiddish and took up the violin, which he played well, but in a gloomy manner.

John was flying in a unit fifty miles up the line with the dog Fritz he had inherited when Chunky went, as his only companion in the cockpit. John had threatened his C.O. with a Very pistol cartridge up his arse when the C.O. tried to force on the squadron a plane with elevator controls the factories had put in wrong.

John wrote me, "It's a very starchy war for our Limeys, but you get up there among the cumulus clouds in an FE-2 with the 250 h.p. Rolls-Royce engine and they can keep the old crazy worn-down earth. There's a whole universe unused. Say, you long-haired bastard, you ever read Faust? *We fear the blows we never get. And those things we never lose, are what we lament.* Damn good for a Heinie. Faust differs from all other intellectuals in that he hunted experience, besides knowledge. To hold life in total vision is damn hard. If we can get poor Chunky's auto working, we'll come down maybe to your field soon with some native fellows we've been bunking with, of the *12ième Groupe d'Escadrilles de la Chasse*, the French elite squadron. Only we call them the Storks. I'm in a bad way, as the poet Hafiz said, "Who can't drink, can't love." I've got an ulcer the Doc thinks. No letter from Sue, who is now some place in the Near East with the Red Cross. I don't know, Bill, I'm scared."

That set me back on my heels a bit, solid John cracking.

Tony and I were taking up a wing of twelve. The trouble was that usually there was a strong wind from the west, so that if we took our sucklings, just out of solo school, too far over the German lines and a dogfight broke us up, they'd drift so far east in their excitement they'd never have the petrol to make it back. They were all as eager as bridegrooms who had read it all in a book. But green, green, *green*.

The Germans had their Aviatik two-seaters out, and we had no backup at all in the air except from the Escadrille Lafayette at Bar-le-Duc. We didn't get on too well with them. They had been the Escadrille Américaine, N.124, flying the Vosges sector. They felt it was not playing the old ball game for Tony and me to be flying with the lousy Limeys when we could fly with them, real solid American he-men, who were going into the Hat-in-the-Ring group, U.S.A. But they could fly, and could die.

Tony in his flying pants, unshaved, eyes bloodshot, was to fly wing for me and the sucklings. The planes snorted and stank on the flying field, hustling at their wheel blocks, the castor oil a fearful odor, blue smoke tossing pebbles among the dying weeds. I got in my crate, raised my hand to get in the saddle, and we took off into the rising day, bluish shadows in the plane trees we just got over, the air warm as English beer, the day still dark to the East.

The sun was slanting on our left as we wheeled up and up in case the staffel of the late Herr Immelmann were in a paranoiac mood and were hunting our ass. I let the airstream clear my head. I hoped to endure, with care. I was living on coffee, raw eggs, and brandy again, and any day I hoped to hear the major say I'd been elevated out of combat and could go to a nice rest in London. Bathe, see a doctor about my nerves, get my teeth fixed, read a book. . . .

Tony was wagging his wing. To the far left I saw were a herd of *drachen*, German kite balloons up to observe and direct artillery fire. I signalled no. We had to ride a contact patrol with some land action. And the *drachen* were protected by nasty A.A. fire, and Boche pilots lurked some place in the clouds nearby to take care of the foolish fighter who was sucked in by balloons.

I gave my Lewis guns a burst to clear them for action. They often jammed. I was thinking that this horse's nuts air fighting we were doing had no real military value, merely anonymous butchery that the press wrote up, when *zam!* we walked right into it. The clouds having drifted away, we were blinded by the sun. In two layers, red-painted triplane Fokkers were down on us; black crosses and mean. They had been stacked just above the cloud bank. My sucklings ganged up like fox-nervous hens. I dumped my retrospective thoughts, kicked the rudder, went into a roll, saw the babies under my wing try and follow. Tony pulled up in a loop, always a crazy fine flier, and he came around and to the left, firing in bursts. A red-nosed Boche went down and around, wind screaming like a fury through his wires.

A dogfight is a rocketing chaos; chasing tails I had enough to do. Some of the Huns' new planes were firing one-pound pompoms. I saw one of my babies go crazy in a tailspin and pour black smoke and come apart. I suppose he forgot his belt for he fell out screaming, but I was in trouble myself. I put on rudder without banking. I had two enemies, one above me, and the one below in the blind spot was pumping slugs into me. I could feel canvas and wood splinter and tear and I prayed ohshitandpiss, if I get it now, give it to me a fast one right through my brain or heart, as I gave a few. No burning no burning no falling falling to mash into a field. ("He fell at dawn on a clear quiet day.") I kept the trigger finger ready, and kicked up and let the top Hun feel my guns. I let go half a drum, twenty-four rounds, but he ate it all and I knew it wasn't my day. I jabbed at the rudder bar, pushed the stick over and went into a steep dive. But they followed me down. The unshaved bastard behind his goggled eyes was staring at me. I panicked, but my deep inner nerves—who didn't give a damn about my surface ones—they told me what to do and how to do it.

I took a quick look in the blue quadrangle of sky. My flight had blown apart. Some of my babies were scattered, or falling burning or breaking up. Tony—I hunted his ship—he had a thumb-on-nose insignia painted on his fuselage. He was flying far below, near the treetops, dodging three Heinies on his tail, trying to lure them low enough to crash them into the ground. I didn't see more. I was off to the north and they east—the horizon spinning like a fever dream—trying to get clear. One bastard clung just below in the blind zone, and I knew if I kept up going east, I'd run into Jagdstaffel interceptors.

I poured on coal to get a black exhaust, suddenly stalled and went down tail first, hoping I could get out of it in time. The Hun shot out in front of me. I came out of the dive, roared up and around and over him. I fired the rest of the drum, put in another drum (try it sometimes if you ever find an old Camel in a museum) working stick, rudder, your elevator controls, feeling the oil gage drop—one hand loading, wind tearing at you, the Hun circling to get behind and below.

And he had me. My motor sounded like a grease-spitting iron skillet frying flounders.

It's marvelous for your nerves, dying in a sodden sun. Makes you think, repent, shrinks your scrotum. I could feel the plane shudder as he fired short bursts, but lots of them. Then there was the sound of a Klaxon (we carried them to signal ground patrols) and a big blue fighter with English oval insignia was to the left of us. It had two fixed Vickers guns firing through the air screw, and the Hun just went up into an exploding rose. Breaking at once into fragments. The blue Nieuport wagged its wings. I made a feeble superflous gesture of thanks—held my hands in prayer position. Then it was that I felt my right leg and hip burn, and I put down a glove furtively to investigate. It came up smeared with black blood. Funny, I hadn't felt it during my funk. I gave a curdled smile. Was I dead or out of the war?

I didn't think I could make it back to the field, so I began to look for a place to bring down my ruptured duck, oil spitting in my face. I couldn't work the rudder, so I used the tail surface for some kind of wearing around and the engine was pissing hot rusty liquid in three places. I couldn't see and the goggles were smeared. I pulled them off. It was a fun day and I didn't want to bleed to death at two thousand feet. Tony kept above me on guard, and I came down hard—too hard in the front-line trenches of a Canadian outfit, The Princess Pats. A colonel with the A.D.C. said it was a damn improper landing when they brought me through the wire. I smiled and said, "That's right." I passed out there and woke up in hospital with a little New York City doctor shouting: "Beautiful, beautiful. It's a hip wonderful to work on. Give the *povero diavolo* another whiff of ether, Miss Bedpan." I fell way down into happiness and quoted Buddha to myself: "The sword follows space without exertion to the wound." I felt good. The war was over for me. I was a human being again. I hoped the wonderful wop didn't take off the leg; my last thought was—how embarrassing to get into bed with a woman with my leg off—sorry baby, this is *all* of me. The ether sang in my head. Survival is all. . . .

"W. W. Windstaff" does not give the date of his wound, but it was sometime early in 1918, as I gathered from talks while working on his memoirs with him. I am full of hope I can get some publisher to issue the entire book, which is an amazing document and carries his life forward into the era of Gertrude Stein's "Lost Generation" days in Paris. Only twenty-five copies were privately printed in 1930. "Windstaff" was killed in an auto accident in 1931.

PART V:
Change of Mood

CHAPTER 18

PEACE FEELERS

The first time I was ever in bed with her (we did not
go to bed the first time we were lovers . . .) we heard
suddenly a shout of bestial triumph in the street. I
leapt out of bed and saw a Zeppelin falling in flames . . .
— BERTRAND RUSSELL, *Autobiography*

As the war ground on, even the fliers despaired—despair that was only slightly eased by leaves. Frank X. Percy remembers those leaves:

> . . . to the London stage at the time of the Kaiser's war when I was a member of the Royal Flying Corps. Those were the days when a young flying officer spent his leave on Shaftesbury Ave., the Strand, Haymarket, and the immediate area similar to New York's 42nd St. and Broadway . . . tickets were generally arranged through the regimental clubs of London. It was under such circumstances that I was able to see such shows as *Chu Chin Chow, Our Miss Gibbs, The Bing Boys on Broadway* . . . the list is long . . .

And in the country an English gentleman wrote: ". . . Played tennis on Sunday, but were driven in by the rain . . . played Bridge . . . guns in Flanders were heard very distinctly on the terrace at Glynde . . ."

For the General Staff, the old school tie still ruled supreme. When Lloyd George (appointed Prime Minister in December 1916) questioned Foch on the failure of Haig's dismal British military strategy and its supercilious, incompetent planning, Sir

Douglas Haig had to say, "Never could have believed that a British minister could have been so ungentlemanly."

Chief of the Imperial General Staff, Sir William Robertson—"Wully" to Haig—wrote the field marshal: "Lloyd George is a bad 'un." (The use of schoolboy slang among the staff is both pathetic and revealing.)

If the generals acted like diabolical schoolboys (wrote H. G. Wells of the professional military mind, "by necessity an inferior and unimaginative mind; no man of high intellectual quality would willingly imprison his gifts in such a calling . . ."), often the fliers on leave acted like madmen. Drink and women seemed to be foremost in many overkeyed, tight-coiled minds.

The generals could sound impressive. Joffre had said in an order: "At this moment when the battle is about to begin on which depends the salvation of France, the time has passed for looking behind us . . ."

The Germans had fallen back halfway to Belgium. The war bogged down and trenches were dug and reinforced. No decisive victory was possible. The stalemate would last until almost the end of the war amid this same debris of rotting men and horses, broken landscapes, and unreasoning destruction of human life. Many young men asked to be transferred to the air services. The only things they saw that moved freely over the opposing deadlocked enemies were the airplanes. In the Somme offensive, a few miles of broken men and debris would cost the British three-quarters of a million soldiers.

With fighter planes roaming the skies, it was no longer a picnic for important persons to visit the front. There is a comic haste in reports of the Kaiser almost sneaking up to the front and hurrying away again before enemy planes could spot the ceremony of his visit. It was east of the Somme, with French guns roaring and German cannon thundering replies, that the German emperor unexpectedly appeared in a little village behind the front, reviewed a hastily improvised parade, and decorated some officers and soldiers. He addressed the men briefly, and was then whisked on to an advanced position. His visit was known only to a few high-level officers and came as a surprise to the troops. On a level plain by a French château, all the troops in the immediate neighborhood were collected. With the emperor was Prince Eitel Frederick, an admiral, several generals. The troops were drawn up in a hollow square. His majesty was described as "looking trim and fit, perhaps somewhat wearied." He quickly passed in review, shook hands with officers he knew, saluted soldiers who stood at present arms "as correctly as they would have done at a parade in Berlin."

Then off to safety, as Allied planes were scouting in the neighborhood.

The novelty of reporting from the air intrigued Cyril Brown of *The New York Times*, flying over the 25-mile Somme front:

. . . a far-flung parabolic battle-line unrolled like a painted scroll. The center was marked by giant smoke-pillars of burning Peronne, where German soldiers, at the risk of their lives, under heavy French shellfire, were dynamiting blocks of houses to stem the conflagration. Far to the north the smoke-pall of battle festooned the British front, and just north of the Somme there was a sea of smoke where the French and German artillery were grappling with drumfire. Just south of Peronne was the village of Blaches, in German hands, and close to it one of the burning points of the Somme battle, now smiling in sunlight and comparative calm, the small hill of La Maisonnette, whose toll in blood approximated the human sacrifice laid on the altar of Notre Dame de la Lorette . . . the German and French first lines were a tangle of trenches chiseled sharply in the checkerboard pattern of the Somme landscape.

The men in the air became more and more divorced from the reality of the ground war. The despair of the Poor Bloody Infantry was showing as they sadly sang: "Take Me Back to Dear Old Blighty!" Romantic lyrics were gone from the soldiers' songs, the glory of war. Now it was a flat statement of the miserable life in the reeking trenches.

> *We're here because we're here*
> *Because we're here, because we're here . . .*

Hasty seduction and fornication on leave became the themes. Even the fliers sang of the lure of female flesh.

I love the ladies,
I love to be among the girls . . .

The enemy, too, had gone sour in his sentiments. No more verse of knighthood and Teutonic glory, but a lament of turning away during air battle from a falling friend:

I can't give you a hand.
You're going to the Promised Land
My comrade, good and true . . .

And the news reports read: GREAT ALLIED BREAKTHROUGH PLANNED . . . IM WESTEN NICHTS NEUES.

The airmen on leave still found the old recruiting posters and the song that went with them, heard dimly on a scratchy gramophone disc:

Oh, we don't want to lose you,
But we think you ought to go,
For your King and your Country
Both need you so . . .

It was not a tune in keeping with the young widows' weeds, the thin, undernourished children the airmen on leave saw at home.

We shall want you and miss you,
But with all your might and main
We will thank you, cheer you, kiss you,
When you come back again . . .

By 1917, there were nearly a million English who would never come back again. Not all fell in brave action to the enemy. The journalist and novelist, Philip Gibbs, described the end of a young officer sentenced to die "for cowardice (there were quite a number of lads like that). He was blindfolded with a gas-mask fixed on the wrong way round, and pinioned, and tied to a post. The firing party lost their nerve and their shots went wild. The boy was only wounded, and screamed in his mask, and the A.P.M. had to shoot him twice with his revolver before he died . . ."

Most likely he was not in the RAF, for while the air groups had as many cowards and sensitive men who broke down as any unit of the service, the air squadrons were better able to protect their ruined young men, get them carried off out of the way of the firing squads.

There is a great graveyard today to the third Battle of Ypres (July 1917) and a monument to 56,000 British, fliers and others, whose bodies were never found. The rest lie in Passchendaele, biggest British boneyard in the world. In all, 174 British grave-yards crowd one sector of the old front, on land "conceded in perpetuity to England." There are 40,000 graves in the Ypres area alone. All but the fliers lie under white crosses. For the airmen, if a recovered body existed, there was a sawed-off propeller driven into the earth to mark the flier's final landing.

At each cemetery there is a Cross of Sacrifice, engraved: "Their names liveth for evermore." And at home the widows of pilots stood in line with the rest in the interminable queues below the sign: WHITE LOAF OF BREAD IN EXCEPTIONAL CASES ONLY.

The Germans kept making feelers for peace, but the magazine *John Bull*, which fliers often carried back to France, gave the Allied answer: "No more peace parleying with the enemy, no more damned nonsense about consulting the wishes of the niggers in the captured German colonies!"

Mr. Lloyd George—busy producing planes, shells, guns—was often more worried about his own War Office than about the Germans. The military wanted to run things, and their policies were destroying the Empire. The generals' figures of results were hardly worth reading. The military, Mr. Asquith sadly said, kept three sets of figures, "one to mislead the public, and another to mislead the Cabinet, and the third to mislead itself . . ." (How like the modern Pentagon press releases all this sounds.)

Except for continued air action, military paralysis had set in by 1917. Costly frontal attacks had gotten nowhere. From the Channel to the Swiss border a great mass of armies still lay buried in the earth and filth—the living as well as the dead. The wheeling scout planes looked down on the desolation made by Field Mar-shal General Douglas Haig, whose concept of war was still the costly breakthrough, then send in the horsemen; for he had noted "the role of cavalry on the battlefield will always go on increasing . . . bullets have little stopping power against a horse." Said an observing French officer of this kind of thinking, "The British cavalry officer seems to be impressed . . . he can dash and ride over everything, as if the art of war were precisely . . . fox hunting." Haig—who had frightened George Bernard Shaw, "He made me feel the war would last thirty years"—was a man devoted to spiritualistic séances, and at one tapped table he had been told, "the spirit of Napoleon is always near you." He had consulted mediums on military matters, gaining advice on battalions and army procedures not taught at military schools. He added, "Every step in my plan has been taken with Divine help."

It was said of some other general but it fitted Field Marshal Haig: "He was Napoleon devoid of genius."

To the Americans flying with the British and the French, a great weariness was also setting in in the third year of the conflict. They, too, were waiting for Woodrow Wilson to be lured into the war. At last, on April 6, 1917, came celebration of the U.S.A. as an Ally, and among Americans flying with the Allies there was great drinking. Recalls "W. W. Windstaff":

> America has been sucked into the war. Oh, my grandmother's balls, how the USA has been sucked in. Everybody at the field who can get drunk got drunk, even the fliers going out on patrol. The older ground officers see American guns, planes, dollars, *lots* of lovely dollars. They asked me about American whisky, "Bourbon, I believe you chaps call it." I said it was a skull cracker. We all stood up and drank at mess to the King, to the President, to victory. Until the batmen had to take most of us off to bed . . .

But something was seriously wrong at the front. In May 1917, fliers noticed strange commotion in the French trenches, and disordered ranks behind the lines. They heard rumors. The French army was in a huge mutiny. The 21st division of Colonial Infantry had refused to fight. The 120th Regiment withdrew from action. Others joined in, crying, "Never shall we enter the trenches again!" Sixteen army corps mutinied. More would. No more suicidal attacks into machine-gun nests. French troops moving up often marched baaing like sheep: "We are not stupid enough now to march against machine guns!"

It was soon clear there was no French army. Only the French air force existed still to serve the war. Fliers hovering over these hundreds of thousands of men deserting the fronts could only wonder at what would happen to the war. They withheld their bombs, their machine-gun fire from their own army, even if there were suggestions in some places, "To the wall with the bastards! It's the Paris Commune again! We shot thousands then!"

Delegations from war-weary regiments were sent to Paris; the soldiers at the front stayed in rest sheds. A general fell into their hands and was clobbered. Over 22,000 soldiers deserted and went home; others tried to. Officers who got mean were killed, or had their heads or limbs broken. Trains were burned, lorries overturned. Fifty-four divisions, nearly a million French soldiers, refused to go on with the war. The value of war stocks fell.

On the airfields some French and British commanders wondered if the time had not come to bomb and fire on this vast mass mob, refusing to die for—for what? Few could say, more than honor, flag, country; all abstractions to the soldiers. But there were too few planes and so many of *them*. The orders to fire never came.

Hysteria and panic held the French Deputies, hunting a way to face this sudden, unnatural idea that soldiers do not have to die. On the Champagne front only two divisions out of sixteen manned the trenches. What if the Germans knew of the collapse of the French army? Somehow they didn't; in spite of all the talk of the high skill of German Intelligence, they did not find out about the Great Mutiny.

Wrote Paul Painlevé, Minister of War in charge of the army: ". . . daily quarrels take place between the infantry, the artillery, and the airmen. The former reproaching the latter for having massacred them or left them to be massacred." If the airmen answered this charge of massacre, it is not on record.

The man to end the Great Mutiny, it was decided, was Henri Pétain. A tried, loyal Frenchman, undemocratic, true, but cool, not liable to panic or let the lousy soldiers loose on the folks at home. He rounded up 250 French soldiers, drawn by lot, guilty or not guilty. He packed them out to a field and simply had them murdered by French artillery fire. For show purposes, twenty-three soldiers were sent to die before firing squads, attended by priests; Pétain was a pious man. A couple of hundred soldiers were exiled to hell holes in French colonies. All this firmness by the general successfully broke the mutiny. Being blown to bits by one's own artillery was nothing to look forward to. Pétain then promised more home leaves to the frightened poilus. He also shrugged his way into a solution: "We must wait for the Americans and the tanks."

Air patrols moving over the front saw long lines of soldiers moving back into the trenches.

The British, too, had been waiting for American aid. Field Marshal Haig wrote in his 1917 diary:

> 1. Send to France every possible man.
> 2.   " " "   "   "   aeroplane.
> 3.   " " "   "   "   gun.

It will be noticed that by now he was *not* asking for horses, and had apparently accepted the airplane. Tanks advancing at one to three miles an hour were assigned airplanes to protect them.

The fliers knew their worth, knew air warfare settled no war, had little hope of one more bloody ground attack to end the conflict. They passed back and forth over the weary lines of Tommies moving up to the front, smoking their Woodbines to the last shred.

All waited for the Americans. Not just the English and the French, but the scattering of Belgians, black African colonials, Portuguese, Australians, New Zealanders. Douglas Haig had his private railroad command car set up under the shade of ancient trees west of Ypres where he was to attack just once more in force, an ambitious new offensive (the third at Ypres), beginning by sending the Fifth Army over the top. His scout planes had little to report. He wrote in his journal: "Morning dull and coldish. The bright weather reported as coming is slower . . ."

By that August it was clear that the attacks had failed, and the planes reported the Germans strengthening their lines—also waiting. The British and French losses in manpower in these attacks were a staggering 74,000.

"Why does the waste and killing go on?" demanded H. G. Wells in the *Daily News*. "Public policy on both sides remains childish, vague and disingenuous . . . imbeciles, while civilization bleeds to death."

The Allied generals feared most another German peace feeler. Talk by neutrals seeking a peace was answered by *The Times* (London) as being: "Pro-German and anti-Ally . . . permeated with German ideas . . ."

In the air both sides threw in new planes, new pilots. Flanders mud held the trenches; the war did not flow there. Pétain still waited and Joffre called him *"trop negatif, trop timide."* Patrols raided wherever a scout plane reported some movement in No-Man's-Land, and desperate voices came across the wire, *"Raus, raus die Englander . . ."* and "Fuckin' bloody krauts . . ."

Meanwhile, air heroes were promoted, aces feted, as the bad news and the lists of the newly dead swelled. Lloyd George grew angry at this journalistic build-up. "G.H.Q. could not capture Passchendaele ridge, but was determined to storm Fleet Street . . . here strategy and tactics were superb. The Press correspondents at the front were completely enveloped . . ."

To the press the fliers remained the only glamorous branch of the services. Little of the true horror of the air war reached the daily printed page.

A lieutenant with the Military Cross—he was not a flier—Siegfried Sassoon, spoke up, to outraged screams and threats. "I believe the war is being deliberately prolonged . . . a war of aggression and conquest . . ."

In Kiel the unrest among the German High Seas Fleet crews was gathering radical speakers and revolutionary plans. Sailors refused to stoke up the boilers. But the air forces on both sides—search the records as one can—seemed numb to any idea of a mass revolt for peace. They groused and swore, they lost their minds and senses at times, but the records show almost nothing in any country of the pilots moving toward a serious protest against the conduct of the war, the refusal to accept peace talks.

A British newspaper cried in black type: "To Hell with pacifists!" Lytton Strachey, homosexual leader of the Bloomsbury avant-garde, was questioned as a conscientious objector: "Mr. Strachey, what would you do if you saw a German soldier trying to violate your sister?"

"I would try and get between them."

John Bull, much read in the airdromes at the front, had the only true answer; it told readers, "We're out for War—let it be War to the death!" *The Times* was more gentlemanly, still rejecting German peace feelers. For "Illusory peace proposals of Germany the Allies with one accord have given a definite negative." It all sounded like a viceroy in India punishing natives: "Germany's conduct demands penalties, reparations and guarantees." Even General Pershing was fooled by false claims of victories at the front. He wrote Haig that his valor gave a "striking answer to weak-kneed peace propaganda." Wrote one flier home, "You can't blame the generals for wanting the war to go on. It's a good living."

German planes dropped leaflets. Secret talks of peace offers were to start in the autumn of 1917. Baron Richard von Kuhlmann, German Foreign Minister, made overtures in private: Germany would return Alsace-Lorraine, set up an independent Serbia again, give territorial loot to Italy and colonies to England, move out of Belgium. But both Lloyd George and the generals, out to humble Germany publicly in battle, agreed (for once) never to accept "a premature peace."

America had promised great air fleets.

One of the most daring or foolhardy exploits of the air war took place at this juncture in the war. It was carried out in June 1917 by Captain William Avery Bishop, a Canadian flying for the RFC. Working on a plan he had often thought out carefully, he took off at dawn and flew to a German airfield, arriving as the planes were just warming up their engines. Bishop guessed that the enemy planes would be unwary targets for anyone waiting for them upstairs as they took off.

He shot down the first three in close order as they rose. The fourth gave him some trouble. As he remembered it:

> I opened fire on him. I was now greatly worried as to how I was to get away, as I was using up all my ammunition. . . . But there was no chance of running from this man—he had me cold—so I turned on him savagely, and, in the course of a short fight, emptied the whole of my last drum at him. Luckily, at the moment I finished my ammunition, he also seemed to have had enough of it, as he turned and flew away. I seized my opportunity, climbed again, and started for home . . . feeling very queer at my stomach. The excitement had been a bit too much. . . . The thrills and exultation I had at first felt had died away, and nothing seemed to matter but this awful feeling of dizziness and the desire to get home . . .

It was a startling feat; and it earned Bishop the Victoria Cross.

Billy Bishop had joined the Canadian militia in 1911. When war came, he was commissioned an officer of the Mississauge Horse Troop of Toronto. He sailed for England, a journey memorable for the stench of both horses and men. In England it rained, and kept on raining. The horse grounds were seas of liquid manure, mud mixed with horse litter. Billy Bishop decided he had had enough of "days of cavalry mud, and I was convinced that to be an observer in the air was far better." He had trouble getting transferred into air training; once in, he got airsick and green every time the shaky training plane took off.

He wanted to be a pilot, not an observer, but no one thought he had the coordination, the ability, to fly a plane. In France he served as an artillery observer and kept asking, begging for a pilot's seat.

Asked by a superior, "But how can you be sure you are suited to handle a plane?" Bishop had no answer. He walked out, without a word, disheartened. However, when he came back from a leave in June 1916, he found himself posted for pilot's lessons. The war was chewing up fliers at a disastrous rate and pilot replacements were needed, badly needed. His training in a Farman went miserably. Bishop did not fly well: "My instructor and I both suffered tortures. So when suddenly one day he told me to go up alone, I had my doubts as to whether it was confidence or desperation that dictated this decision. I didn't worry very long as to which it was; I was willing to take the chance."

It was a dismal solo in the test Farman machine. The sight of an ambulance pulled up on the field didn't help. Bishop became airsick again, lost the horizon; he nearly crashed the plane in landing, coming down like an elephant falling from a height. The Farman was an evil training ship; it had few instruments, and killed many young pilots in training. So the survivors were a special lot. Bishop survived, just.

In March 1917, he was sent to the front where they flew Nieuports. He was like a child with a treasured new toy, and in his description of his Nieuport we get a fine picture of how a sky fighter saw his machine:

> . . . the power of 200 horses throbbing in its wonderful engine. . . . Some of the machines are very slender of waist and almost transparent of wing. Airplanes do not thrust their warlike nature upon the casual observer. One has to look twice before definitely locating the gun or guns attached so unobtrusively to the framework, and synchronized, where necessary, to shoot through the whirring propeller in front. Such guns are connected to the engine itself by means of cams, and are so arranged that they can fire only when the propeller reaches a given position, thus allowing the bullets to pass safely. . . . The nacelle, or cockpit, of the modern machine, I have heard people say, suggests to them the pilot house of a palatial private yacht in miniature. They are generally finished in hardwood and there are polished nickel instruments. . . . There are ingenious sights for the guns and rangefinders for bomb-dropping. When he is tucked away in the nacelle, a little well-like compartment about as big around as an ordinary barrel, only the pilot's head is visible above the freeboard of the body of the machine. . . . Directly in front of the pilot is a little glass windscreen, a sort of half-moon effect.

No screen cowboy loved his horse better than Bishop his Nieuport.

But his first mission in the war sky was a jinx. Flying in the tail position of a six-plane formation, Bishop was told to watch and see that no enemy plane overran them from the rear. He couldn't control his speed, so he either lingered too far behind or went too fast and almost rammed the plane ahead. As a straggler he was tempting bait for some quick German to knock off the Tail-End-Charlie before anyone was aware of it.

The next day was worse. German antiaircraft fire lifted and tossed his plane like a feather in the wind. Bishop dived 300 feet before he got control of the plunging, bucking machine. Control of an aircraft came hard to him; he still had trouble maintaining it even when *not* under attack.

Describing his first sight of enemy fighters, Bishop is very frank. He suffered the usual disturbing, despairing speculation of death in the evanescent clouds.

Like nearly all other pilots who come face to face with the Hun in the air for the first time, I could hardly realize that these were real live, hostile machines. I was fascinated by them and wanted to circle about and have a good look at them. The German Albatros machines are perfect beauties to look upon. Their swept-back planes give them more of a birdlike appearance than any other machines flying on the Western front. Their splendid graceful lines lend to them an effect of power and flying ability far beyond what they really possess. . . .

I flew straight at the attacking machine from a position where he could not see me and opened fire. My tracer bullets . . . began at once to hit the enemy machine. A moment later the Hun turned over on his back and seemed to fall out of control. This was just at the time when the Germans were doing some of their famous falling stunts. Their machines seemed to be built to stand extraordinary strains in that respect. They would go on spinning down from great heights, and just when you thought they were sure to crash, they would suddenly come under control, flatten out into correct flying position, and streak for the rear of their lines with every ounce of horsepower. . . .

Bishop was closer to the normal average man (admittedly a

group one hesitates to define) than almost all the great fliers of the war. Under tension he would play practical jokes. Also under the prolonged stress of flying in the war he would get the shakes. He was aware that battle brought out long-latent proclivities to violence in men's direct personal combats. War he knew sometimes liberated a personality in strange directions. But Billy Bishop never gave in to drink, orgy, or mental collapse; there was too much of the bland Canadian in him. New areas of sensation, new sensitivities were developed as he killed. He tried to see it all as a game, but his nerve ends revolted and his limbs would begin their embarrassing shaking, his teeth chattering when he was under prolonged strain.

In the air he found that individualism was more complete, but the loneliness became intensified. He was not a deep thinker. Indeed, if one goes by what he wrote of his war experiences, he was a surface personality, prone to attacks of nerves he never fully probed. For him flying and the air war meant a richer, more dangerous experience, a deeper susceptibility to the proximity of death. Beyond that he could not or would not probe. He tried— as many did—to pass it off as a game, like popping over ducks in a shooting gallery. When he wrote it down, however, it did not make very convincing reading.

Bishop had a broad, frontier sense of humor. Once when bored, he acquired some ducks and painted them with the English national colors, red, white, and blue; he admitted he had trouble trying to get them to march in the proper order as a living flag. In France he borrowed a fat pig and covered it with large Maltese crosses.

Bishop was a fine marksman and in time became a good pilot, as he learned to move with speed, drive, and knowledge of his own plane, acquiring all the tricks of the enemy in an attack. For him the colossal perspectives of war came down to one plane and the moment of its destruction.

It was Bishop who invented the game of "chicken" in the air. The rule was to speed directly at the nose of an approaching enemy ship, not pulling out but waiting to the last moment until the enemy pilot became confused and panicked, then sending a burst of bullets into the enemy engine—a burst held to the last split second, then a quick bank and away. It took perfect control, steel-jacketed nerves to play "chicken" at 100 miles an hour.

Needless to say, Bishop by now was Tail-End-Charlie no longer but patrol leader, and was winning victory after victory in his direct charge at an enemy plane, firing and pulling up just in time.

I led my companions up to 12,000 feet before heading across the trenches just south of Arras. Once over the lines, we turned to the north, not penetrating very far into Hunland because of the strong wind that was blowing about fifty miles an hour from the west. These westerly gales were one of the worst things we had to contend with at the front. They made it very easy for us to dash into enemy territory, but it was a very different story when we started for home and had to combat the tempest. If an airman ever wishes for a favoring wind, it is when he is streaking for home.

One March day in 1917 over German positions, at 10,000 feet, he observed three enemy planes heading for the Allied lines, and below them two other planes. Bishop decided to raid the two lower planes before the upper three could come down on him. He attacked the first enemy, but was tailed by the second, whose bullets grazed his flying helmet and also sent a slug through the center of his windshield.*

The three enemy planes overhead were now coming down in a rush to get him. Bishop at once began to climb up to meet them and their firepower as they sent down bursts of fire. It is strange to record, but none of the three Germans could face him. One backed away, and the other two went into long dives to escape Bishop. The two lower planes had long since made tracks in the sky. There he was, a lone flier who had taken on five enemy planes and been left in possession of the sky, with a tattered helmet and a hole in his windshield to show how close he had come to his last fight. The furious impulse to aggression was suicidal—but not to Bishop.

---

* Bishop kept the windshield and its bullet hole at home until the day he died.

His CO, reading his report of the battle, nodded. "Well, Bishop, after that lot I think you'd better have a rest."

Bishop thought of a fine leave in London, its baths, its glitter, a chance to wear his best uniform. Yes indeed.

The CO looked up. "Take the afternoon off."

At the Battle of Arras (begun on April 9, 1917), the British fliers started to sweep in over enemy gun emplacements, firing away. But by mistake some got caught up in a British barrage (called a "creeping barrage") which the planes were supposed to be kept behind as it advanced. Bishop had a wingtip shot away.

It was a dismal, ghastly battle, and the sight below of thousands of young men advancing to their deaths touched Bishop. He never would become toughened to the senseless killing of war.

On the fourth day of the grim battle it was snowing hard. But Bishop went up, and discovered a strange new universe—a battlefield so silent, so dead, the shell holes all hidden under a bone-white blanket of fresh snow. As he waited at 500 feet the first advance of that day started for the German lines below him, the slow steady walk of ghosts leaving thin trails in the snow. Bishop glided down, engine off, to observe this white war close up. Germans in a hidden machine-gun nest began to knock over the advancing soldiers like toys in a boy's floor game. Bishop dived at the machine-gun nest, firing directly down and from their rear, wiping it out. The Tommies waved their gloved thanks to him.

Bishop was made a captain. He decided that he wanted a personal color for his plane, to match von Richthofen's scarlet one. So he had his ship painted a solid robin's-egg blue and a new nose made for it.

The war now began to harden him somewhat.

An enemy going down in flames is a cause of great satisfaction. You know his destruction is absolutely certain. The moment you see the fire break out you know that nothing in the world can save the man, or men, in the doomed airplane. You know there is no "camouflage" in this, and you have no fear that the enemy is trying any kind of flying trick. . . .

There is a hint here that the warplane is a sexual object and the battle an affair without tenderness—a satisfactory rape.

Like the tough young kid in a Western town who wanted to make a reputation fast by taking on the fastest gunslinger around, among the young fliers in the Allied air force there was always the fantasy of wrestling down the Red Baron, von Richthofen himself. The baron flew his scarlet machine, heading his squadron, then peeling off to take on individual challengers. The strength of his reputation was such that many of his victims lost their coordination and thus vital seconds in their timing. Down they went in that last rolling plume of smoke and fire.

There was only one meeting in the air—in mid-1917—between Bishop and the Red Baron. There had been a morning of active flying against German air patrols. Bishop back at his airdrome had just finished lunch and had walked over to the airstrip. He studied the sky, wondering if the weather would hold for another hour in the air. He went inside to brush his teeth as he did after every meal. Then he decided to take advantage of the weather while it lasted and had six of his squadron routed out of their sleep. One man protested. Why waste petrol? Bishop made a small speech about there being a war on, and if they couldn't fight it here, maybe they preferred the peaceful life? With smiles they agreed to fly if he wanted them to.

Bishop led his flight of Nieuports past the German front lines. It was a silent front, as if some sort of recess had been declared. They had been fifteen minutes in the air when they sighted five Albatroses to the south of them. Bishop led his planes in a dive that would put them right on the enemy's tail and able to get off a few blasts of their guns.

Then out of the corner of his eye, to his right, Bishop suddenly saw four red-decorated Albatroses. They looked closer than the others. There was a tingling in Bishop's scalp: red planes. Was it von Richthofen? He gave the signal and they moved toward the red ships, Bishop picking out the leader who could only be the Red Baron. It had to be, the way the German met his challenge, both firing at each other as they twisted, banked, and turned for advantage. Both sides mingled in a dogfight. Bishop said later he expected death at any moment. When von Richthofen turned, Bishop tailed him, holding back his fire to save his ammunition until he was sure of his shots. The baron got clear of the dogfight, as if drawing Bishop to the uncluttered open sky for a fight between the two of them. Bishop let go a few blasts of his guns, but they did no damage. As Bishop closed in, he knew there would be that *one* moment when he could pour a murderous blast of firepower into the scarlet body of the enemy machine. That decisive moment of the kill.

The split second came. He had the German dead in his sights. Bishop pressed the trigger. *Nothing.* His gun had jammed. For some reason von Richthofen paused, perhaps to look around the sky and see how his fliers were doing. Bishop cursed and tried to unjam his gun. The gear cleared under his blows, and there still in front of him was the baron's plane. Bishop began to fire, neatly etching a row of bullet holes into the scarlet fuselage. But von Richthofen never presented himself as an easy, constant target. Shifting and banking, outflying Bishop by his masterful handling of his plane, the baron evaded the death burst. Bishop tried again to get in position for firing, just as he saw four triplanes approaching.

If enemy, the fight was over; he'd try to run for it. But they were English naval planes. The Germans took a look at the new enemies and ran, Red Baron and all. So the British went home too. There were seven bullet holes in Bishop's plane, all of them within inches of his body. He said, "Close shave, but a wonderful, soul-stirring fight."

He respected the enemy fliers, von Richthofen's men and their planes. "Their machines were painted a brilliant scarlet from nose to tail—immense red birds, they were, with the graceful wings of their type, Albatros scouts. They were all single-seaters, and flown by pilots of undeniable skill. There was quite a little spirit of sportsmanship in this squadron . . ."

Once, chasing three enemy planes, Bishop boldly went hard after them:

> I saw that all three were firing at me from their back guns. I was so much faster than the Huns I could zigzag on my course—wondering as I did so if I resembled an ocean greyhound dodging a submarine. Finally, I closed to within twenty yards of the

fleeing Germans and let go at them. The rear machine was my easiest target. Soon I saw my bullets going into the observer's body and I feel sure that some of them must have passed on from him to the pilot who was seated directly in front. The observer's face was white as a sheet, and out of pure terror, I think, he had ceased to fire at me. The pilot was now gazing back over his shoulder and was too frightened to maneuver his machine. He had turned into a sort of human rabbit, and was concerned only with running for his life. Fifteen rounds from my gun sufficed for that machine. Down it tumbled . . .

Four Germans then tried to ambush him, but he escaped into a cloud. In a bad state of nerves, Bishop lost control of his ship as he dived a mile into space. It was his fourth fight of the day . . . The medical officer insisted then on Bishop's taking a spot of leave in England. His shakes were very bad; he was told to go to the English countryside and have no distractions of any kind. But a week of trees and hedges was enough for the restless man and he went down to London for a spree. He was still shaky, but his nerves were under control when he went back to his squadron.

To act as a crutch for his condition, Bishop invented a rococo philosophy about the death of German pilots by his guns. It was all

. . . just a wonderful game. To bring down a machine did not seem to me to be killing a man; it was just like destroying a mechanical target, with no human being in it. Once or twice the idea that a live man had been piloting the machine would occur and recur to me, and it would worry me a bit. My sleep would be spoiled perhaps for a night. I did not relish the idea even of killing Germans, yet, when in combat in the air, it seemed more like any other kind of sport, and to shoot down a machine was very much the same as if one were shooting down clay pigeons. One had the great satisfaction of feeling that he had hit the target and brought it down. . . .

Here was a philosophy that Orwell would predict—the human species as we know it scrapped, to be replaced by shapes conditioned to some vast game, strange rules.

As the autumnal weather of 1917 began, Bishop's roundel-marked plane had run up forty kills, not counting two balloons. It was then that he was mentioned for the Victoria Cross and his blue plane with its red and white markings became the hunted game of the entire German air force in the Ypres areas.

Due for leave again, Bishop went up into the air once more, burning an enemy plane out of the sky at 13,000 feet. He watched it fall and break up in its long crippled dive and thrust to earth.

In London, at Buckingham Palace (he got lost and had to ask his way), his new boots squeaking like violins tuning up, Bishop walked across a large, crowded room. He stood while his deeds were read out to lords and admirals, generals, diplomats, and royalty. The little king with his little trimmed beard and curled mustache pinned three medals on Billy Bishop, saying: "I have never before presented any officer with the V.C., the D.S.O., and M.C. simultaneously."

All in all, Bishop was credited with seventy-two air victories. Then he was ordered back from the front to headquarters in London as being too valuable to lose.

In World War II, he became marshal of the Canadian air force, and his son a fighter pilot under him. Bishop died in 1959, one of the few aces of World War I to survive and take an important position in the second war. Beside his English awards, Bishop also received the Croix de Guerre with Palms, the Croix de Chevalier, and the Legion of Honor.

CHAPTER 19

FOKKER'S PROBLEMS

While the war had started with some monoplanes, the popular war plane soon became the biplane. But as more lift seemed indicated, in the hope it could make quicker turns, there were triplanes. The British Sopwith triplane came out in 1917; only 150 were delivered from the factory, the lowest fighter order in the war. It was slower than expected, didn't climb with any dash, and could handle only one gun. All told, it was a disappointment. But Fokker decided that the idea was a good one, and that he would make a better version of the triplane for the Germans.

In a flurry of activity he came up with the Fokker triplane, the Dreidekker. It was not as fast as the French Spad (the initials of the *Société pour l'Aviation et ses Dérivés*) or the Sopwith Camel, but Fokker's plane handled better at the controls. His Dreidekker had a 110-horsepower Oberursel rotary engine; the wing area came to 200 square feet, and the airfoil section was thick. This was by now of the accepted Fokker steel-tube construction, the bar spar wings being hollow. It was an amazingly light plane at 1,200 pounds, the average German fighter weighing precisely 1 ton.

The Fokker flying machine could outturn anything in the air, besides climbing like a mountain goat. Whereas the Sopwith triplane needed five minutes to climb a mile, the Fokker Dreidekker cut the time in half.

Fokker's planes again ruled the skies. Von Richthofen's men would fly no others. According to the ace Hermann Becker, the best German scout machine of the war was the Fokker D-VII. From April to November 1918, 3,000 D-VII's were at the front.

It used two different motors, either the 160-horsepower Mercedes D-III, or the 185 horsepower BMW-IIIa, both six-cylinder water-cooled in-line engines. Again, it had the Fokker welded-steel tubing, and while the body was cloth-covered, the engine had sheet-metal protection, a move toward the all-metal plane. Its cantilever wings were of one-piece construction, the lower plane wing being attached under the body, unlike other planes whose lower wing was really two wings. The plane could only stall forward, didn't lash around in a spin. Best of all, it could be put together in mass production when the German war effort was failing and there was a shortage of everything.

For grace and beauty of design, most German fliers spoke glowingly of the Albatros C-XII, a two-seater with plywood fuselage and a 260-horsepower Mercedes D-IVa motor. It had one bad and dangerous habit: the carburetor froze at high altitudes. Late in 1917, Leutnant Theobald von Zastrow and his pilot Leutnant Rochling were over a bleak winter forest on the Russian front in an Albatros C-XII, brushing the cirrus clouds at 16,000 feet, the crackle of freezing air blowing around them. They huddled in their heavy fur-lined coats and fleece-lined helmets and gloves. Nothing is grimmer than a Russian winter; it devours all intruders.

Suddenly the motor coughed, began to miss; the carburetor had frozen. The pilot did a dive to try to keep the propeller alive, but it was a dead stick. To fall into Russian hands usually meant a Siberian prison camp, if they survived a crash. They turned toward the German lines hoping for a *very* long glide. Oddly enough, neither flier suspected they had a frozen carburetor, which they could have fixed with a quick landing and takeoff. The Russian-held landscape looked unappetizing, and in those forests might even lurk the gray wolves of popular Slavic stories.

They glided on, losing half their height. Then, ten miles from their own lines, they saw by the action of the wind on a lake that the wind was against them, blowing from west to east. A head wind that their failing height and dead motor could not buck. At tree-top level, Russian soldiers began firing at them, popping away and coming closer. The pilot was hit three times. Leutnant von Zastrow tried to reach the controls but, at that moment, the plane crashed solidly into the trees, tearing off its wheels. It nosed over and the leutnant observer fell into the bog below. The pilot tried to set fire to the plane, strapped in as he was, but couldn't find his cigarette lighter. They were taken prisoner.*

Fokker's luck held almost to the end of the war. He had spending money (his own, for his income was huge, his father and friends having sold out to him). He had bought into the great Hugo Junkers business at the cost of 3 million marks, but as usual discovered that partners were not for him, and at a loss bought himself free again for 1,500,000 marks. He had then put 4 million more into the companies building the Gnome and Le Rhône engines, and this paid off handsomely.

Fokker's first planes became outdated; the early ones had been able to do little better than 70 miles an hour, never above 6,000 feet. During power dives his first planes' wings had a habit of wrinkling, then falling off. They were superior only to the soon-to-be-replaced British and French Farman, the BE-2C, and the Morane-Saulnier. Then information came through German Intelligence (from Mata Hari?) that the 110-horsepower French Nieuport was being built to outclass Fokker's 80-horsepower Gnome.

He went back to the drawing board.

As a human being, Fokker remained an enigma. There was never much apparent feeling for the men who faced his deadly inventions, his special gunmounts, his faster killer planes. He was not a German, nor did he have much interest in the outcome of the Great War, or any other war he armed. Fokker had that dreadful sweet reasonableness about his work—considering it expedient, convenient, and rewarding, labor well done. Some who worked with him felt he remained musclebound so far as the sensibilities of others were concerned. He seems to have been a totally scientific, disengaged egotist, who would have built planes for Satan if there was a machine shop in Hell and a fairly decent landing field.

---

*Von Zastrow escaped from a prison camp while the Russian Revolution raged around him. Somehow he got back to German-held country, to fly again at the start of 1918. One of his last adventures was almost being shot down by a Nieuport bearing a strange device, a tall hat of Uncle Sam in a ring; it was one of Captain Eddie Rickenbacker's 94th U.S. Aero Squadron.

Special bullets were perfected as the strength of planes increased. For shooting at balloons a really ugly slug was produced. The enemy called these outlawed bullets (which the Germans themselves were often known to use) "dum-dum" bullets. The RFC issued fliers going for balloons a blue card which stated he was only going to use the Buckingham incendiary (loaded with phosphorus) against hot-air bags and *not* against the ground crews, so that if captured, he could present his card, like a schoolboy bringing an excuse to teacher. Twenty-six million rounds of these bullets were issued. The Brock bullet exploded between the outer and inner skin of a Zeppelin. The Pomeroy was designed to penetrate and not explode until deep inside the vitals of the balloon. Usually a mixture of the three types was loaded onto a belt, just to make sure one kind or the other did its duty. The RTS was a double-duty bullet, both an explosive force and a firesetter. In 1918, 200,000 RTS's a week were in use.

In 1916 the Germans had also developed a powerful bomber, the twin-engined biplane Gotha, with Benz engines of 220 horsepower: a slow plane averaging about 80 to 85 miles an hour and carrying 600 to 1,000 pounds of bombs. Each was armed with three machine guns and had the range to wander all over southern England.

In May of 1917, twenty-one German Gothas, called "the *England Geschwaders*," hit the Kentish towns, coming across from bases in Belgium. It was their lucky day. They killed or wounded 120 soldiers at Shorncliffe Barracks, and in Folkestone scored a bull's-eye on queues of women shopping, killing or wounding 163 of them. In June, they were over Sheerness, coming out of the high-piled cumulus clouds; result: 45 killed or injured.

On June 13, 1917, London had its first sight of the Gothas. The visit was lethal; forty-six children in a Council school died in their classrooms and twenty people were killed by fragments from British antiaircraft shells. In all, nearly 600 died or were injured.

Raids went on as the 56th Squadron came home from France to try to stop the Gothas. On July 7, twenty-one enemy bombers reached London. The BE-2C's of the British couldn't reach the bombers or climb fast enough to get anywhere near them. The enemy bombed the City (the Wall Street of London—the area around St. Paul's). But as they returned downriver to Tilbury, they had a surprise. The Irishman Major James T. B. McCudden was there with his Sopwith Pup painted baby blue on its bottom to match the sky. He was high up as the bombers passed him and remained unnoticed from his place in the sun. He dived at the last bomber in line. He got off a full drum on his Lewis guns and came so close he had to pull back fast and broke the seat supports under him. Reloading, he came down on number two, and shot off the fresh drum at nearly 50 yards from the big ship. Wounded, the plane flew on, wings and fuselage chewed up.

McCudden pulled away; he had run out of ammunition. As other British planes came up to join in, it was clear their speed and gun power wasn't much of a help against the bombers. McCudden began to try to delay the bombers by playing tag among them. He got a burst of slugs through his windshield. One British plane was shot down, and there were casualties among some of the other fliers. McCudden, unharmed, followed the Germans 30 miles out over the sea, but none fell.

Watching the air fight instead of taking cover, many people were killed or wounded by British antiaircraft splinters. One of the results was the creation of the RAF, the Royal Air Force, which was to merge the battling RFC and the Navy's RNAS. In addition, an air defense system was set up for London, with Brigadier E. B. Ashmore in charge.

McCudden became the fourth-ranking British ace with fifty-seven victories in the air. He came to flying early for those days, having started as a bugler in the Royal Engineers in 1910. By 1913, he was a first-class air mechanic with the 3rd RFC Squadron. He was with the first fliers to cross the Channel, doctoring and nursing the Blériots and Farmans. (The Farman was "a bastard," called by the fliers the "bird cage," its biplanes needing so many wires and struts.) By the start of 1917, McCudden had his pilot's wings leading the 56th Squadron patrols, with seven kills to his credit. Amazingly, only seven months later, when he left to teach flying in England, his score was fifty-seven confirmed kills.

Like most pilots of those days, he was a small man. He had red-

blond hair, delicate features, blue eyes. His favorite ship was the
SE-5, to which he contributed his own idea of high-compression
pistons that added 10 miles an hour to the ship's speed. He had no
illusions about air killing. "After all, we are nothing but hired
assassins."

He was calm, controlled, not at all the stage Irishman. He prepared his ship, and himself, carefully. He liked to fly high, up to
20,000 feet, and wait in hiding for an enemy; he never fought in
close if he could help it. A great shot, McCudden could, and did,
hit a plane and down it with a burst at a quarter of a mile range.
He did not believe in gallantry for its own sake, or in the use of
dash and skill just to show off. The objective was to kill. His
advice as to how to get an enemy "is to find him before he finds
you . . ." He always remembered an early flying accident:

> . . . The upward pressure was so great that all my ammunition
> drums shot out of my plane over the top wing and into the
> revolving propeller, which, being a pusher, was behind me. . . .
> There was a mighty scrunch and terrific vibration as three of
> my four propeller blades disappeared in a cloud of splinters. I at
> once switched off and removed my gun from my knees, where
> it had fallen after having been wrenched from its mounting
> and thrown into the air, owing to the terrific vibration caused
> by my engine doing 1600 revs per minute with only one pro-
> peller blade . . . and I just had wits enough left to make a
> landing successfully.

On July 9, 1918, having been given command of the RAF 60th
Squadron as major, McCudden took off from the airfield at Aux-
le-Château. His engine suddenly died. As a teacher, he had always
warned his fliers *never* to turn downwind with a conked-out
engine for a dead-stick landing. It was "the surest form of suicide
by airplane."

Yet this is what McCudden did at Aux-le-Château. He tried to
turn downwind for a quick landing and died in the crash that
followed. McCudden had a mind of extraordinary penetration
where plane motors and gunnery were concerned. Yet, like so
many skilled long-time fliers who died, he had perhaps begun to
fly fully automatically, with an indifferent appraisal of what a

plane faces, what its motor and control areas encounter at takeoff.

There was a touch of acid in McCudden's Irish charm. He liked the lilt of the old Irish benediction:

> *May the roads rise with you,*
> *Fair weather at your heels.*
> *May the wind ever be at your back . . .*
> *And may you be a long time in Heaven*
> *Before the Devil knows you're gone.*

In July 1918, something grotesque and epoch-making was added to the history of air warfare: *HMS Furious*, built as a cruiser, armed with two 18-inch guns, appeared as an aircraft carrier. (Before this, seaplanes had been dumped over the side to fly or sink, and were recovered by a winch. Sometimes wheeled planes had taken off, but were forced to fly somewhere else to land.) *HMS Furious* still had her funnel right in the middle of things, but she did have two landing decks. She went to war on July 19, protected by the 1st Light Cruiser Squadron. She stood 80 miles northeast of the Tönder Zeppelin hangars, preparing to send up seven Sopwith Camels, each carrying two 50-pound bombs.

Captain W. D. Jackson led off and scored on one Zeppelin hangar containing the L-54 and the L-60, destroying them both. The return for the fliers wasn't easy. Two crashed into the sea; one ducked down by a destroyer's bow. Three had to land in Denmark. But only one pilot was lost.

The oddest carrier attack was made on August 11, 1918, by destroyers pulling barges on which were three seaplanes and a Sopwith Camel. All were headed for Heligoland, the Bight, long a dangerous thorn in the British navy's side. But the seaplanes never got into the air. The weather was too rough and there was no wind for lifting power. The Sopwith, with Lieutenant Stuart D. Culley, had taken off once on a test run from the barge. It fell into the water as it left the ship and the barge ran over it, but both flier and plane were recovered, to try again. This time, the Camel got into the air, which gives some idea how tough a bird it was, after its former troubles.

An hour later, the Camel found a Zeppelin and shot it down. It was the L-53. Lieutenant Culley came down in the water (there was nowhere else to land) and was picked up in two hours. A successful launch. A whole fleet of motorboats that accompanied this raid were knocked out by German seaplanes, however.

The British air arm went after the U-boats. Hero of the anti-submarine fighters was J. C. Struthers, serving with Coastal Command. In 1917, he attacked nearly a dozen U-boats, but the results were never known for sure. In September, he sighted a conning tower 15 miles southeast of The Lizard, and dropped two 100-pound bombs about 330 feet ahead of the U-boat just as she crash-dived. Up came a boiling mushroom-shaped explosion, then oil, then air bubbles. Hours later, the oil slick covered miles of sea. There was no way of knowing just which U-boat it was; she would be entered in German official records among those "Vanished at sea under conditions unknown . . ."

CHAPTER 20

ITALY AND THE EAST

1. | Two Italian Aces

*There was fighting in the mountains and at night we could
see the flashes from the artillery.*

—ERNEST HEMINGWAY

The Italians made war at times the way they cooked and sang
their operas, with a pleasant bathos and careless gestures. But the
war punished them, and their losses were so heavy that in the end
they fell away into fatalism. As fliers they were often excellent.
They were also early, having set up a flying school in 1908 at
Centocelle for soldiers and citizens. Other schools were created,
so that by 1910 there were thirty-eight licensed pilots in the boot
of Italy; being a people who avoided the innate nonsense of taxes
and most legal formulas, no one knows how many additional
unlicensed Italians went up in planes.

The First Aeroplane Flotilla of Tripoli served in Libya, during
the Italo-Turkish War, and another at Bengazi. ("If we must fail,
let us fail shouting.") Mostly they were for show and some little
scouting. Just before World War I, there were over a dozen
military airdromes where Italians were flying Blériots, Savoia-
Farmans, Nieuport-Maccis; and by 1917, the Italians were in
Spads, Caudron G-4's, and Hanriots. Nearly fifty fliers were
called aces; mostly this was a gallant gesture to brave fliers. Like
many such lists, the Italian ones are not trustworthy.

Francesco Baracca was a landowner and a well-off country
gentleman, the kind of overseer of his land usually known as a

"gentleman-farmer." He had begun war training on horseback. From the 2nd Cavalry he went to France in 1912, and studied as a flier. When Italy entered the war in 1915 on the Allied side, he flew a Hanriot two-seater.

In September 1915, Baracca was at 4,000 feet over Palmanova when he sighted an Austrian plane. He made some graceful ballet-like passes around it, but his machine gun kept jamming and the enemy plane flew off. (His gun jammed on several other meetings in the air.) Flying as patrol leader of the 70th Squadron in a Nieuport Baby Scout, he knocked down a two-seater Aviatik. *Digito Mostrare!* Wine flowed that night in the mess, and there was antipasto and pasta and much singing. Enhanced prophecies were made as to Baracca's future in the air.

Io dico cosa incredibile e vero: La ringrazio! Italian air force records seem as erratic as their machine guns. Tenente Francesco Baracca is credited with thirty-four kills. He died in June of 1918, while flying a Spad. His air force companions said he was brought down by ground fire; more reliable evidence has it that an Austrian fighter shot him down.

The second Italian ace was Silvio Scaroni, who went from the artillery to the air force, ending up on the Austrian front flying observation among the dangerous peaks of the snow-covered Alps. It was a remote cold white world of mountain fighters and skiers; planes on both sides were shot down over the peaks and broke up, or had accidents or dead motors and fell into the crevasses.

Scaroni was hit by an aircraft shell while flying a Caudron near Trieste; his engine was struck so hard it shook and came free from its bearings to crash 6,000 feet to the ground.

Scaroni fought the controls and managed to land his instant glider. Later that year, he took nearly a dozen bullets through his flying jacket, but none through his skin. His observer was killed. Scaroni again brought home a wreck.

The great Italian collapse and rout at Caporetto moved Scaroni from bombers to fighters. Taking up his first Nieuport one day in November 1917, he was jumped by two Albatroses from a Jagdstaffel flying boldly out of a captured Italian airfield base. The Italian's plane was raked by enemy fire, but one of the Germans carelessly blundered in front of Scaroni's plane and was shot down. *Render pane per focaccia*—to give bread for bun, or tit for tat! This victory made Scaroni sure of himself. In a couple of weeks, full of confidence, he shot down nine enemy planes; in one attack alone he got three kills.

In July 1918, flying a Hanriot, Scaroni was protecting artillery spotter planes when an enemy flight caught him and he went down firing, in a wild spin, 5,000 feet, before he recovered his senses. Coming down behind the Austrian lines, he rose again and made for home. But he crashed between the lines and fell into a shell crater. Italian troops rescued him. Broken but alive, he went into hospital for five months of body repairs. He was so badly wounded, he was still in bed when peace came. For what it may be worth, his official record is given as twenty-six victories.*

The Italians made ardent fliers and, in many cases, good fighters, but their service of supply, their armament seemed faulty. It was not just the problem of machine guns that jammed; the entire Italian war effort had moments of high elation alternating with periods of black, deep despair. An American who was with the Red Cross service in Italy near an Italian airport wrote home:

> Most daring bastards in the world, the Wop fliers, crazy for the girls, the *vino bianco*, and gramophone records of *Trovatore*. Good friends and full of gestures. Always crossing themselves, wearing saints' medals, mocking the priests and the Pope. Much contempt for the peasants—The gents are lazy, bone lazy, but grand in their uniforms, and scented like a Kansas City whore. They fly crazy and with dash and a smile. . . . And wave to you, *'ello, paesano*. Off duty, they brag about their flying, play *caffé-biliardo* in the cafés, and the young tenentes go off to the brothels. They sure come back full of grappa and are very polite and laugh too much. They all invite you to visit their parents in Rome or at some hill vineyard after the war. Two or three die every week. The wounded, when recovering, look at you with those big black eyes and ask you is it truly a dreadful wound.

---

* Between wars, Silvio Scaroni was the Italian air attaché in Washington, a charming scarred Latin at the capital's cocktail parties. When World War II came to his nation, he went home to Italy, later to become a general.

The Italian air force had one special flier who came from America. He was Representative Fiorello La Guardia, later to become the duck-shaped feisty little mayor of New York. He had been raised as an army brat, his father an army bandmaster at various posts. La Guardia, during the war, flew a Caproni bomber on the Italian fronts. It should be noted that he had testified before a congressional committee when people spoke of winning the war by the use of planes—"about this war being won with the airplane . . . this war will be won in a much more cruel and less spectacular fashion . . ."

2. | To the East

> *The creed of the desert is an inheritance.*
> *The Arab does not value it extremely . . .*
> —T. E. LAWRENCE

The focus of attention remained chiefly on the Western Front. There the war would be decided, there the major powers were struggling in agony for some sign of victory. Both sides knew that this was the ultimate theater of war. Victory or defeat would come here, unless both sides committed suicide (and the antagonists were close to suicide in their mixture of intrigue, mutiny, disorganization, graft, and new industrial millionaires making more planes, guns, tanks).

Yet there were other battle fronts where the airplane played a significant role. In the Balkans, across Sinbad's fabled Arabian deserts, the roar of motors in the sky was heard, the chatter of machine guns, the thud of bombs on camel and Bedouin, Turk and village leper. The plane was often the only way to supply troops in a tight corner. There were failures: the German airship that went to South Africa to aid the Korps there which arrived too late; the disaster at Galliopoli where the British tried to use torpedo bombers; the failed airlift to men besieging Kut-el-Amara.

The planes flew over Macedonia, Crete, Bulgaria, all over the Aegean Sea. At the start of 1917, the Germans sent Hauptmann

Heydermarck out to man four planes against the English forty-odd craft. Their one ardent warmaker was a Leutnant von Esch-wege, in the sole Albatros scout.

Eschwege was active in Drama, Macedonia. Here he suffered heat, fleas, hordes of bedbugs, and malaria from the Struma marshes. Half the British fliers were down with the fever. Over the Aegean, the temperature ran to 110° in the shade. Heat stroke was common, and ordinary motor oil ran like water. Engines lost power in the air and pilots died as a result.

The whole Mediterranean theater was haunted by heat, fever, poor planning. Planes went out scouting, British warships shelled shore installations, the *benzinas*—motorboats mounting machine guns—brought war to the goats and the eroded hills, to the 10-drachma whores who serviced some airmen in the *tavernas* of Piraeus. It was hell on the airfields, all dust. So hot, time only for a hasty burial in the heat if one died of fever or dysentery, or was recovered from a shattered plane. The British found the bodies of two German airmen washed ashore, and held a Church of England burial. It seemed a pleasant change from the heat rash, the revolting food, the foul *ouzo* and *retzina* they were drinking.

The bloody war on the Western Front seemed very far away to these fliers, both German and English, who had at each other in a burnished sky. Letters home spoke of the martyrdom of rancid olive oil, fleas, and lizards, the fevers that laid one low. There was a bit of all right if they managed to get a few hours visit on one of His Majesty's ships of war. Then back to dirty airdromes, the repatched planes, the masklike Mycenaen faces of the natives, their Peloponnesian smells (and some "greasy Greek priests making indecent offers"). The Turkish coffee was all grounds. "Oh, to be home at Christmas . . ."

It was no wonder the airmen gambled, became drunkards, "went to the whores with the unshaved armpits." A few killed themselves in clumsy ways. The rest ate the tough roast Corfu goat and talked of the Arabian theater of war where Allenby was marching his men under pith helmets—he used scout planes and did a little light bombing from the air.

A few of the fresh young men—replacements—went viewing

some crumbling Byzantine church, and debated whether the Deluge really landed the Ark on Mount Ararat. It was almost a pleasure to take on the morning air patrols and go humming into the heated sky, wary of the Eschwege beast that trapped new young pilots by dropping out of the sun to make his kill. It was rather a change, too, to assist the British naval squadron that stood in to bombard Kavalla; here Eschwege got a Farman that fell a victim, its wings torn off before it hit the sea.

There was nothing physically heroic-looking about Eschwege. He was military-academy bred, had served with a regiment of Horse Jaegers. Six months of trenches, and he went to study flying. It was almost the exact pattern of so many other great fliers. He had a hard time learning to fly, and crashed over a half-dozen planes; he got hopelessly lost in the air, made a mess of his navigation. He was disliked by his comrades as a dud. Flying as a scout in France, he went on into training in fighters. Then he was shipped out east to Drama, 80 miles south of Salonika, known as the "Bedbug Front." This front fought the Germans with a strange army, or armies, of assorted French, English, Italians, Serbs, Venizelist Greeks, and bandits. To aid the Germans, some Fokkers came in and a few Halberstadts.

Eschwege was a bit of a madman, which was not much noticed in the battle, camp, and airdrome areas. He tried to invent his own weapons and was almost killed when one of his breech blocks blew up in his face. At takeoff, Eschwege never eased himself into the air; he used top punching power to streak into the air like a rocket.

One day in the air, he forced two Serbs flying a Farman to set down without a fight. Then, just for kicks, he took up the Farman himself to see how it flew.

The British star in the area was Captain G. W. Murlis-Green, who flew a single-seater BE-12, not as good a plane as the German ones, but he managed to knock many enemy fliers into the Aegean with it.

The British sent over a message to the Germans: ". . . we have met so often in the air and peppered one another, we should also be very pleased to make the personal acquaintance of the German airmen of Drama. Give us your word of honour that you will not take us prisoners, and then we will land a motor-boat on the shore of Lake Takhino to meet you."

Eschwege was all for the party, but his commander Heydermarck said no; the official war texts forbade such meetings.

Murlis-Green liked to come over when the Germans were at their food—miserable, olive-oil-drenched, canned food it was—and shoot them up as they chewed, spoiling their digestions. Eschwege had a great vanity, and saw himself as ordained by the gods of war. He became "Green-conscious" and dreamed of killing the British ace, who liked to lurk in the sun and come crashing down on a victim (guns flashing), then back to tea at his base.

Some claim that the two men met in the air a couple of times; if so, nothing was decided. Eschwege went on doing insane battle in the air, against any odds, somehow always coming out alive. Once, when he was wounded and had two slugs in one arm, he came down, had his wounds dressed, and went straight up again, tearing off the bandages when they interfered with his flying. The man seemed doomed, but no matter how many traps the British set for him, he always managed to get away and knock down more planes. It made for excitement in that infinity of boredom, the Green front.

By October 1917, Eschwege had sixteen kills in an area where planes were not as thick as on the Western Front. The British were not his only problem; the Turks, ostensibly Germany's ally, manned a deadly antiaircraft fire aimed at anything, including German planes. They explained it was for religious reasons: those infidel black crosses painted on the wings of the German machines.

It looked as if Eschwege was going to survive the war. The British were putting up balloons but he sneered at them; "that is not my line." However, the fat objects swaying in the heated air attracted him at last, and he began to shoot them down. Once, after getting a balloon, as a bonus he also shot down the protecting BE and a Sopwith.

On November 21, 1917, Eschwege was up early. He had 19 kills over British planes. It was said it was the bedbugs that kept him in the air; it was more restful up there. He flew to investigate an English balloon going up. The British, instead of pulling it down when they saw Eschwege coming, began to let it out even faster on its cable. When it was about 2,500 feet into the air, Eschwege went for it like a cat for catnip. The observer in the balloon basket seemed to be asleep. The German flier began firing. There was a huge explosion in the sky, thick smoke scurried into the air. Eschwege's Albatros shook, tumbling end over end. Twisting like a duck with a broken neck, it fell as if to a sportsman's aim. The "observer" in the balloon had been a straw-stuffed dummy; the basket held 500 pounds of high explosive, set off by an electric charge from the ground.

In the afternoon, a British plane flew over Drama Airdrome and dropped a streamer-hung object. There was a message:

> The officers of the Royal Flying Corps regret to announce that Leutnant von Eschwege was killed while attacking the captive balloon. His personal belongings will be dropped over the lines some time during the next few days.

L. W. Sutherland and Ross Smith were the best-known fliers in the dismal Turkish adventure of the British at Gallipoli. Both were sick with enteric fever there, and were placed in a ship's isolation section—in this case, a lifeboat that was also the living quarters of the crew's Christmas dinner, a protesting pig. After they had recovered (and developed a hatred for pork), they took to flying cloak-and-dagger missions, aiding Lawrence of Arabia and his scabby, irregular cutthroats.

The Australians, unlike the Britons on that front, were inventive. They used a Ford truck to hold a captured German cannon and a machine gun for ground fighting. And a floating item called a "Mimi" (floats on which an airplane engine was mounted) that damaged Turkish shipping. "Agnes" was a railroad flatcar run by an airplane motor and its propeller.

Jackals were also a problem to desert-based fliers, the story being that the bastards would sneak into your tent at night and snap off your genitals before you came fully awake. Sutherland produced a jackal-killing balls-protecting dog from some place, and took it flying. The dog was cold one flight and the flier tucked it into the front of his flying suit. A German plane attacked them and the cowardly dog crept into his pants leg and hampered the fighting. But Sutherland got away.

Another time, the fliers found out where the nurses' bathrooms were located at a field hospital. They carried out low-flying exercises by the bathroom windows, until an order went out, "Pilots must refrain from using their aircraft to further their matrimonial prospects."

It was a deadly, hothouse form of warfare: disease, humidity, bugs, bad food, strange obscure fevers. The lousy Arabs were known to torture and kill fallen fliers. There was the example of a captive like T. E. Lawrence being used for homosexual rape. One flier noted in his journal, "The damn Arab has a saying: a woman for sons, a boy for pleasure, but bugger a melon for Paradise . . ."

The Turks had a reward of 40 pounds of gold for the capture of each British pilot. Prisoners were treated like animals, and many died in filthy Arab and Turkish prisons. It was a dreary second-class war.

The British losses, by the time Allenby took the Judaean Hills and entered Jerusalem on December 9, 1917 ("A Christmas present for the nation") and arms were grounded, were 52,000 killed in enemy action. Nearly 504,000 were laid out by malaria, cholera, dysentery, venereal diseases. Many an airman died of disease or fever rather than in the air.

The warfare among the Greek Islands, on the fringes of the Turkish Empire, was also demoralizing. The fliers drank too much and became involved with whatever raddled female flesh was available. Heat and the fevers and bowel disorders killed too many. Rupert Brooke died on a hospital ship of a fever, his body disposed of in haste on a nearby island—Lemnos; a rather sordid end for one who had produced the romantic finish to a popular war verse:

> *If ye break faith with us*
> *Who died, we shall not sleep . . .*

Allenby's attack on the Turkish front was moving planes, men, horses, and weapons across choking deserts and wadis. What German planes there were were soon put out of action. The English and Australians in their machines held the heated dusty sky, while the Turks reeled back. The last cavalry charge took place as Turk and Australian horse fought it out under the eyes of pilots overhead.

Captain A. R. Brown on September 21, 1918, led a flight of planes that found a big Turkish force moving in haste through the Wadi el-Far'a. It was a canyon miles long and open to the air, "a giant gray-black snake nine miles in length," remembered L. W. Sutherland. The head of the "snake" was thickly bombed, then racked by machine guns. Sutherland took on the tail and punished that with bombs and gunfire. All day, every three minutes, bombers moved over the wadi. Horsemen, baggage, animals, all were huddled together panic-stricken, men died pleading for mercy from the air. Next day, the dead men, horses, and camels made up a Bosch painting of complete horror. The survivors stood and waited for death from the air. They were in Allah's hands. The slaughter of Wadi el-Far'a went on to the very end. The British victors counted 1,000 transports and 100 cannon. No one totaled the dead.*

* Not until the Israeli armor and air force trapped Nasser's Egyptian forces, splendidly armed by the Russians, in the Sinai in 1967 was there to be a greater rout of a modern army in a desert.

CHAPTER 21

RUSSIANS WITH WINGS

"Russian excitability quickly gives way to fatigue . . ."
—ANTON CHEKHOV

With the revolutionary stirrings within Russia making ominous sounds on the horizon, the country still had an air force of sorts. It was to be used, the czar suggested, to inspire confidence in air support. But Igor Sikorsky was the only really talented Russian designer, and he saw his ideas misused. The czar had issued orders that Sikorsky "must *not* be permitted to fly." He was too valuable to think of flying in his own giant plane, the Ilya Mourometz, which therefore took off to battle without him. It was promptly waylaid by three German fighters who racked its cumbersome whale-shaped fuselage as it was trying to sideslip to safety. One Russian gun jammed, the other was on the wrong side of the huge plane. The pilot tried to get the active gun into battle by moving in a tight circle, and his gunner hit one of the enemy planes. Another German came up into the blind area in the plane's belly and put over a dozen slugs into the fuel tanks. Protected from catching fire, the fuel just dripped away, turning, in the freezing altitude, to vapor which the attackers mistook for smoke from a burning plane. They cut off the fight, and the crippled giant started for home.

But a fresh German appeared in the sky and wounded the Russian pilot. The observer meanwhile was trying to patch the leaking metal gas tanks. He froze stiff and motionless at the new attack, leaving his hands flat against the cold tanks at two miles up. He tried to pull them free, then in Slavic fury tore them loose, leaving the skin of his palms frozen to the metal tanks. Slowly the big plane moved over Krasnostav and came to the ground. As they landed, they saw the hunched figure of Sikorsky seated on a camp stool waiting by a hangar. He rose, came over, and stood looking gloomily at his battered ship and the two bleeding fliers.

The Russians did manage to produce other planes, in that slipshod, hasty way of Russians (whether under czar or early commissar), many of them sturdy and effective. A reporter from the London *Morning Post* visited an early World War I plant:

> . . . Accorded the exceptional privilege in wartime, even for an ally, of visiting one of the Russian great airplane factories. Several have been established to keep up the large supply required. The one I visited can turn out five planes per day, or thirty per week. Imagine a London railway terminus, considerably reduced in size and with a broad gallery running round halfway to the roof. That is the fitting department. The whole floor area is crowded with complete airplanes in the rough, some awaiting their engines and others certain other pieces of mechanism used in the active war in the air. Around this central hall and communicating with it are a series of buildings for the preparation of the various parts, for everything including the engines is entirely constructed on the spot. Construction has been standardized, and many are the ingenious contrivances for simplifying the various processes of manufacture. . . . When completed they are lowered down from the gallery to the floor of the great hall. Thence they proceed to the flying grounds for the testing of the engines, and they have to be passed by an inspector, a skilled aviator, before being dispatched to the army. As boxed for the railway the entire airplane is got into a solid packing case which might contain, say, a couple of grand pianos, but rather longer. Thus packed, they fear nothing in transit. . . .

The ace of Russian fliers was Captain Alexandrovich Kazakov. A blond giant, just over six feet tall, egg bald, spur-mustached, with blue eyes. Austere and overdignified as a *gospodar* in public, he resembled one of Tolstoy's characters in *War and Peace*, or one of those career officials in a Chekhov story who reveals himself with all his nuances under some social pressure. Those who knew said that Kazakov was actually quiet, modest, unassuming, rather naïve. He always carried an image of St. Nicholas into the air with him; and his love of horses caused him to bring his favorite mount along to every airfield he flew from.

From a cavalry officer, he had turned himself into a pilot by February 1915. Flying from Sevastopol, he thought up and designed a device for grabbing enemy planes from the air with a grappling hook on a long cable. In March, his cable failed to unreel, and one of the Germans in the Albatros he was fishing for began to take potshots at him with a rifle.

Kazakov, with that Russian fatalism (which they assure us, with a shrug, doesn't exist), dived at the German plane and hit it hard with his wheels and undercarriage. The Albatros sank like a stone to its death. Kazakov discarded his grapnel. It hadn't proved worth a kopeck.

Soon the Russians had machine guns in planes, and Kazakov was given the leadership of an *otryad* (squadron). By 1917, he was commanding four groups of the Death's Head fliers, who painted skull-and-crossbones on their Morane-Saulnier and Nieuport imports from France.

With the arrival of Lenin in Petrograd in 1917, the war changed in Russia.* The Germans had hoped Lenin would get Russia out of the war and the October Revolution did just that. From then on, the Allies trying to keep Russia in the war were like Gogol's character Chichekov, hunting for dead souls. The Allies bought Russians to continue the war. Most of the Russian fliers tried to join British and French units on the Eastern Front, and then went over to the counterrevolutionary forces of the rightist Whites supported and supplied by the Allies.

The U.S. Ambassador to the Russians, David Francis, was a bourbon-loving Kentucky political hack with a fine wild skill at the poker table. He had brought along a Negro valet, but left his wife back home in the bluegrass country. He paraded a mistress,

---

* The "sealed train" legend is nonsense—the doors were not locked, and Lenin and his party descended from the cars at many stations to stretch their legs.

a Madame de Cramm, who practically lived at the American Embassy and was escorted around Petrograd as "my French teacher" by Francis.

Raymond Robins, assisting the inept Ambassador, soon saw the true turn of events: "Trotsky is a four kinds of a son of a bitch, but the greatest Jew since Christ." Trotsky brilliantly organized the Red armies fighting on over a dozen fronts against the Whites and the Allied interventions. He gathered up a collection of oddly patched, motley models from wherever he could find them. Trotsky's main strength lay in the citizen armies, ex-soldiers, ex-fliers, the last great hordes of cavalry, and in his improvising of armored cars and armored trains. But there was also a Red air force. To meet it was a much stronger White air force, supplemented by Allied planes, although compared to the air forces on the Western Front of much less power and strength, and lacking the ability to replace lost or damaged planes.

British troops and some planes occupied Baku, Batum, and other areas of Russia. Sir John Hill, who led the British military mission in Russia, sent Kazakov and over thirty other Russian pilots to join British forces that had come ashore at Archangel, Murmansk, and other points. Kazakov became a major in the Salvo British fliers. He had shot down seventeen German planes (or said he had). Fifteen Bolshevik planes were to fall to him in the next year, when he was flying Sopwith Camels and Nieuports. Russian record keeping has not been too well accepted by many historians, but there is no doubt that Kazakov was an excellent flier— the mere fact of his remaining alive proved that.

By 1919, it was clear the Red armies were winning, and the Allies prepared to pull out. Kazakov became moody, the old days of singing Christmas *Kolyadki*, taking steambaths with gentlemen, were over. He became bitter, withdrawn, acting out the typical Russian character of the great novels. In early April, he went out to his plane, opened the throttle wide, and, of course, stalled the motor. The engine was started again. He took off low, keeping just a couple of dozen feet off the ground, then pulled up for a hard, labored climb. He began to loop the ship madly, insanely. On a wild turn it stalled and fell, tail down, then smashed vertically into the ground. The major, if he had a parachute along, made no effort to use it.

The Russians had another hero in Lieutenant Commander Alexander P. de Seversky. Flying from Oesel Island in the Baltic, in July 1915, his seaplane was shot down in the Gulf of Riga, and to add injury to defeat, the fury with which it fell into the Gulf set off a bomb in the cockpit, removing one of Seversky's legs. He recovered, and having shot down two German planes in one day was awarded the Order of the Gold Sword of St. George. Seversky is credited with thirteen air kills in all.

The Kerensky government in 1917 sent Seversky on an air mission to the U.S.A. When the Soviets came to power, he decided to stay there and become a naturalized citizen. He was a test pilot and plane designer, but his brief moment of fame came much later when he wrote a best seller in 1942. The book was *Victory Through Air Power*—his theory of winning wars from the air, in an age before the Doomsday bomb.*

There is a sort of Keystone Cops epilogue to the American intervention in the Russian civil war. Admiral Dewey's old flagship in the Spanish-American War, the rusting cruiser *Olympia*, was sent to Murmansk to bolster the White forces fighting the Reds. The "Bolos," as the Reds were then called by the Americans, began to harass the U.S. navy sailors with gunboats and armored trains.

Planes flew overhead and the naval officers assumed they were planes of the White forces, since in newspaper cartoons it had been made clear that the Reds were bearded bums who carried sputtering old-fashioned round bombs and were thus incapable of keeping an air force in operation, let alone piloting a complicated airplane.

One of the planes crash-landed, and to assist it, a U.S. army major ran forward to help, crying out: "Don't fire! We are Americans!" The plane answered this identification with a round of machine-gun fire. The major hastily took cover on the cold

---

* Most historians feel that Seversky's ideas were proved wrong. In World War II, in Korea, and in the overkill bombings of Vietnam, airpower failed to bring automatic victory.

ground in a freezing swamp. When the American rescue party came up, they found the Red plane's crew gone, and a chilled, disillusioned major. Shortly thereafter the Americans withdrew and Leon Trotsky, who mapped out the Soviet military victory, began his long pilgrimage toward assassination.

CHAPTER 22

THE DEATH OF
THE RED BARON

"The President of the Immortals . . . had ended his sport . . ."
—THOMAS HARDY, *Tess of the d'Urbervilles*

Baron von Richthofen's score had risen to above fifty by early 1917, but his mortality was beginning to show through the scarlet paint of his plane, the chest covered with enameled metal and ribboned decor. The adulation of women, the cheers of Germans for their Red Knight, showed signs of expectation that he was a monument, already a memory.

There was no true rapprochement between the baron and the hungry, tattered, ordinary German civilian, living like a well-trained beast of burden.

The fliers remained cut off from most of the true condition of things, the hopeless ground fighting, the outer world beyond their airfields. On their woozy and hectic leaves their vision was imprecise and diffused. Conditions on the German home front were depressing; thousands of widows and cripples filled the cities. But von Richthofen even when on leave continued his killing—at Freiburg it was pheasants. He met another Prussian hero, von Hindenburg, a square figure with a head as if crudely carved from a block of German oak. It was a long meeting, and no doubt they saw each other as the proper father and son images. Their backgrounds merged: the Prussian acres and forests. Each mystic shapes his own God, and these two approved of each other; a cadence, unique yet very German, full of omens and portents, was common to both.

The baron's brother, Lothar, had been shot down in air combat, and was in serious condition, badly wounded in both legs.

The baron hurried back to his men. The enemy was putting better and better planes into the air against them: the SE-5 fighters (single-seaters), Bristols, DH-4 fighter-bombers. They were very fast and balanced off the advantage the baron's Albatros had held. The Germans, jumpy, began to plan to combine the old staffel system into single sectors, called *Jagdgeschwaders*, of four squadrons each. The whole to have nearly fifty planes ready for action and be able to move around to any part of the front that needed them.

In July 1917, the baron was listed as having fifty-seven air victories. Then he came up against Flight Commander A. E. Woodbridge and Captain Pilot D. C. Cunnell, of the RFC 20th Squadron. In a few moments the encounter was over. Something —perhaps only the odds—was against von Richthofen that day. Suddenly he felt a tearing pain in the skull and barely brought his plane down to earth, to fall among thorn bushes.

It was a close thing for the Red Baron. He lay in a hospital in Courtrai. The machine-gun bullet had parted his scalp and laid bare his skull and splintered some bone. The surgeons did their utmost for the national hero, but the wound failed to heal properly, and when scar tissue did develop on the shaven head, the pain continued. It was now discovered that thorns had also injured the flier's head when he fell into a bush on landing. Their points had been left imbedded in the scalp, to the disgrace of the German medical service. Bone splinters, too, were surfacing under the scalp. The wound was reopened and the bone fragments removed. But the thorn points were now firmly imbedded and were not taken out.

The pain was maddening. Von Richthofen suffered headaches in close-paced waves. Most nights, he was kept awake by Allied bombers active all around the hospital. When day came there were the army surgeons with their torture tools, probing his open wound and trying to keep it from infection. In his agony, they seemed like flesh-snipping carnivores, not healers.

Debacle or victory, all round the baron was aware that the

young men were dying. And he knew the war was going badly for the Germans. Gone were the tribal helmets of early days, the social elation of highly honored regiments, of *Korpsbruder*. The elite of the army lay dead on the Marne, at Loos, the Somme, Arras, Polygon Wood. The horsemen were usually on foot now —and dead horse was valued as food, for the Allied blockade had cut off suppies. As the baron left his bed, he noticed the black eagles of the Teutonic empire on public buildings. For the baron, the Germans still waged a war in the Roman, Caligulan mold: "*Oderint dum metuant*. Let them hate us, just so they fear us." Wounds and pain had not touched the inner core of the man.

Baron von Richthofen came out of hospital, pale, thin, wearing a helmet of bandages on a battered skull with thorns in it. He was now a captain with five Jagdstaffels under his command. There was a convalescent leave to taste *Liebe Mamma*'s jellies. Back flying, he seemed to have lost his coordination in the air. After going up for nearly two weeks, he had made no kill. When he did strike down a British plane, he wrote home, "I became deadly ill."

But by September he had recovered most of the old timing, to claim his sixtieth kill. Christmas, he went on leave and to parties organized by high-born society ladies. He visited Brest Litovsk, where the Russians were at low ebb. He hunted four-footed game in the Bialowicka forests with Lothar, who had recovered safely. Back to flying, he was good; he sent a gift to his sixty-fourth victim, lying in a hospital. Second Lieutenant H. J. Sparks got a box of cigars.

The baron's last victory was number 80; the victim hit the ground with a tremendous bang. But Lieutenant D. E. Lewis walked away from the smashed plane. Swooping low overhead, the baron waved and smiled at his foe.

April 21, 1918: There should have been the thunder of Wagnerian drums in the clouds, the flash of heroic lightning in the night. From Bertangles, three flights of five British planes each took off. A Canadian, Captain Roy Brown, headed this formation of the RFC's 29th Squadron. It was a sky of brilliant blue taffeta. The British knew the Red Baron was in the district; they had flown against him, fought his pilots. Near the village of Hamel, the fighters were hovering over Australian camera planes, protecting the slowpokes. Four Fokkers appeared to try for the camera planes. Captain Brown scanned the sky for a quick look around. He saw an Albatros coming to join in. He signalled his group—they were flying Sopwith Camels—to dive directly into the gathering fight.

Thirty planes crisscrossed and fired blasts from their machine guns. All were jockeying for position, slashing past vapor trails, turning, banking, wings chasing wings. This went on for ten minutes. A young untested Canadian, a Lieutenant Wilford "Wop" May, lost his nerve and tried to flee the fight. He pushed his Camel into a steep dive and saw, to his horror, a scarlet plane on his tail. He increased his dive, with a prayer that maybe he could shake off the legendary Red Baron coming up close behind him.

Captain Brown, eyes alert, saw the chase. He came to May's aid. Diving, he barreled in at 1,000 feet, trying to get his ship alongside the scarlet one. But the baron's Albatros was very fast, and Captain Brown fell behind. He banged out a burst of bullets from his Lewis guns, hoping some had hit the quick enemy machine. Then, to his fellow pilots' amazement, the scarlet Albatros began to dive in the movement of what could only be a hurt machine (or pilot), so swift was its passage. Below were ruins, the jagged brick teeth of a once fine village, Sailly-le-Sac, now a reeking, mired horror. It was part of No-Man's-Land between the two armies.

The scarlet plane crash-landed near the Bray-Corbie road. Australian gunners nearby watched open-mouthed. One Aussie, with a whoop, ran out with a rope which he made fast to the wreck. With a heave and a ho, they pulled the plane out of No-Man's-Land and gathered round for a look-see at the dead pilot.

Captain Brown never claimed he actually downed the baron, just that he fired at him and that pilots of his flight had seen the scarlet plane go down. Claims were later put in for the kill by some Australians manning a Lewis gun post near the road, protecting a battery armed with 18-pound field guns. The Australians had opened fire with their Lewis guns and the artillery also fired on the scarlet plane; they watched the baron's Albatros make a quick right-hand turn in the air and fall into a steep dive. So no one knows for sure who downed von Richthofen. Most accounts give the credit to Captain Brown, however. (This bears out Tolstoy's famous dictum: "As soon as an event has taken place, it becomes as many events as it had witnesses, for they all tell different versions . . .")

What is known is that a rigid figure was still at his controls in the scarlet plane. From the open mouth blood, thick and red, gushed as from some wine fountain. The body was searched, pockets emptied. Papers went around in grimy gunners' hands. "Jesus Christ! That's Richthofen, the bloody Baron himself." (The language may have been stronger, but such is the report that was given out.)

It was decided by the victors to hold a grand funeral. The entire burial was like some ritual scene from a Gilbert and Sullivan operetta. The British, having made plans to honor the dead German flier, overdid the thing to the point of satire. Deadpan, and of course with no idea of how it would all look in saner times when the war was over.

The body was shrouded, laid on the bed of a military truck, bedded deep with flowers. A stiff correct escort of six officers from the RAF's 209th Squadron, captains all, walked in solemn parade step behind the slow-paced lorry. The body was removed to a hangar and prepared for burial. For interment, "a choice plot" (as one historian puts it) had been picked in the shade of a lordly hemlock. The body of the Red Baron had lain in state during the day, and hundreds of British officers and rank and file, ground crews, anyone interested, had filed past the dead enemy. He lay, it seemed, untouched, for the bullet that killed him had not marred his features. (The postmortem showed the slug had entered one chest wall, banged against the spine, gone through the heart, and moved on through the other chest wall.)

One overemotional eyewitness wrote, "So when a staunch foe of long standing passes on, you find you strangely miss him . . .

a certain piquancy was found lacking in the ensuing weeks of action . . ."

Now came the actual burial in the French earth, with full military protocol. The coffin, carried by the six air captains wearing black armbands, went into a Crosley utility car painted black. Wreaths were piled on the coffin, one lettered "TO OUR GALLANT AND WORTHY FOE."

On command, off moved the fourteen-man firing party, rifles reversed in the traditional ritual position, to match the pomp of mourning, leading the cortege. Next came the carrier and the honorary pallbearers (the captains). All in bare sunlight at a slow regal pace.

At the cemetery gate, the riflemen formed two lines facing each other. The captains carried the flower-draped coffin past the riflemen at salute position. All were led by a well-fed, neatly robed chaplain of the Church of England, prayerbook in hand. An orderly crowd of soldiers, and whatever townspeople were available in the ruined village, gathered around under the best surviving hemlock tree mentioned in the report. The chaplain recited the Church of England ritual for the dead . . . words once powerful, now worn meaningless by constant casual use. A eulogy was said. Then the coffin was lowered into the fresh-dug grave. A crisp officer's bark stiffened the firing party into position, with the calls: "Load! Present! Fire!"

Three times in paced order volleys were pressed off. A bugler stepped forward, wet his lips, and blew "The Last Post."

The next day, a four-bladed propeller was lopped off to make a cross, onto which was screwed a brass plate with the dead baron's name and rank. His age was wrongly engraved as twenty-two.

Official pictures were taken of the burial. Thus was Manfred von Richthofen interred. A legendary hero so easily destroyed by one burst of desperate gunfire from a lagging enemy.

Von Richthofen was a fitting example of his class, his place, and his time. Napoleon had said: "Prussia was hatched from a cannonball." Now the full legend of the Red Baron could begin. The true baron would somehow become changed, modified, glamorized. Become, even to the enemy, someone who could be spoken of with other folk heroes: Daniel Boone, Sherlock Holmes, Bonnie and Clyde, Churchill.

The British helped begin the strange sainthood. They dropped photographs of the baron's burial over his airdrome at Cappy, with the message:

TO THE GERMAN FLYING CORPS:
Rittmeister Baron Manfred von Richthofen was killed in aerial combat on April 21st, 1918. He was buried with full military honours.

From the British Royal Air Force

The body of von Richthofen did not stay in Bertangles. The Germans later, in rising arrogance, held to the boast that they had not lost the war but had been betrayed on the home front. The baron's body was moved to Frecourt, where 18,000 German corpses were interred. In 1925, his young brother Bolko went to find Manfred's grave, intending to ship his remains in a zinc-lined casket to Silesia and home. The remains were dug up and a decorated train carried them solemnly to Berlin. There they lay in state for two days, before being moved to the memorial shrine for dead heroes—The Invaliden. They were never sent home.

A German editor of a religious paper elevated the baron into a saintlike figure: "An airplane seen against the sky from below has the look of a cross, and on such a cross as this, have Richthofen and a multitude of so many brave martyrs, both friend and foe, paid their awful atonement for humanity's sins of war."

The *Deutsche Tageszeitung*, however, brushed off the British photograph and the rites:

This homage is simply the latest self-advertising of British sportsmanship and knightliness. . . . The Allied press is full of this cant . . . this stale trite way, beating a big drum of absurd British magnanimity. . . . But nothing is said of how many and how big were the cash prizes for whomever succeeded in killing Richthofen. The sum must have been enormous. What else can explain the ghoulish fights that took place around the body? . . . A fortune was there for the man who inflicted the fatal wound. The very fliers who carried the coffin to the grave were paid off in blood money. . . .*

As for Captain Roy Brown, two days after he brought the scarlet plane down, he suffered desperately painful stomach cramps. Examination showed dangerous ulcers. He was hurried to hospital and underwent treatment. Invalided back to England, he never again flew in combat. Today, the public cannot easily place the name of this Jack the Giantkiller.**

* This is nonsense. No offer (or reward) to kill the baron existed.
** As for the von Richthofen legend, it was still valid in the comic strip world, even if come on dog days, as reported in a news item of March, 1969: "While a formation of three old Stearman biplanes droned over San Mateo, Calif., the Hamilton Air Force Base band burst into 'Anchors Aweigh.' The fliers of the U.S. Air Force and Navy, along with half a dozen civilian aviation groups, decided it was high time to pay tribute to Snoopy, pilot par excellence and fearless scourge of the Red Baron. As the peerless pup's creator, cartoonist Charles Schulz, inventor of Charlie Brown and his friends, stood at attention, they gave him a pair of gold wings and a picture of Snoopy in fighter-pilot gear."

CHAPTER 23

HERMANN WILHELM GOERING (1893-1946)

"I'll have them wall all Germany with brass . . ."
—CHRISTOPHER MARLOWE, *Dr. Faustus*

A number of men who were involved with the German flying efforts in World War I survived to become important figures in World War II's Luftwaffe: Udet, Fokker, and, of course, Hermann Wilhelm Goering. The last was not then the sinister fat clown of that later conflict, but the slim, romantic, scheming ace of the earlier war, whose official record was twenty-two air victories. He was one of those silver-spoon babies, who for as long as he could remember had been told he was of a great family that could trace its fine blood ties back to royalty, to Hohenzollern and Wittelsbach ancestors. *Gott will es.*

Those who earn a living by it have traced Goering's family line back to the twelfth century. The findings of the experts were always intended to show he was of "pure Aryan stock" and descended from the line of Wolfgang von Goethe, from the Bismarcks, from the Count Zeppelins. Because of Hohenzollern ties, Goering could claim kin to Wilhelm II (usually referred to by democratic Americans as "Kaiser Bill") as well as to Queen Victoria.

Naturally the Goerings were soldiers rather than poets, music makers, or painters. Hermann was born in 1893, but was almost at once sent away with a nurse and did not know his mother and father until he was six. He was born in a sanitarium at Marienbad in Bavaria. His mother, Fanny, had rushed across the ocean from Haiti where his father Heinrich, of Prussian-Austrian stock, was German Consul, to ensure that Hermann was born in the *Vaterland*.

There is no doubt that being left without a mother and father during these early years predisposed the boy to grow up a confused child, and a strange adult. He always claimed he was Bavarian, as if the Marienbad Sanitarium was his homeland, the place of his birth. Six weeks after he was born, Mamma was gone. His actual caretaker was a Frau Graf, whom he called "Mamma." He grew into a pretty child, lonely, brooding over the mother, father, and older brother and sisters he had never seen. He began to invent fantasies early, bragged to other children. He was spoiled, overbearing, and cruel as only maladjusted children can be. Frau Graf was an old widow, and had no place in her dry heart for this child left on her. Hermann got no affection, and he made no real friends with other children.

When the family returned to Germany, they settled in Berlin. The father retired. It was an upper-middle-class world of army talk, of civil posts around the world, of Germany's place in the sun. And of those damn French, the eternal enemy; also, of course, to the eager boy with the receptive mind, of the glory of the Goerings. There were parades in polished boots, goosestepping at Potsdam, fine swords, helmets with feathers, and headgear thick with horsehair. The last, at some Goering parties, little Hermann liked to handle and try on. He had a costume designer's love of finery.

The boy had a collection of toy soldiers (of which Germany was the largest producer in the world), painted in all the glory of uniforms of the past. These were his passion. He maintained a huge collection, even as an adult. And with the aid of a mirror, he imagined he had twice as many soldiers. The fantasy that was so much a part of his brutal nature, his selfishness, was actually a dream world in which he hid, to picture himself immortal and able to create miracles.

Hermann was a bad student; by the age of twelve, five schools had tossed him out. By nature he was vain, self-glorifying, had no respect for teachers. Uniforms, not chalk and books, were his dream, and he was delighted to be taken in by the Karlsruhe Academy. It was a school where the soldier-like stance, the rigid mind, orders, came first. Here Hermann expanded, becoming the perfect soldier, the disciplined robot on parade. Here was the security of old soldiers, barked orders; order in everything. He was, on the surface, no longer insecure. Precision and direct punishment, a pat on the shoulder, a word of crisp praise for duty well done, replaced a lost mother. He developed a veneer of German idealism, eager for Germany to seize its rightful place in the enemy world. This was a successful façade for the hurt, warped ego of a discarded child. But under the polished surface, he never felt at ease unless he was jesting, being funny, even witty. For he had a good intellect, though totally lacking in true learning. Never a scholar, the sly, ingrown boy turned into the school charmer as a protective covering for his still sensitive fear of rejection. This, crossed with all those ancestors who had taken cities, chopped off heads, fought in Crusades, and died on the best horses to the smell of gunpowder, made for a complex youth.

Hermann ached for friendships; he now wanted to be liked, well liked. The real Mamma had been unfaithful to him, so his friendships were in some ways the search for a warmth he had failed to find at home. A historian was to write of him: "in a figurative sense, Goering is a breast sucker . . ."

When the war came, he cheerfully, hopefully, became a leutnant in an infantry regiment where he served with no great glory in some early battles. But even this action in the field was denied him when his legs grew stiff. In hospital at Freiburg, he was told he had rheumatoid arthritis. His army days were over. A friend, Bruno Loerzer, was sent on to the front as a pilot and Goering escaped from the hospital (it was to be called "deserting") and followed him. They bluffed their way into getting a plane, without proper orders, and acted as a training crew without permission. Somehow, in the confusion of war, the stunt worked and they were moved on to Feldfliegerabteilung 25, ready for action. Procedure was not too well handled, even in the German army. Meanwhile, Goering was tried, *in absentia*, by a military court for being absent without leave. The verdict was three months in the military clink; but in the confusion of a hard-fought war, it was never put into effect.

Goering was passing himself off now as a trained observer. The two friends flew together, and flew well, downing a French plane over Verdun. The other fliers called the strange pair "The Odd Couple." Goering took pilot's lessons and was soon flying two-seaters for artillery spotting.

In 1916, Loerzer was in charge of Jasta 26, and Goering came over, now flying single-seater fighters, to become second in command. He was wounded in the thigh, but returned to head his own Jasta, the 27th. Goering was a good pilot, but not a great one. He was, however, an intelligent flier and made the most of what skill he had.

In the huge air struggles that were part of the big German attacks of March 1918, Goering was awarded the Ordre pour le Mérite. The Richthofen *geschwader* was up for offers, another of its leaders, Kapitan Reinhard, having died. Goering got the job. There was talk of family background, of pressure in high places; actually, Goering was the leader type. He admitted it often. And a really great flier at this stage of the war was not too easy to find; anyone who could fly was needed.

He was getting plump; his figure was short and square, his stare blue-eyed and steady; the big jaw at this stage was still firm. Goering had four months of glory before the war ended. He was based at Tellencourt when the Armistice came and the group was told to fly to Darmstadt to await orders. The city was in the hands of a revolution, led by street fighters and soldiers, who stripped the first planes to land of their weapons. Goering roared that if the weapons were not returned to his fliers, he'd call in the entire unit and bomb and machine-gun the town. They got back their guns and took to the sky for Aschaffenburg. Here, under Goering, the Richthofen Circus finally went out of business, disbanding its glory with the usual tears, body hugs, and swearing of eternal friendship. And oaths that the old Germany would rise again. *Die Natur weiss allein was sie will!*

There is no doubt that Goering's mind, in the shock of defeat, was already back in the fantasies of his childhood. Revenge became paramount, and some high destiny awaited him.

Goering's part in Hitler's ascendancy in World War II is well known, as is the failure of his Luftwaffe to subdue England. His later grossness was expressed in luxurious living, the fantasy more and more replacing the actual facts of the second dreadful war. His art collecting, his looting of museums, his uniforms, the decor, took over. This led to that final moment when he sat in Nuremburg for the trials of 1946. One caught, in a glance, the blubbery wreck of a man, crafty, almost cheerful, in a worn Luftwaffe jacket with no insignia, still proud, amused; the bruised child acting up for company, the enemy. He heard himself called by a fellow Nazi the "last remaining Renaissance man," and could only agree.

Two hours before he was to be hanged, Hermann Goering swallowed poison, said to have been kept hidden in a small vial in his navel.

PART VI:
Epilogue —
The War to End All War...

*The war to end all war was to be followed by
the peace that would end peace . . .*

—H. G. WELLS

No matter how dreadful the war, no matter how much the muck and filth and madness of it filtered through to the airmen, the soldiers, and even to the people back home, the romantic glow lingered on for some perverse reason. The voices that rang out sang loudly:

> *Over there, over there,*
> *Send a word, send a prayer over there*
> *Say the Yanks are coming . . .*

This was the kind of romantic mist that enveloped the airmen, as kept alive in William Faulkner's fantasy memory (he never got to France; only a little time with the Royal Canadian Air Force, and a quick discharge). Like Fitzgerald, Faulkner knew the war would end the fliers' youth:

Because they are dead, all the old pilots, dead on the eleventh of November, 1918 . . .

The bitterness at the end was mixed with the hardness that came from the experience. Malcolm Cowley, who served with the American Field Service on the Chemin des Dames, summed up for the pilots:

Others, especially the airmen, had lived more intensely than they would ever live again and felt in a vague fashion that something in them had died on the eleventh of November, 1918. All the young men had been exposed to a variety of strong emotions. Their individualities had been affirmed, even in the anonymous disguise of a uniform. . . .

On that November 11, 1918, morning, another flier, Capitaine

Jacques Leps, commander of the French 18th Squadron, sat in his Spad. He was about to take off with his fliers and their planes, all marked with the insignia of a leaping hare chased by a greyhound. The engines were turning over, the props spinning silver.

It was time to get into the air, to escort a major bombing raid on Metz. As Leps raised his arm to signal the takeoff, someone came running from the airdrome's communication room, running agitatedly, arms waving.

"La guerre! C'est finie, la guerre!"

Jacques Leps took in the heart-bursting news. He switched off the Spad's engine. The engines of the rest of his fliers went silent, one by one, as the cry *"C'est finie, la guerre!"* spread throughout the field.

Capitaine Leps unfastened his safety belt and slowly got out of the cockpit.

Finie.

In the sooty skies over New York Bay, the guttural *geek-geek* of the sea gulls inspecting debris was disturbed by the roar of two U.S. army planes and a dirigible, all circling an old Hamburg-Amerika liner renamed the *George Washington* as the ship left her dock in Hoboken, New Jersey. It was the vessel that was to carry President Woodrow Wilson eastward to a battered Europe —a continent starved, death-filled, impotent—to make peace. From government harbor posts came a 21-gun salute. The President carried hopes of permanence and calm at last as he gazed upward at the planes, the circles and stars of their insignia clearly seen on the wings.

Out to sea, beyond the harbor's crisscrossing traffic, there was a suggestion of gray cumulus clouds and thunderheads. The planes continued to circle the ship ceremoniously as she reached the main channel of the harbor. The crowds packing Battery Park waved flags and cheered the passing vessel and her escorts.

Then the army planes turned and banked, moving off toward their base; the dirigible took more time to change course. The President moved toward the freshly agitated ashen landscapes of

Europe. Cheers drowned out the last hum of the motors as the planes grew distant in the sky.

> *Lo, the dread empire, Chaos, is restored;*
> *Light dies before thy uncreating word:*
> *Thy hand, great march, lets the curtain fall*
> *And universal darkness buries all . . .*
>
> **ALEXANDER POPE**

THE OFFICIAL RECORDS
OF THE FLIERS' VICTORIES

The word "official" is not accepted by most historians as a guarantee of the accuracy of the number of victories given. The most that can be claimed of the following lists is that they are fairly reasonable in a majority of cases.

BRITISH EMPIRE

Major Edward Mannock	73	Major Roderic Dallas	39
Col. William A. Bishop	72	Capt. W. G. Claxton	39
Major Raymond Collishaw	68	Capt. F. R. McCall	39
Capt. James McCudden	58	Capt. John Gilmore	37
Capt. Donald McLaren	54	Capt. Henry W. Wollett	35
Capt. A. Beauchamp-Proctor	54	Capt. Frank G. Quigley	34
Major Philip F. Fullard	53	Major G. W. Murlis-Green	32
Major William G. Barker	52	Major Albert D. Carter	31
Capt. G. E. H. McElroy	48	Capt. W. L. Jordan	31
Capt. Robert A. Little	47	Capt. J. L. M. White	31
Capt. Albert Ball	44	Capt. M. B. Frew	30
Capt. H. J. Larkin	41	Capt. S. M. Kinkead	30
Capt. F. T. Hazell	41	Capt. C. E. Howell	30
Capt. J. I. T. Jones	40	Major A. E. McKeever	30

FRANCE

Capt. René Fonck	75	Capt. Armand Pinsard	27
Capt. Georges Guynemer	53	Lt. Guerin	23
Capt. Charles Nungesser	43	Lt. René Dorme	23
Lt. Georges F. Madon	41	Lt. Claude Marcel Haegelen	22
Lt. Maurice Boyau	35	Sgt. Pierre Marinovitch	22

BELGIUM

Capt. Willy Coppens	36	Lt. de Meulemeester	10
Lt. Thierry	10		

UNITED STATES OF AMERICA

Capt. Eddie V. Rickenbacker	26	Lt. David Putman	12
Lt. Frank Luke, Jr.	21	Capt. Elliott W. Springs	12
Major Raoul L. Lufbery	18	Capt. Field E. Kindley	12
Major G. A. Vaughn	13	Major Reed Landis	10
Sgt. Frank L. Bayliss	12	Capt. J. N. Swaab	10

RUSSIA

Capt. Alexandrovich Kazakov	17	Capt. Kroutenn	6
Lt. Alexander P. de Seversky	13	Lt. Pachtchenko	5

GERMANY

Manfred von Richthofen	80	Lt. Paul Billik	31
Oblt. Ernst Udet	62	Lt. Gotthardt Sachsenburg	31
Oblt. Erich Lowenhardt	56	Lt. Theo Osterkamp	31
Lt. Werner Voss	48	Lt. Karl Allmenroder	30
Lt. Fritz Rumey	45	Lt. Karl Degelow	30
Hpt. Bruno Loerzer	45	Lt. Heinrich Kroll	30
Hpt. Rudolf Berthold	44	Lt. Josef Mai	30
Lt. Paul Baumer	43	Lt. Ulrich Neckel	30
Lt. Josef Jacobs	43	Lt. Karl Schaefer	30
Hpt. Oswald Boelcke	40	Hpt. Hermann Goering	22
Lt. Franz Buchner	40	Lt. von Eschwege	19
Oblt. Lothar von Richthofen	40	Oblt. Max Immelmann	15
Lt. Emil Thuy	32		

BIBLIOGRAPHY

Here is a list for those who want to do some added reading on the subject matter of this book, all in English. Some may be difficult to locate, but most can be found without too much hunting.

Editors of American Heritage, *American Heritage History of Flight*, New York: 1962. A picture book with text, and a good section on World War I.

John R. Cuneo, *Winged Mars: The German Air Weapon, 1870–1914*, 1942.

Christopher Draper, *The Mad Major*, Fallbrook, Calif.: Aero, 1962.

Elsbeth Freudenthal, *The Wright Brothers and the Air Age*, 1949.

Charles H. Gibbs-Smith, *The Aeroplane*, 1960.

Margaret Goldsmith, *Zeppelin*, 1931.

Emile Gouveau and Lester Cohen, *Billy Mitchell*, 1942.

William Green and John Fricker, *Air Forces of the World*, New York: Doubleday, 1958.

Charles G. Grey, *The History of Combat Airplanes*, 1941.

Gene Gurney, *Five Down and Glory*, New York: Putnam, 1958.

Basil H. Liddell Hart, *The Real War, 1914–1918*, Boston: Little, Brown and Co., 1930.

Eric Hodgins and Alexander Magoun, *Sky High*, 1935.

R. H. Kiernan, *Captain Albert Ball*, 1933.

Cecil Day Lewis, *Sagittarius Rising*, 1936.

Alexander McKee, *The Friendless Sky*, New York: Morrow, 1964.

Edward V. Rickenbacker, *Fighting the Flying Circus* (paperback), 1970.

Elliot White Springs, *War Birds*, 1938.

John W. R. Taylor, *Combat Aircraft of the World*, 1909 to the present. A reference work that lists 800 types of combat planes with pictures and full details, statistics. 1969.

APPENDIX

More than a half century after World War I, its planes, those that survived, still have an appeal, and people who will pay fortunes for them, as reported in the *Los Angeles Times*.

May 13, 1968

PLANES FAMED SINCE DAYS OF
RED BARON WILL BE AUCTIONED

Vintage Aircraft Covering Era from World War I to II
Go on Sale at Orange County Air Museum on May 29

Would you like to own a World War I Spad, the chunky little French pursuit plane that fought its way into history over the Western Front?

Or perhaps a Fokker D-VII, the deadly German scrapper of the same dogfighting era, or a British S.E.5a, a snub-nosed Sopwith Camel, a Nieuport 28, a Pfalz D-XII with original Spandau machine guns?

Such vintage planes, along with many veteran aircraft of later years into World War II, will be sold at a unique auction to be held May 29 at the Movieland of the Air Museum, Orange County Airport, Santa Ana.

If you're a World War I flying buff—remembering the fascination of *Wings* and *Battle Aces*, the derring-do pulp magazines of bygone years—you might like to acquire a mixed squadron of your own.

About 30 planes will go on sale at the auction, part of the collection gathered and combined by two noted stunt pilots and movie fliers—Frank Tallman and the late Paul Mantz.

They were acquired more than a year ago as an investment by two Nebraska firms and will be sold by Parke-Bernet of New York, the nation's largest fine arts auction gallery.

May 30, 1968

"Here's the World War I Sopwith Camel selling for $40,000—Good grief!"

Snoopy, famed ace of Peanuts comic strip fame, probably would have voiced his surprise in such words Wednesday had he seen his pugnosed little pursuit plane sell for such a price, particularly when the Camel cost but $8,000 in 1918.

The British fighter brought top money at a unique auction of vintage and veteran aircraft that collected $286,620 in spirited bidding not only for planes, but everything from machine guns (rendered harmless) to a World War I field ambulance.

About 500 persons, present by invitation, packed the Movieland of the Air Museum at Orange County Airport for the auction conducted by Parke-Bernet Galleries of New York City.

Bought by New Yorker

The Camel was purchased by an unidentified New York collector who had entered a preauction bid of $35,000 and then upped his offer by $5,000 at the last minute in a worried telephone call.

As it was, he almost lost the plane to the representative of a New Jersey museum group who bid $37,500 for the Camel—one of the few World War I aircraft he missed among those he sought to purchase.

In all, Gustave Hulkower, bidding for the Aeroflex Museum, now being organized by the Aeroflex Foundation, bought six aircraft for $96,500, plus various aeronautical accessories also up for auction.

They included a 1914 Maurice Farman pusher biplane, $20,000; a 1918 German Pfalz pursuit, $16,000; a 1918 DeHavilland D.H.4 biplane, $15,000; a 1918 French Spad pursuit, $16,000; a German Fokker D-VII pursuit, $20,000, and a British SE-5a pursuit, $9,500.

In addition to missing the Camel, he lost out on a sleek little French Nieuport 28 pursuit that went to grand prix race driver Jim Hall for $14,500.

Hall, delighted with his prize, said he intends to fix up the rotary engine Nieuport and fly it himself just for fun.

There are not many of the aces left. A news item of January 1970 checks off another one.

F. W. GILLET, 74; WORLD WAR I ACE

BALTIMORE, Md. (AP)—F. Warrington Gillet, a retired businessman and World War I flying ace, died Sunday at the Greater Baltimore Medical Center after a short illness. He was 74.

He was president of Gillet-Wright Inc., a liquor importing company.

Gillet, who learned to fly in the Canadian Royal Flying Corps at 19, went to England in March 1918 and was assigned to the British at the Flanders front.

He brought down 10 German planes in September alone.

By the end of the war he was credited with 21 kills.